HERO OF THE AIR

HERO OF THE AIR

GLENN CURTISS and the
Birth of Naval Aviation

WILLIAM F. TRIMBLE

NAVAL INSTITUTE PRESS
Annapolis, Maryland

Naval Institute Press
291 Wood Road
Annapolis, MD 21402

Library of Congress Cataloging-in-Publication Data
Trimble, William F., 1947–
  Hero of the air : Glenn Curtiss and the birth of naval aviation / William F. Trimble.
    p. cm.
  Includes bibliographical references and index.
  ISBN 978-1-59114-879-1 (alk. paper)
  1. Curtiss, Glenn Hammond, 1878-1930. 2. Air pilots—United States—Biography.
3. Aeronautical engineers—United States—Biography. 4. United States. Navy—
Aviation—History. I. Title.
  TL540.C9T75 2010
  629.130092—dc22
  [B]
                                        2009052948

Printed in the United States of America on acid-free paper

15 14 13 12 11 10   9 8 7 6 5 4 3 2
First printing

Book layout and composition: David Alcorn, Alcorn Publication Design

To Richard K. Smith

Contents

Acknowledgments

I t has been said that timing is everything. In early 2002, Paul Wilderson at the Naval Institute Press approached me with the idea of a book on Glenn Curtiss and early naval aviation. I agreed with him, but told him that I would have to put it off because I was totally wrapped up in a book for the Press on the Navy's seaplane striking force, not to mention my responsibilities as chair of the History Department at Auburn University. A few years later, in a fortuitous coincidence of procrastination and the calendar, it became apparent to me and Paul's successors at the Press that the Curtiss project would coincide nicely with the centennial of naval aviation in 2010 and 2011. I am especially indebted to Mark Gatlin, former editorial director at the Press, for committing to the book, and to Susan Todd Brook, the current acquisitions editor, for seeing the project through to completion. Jehanne Moharram expertly copyedited the finished product.

Through the masterful scheduling expertise of Anthony Carey, who succeeded me as department chair, I had a generous block of time to finish my research and draft the bulk of the book manuscript during the 2006–2007 academic year. At the Library of Congress, where I spent most of my time on this project, no one could have been more helpful than Jeff Flannery. I encourage anyone working on the early history of aviation to spend time with the archival materials at the Glenn H. Curtiss Museum in Hammondsport, New York, where Trafford Doherty and Rick Leisenring tolerated my presence during an all-too-brief visit in the summer of 2006. As always, George Cully suggested promising avenues of research and new ways of looking at airplanes and people; he also generously provided information on specific aspects of Curtiss' life and work. Richard Hallion offered insight into the broader implications of Curtiss' aviation career. Friend and former student Larry Lee helped dig out information on Curtiss' Hammondsport wind tunnel, in addition to verifying how Curtiss and his exhibition team traveled across the country by rail in the early part of the last century. At the National Archives, Rebecca Livingston and Charles Johnson ferreted out materials on Washington Chambers and the Curtiss company in the Bureau of Aeronautics and other record groups.

Dan Hagedorn and Dennis Parks went out of their way to locate and send me photocopies of materials on Curtiss and his business interests from the Wright Collection at the Museum of Flight in Seattle.

Tom Crouch at the National Air and Space Museum furnished a much-needed assessment of the book manuscript from his perspective as both a friend and as the foremost scholar of the Wright brothers and early aviation. I am also much obliged to Tom Wildenberg, author, naval historian, and another good friend, who turned his sharp editorial eye on the manuscript at a stage when it demanded precisely that kind of critical attention. Phil Edwards, Mark Kahn, Jeremy Kinney, Melissa Keiser, Alex Spencer, Larry Wilson, and other friends and former associates at the National Air and Space Museum were supportive of my work in ways that I cannot hope to acknowledge fully. On research trips to Washington, Karen Babich welcomed me to her home on the Bay. My colleague at Auburn, Jim Hansen, now director of the University Honors College, provided funds through his program that allowed me to spend a week in Washington tying up loose ends at the Library of Congress and to make a quick trip to Gainesville, Florida, to look at a collection of Curtiss materials. Also at Auburn, David Burke located Curtiss photos from the National Naval Aviation Museum and Carey Cauthen reworked photos into formats more compatible for publication. For the last time, sadly, I thank Paul Sirovatka, my good friend since undergraduate days, who died early in the fall of 2007. His widow Harriet, son Jonathan, other members of the family, his many friends, and I will miss his intelligence, wit, and dedication to his profession. More happily, to my sons Will and Mike, their wives Andrea and Ashley, and to my wife Sharon go my everlasting thanks for their love and support through this and all of my book projects.

Introduction: The Aviator

It was one of those bright, clear spring days that seem naturally to draw the eyes skyward. A Sunday in New York City can be special under even the most ordinary circumstances, but this next-to-last day in May 1910 had the whole metropolis buzzing in anticipation of something even more dazzling than the noonday sun. Barely six and a half years after the Wright brothers had broken the bonds of earth in a heavier-than-air flying machine, thirty-two-year-old Glenn Hammond Curtiss had taken off in his single-engine biplane from Albany some 150 miles up the Hudson and was winging his way south. Two and a half hours later, he arrived over the city, orbited the Statue of Liberty, and alighted at Governors Island to claim the $10,000 prize offered by Joseph Pulitzer's *New York World*. The flight was one of the most spectacular accomplishments in the early years of aviation, a stunning achievement that gripped the imagination of millions and underscored Curtiss' already lofty reputation as the one of the world's most accomplished aviators.

Predictions about the future of the airplane flew off the pages of the popular press, most of them outrageously optimistic about what the new technology meant for people around the globe. Flush with the optimism of the Albany-to-New York flight, the *World* editorialized that the accomplishment "was what men have dreamed of since Daedalus—actual Travel in the Air." A. Leo Stevens, veteran balloonist and member of the Aero Club of America, foretold that the flight "means that in a few years heavier than air machines will be crossing the Atlantic." According to the *New York Press* Curtiss had demonstrated that "the complete conquest of the air is measurably in sight. We have gone from the poetic to the prosaic."[1]

But one observation stood out from the rest. Responding to reporters' questions about what he hoped to accomplish next, Curtiss pronounced that he would concentrate on perfecting an airplane that could reliably operate from the water. Once that had been done, a new world beckoned for the airplane as a naval weapon: "Someday soon," he said, "aeroplanes will have to start from the decks of battleships and from the water and I am not sure but what they could be launched from a battleship going at top speed now." The

World went even further to predict that an airplane "high overhead" might well deliver a "rain of bombs" onto the deck of a dreadnought and that a fleet of airplanes could be acquired for the cost of two modern battleships. At altitude, Curtiss would have been nearly impossible to hit with defensive fire, and even if he had been, another "bird of destruction" would follow and still another until they fulfilled their devastating mission.[2]

How many thoughtful Americans took such definitive statements about the future of the air weapon seriously is open to debate. It is not clear whether Curtiss himself truly believed that his flight presaged the imminent demise of the battleship. But Curtiss used this vision as a blueprint for his work in aviation over the next half-decade, with the result that by the outbreak of World War I the United States Navy had taken the first tentative steps toward integrating the airplane into the fleet. That a self-tutored mechanic, inventor, and flier from a small town in the Southern Tier of New York State with no formal education beyond the eighth grade, would, within less than a decade, become inextricably linked to a new naval technology is an unlikely, improbable, and fascinating story, worthy in and of itself of telling. Curtiss was complex, like all of us made up of a contradictory amalgam of strengths and weaknesses. He was a skilled, knowledgeable, and resourceful engineer, daring yet calculating about risk, patient and tolerant, quiet yet not hesitant to speak his mind when need be or to defend what he considered right. He was innovative and usually open and willing to share his ideas, but at times he could be evasive and secretive about his projects and inventions. Yet, though a century removed, the story of Glenn Curtiss and the formative years of naval aviation resonates on a level beyond the personal. Through the lens of an individual, we can resolve a fine-grained view of the dynamics of technological change within shifting patterns of bureaucracy, weapons acquisition, personnel, and policy.

Curtiss' life and his role in the invention of the airplane is a tale polished smooth by many previous writers—some of their work bordering on anti-Wright polemicism.[3] It needs to be clear from the outset that the Wright brothers, Wilbur and Orville, invented the airplane, not only its proof-of-concept version at Kitty Hawk, North Carolina, on that momentous day in December 1903, but also the first practical heavier-than-air flying machine following two years of intensive development and flight testing in Dayton, Ohio. It may now seem like a purely academic issue, of no real consequence to us in the early twenty-first century, but in the first years of the last century, it meant much to the Wrights, Curtiss, and those with a financial stake in the new technology.

Furthermore, the question, as it played itself out in a long and contentious patent dispute, had consequences for the development of the airplane in the United States. More open to debate is the significance of Curtiss' contributions to airplane control, in particular the use of the aileron and a more logical, "user-friendly" system of hand and foot controls that contrasted with the awkward and less intuitive Wright method, which relied on a complex system of levers to achieve three-axis control. The rugged simplicity of the Curtiss design was another factor in its favor. Weighing on average 40 percent less than contemporary Wright airplanes and having only a single propeller and no chain drive, Curtisses could be manufactured and sold more cheaply than their competitors and were relatively easy to maintain and repair.[4]

Important for the expansion of aviation in the second decade of the century was the widespread availability of the Curtiss airplane design. Compared to the Wrights, Curtiss made details of his airplane construction available to everyone and they were widely copied, especially by amateur fliers—a precursor to what in the computer world is now known as "open architecture." As brilliantly innovative as the Wrights were, particularly in seeing the airplane as a system made up of interconnected and interdependent subsystems, they had difficulty looking beyond their invention and imagining the airplane in a wider socioeconomic context. They predicted only limited applications for the airplane, whereas Curtiss' more comprehensive vision foresaw the airplane evolving both as a practical means of public transportation and a weapon of potentially great destructive power, with aircraft manufacturing companies drawing profits as a result.[5]

A contemporary and friend of the Wright brothers, Grover Loening, wrote that although he had a "high appreciation of [Curtiss'] qualities as a flyer and a promoter," he did not hold his "talents as an engineer or scientist" in high regard. On the other hand, John H. Towers, one of the Navy's earliest aviators and a close friend of Curtiss, recalled that although Curtiss "had no engineering degree . . . he was an engineer of the highest order." According to Towers, "Curtiss just had a very natural genius for being able to visualize the right answer," and he "was extraordinarily clever in figuring out what wing curve would be best." He did not need mathematical calculations because "he just felt how the curves should look." Richard K. Smith, the noted historian of naval aviation, provided another perspective: "Curtiss was one of the world's great pioneers of aviation. . . . [U]nlike the Wrights he was less a research man than a developer." "Curtiss," Smith noted, "was a great ad hoc engineer whose genius was in his ability to improvise, synthesize, and simplify promising ideas and devices at hand, and to transform them into something immediately useful—and marketable." Placed within a common model of technological change, the Wrights were responsible for the invention phase of the airplane, and Curtiss was instrumental in its development or innovation phase. Another way of looking at it is that Curtiss enjoyed the benefits accruing to the innovator who was the "fast second"; that is, he knew that the Wrights and others had demonstrated the feasibility of powered heavier-than-air flight, and he could therefore expand on and exploit the marketing potential of their pioneering work.[6]

These differing but essential contributions to the eventual maturation of the airplane as a technology were complementary, yet as time has passed they have been presented as dichotomous. This was due partly as a consequence of the long and highly publicized patent war between the Wrights and Curtiss, which many at the time thought left American aviation languishing while Europeans forged ahead. Not surprisingly, the legal battles brought out the worst on both sides, while at the same time making it hard for us to view the dispute with any semblance of objectivity, even more than a hundred years later. Sides were chosen early, lines drawn in the sand, and accusations and threats flung across those lines with little regard for the personal and professional consequences. Lamentably, the episode tarnished the reputation of the Wrights and even embarrassed the august Smithsonian Institution. To complicate matters even more, Curtiss himself filed for and received patents and did not hesitate to protect them with litigation. In truth, little of this affected the Navy, whose aviation leaders committed themselves to Curtiss and his airplanes more than a year after the Wrights filed their first lawsuit. Thereafter, symbiotically joined, Curtiss and American naval aviation followed a generally upward trajectory from 1910 to the eve of World War I, setting standards that Europeans were forced to emulate.[7]

The Curtiss-Navy partnership underscores one dimension of larger changes within the service as it grappled with the assimilation of new technologies at the start of the twentieth century. Within a decade, the Navy more or less successfully adjusted to the professionalization of its engineering corps, centralized its command and leadership functions, introduced the all-big-gun battleship, complex fire control systems, and new undersea weapons, developed wireless communications systems, and sought ways to integrate aviation into the fleet. It is overly simplistic to conclude, as some have, that the naval establishment, steeped in conservative traditions, resisted the airplane, viewing it as little more than a nuisance dripping oil on their polished teak decks.

Generally, and contrary to conventional wisdom about institutional resistance to innovation, the Navy's leadership and bureaucracy adjusted well to aviation and other changes, adding weight to the historian Ronald Spector's assertion that on the whole navies were more amenable to new ways of doing things than they and their leaders are given credit for.[8] Early on, advocates of aviation in the Navy, chief among them Capt. Washington I. Chambers, recognized that the Navy had special requirements for airplanes and their operations, and for aviators and their training. It is generally understood that the sea environment places extraordinary demands on equipment and personnel that are not usually encountered in other military aviation activities.[9] Chambers bound the Navy's fortunes to Curtiss, who more so than other early experimenters was willing and able to meet the Navy's special requirements, particularly in designing and developing airplanes with the potential for operating with naval vessels at sea or in conducting long-distance flights over water. That is not to say that others did not have the expertise or potential to work with the Navy in meeting its needs. Curtiss' chief competitors, Wilbur and Orville Wright, had all the necessary skills and experience, but were so involved with providing airplanes and aviators for the Army and for other countries that they did not have the time, energy, or inclination to collaborate with the Navy.

It is not possible to understand Curtiss without comparing him to the Wrights, especially because the intense rivalry fueled in part by the patent dispute forms such an important backdrop to the early history of aviation. They were roughly the same age, they ran profitable bicycle sales and repair businesses, and as mechanics they knew and enjoyed working with a wide variety of machines. But there the similarities end. Curtiss had no formal education beyond the eighth grade. Wilbur Wright completed high school and was set to attend Yale had he not suffered an accident that required a long recuperation, while Orville completed advanced college preparatory courses before dropping out of high school at the end of his junior year. The Wrights' approach to the problem of heavier-than-air flight, while hardly scientific or theoretical, derived from their mathematical skills and relied on systematic laboratory testing correlated with field experimentation.[10] Curtiss, instead, based his approach on his "feel" for the performance of machines and almost always eschewed laboratory work for "cut-and-try" methods. Drawn to aviation through his competence in designing and manufacturing lightweight motorcycle engines, Curtiss saw flight unidimensionally as a challenge to be met with more power. The Wrights, in contrast, viewed the airplane as a complex system, made up of subsystems, the most important of which was control, while propulsion was the least important. Unlike the Wrights, Curtiss did not systematically document his aeronautical experiments, nor is there a large central collection of Curtiss papers such as there is for the Wrights, making the historian's task in coming to grips with Curtiss and his achievements all the more challenging.

Most important, Curtiss and the Navy continued a long-standing trend of government-private sector cooperation in the introduction and development of new technologies. The so-called military-industrial complex was not new, with the Navy in particular going back at least to the nineteenth-century collaboration leading to steam power, armored warships, and large-bore artillery. Moving beyond its negative connotations, examining the "complex" is instructive about the interactive dynamics of weapons procurement and technological change within a large bureaucracy. In a remarkable conjunction of civilian and sailor, Curtiss, with no family background in the military or personal experience with the profession of arms, allied with like-minded naval officers to make aviation a reality, and for the next two decades the company bearing his name became virtually synonymous with naval aviation. He moved as easily within the Navy bureaucracy as did any mid-to senior-level officer and they in turn learned firsthand the business of aircraft design and manufacture in his homes and factories. Simply put, Glenn Hammond Curtiss was the essential figure in the cooperative venture that saw the emergence and early development of naval aviation, and was the person most responsible for bringing to reality a technology now universally accepted as integral to the power and reach of the modern United States Navy.

—1—

Young and Restless

To visitors a century ago the village of Hammondsport at the southern tip of Lake Keuka in Steuben County, New York, could easily be mistaken for parts of the Rhineland. Neat, freshly painted houses lined the streets of the village. In the distance well-tended vineyards reached down from the lofty heights to the narrow and winding lake, which at a glance resembled the Rhine itself. But it was not grapes that attracted settlers to this idyllic setting at the turn of the nineteenth century. Rather they saw opportunities for growing wheat and other crops and raising livestock, which in the absence of anything approximating a road network they could transport to market by water. Keuka is one of New York's scenic Finger Lakes, chiseled from bedrock at the end of the last Ice Age. Viewed from space they look more like gigantic claw marks on the landscape than outspread human fingers. By 1796, John Shethar had a homestead fronting on the lake—then known as Crooked Lake for its characteristic Y-shaped configuration—where he operated a store and a flour mill. In a little more than a decade Lazarus Hammond bought the property, laid out lots and streets around a central square, and named the place Hammondsport. Agricultural products warehoused in the town found their way onto lake boats for the twenty-mile voyage north to Penn Yan, where a feeder canal provided access to the Erie Canal and points east and west.[1]

Commercial activity declined in the 1850s when a branch line of the Erie Railroad reduced lake traffic, but almost simultaneously viticulture emerged as a new and lucrative industry. The temperate climate and well-drained soil along the shores of the lake were ideal for varieties of North American *Vitis* used in making sparkling wines, whose effervescence masked their peculiar "foxiness." First was Charles Champlin's Pleasant Valley Wine Company, located between the hills south and west of town, followed by Walter Taylor's enterprise, and others. Winemakers from France, among them Jules D. Masson, followed the

I

grape to Hammondsport, introducing new varieties and cleaving deep cellars into the hillsides around the town and above the lake. Meanwhile, vacationers from Buffalo, Rochester, and other nearby cities discovered the pleasures of summer in the village, made more accessible by the Bath and Hammondsport Railroad, which in 1874 connected to the Erie at the county seat of Bath eight miles to the south.[2] For reasons perhaps only known to its 2,082 residents in 1870, Hammondsport evoked a powerful sense of place transcending its modest size and population.

The Reverend Claudius G. Curtiss was a relative latecomer to Hammondsport. An otherwise undistinguished Methodist minister, Curtiss arrived in 1876 with his wife Ruth and one of his two sons, Frank, who soon wed Lua Andrews, whom he had met in nearby Jasper where Claudius had had his previous church. After his marriage, Frank struck out on his own to open a small harness-making and repair business, while still living in the church parsonage on Orchard Street. On 21 May 1878, the couple delighted in the birth of a son, Glenn Hammond. Tradition has it that Lua named her son after the Glen, a cool, rocky valley with a series of cascades within walking distance of the town square, adding the "n" to the infant's first name as an affectation. When the elder Curtiss left for a new ministry, the couple acquired a comfortable white frame house on Castle Hill above the town, supposedly built by Lazarus Hammond and complete with a vineyard. On 15 February 1881, Lua gave birth to a baby girl, named Rutha in honor of Frank's mother but with an extra "a" characteristically tacked on at her mother's insistence.[3]

Life for the Curtisses took a less agreeable turn in the next few years. Suffering from failing health, Claudius retired from the ministry and returned to Hammondsport with Ruth to live with Frank and his family, only to die a short time later in 1882. Barely had the family recovered from this loss when Frank himself died in January 1883, leaving the two Curtiss matrons alone to carry on with raising the two young children. It was not easy. Lua taught piano and played the organ in one of the town churches, while the family supplemented its income by selling grapes harvested from their small vineyard. As if the deaths in quick succession of the two Curtiss patriarchs were not enough tragedy for one small family, Rutha came down with meningitis in 1887, which left her deaf and in need of special attention if she was not to lose her speech as well. Two years later, Lua decided to leave Hammondsport and place Rutha in the Western Institution for Deaf Mutes in Rochester, where she would receive speech training and learn lip-reading. Eleven-year-old Glenn remained behind to be cared for by his grandmother.[4]

Distant from his mother emotionally and physically, Glenn naturally was close to his grandmother Ruth, and she to him. As with most grandparents, she took a generally more tolerant attitude about his upbringing, while still setting behavioral boundaries within which Glenn knew he had to stay. The result was that Glenn had the security and love all children need, as well as a sense of independence and self-reliance that served him well later in life. Glenn attended the public school on the corner of Lake and Main streets, where he did just well enough to get by, although he did show an exceptional grasp of mathematics. He read voraciously, but not in great works of literature. Instead, he devoured every magazine, pamphlet, and brochure that offered information on mechanical devices and practical engineering. Outside the home and school he explored the hills around the town, and like everyone in the village was drawn to the lake with swimming and fishing in the summer and skating in the winter. He was selective in his friends, joining with them as the "uptown boys," who often found themselves opposed to rivals from the "low town" closer to the lake. A natural competitor from an early age, it was not enough just to go fishing, he had to catch more and bigger fish than his companions. Wintertime sled riding was not real fun for him until he had designed and built a sled that was faster than the other boys'. He followed his victories with the boast: "There, I planned your defeat a long time ago, and now I'm satisfied."[5]

Along with self-confidence, Glenn acquired a sense of independence early in life, in part out of family uncertainties. To help out with the finances he undertook a variety of jobs, including a delivery route for the *Hammondsport Herald*, minor electrical repairs for neighbors and friends, and rabbit breeding. For the paper route he rode one of the early "safety bicycles." Unlike the dangerous high-wheel "ordinary," the safety bicycle featured two wheels of equal size, pneumatic tires, and pedals and crank connecting a chain drive to the rear wheel through a system of sprockets; it optimized human muscle power in a way hitherto unprecedented. In the spring of 1892, when he had just turned fourteen and had completed the eighth grade, Glenn dropped out of school, a common occurrence in nineteenth-century America where high school diplomas and college degrees were usually exclusively held by the social and economic elites. At the same time, he left Hammondsport to live with his mother and sister in Rochester, then a prosperous commercial and industrial city of about 130,000 residents seventy miles north of Hammondsport. Situated on the Genesee River, Rochester was ideal for water-powered manufacturing, later augmented by banks, financial institutions, and companies specializing in clothing, shoes, tobacco, and beer. Just before Glenn arrived, the Eastman

Kodak Company had been incorporated. Founded by George Eastman, the company had become a major employer in the city, specializing in roll film and inexpensive handheld cameras marketed under the brand-name Kodak.[6]

Glenn got a job as a grocery delivery boy and then in the summer of 1895 employment at Eastman's new Kodak Park film-manufacturing plant north of the city on Charlotte Boulevard. There he and others were responsible for marking the image numbers on the paper backing of the film. Finding the work tedious and repetitive, Glenn designed and built a prototype machine that imprinted a hundred strips of film simultaneously, then persuaded his boss to adopt the machine and institute a piecework pay system. The result was a tenfold increase in production and a bump in pay for Glenn and his fellow workers. At Eastman's big Camera Works factory downtown on State Street he also got a firsthand understanding of the principles of photography and camera making. A year later, a decline in Eastman's business led to a lay-off, forcing Glenn to look for a new job. He started delivering telegrams for Western Union, which allowed him to earn money while gaining more confidence and experience in bicycle riding. As often as time and money permitted he rode his bike back to Hammondsport to visit his grandmother and catch up with his former schoolmates.[7]

About the same time, changes came to the Curtiss family, starting with his mother Lua's second marriage in 1895 to J. Charles Adams, a moderately prosperous vineyard owner from Rock Stream near Seneca Lake in Yates County. For a while the couple maintained separate residences, which allowed Rutha to continue her schooling in Rochester—until Lua became pregnant, at which time she moved to Adams' home in Rock Stream, leaving Rutha behind to board at the institution. Before the end of 1897, Lua gave birth to a son, G. Carl Adams, Glenn's half-brother.[8]

On one of his forays to Hammondsport, Glenn met C. Leonard Waters (nicknamed "Tank"), who was so impressed with his riding skills that he invited him to join a local group of bicycle racers known as the Hammondsport Boys. Waters worked for James H. Smellie, a local entrepreneur who owned and operated a drugstore on Shethar Street downtown and who capitalized on the bicycle craze of the 1890s by getting into bicycle sales and service. Glenn joined Waters and the Boys at Stony Brook Farm, about two miles outside town where Harry M. Champlin, whose father had founded the Pleasant Valley Wine Company, let them ride on the track he used for his trotting horses. It did not take long before Waters and Smellie saw in Curtiss the unusual combination of raw talent and competitive spirit needed to win bicycle races, and Glenn did not disappoint them. With light blue eyes and a high forehead, the lanky and muscular youth weighed about 150 pounds soaking wet, without an ounce of fat—an ideal bicycle racer. He won a Memorial Day road race in Pleasant Valley in 1897, riding one of Smellie's Stearns Specials. Two more victories followed in Fourth of July races in nearby Weston and Wayne. With the Hammondsport Boys he entered other competitions throughout the area, usually riding his bike to the events in the morning and competing in the afternoon.[9]

The bicycle had created a nation on wheels by the middle of the decade, with hundreds of manufacturers churning out more than a million vehicles annually. For the first time, people had a means of personal transportation that was relatively inexpensive and easy and safe to operate, especially compared to the horse. Women especially reveled in the liberation offered by the new technology, which transformed long-established patterns of dress and behavior. By the early 1890s, bicycle racing, with amateurs and professionals alike streaking along roads and around dirt and wood tracks, satisfied a populace fascinated with speed and addicted to sports of all kinds. As for technology, the bicycle helped introduce metal stamping, electric welding, bearing design, and new power transmission concepts. Equally significant, bicycle manufacturing and repair provided a generation of engineers and mechanics with metalworking and other skills applicable to the automobile, and later, the airplane.[10]

Absorbed with the bicycle and racing, Glenn had little time to make the acquaintance of young women in Hammondsport, except for Lena Pearl Neff, whom he had known for a number of years. Lena's aunt, her mother's sister, was Mrs. George Osborne, whose husband was a good friend of the Curtisses. Mrs. Osborne recalled: "I remember well when Glenn and Lena met. It was at my house and the children were playing hide and seek. Glenn always liked her and never had very many girls." At the time of her birth on 14 September 1879 Lena's parents, Guy L. and Jennie Neff, were living in Wheeler, about eight miles west of Hammondsport. Sometime in the early 1890s, about when Glenn left for Rochester, the Neffs moved to Hammondsport, where Lena's father owned and operated a sawmill and a freight-hauling business. His brother Frank, Lena's uncle, ran a machine shop in Hammondsport that made wire retainers for champagne corks, which he marketed locally and to wine makers in France. By the end of 1895, the friendship between Glenn and Lena had matured into love and, in keeping with the custom of the time, Glenn received Lena's permission to call on her. He was a guest at her home in June 1896, and accompanied her, her parents, and the Osbornes to the wedding anniversary celebration of one of their out-of-town relatives in October 1897.[11]

Lena's companionship and his commitment to bicycle racing in 1897 drew Glenn back to Hammondsport, where his grandmother Ruth was more than happy to welcome him into her home on Castle Hill. Glenn found work with H. E. Saylor, one of the photographers in town, and continued to pick up other jobs as needed, among them bicycle repairs for James Smellie. Glenn proposed to Lena before the end of the year, and the couple exchanged vows at the Presbyterian parsonage in Hammondsport on 7 March 1898; Glenn was just nineteen and Lena eighteen. The newlyweds lived for a time on Davis Avenue, but within two years Ruth invited the couple to live with her in the house on the hill. Lena and Glenn proved a superb match, each bringing qualities to the marriage that rendered it greater than the sum of its parts.[12]

When patriotism and a desire to help win the war with Spain led Tank Waters to enlist in the Army in May 1898, Smellie hired Glenn to handle the bicycle end of his business, increasingly seeing him more as a protégé than as an employee. By June, Glenn piggy-backed on his work for Smellie and began selling bikes on his own; an illustrated ad that month declared that "Wise Buyers Buy White Flyers. . . . G. H. Curtiss sells them." In March 1899, Glenn opened a bicycle sales and repair shop, on the north side of Pulteney Street opposite the town square, with the help of Mrs. Melinda Bennitt, a well-to-do widow and one of the founders of the *Hammondsport Herald*. He expanded the business the following year to include National, Cleveland, Orient, Reading, and Corsair lines, among others, and opened a second shop in nearby Bath, the county seat. In June 1901, Smellie finally got out of bicycles altogether, turning everything over to Curtiss, who now was the local franchisee for all the big-name marques. Growing more confident and knowledgeable in the ways of the business world, Curtiss hired his first workers and established his own brand, which he realized was more profitable than selling bicycles manufactured by others. He arranged a deal with a machine shop in Addison south of Bath to fabricate them using the Hercules name.[13]

With the expansion of the Curtiss business in 1901 came also a new member of the Curtiss family. On 8 March, Lena gave birth at home to the Curtisses' first child, a boy they named Carlton. Soon it was apparent to the couple that their son had a serious health problem: he was what was then called a "blue baby" due to the cyanotic appearance of his skin caused by a heart malformation that prevented adequate oxygenation of the blood. Today surgery is possible, but at the start of the last century there was nothing to be done. Still, Carlton was well enough to travel short distances and seemed to be improving during the fall, only to succumb suddenly at noon on 8 February 1902. Following services at the Methodist Episcopal Church, the bereft family interred him in the snow-covered ground at the Pleasant Valley Cemetery.[14]

Emotionally scarred from having lost his son, Curtiss focused all his attention on the bicycle sales and repair business, which earned enough for the couple to live comfortably but did little to satisfy Glenn's mechanical and speed aspirations. By the turn of the century, manufacturers in Europe and the United States sought ways to apply mechanical power to bicycles in an effort to widen the market for personal transportation. In 1893, the Hildebrand brothers in Munich successfully adapted a four-stroke engine to a two-wheeler, which they later placed in production. After the turn of the century, manufacturers generally located the engine low in the vehicle's frame to improve handling and road-holding. To transfer power to the wheels, they used belt drives—chains were thought to be more robust but also prone to roughness and vibration—with pulleys to compensate for varying engine torque loads.[15]

With his appetite for mechanical and engineering literature, and his knowledge of bicycles, Curtiss was interested in motorcycles, especially those from the E. R. Thomas company in nearby Buffalo. Thomas is generally accepted as the first American maker of motorcycles, starting in 1900 with the air-cooled single-cylinder Auto-Bi. Sometime before the fall of 1900, Curtiss made rough drawings of an engine and obtained castings from the Thomas company, which he sent to Lena's uncle Frank, whose machine shop could do the finishing work to Curtiss' specifications. The result was a single-cylinder motor with a 2-inch bore and a 2½-inch stroke (now referred to as undersquare) putting out an indeterminate amount of horsepower at about 3,500 revolutions per minute.[16]

Like other manufacturers, Curtiss installed his engine as low as possible in a reinforced bicycle frame, driving a large pulley on the rear wheel through a leather belt. To ensure a hot spark, he borrowed an electrical coil from a local physician who had used it to increase the voltage of an instrument for treating patients with electrical stimulation. A drip system Curtiss used for acetylene gas lighting systems was the model for the engine's carburetor, crafted from a tomato can, a piece of fine-mesh screen, and plenty of solder. He retained the bicycle's pedals, using them to get the machine up to speed before engaging the belt-and-pulley transmission to start the engine. The end result was similar in concept if not appearance and construction to modern-day mopeds. By the summer of 1901, the motorcycle, which had earned the nickname Happy Hooligan from dubious townsfolk, was ready for its first test run. After several laps around the square and fiddling with the carburetor and coil, Curtiss got the machine to fire and clattered down the street toward the lake. Town lore has him bailing out on the bike before it would have plunged into the water, having evidently not considered means of cutting the motor or stopping the machine. In reality, Curtiss knew full well how to turn off the engine and had fitted his first motorcycle with more than adequate brakes. His big problem was that the machine was heavy and had nowhere near enough power to pull the steep hills in and out of town.[17]

The experiment convinced Curtiss that he needed a bigger engine. He went back to Thomas later in 1901 for another set of castings, the largest they had in stock, which once more he had machined by Frank Neff. The result was an engine with a 3½-inch bore and 5-inch stroke that promised sufficient power, but it was heavy and ran so rough that after a short ride on the roads outside town Curtiss said it "almost tore itself loose from the frame."[18] Engineers often learn more from failures than successes. This second effort was all Curtiss needed to conclude that it was better to build a lightweight engine of his own design and that he needed a frame specially designed and crafted to cope with the power and vibration of a motor. Curtiss may not have realized it at the time, but through the internal combustion engine and the motorcycle he was developing skills that placed him at the cutting edge of a new engineering discipline, requiring a sophisticated understanding of the properties of materials, gas flows, heat transfer, and control and power transmission systems, all of which in a few years proved central to transportation technology in the twentieth century.

John Kirkham, the proprietor of a modest machine shop in Taggarts just down the road toward Bath, was the person Curtiss needed to transform his ideas about a motorcycle engine into metallic reality. Curtiss contracted with Kirkham to provide fully-machined castings to Curtiss' own specifications. He assembled the castings into an engine with a 3-inch bore and 3-inch stroke and installed it in a frame of his own design and fabrication. By early 1902, satisfied that he had a practical machine, Curtiss began production under the Hercules name. He sold his first example to a customer in Pennsylvania, then quickly moved on to design and build a larger 2½-horsepower two-seat model, which he personally delivered to a buyer in Corning, riding the machine all the way from Hammondsport. In June, the *Hammondsport Herald* remarked that Curtiss "is meeting with quite a demand for his motor cycles. . . . He has had many inquiries, and hopes to place a large number of machines before the season closes."[19]

Curtiss' belief that he had a superior motorcycle and his conviction that racing was the best way to generate public interest and a customer base meshed with his intense desire for speed and competition. Bicycle and motorcycle races were often combined at the same venue in the early part of the century, so it was relatively easy for Curtiss to make the transition from successful bicycle racer to motorcycle racer. Possibly the first American motorcycle speed event took place in Boston in July 1900. Thereafter, motorcycle racing took a variety of forms, including short dirt tracks at county fairs, board tracks, hill climbs, and endurance road races. Curtiss' baptism in the sport came on Labor Day, 1 September 1902, when he entered a ten-mile handicap on Coney Island Boulevard in Brooklyn, finishing third, a little more than a minute behind the winner. The *Hammondsport Herald* commented that even though Curtiss did not win, he "gave them a race for their lives," and that he "was complimented on every hand for the excellence of his machine." That was precisely what Curtiss wanted to hear as he sought new customers for his products.[20]

Curtiss brought out his first motorcycle catalog in February 1903. In it potential buyers found the Hercules had an air-cooled, single-cylinder motor situated vertically in a triangular frame, with a cylindrical fuel tank attached to the horizontal top tube and the batteries and coil in a separate metal box under the seat. As on his early machines, the power from the engine was transmitted to the rear wheel via a leather belt attached to a large pulley mounted on the wheel. In contrast to modern practice where the rate of fuel delivery is used to regulate engine speed, Curtiss controlled his by advancing or retarding the spark using a lever on the handlebars. The Hercules was well designed, well finished, and quickly gained a reputation for combining light weight with rugged dependability. For more performance, Curtiss introduced a 5-horsepower 2-cylinder engine—one of the first of its kind—in 1903. Curtiss employed the same 3-inch-bore cylinders from the single, arranging them in a V-configuration mounted longitudinally in the frame, along with the same pistons and only minimal modifications to the crankcase. By 1903, all Curtiss machines featured a narrow, boxlike fuel tank attached to the upper tube of the frame (now further reinforced), and used an increasing number of precision, interchangeable parts. As orders began to arrive from all over the country (and inquiries from as far away as New Zealand and South Africa), Curtiss found himself overwhelmed. In the spring of 1903, he shuttered his

Corning bicycle shop, built an addition behind his Pulteney Street facilities, and hired his first employees.[21]

With seemingly boundless zest and energy, Curtiss juggled motorcycle manufacturing with racing in 1903, tapping deeper into the flourishing American motorcycle market. On 30 May 1903, Curtiss rode a 5-horsepower twin to victory in a Memorial Day hill climb sponsored by the New York Motor Cycle Club at Riverside Hill in Kingsbridge, a bucolic neighborhood in the Bronx Borough of New York City. As if that were not enough for one day, he also came in first in a five-lap race for amateurs on the mile-long Empire City track in Yonkers, just north of the Bronx. More than five thousand spectators were present to see him finish in a little more than six and a half minutes, completing one lap in less than sixty seconds. Hailing Curtiss as a national champion, even though the accomplishment was considerably more modest, Hammondsport businessmen surprised him with a cut-glass trophy on his return home. Meanwhile, the *Hammondsport Herald* predicted that the dual triumphs showed the world that Curtiss had "a wonderful machine, admirably suited to all road requirements. . . . The result of these Memorial Day victories will doubtless give the Hercules a great boom." The paper further reported that the Curtiss shop had fifteen workers who had finished twenty machines so far that year and had at least that many more on order. But as all racers understood, disappointment was often just around the next corner; in a two-mile race in Syracuse on 12 September Curtiss did not finish due to an ignition problem. A more profound personal loss came less than two weeks later when Curtiss' grandmother Ruth died at the age of seventy-nine. Her death, while not unexpected after several years of ill health, was nevertheless hard on both Glenn and Lena, who had drawn closer to her during the time they had shared the house on the hill.[22]

The year 1904 saw more racing and more victories for Curtiss, who now was living up to the *Herald*'s confidence in his competitive prowess. In January, he was at Ormond Beach, a thirty-mile stretch of compacted sand in Volusia County on Florida's east coast. Ormond had been used for a year or so by automobile and motorcycle racers seeking more room for speed events. Among the first competitors there had been early automobile racer Barney Oldfield and manufacturer Alexander Winton, whose 60-horsepower *Bullet* had set a record for the mile in March 1903. Curtiss arrived at Ormond with one of his 2-cylinder motorcycles on 27 January, encountering unusually cold weather and in his own words "expending a small fortune" having his bike transported to the beach. After spending the next two days sorting out the machine, which had not been tested before he left home, Curtiss easily won a mile-long handicap race. In the feature event, a ten-mile contest on 30 January, Curtiss covered the distance in 8 minutes, 54⅖ seconds, shattering previous world motorcycle speed records and for the first time gaining genuine national recognition. The *New York Times* called it "one of the sensational records of the meet."[23]

Curtiss was in more familiar territory on 30 May for the annual Memorial Day hill climb in the Fort George Hill neighborhood of Manhattan. On another of his twin-cylinder machines, Curtiss was runner-up, finishing two seconds behind the race winner over a half-mile course that featured a challenging mixture of Belgian block and macadam surfaces. In a three-hundred-mile endurance contest from New York to Cambridge, Maryland, starting on 6 July, he led all twenty-seven riders into the control station in Philadelphia, only to have a runaway team of horses force him to veer off the road halfway between Wilmington and Dover, Delaware. The damage to the machine was so severe that he could not continue the race.[24]

Not too many months into 1904, it became obvious to Curtiss that the bicycle shop on Pulteney Street was not adequate for his rapidly growing motorcycle manufacturing business. Possibly aware of the situation, a group of businessmen of Owego, in Tioga County about sixty miles southeast of Hammondsport, sent out feelers to see if he were interested in relocating there. Curtiss met with them in May but determined that it was in his best interests to expand his operations in Hammondsport. By November, he had constructed a twenty- by sixty-foot, two-story building next to his Castle Hill home, reserving the Pulteney Street location for bicycle repairs only. Some 1904 Curtiss models featured twist-grip handlebar engine controls, using flexible Boden cables instead of the complicated articulated rod linkages found on some of his competitors' machines. Before the year was out, Curtiss discovered that someone else had trademarked the Hercules name. He decided to replace the former brand with his eponym, painting "Curtiss" on the tanks of his motorcycles in a distinctive scroll-type script.[25]

It was perhaps inevitable that the reputation Curtiss engines had for their combination of power, light weight, and reliability would come to the attention of inventors seeking means of propelling airships, or lighter-than-air flying machines. Of the many telegrams that arrived at Curtiss' office in Hammondsport, the one from Thomas S. Baldwin on 2 August 1904 requesting delivery of no fewer than five 2-cylinder Hercules motors was the most remarkable, for it was the largest single cash order he had yet received. Baldwin was one of those intriguing figures who occasionally find their way into the historian's world, an enigmatic man whose middle name is usually given as Scott but that in reality was Sackett. Born in Decatur, Illinois, in 1858, he became one of the most popular circus performers of the 1870s, renowned for his tightrope walking and expertise as an acrobat. His career as an aeronaut began in 1887 with a parachute jump from a balloon in San Francisco. Over the next decade, Baldwin, joined by William Ivy, also known as Ivy Baldwin, toured the United States, Europe, and the Far East, earning fame (and some fortune) for sensational feats of aerial acrobatics, daring parachute leaps, and fireworks displays, before settling down to manufacture balloons at a park and fairgrounds in Quincy, Illinois.[26]

Still the entrepreneur and promoter, Baldwin understood that the paying public had become jaded with balloon ascensions and craved something more exciting. He also knew that unless there were some way to provide more control over the balloon in flight it would never achieve widespread practical application. Relocating to San Francisco, he experimented with an airship powered by an automobile engine, which he managed to get into the air but was unable to control directionally. Inspired by airship pioneer Alberto Santos-Dumont and Europeans who after 1900 had married elongated envelopes with lightweight frameworks and gasoline engines, and enticed by a huge prize to be awarded for flights at the 1903 Louisiana Purchase Exposition in St. Louis, Baldwin was more determined than ever to build a successful machine. As it turned out, neither he nor any of the other potential competitors were ready for the opening of the exposition, but they got a second chance when the organizers extended the fair into 1904. In the interval, Baldwin had learned of Curtiss and his motors from one of his catalogs and quickly dispatched an order to Hammondsport. He received a refurbished 2-cylinder, 5-horsepower engine that he fitted to an airship he was building in San Jose, California, in the early summer of 1904.[27]

Test flights of the fifty-two-foot-long craft, named the *California Arrow*, in late July and early August 1904 convinced Baldwin that he had made the right choice in the Curtiss engine to challenge for the prize in St. Louis. But he also realized that he needed someone more nimble and weighing less than his two hundred pounds to pilot the airship, the balance of which demanded swift movements by the operator in the framework suspended beneath the envelope. To that end, Baldwin recruited Ohio aeronaut A. Roy Knabenshue to fly the new machine. The results spoke for themselves three months later when Knabenshue took the *California Arrow* through nine complete circuits of the exposition grounds, capped by a 3½-mile flight lasting twenty-eight minutes on 31 October. Although he received no prize money when creditors seized the now-bankrupt fair's assets, Baldwin was satisfied that he had taken a giant step toward practical aerial navigation. Less than a month later, Baldwin arrived in Hammondsport with much fanfare to see firsthand his new airship motors being assembled at the Curtiss works. He stayed a few days with Curtiss and even took a ride with him on one of his 2-cylinder motorcycles, posing afterwards for a photo that appeared in the *Hammondsport Herald*. More important, he assured Curtiss that he wanted his motors for a series of airships he planned to build in the immediate future.[28]

Curtiss got on well with Baldwin, but other than supplying him with engines he had no interest in airships or flying, his focus remaining on going as fast as he could on the ground. Then, as now, success in motor sports came more from hard work, thorough preparation, passionate commitment, intelligence, and skill than it did from luck and derring-do. Curtiss had all the necessary attributes to thrive in motorcycle competition, which also demanded a judicious blend of long-term strategy and innovative tactics to win with consistency. What appeared to the spectator as confirmation of Curtiss' reputation as a reckless "hell-rider" was in reality carefully calculated risk. Proof of Curtiss' maturation as a competitor came during the 1905 season, which began on 4 July with a race sponsored by the Chicago Motorcycle Club in the city's Garfield Park. On his 5-horsepower, 2-cylinder machine Curtiss circled the half-mile concrete track ten times in five minutes, five seconds. He was in Waltham, Massachusetts, with another of his 2-cylinder models on 9 August for a twenty-five-mile handicap road race, lapping the field and covering the distance in a little over thirty-four minutes. At the New York State Fair in Syracuse on 18 September he chalked up a victory with one of his single-cylinder machines in a three-mile race, coming in at three minutes, forty-seven seconds. He also set world records in one- and two-mile races, and easily won a five-mile event, leaving his competition "so far outclassed as to be hopelessly out of the running."[29]

Laurels in racing brought other benefits. Needing more capital to keep pace with orders, Curtiss talked with interests in Rochester and Elmira about moving to those cities. The prospect of losing the Curtiss enterprise so alarmed the *Hammondsport Herald* that it urged the town's grandees to do what they could "to retain this promising industry." The locals responded. On 17 October, Curtiss incorporated his business as the G. H. Curtiss Manufacturing Company, with Victor and Lynn D. Masson, sons of wine maker Jules Masson, G. Ray Hall, a life insurance agent, J. Seymour Hubbs, owner of a local wine cellar, George H. Keeler, Hammondsport's mayor, and Judge Monroe Wheeler from Bath among those investing in the new firm. Curtiss held a minority of the one thousand shares in the company (whose total capitalization was $100,000), received an immediate cash payment of $3,000, and became general manager with an annual salary of $1,800. With the infusion of money, Curtiss severed his ties with Kirkham and began manufacturing his engines in-house, doubled the number of his workers to forty, and completed another two-story building that allowed him to meet the expected demand of the 1906 season.[30]

At the New York Automobile Show, held in the recently opened 69th Regiment Armory in the middle of January 1906, Curtiss exhibited a range of new models with carburetors of his own manufacture, roller-bearing crankshafts, better valves, quieter mufflers, new fuel tanks, and generally upgraded fit and finish. A portent of things to come was that the newly formed Aero Club of America put together for the show a special aeronautical exhibit. Hung from the ceiling were balloons, model flying machines, Tom Baldwin's Curtiss-powered *California Arrow*, and a man-carrying kite designed and built by Alexander Graham Bell of telephone fame. Upon his return, Curtiss encountered a three-month backlog of orders, which he tried to meet by putting on a night shift and constructing another building with room for the office and enameling department. He continued racing, too. Triumphs in one-mile and five-mile events in Rochester on the Fourth of July highlighted Curtiss' 1906 racing season. He even gave his workers a day off so they could see him race; many, if not most of them, had never seen their boss compete.[31]

Largely through his Baldwin connection Curtiss became convinced that power plants for flying machines were a small though lucrative market. Determined to pursue prospective customers and knowing of the recent success Wilbur and Orville Wright had had with their airplane, he wrote to the brothers on 16 May 1906 to see if he "might be of service to you in getting out a light and powerful motor with which to carry on your work." With Lynn Masson and George H. Keeler, Curtiss drove to Columbus, Ohio, in a big Frayer-Miller touring car owned by J. Seymour Hubbs and manufactured in Columbus by the Oscar Lear Automobile Company. The route took the party from Rochester to Buffalo, then to Cleveland and Columbus over some excellent and not-so-excellent roads; the year before they had made the same journey and had found it to have been "exceedingly trying" at times. In Columbus Curtiss telephoned the brothers, one of whom politely told him that although they were not interested in a motor he was welcome to visit them if and when he was ever in Dayton.[32]

Meanwhile, the relationship between Tom Baldwin and Curtiss, strictly on a manufacturer-customer basis in 1904 and 1905, underwent a transformation in 1906. Baldwin had visited Curtiss in Hammondsport on at least two occasions in 1905, and Curtiss had followed Baldwin's airship exploits in the press and from periodic telegraphic updates. For testing airship engines and propellers, Curtiss built what he referred to as a "wind wagon," a noisy and dangerous vehicle with a three-wheel lightweight chassis and tiller steering that caused a commotion wherever it went. The collaboration between the two became more intimate in the aftermath of the calamitous San Francisco earthquake of April 1906, which had cost Baldwin his factory and one of his airships. Rather than rebuild in the Bay Area, Baldwin decided to move his base of operations to Hammondsport, a logical step bringing engine and airship construction together under one roof. Not long after Baldwin set up shop in Hammondsport, he and Curtiss completed a new airship with a 4-cylinder inline engine that Baldwin planned to fly at the 1907 Jamestown Tercentenary Exposition.[33]

In September, Baldwin summoned Curtiss to the Montgomery County fair in Dayton to help with repairs and maintenance of his airship's engine. Curtiss was happy to go, as it provided the opportunity to get together with the Wrights, who came over to the fair on 5 September to see Baldwin's airship in action. Introduced to Curtiss, the brothers invited both him and Baldwin to their bicycle works where they showed him photos of their airplanes in flight and answered Curtiss' questions about their construction and operation. Back in Hammondsport, Curtiss wrote on 22 September to thank the Wrights for their hospitality and to inform them about some changes Baldwin had made to the propeller of his airship based on the conversations they had had in Dayton. He added that he was "getting well started" on building an 8-cylinder engine and would let them know how well it worked out.[34]

The new motor was originally intended for Charles Oliver Jones, a former newspaper illustrator who wanted it for a flapping-wing flying machine he had been working on for years. From his experience with inline 4-cylinder engines Curtiss understood that it was relatively easy to align two of those engines at an angle and link them to a single crankshaft, thus creating a V-8 with double the capacity and power. When it was completed in late 1906, the new air-cooled engine was oversquare, its cylinders having 3⅝-inch bores and 3¼-inch strokes; it produced forty horsepower and weighed 150 pounds. Curtiss fitted the motor to a specially built seven-foot-long motorcycle frame, with the seat set well back over the rear wheel. To cope with the immense power he substituted a shaft drive for the more usual belt drive attached to the automobile-sized rear wheel. Neither Curtiss nor anyone else harbored illusions that the monster bike had any purpose other than to go fast, and the only place where that would be possible was the expanse of sand at Ormond Beach where he had set records on his twin three years before.[35]

Tank Waters and Tom Baldwin accompanied Curtiss to Ormond on 17 January for what was called the Carnival of Speed, during which automobiles garnered more attention than motorcycles. Squeezed in among the automobile speed and endurance races were the two-wheeled events, starting on 21 January with Curtiss in one of his single-cylinder machines speeding through the mile in a little more than a minute and five seconds. On one of his 2-cylinder bikes he just beat out a French Simplex-Peugeot two days later to set a world's record for the mile in a fraction over forty-six seconds. Impressive as these victories were, the fans were most interested in seeing what Curtiss could do with his V-8-powered machine. They were not disappointed. On the twenty-fourth, donning a leather jacket and a homemade helmet, Curtiss swung onto the seat of the V-8 and fixed a safety strap around his waist just in case the blast of air at speed knocked him off the bike. After a hefty push start from Waters and Baldwin, Curtiss was enveloped in noise and almost overwhelmed by the fierce acceleration. It took two miles to get to the start of the one-mile timed course, which Curtiss shot through in 26 2/5 seconds at 136.3 miles per hour. As he slowed to ninety miles per hour at the end of the run, one of the universal joints connecting the driveshaft to the engine broke, causing the loose shaft to thrash around but fortunately not resulting in any injuries to the rider. The damage, coupled with a distorted frame, precluded the required return leg, and the speed was not official because the machine exceeded the one thousand cubic centimeter limit dictated by the American Motorcycle Association. Nevertheless, those present knew that they had witnessed something extraordinary; no human being had ever gone faster on two or four wheels, or for that matter in the air, and no one would until 1911 when a giant Benz speedster achieved 141 miles per hour.[36]

Rather than return from Florida by train, Curtiss and Waters opted to take a steamer from Jacksonville. They arrived in New York after a stormy voyage in which they both suffered greater or lesser degrees of seasickness. On 1 February, the day after he got back to Hammondsport, Curtiss canceled the night shift at the factory on the hill and regaled his staff for more than an hour with stories about his exploits at Ormond Beach while treating them to juicy

Florida oranges. The *Hammondsport Herald* believed that at Ormond Beach "Mr. Curtiss has again demonstrated his advanced knowledge of the building of motors and motorcycles, and that he is a nervy, fearless, expert rider." The paper predicted that the publicity from the record runs would result in more orders for the already busy factory, which might have to undergo even more expansion to keep up with demand.[37]

For the start of the 1907 season, Curtiss participated in the New York Motor Cycle Club's Memorial Day hill climb at the Vanderbilt Cup course at Manhasset, Long Island, on 30 May. Curtiss entered both a single-cylinder bike and one of his 2-cylinder machines, won his class in the twin, and was victorious in an open "free-for-all" race. The big event of the year was the sixth annual meeting of the National Association of Motor Cyclists in Providence, Rhode Island, from the first to the third of August. Curtiss was there with Lena and Tank Waters. On the first, he rode one of his single-cylinder machines to victory over a one-mile straightaway course in 56½ seconds, topping that with a win over the same distance in the 2-cylinder machine in fifty-one seconds—only five seconds slower than his record at Ormond Beach. He finished a disappointing third in a five-mile handicap event on a dirt track outside the city, but won a one-mile "free-for-all" in a little over a minute. The next day, he entered a hill climb on one of the city streets, winning the single-cylinder race, and finishing second to a big Indian in the 2-cylinder event. In his third race, an open for 2-cylinder machines, he was thrown from his bike while negotiating the tricky curve at the top of the hill. He was lucky to escape with a banged-up knee and a bloodied hand.[38]

The accident in Providence could have been much worse and signaled to Curtiss that at age twenty-nine it was time to retire and leave racing to younger men, but it did not by any means end his motorcycle business, which continued to expand and earn profits. For the first year or so after its incorporation, G. H. Curtiss Manufacturing was small enough that Lena could still handle the company's bookkeeping as well as the day-to-day correspondence, but as the enterprise grew she could not keep up with the work. In September 1907 Curtiss hired fellow Hammondsporter and long-time friend Harry C. Genung as the company's business manager. Earlier that year, another Hammondsport resident, Henry C. Kleckler, came to work at the factory, his mechanical skills useful in the design and construction of the big V-8. A few months later, Curtiss elevated Kleckler to shop foreman, relieving himself of much of the daily oversight responsibilities in the factory. With the production organization taken care of, Curtiss felt free to travel more. In October and November 1907, he and Lena went to New York along with Waters and Genung for the auto show, where his motorcycles and engines were again on exhibit. Another trip followed in December that took him to Baltimore and back to New York.[39]

A year later, following his return from the New York Automobile Show in January 1909, he began discussions with Waters about getting out of motorcycle manufacturing. Waters' Motorcycle Equipment Company, which had sold parts and accessories since 1905 and complete motorcycles under the Erie name for the last two years, now needed more room for its expanding operations. Curtiss, who had been concentrating more on the design and manufacture of airplanes and engines, did not have time to keep up with the motorcycle business. It made sense, then, to combine the two operations, both of which were located in Hammondsport. The two men agreed to join forces and in July 1909 formed the Marvel Motorcycle Company, capitalized at $50,000 and with Waters as general manager. All motorcycle manufacturing was taken over by the new company, although limited engine production remained for a time at the Curtiss plant. By the end of the year, Marvel had completed a new two-story, 3,400-square-foot factory building just down the street from the Curtiss works.[40]

For Curtiss the motorcycle was the link to aeronautics in much the same way as the bicycle was for the Wright brothers. Like the bicycle, which demanded a degree of skill and sense of balance on the part of the rider to effect full control, the motorcycle brought a quantum leap in speed along with the ability to cover distances without having to exert anywhere near the same amount of physical energy. Moreover, the motorcycle needed a carefully built, powerful, lightweight, and reliable engine, precisely the characteristics required for mechanical flight. Tom Baldwin and his airship initiated Curtiss into the new realm of aeronautics, but his full commitment to the technology of flight came from an entirely unexpected source: the inventor of the telephone and one of the most famous people in North America if not the world, Alexander Graham Bell.

—2—

Bell's Lab

I n 1906, it was hard to find anyone in the country who did not instantly recognize the name of Alexander Graham Bell. Renowned for his invention of the telephone, he was rivaled only by Thomas Edison as an icon of American know-how and the entrepreneurial spirit. Few realized or cared that the celebrated Bell was a Scottish-born Canadian citizen, and still fewer knew that Bell had been absorbed with flying machines since the 1890s. Bell's concentration on heavier-than-air flight went back to 1891, when he began experiments with kites at Beinn Bhreagh, his estate in Baddeck, Cape Breton Island, Nova Scotia, where he and his wife Mabel retreated to escape the summer heat of their home in Washington, D.C. In Washington, Bell developed a close friendship with Samuel P. Langley, third secretary of the Smithsonian Institution and one of the men constituting Bell's tight-knit intellectual and scientific circle. For his part, Langley had begun aeronautical research in the 1880s that had come to fruition with a series of steam-powered model "aerodromes." Bell was present on 6 May 1896 when Langley's aerodrome No. 5 made two flights over the Potomac, one of which covered 3,300 feet in a series of circles—the first sustained flights by a powered heavier-than-air flying machine.[1]

Bell's kite experiments from 1896 on revealed that the tetrahedron—with four triangular sides—combined lift and structural integrity and could be arranged in "cells" that formed "building blocks" for progressively larger flying machines. He also believed that the design promised inherent stability—then thought by many as an essential prerequisite of human flight. By the summer of 1902, Bell was certain that he could assemble his tetrahedral units into a "compound structure of gigantic size," fully capable of lifting the weight of a human being. As with other experimenters, Bell corresponded with Octave Chanute. An independently wealthy retired railroad engineer who since 1890 had acted as a personal clearinghouse for information on heavier-than-air flight, Chanute also provided financial support for experimenters whose work he thought showed the most promise. In 1903, Bell furnished Chanute with detailed information about his experiments with large kites, along with photos and data on their construction, weights, lift, and wind resistance (or drag). Two years later, in December 1905, Bell massed 1,300 cells into a kite more than eighteen feet wide that he named *Frost King*. It had more than enough lift to accommodate a man's weight and, Bell reasoned, could easily have more cells added so that it could be fitted with a lightweight engine.[2]

It is likely that Curtiss met Bell when Bell made a "hurried visit" to the New York Automobile Show on 18 January 1906, where among the exhibits gathered for the show by the Aero Club of America were Tom Baldwin's *California Arrow* and Bell's *Frost King*. From an examination of Baldwin's airship and Curtiss' engines, Bell was convinced that he could secure a motor suited to power one of his big kites. But first he wanted to do more experiments at his laboratory in Baddeck. He ordered a single-cylinder, 2½-horsepower motorcycle engine from Curtiss, which he fitted with a propeller and ran on a twin-float watercraft at Baddeck that summer. Nicknamed the *Ugly Duckling*, the boat proved slow and ungainly, leading Bell to substitute a 4-cylinder engine that proved to be too heavy and did nothing to improve performance. Now convinced he needed a motor that combined light weight with more power, Bell once more turned to Curtiss, who had been perfecting an air-cooled in-line 4-cylinder engine that produced fifteen horsepower. In the first week of December, Curtiss again exhibited his motors and motorcycles alongside Baldwin's latest airship at the New York Automobile Show in the Grand Central Palace, also attended by Chanute and the Wrights. About that time, Bell put in an order for one of Curtiss' new 4-cylinder engines, which he hoped eventually would prove satisfactory in a flying machine.[3]

Aside from these indirect connections with Bell's experiments, the only involvement Curtiss had in aeronautics in the first months of 1907 was through his collaboration with Tom Baldwin. With the coming of spring and good weather in Hammondsport, Curtiss and Baldwin erected a large building on what was known as Kingsley Flats, a low-lying area on the outskirts of town adjacent to the lake, where they assembled the airship intended to take part in the Jamestown celebration later in the year. Baldwin planned to fly the machine at a "gala" planned for 26 June, only to have bad weather postpone the flight until the evening of the twenty-seventh. Up to that point, Curtiss had been content to assist Baldwin on the ground, but the next morning, determined to get a better understanding of how the machine performed, he took it up for a brief flight, the first for him and a milestone in his aeronautical career. Following a "most exhilarating" flight, he reported that he had no problems controlling the craft, even when going against the wind, "although the rudder could not be neglected for a moment," and "it was necessary to steer all the time." Shortly thereafter, Baldwin and Curtiss were in Clarinda, Iowa, where Baldwin made a twenty-mile cross-country flight in the airship on the Fourth of July.[4]

As important as the Baldwin association was in getting Curtiss into the air, the connection with Bell, so tentative at first, proved in the end to be more decisive in pointing him to a career in aeronautics. In the spring of 1907, Bell asked two young men to join him in Baddeck. The first was John Alexander Douglas (J. A. D.) McCurdy, usually known as "Douglas," and the second was Frederick W. Baldwin, nicknamed "Casey." McCurdy, a Baddeck native and son of Bell's personal secretary, and Baldwin (no relation to Tom) had both recently graduated from the University of Toronto with engineering degrees and, being enthusiastic converts to heavier-than-air flight, were more than eager to assist Bell with his experiments. Army artillery Lt. Thomas E. Selfridge joined the team a little later. A West Point graduate in the class of 1903, Selfridge approached Bell in 1907 with the suggestion that he join the group in Baddeck to monitor the experiments, in order to learn enough about the technology to assist the Army in the eventual acquisition of a flying machine. Bell liked Selfridge personally, admired his initiative, and respected his broad knowledge of aeronautics; through his connections in the Roosevelt White House he easily got Selfridge assigned to temporary duty in Baddeck. As for Curtiss, the fourth and most important recruit to the aeronautical circle, Bell and the others valued his hands-on experience with airship engines, his innate mechanical know-how, and his obvious access to manufacturing facilities in Hammondsport. When Bell got back at the end of May from a trip to England he invited Curtiss to visit Baddeck and meet the rest of the aeronautics team.[5]

Not quite comprehending what he was getting into but hardly in a position to turn down Bell's overture to join him at his Nova Scotia retreat, Curtiss left Hammondsport on 11 July, arriving in Baddeck a few days later. Ensconced in one of the bedrooms at Bell's house on the bluff above the scenic Bras d'Or Lakes and struck by the beauty of the vista, he wrote to Lena on the seventeenth that "this is a great place." Bell escorted him around the house, the laboratory, and especially the big "Kite House" where in progress was construction of a structure with three thousand cells intended to provide lift for Bell's first powered flying machine. Curtiss also went out in the *Ugly*

Duckling for propeller tests with his 4-cylinder engine. Good food, drink, and animated conversation enlivened evenings in the big house, where Curtiss quickly developed a special emotional relationship with Bell's wife Mabel who, like his sister Rutha, had lost her hearing as a young child. In the most general sense the group discussed how they might cooperate to expedite Bell's experiments, agreeing that even though the Wrights had solved the basic problem of heavier-than-air flight important research was still to be accomplished in lift, propulsion, and control. Curtiss returned home on 23 July with an entirely new perspective on aeronautics and a sense that he might be in a position to make a contribution to the advancement of flight.[6]

At the same time, there was uncertainty, at least in Bell's mind, about the best way to accomplish the objectives discussed at Baddeck. Bell mused that it might be preferable to hire Curtiss and others, contracting with them for a specific sum for their services. McCurdy and Mabel Bell disagreed with Bell, believing that an association where each had a stake in the outcome would be more beneficial and productive; Mabel was even willing to provide the necessary capital. Baldwin stressed that the "really important thing . . . is to keep Mr. Curtiss," and that the best way to do so was to give him "some authority" and not relegate him to a "mere nominal position." But most significant was a philosophical difference between Bell and his new colleagues. Unaware of the obstacles that the Wrights had to overcome before they flew, Bell believed his many years of labor were close to culmination, needing only a means of propulsion to achieve success with a flying machine. Joining in an association with his young, would-be partners might mean casting that work aside to accommodate their ambitions and starting from scratch with expensive and time-consuming new projects. The solution to the dilemma was to divorce the association from the prior work done by Bell and limit any of the members' benefits to those derived from future activities and innovations.[7]

Regardless of how the organization was to be structured, the association came at the right time for Curtiss, who after the Providence races in August had given up motorcycle competition but who was hardly ready to forgo new challenges and prospects for him and his company. Moreover, with Harry Genung and Henry Kleckler he now had experienced and trusted people handling motorcycle and engine production, leaving him free to pursue other interests. Bell, Baldwin, McCurdy, and Selfridge drafted a proposal for the body, to be known as the Aerial Experiment Association (AEA), and invited Curtiss to return to Baddeck for an organizational meeting. He was more than willing to go, leaving Hammondsport on 3 September and arriving at Bell's estate a few days later. As before, he found genial companionship at Beinn Bhreagh and total commitment among the group "to get into the air." By the terms of the arrangement, approved unanimously, the members agreed to the principle of "working together individually and conjointly" on "the construction of a practical aerodrome driven by its own motive power and carrying a man." The AEA would be temporarily located in Baddeck and would move to a "location within the limits of the United States"—presumably Hammondsport—some time before the end of the year. Bell's aeronautical laboratory was to be available for the association's use free of charge. In a concession to Bell and his primacy in aeronautical experiments, and out of concern that winter weather would soon close in, the group determined to work first on Bell's big new tetrahedral kite before proceeding with other flying machine experiments.[8]

Formal organizational proceedings for the AEA took place in Halifax, where Tom Baldwin was scheduled to fly his airship. The group watched Baldwin make a short flight late in the afternoon on 30 September, then repaired to the Halifax Hotel that evening for dinner, at which Bell presented Curtiss with a trophy for his record mile at Ormond Beach. The interested parties signed the agreement in the presence of the American consul and a notary public, the terms of the document to take effect the next day. Bell was the AEA's chairman, Curtiss was director of experiments, Selfridge secretary, McCurdy treasurer, and Casey Baldwin chief engineer. The association was to be terminated after one year, unless the members voted unanimously to continue it for an additional year. All members shared in any inventions made after the formation of the organization. Mabel Bell pledged to the association the considerable sum of US$20,000, starting with a payment of $2,000. Curtiss received $5,000 in annual compensation, to be reduced by half for time spent away from the AEA on other business. On 3 October, he assured his partners that he was "honored" to work with the association, and that "my plan is to devote myself entirely to its interest. . . . I shall be at the 'scene of action' as much as possible," he added, "but when not, I shall be constantly working to further the interests of the organization." For their part, Baldwin and McCurdy accepted salaries of $1,000 each; Selfridge remained on full military pay and therefore declined payment; Bell, too, refused any income.[9]

Curtiss returned to Hammondsport on 6 October, spending ten days at home before he was off to St. Louis with Tom Baldwin to appear at a weeklong international aeronautics meet starting on the twenty-first. They took two airships, one of which had been designed by Curtiss with a more streamlined envelope, his 40-horsepower V-8, and twin propellers. Baldwin made a couple of flights with the old machine, losing a race to his former student and now rival Lincoln Beachey. Curtiss attempted a flight with the new airship, hoping to get more speed out of it than was possible with Baldwin's machine, but was grounded when he was unable to get the craft to balance properly. Meanwhile, in Baddeck, the AEA had progressed with Bell's powered machine, appropriately named *Cygnet*, because the ungainly complex of 3,400 tetrahedral cells could hardly be mistaken for a mature swan. Curtiss had advised on engine and propeller placement, but he was not present for its first test on 6 December. Perched atop the *Ugly Duckling* and towed behind a lake steamer, the engineless *Cygnet* flew easily with Selfridge aboard, only to be dragged through the water when Selfridge failed to release the towline on landing and was so badly damaged that it had to be written off as a complete loss.[10]

Bell and the AEA members assembled in Hammondsport for a short meeting on 23 December. Castle Hill was not Beinn Bhreagh, but Glenn and Lena were cheerful hosts who warmly welcomed everyone into their home and reinforced the collegiality so integral to the association. After a brief but thoroughly enjoyable stay, the AEA members split up for the Christmas and New Year's holidays. There had been general agreement at Hammondsport that even though Bell's tetrahedral concept had shown promise with the *Cygnet* the research should henceforth take a new direction, starting with Selfridge's suggestion that they construct a glider similar to ones already proved successful. Curtiss agreed to have it ready when everyone reconvened in Hammondsport after the New Year. The result was a biplane glider, closely resembling the diminutive "two-surface machine" designed by Octave Chanute and Augustus M. Herring and flown at the Indiana dunes south of Chicago in 1896. A bright but mercurial engineer, the Georgia-born Herring had assisted Langley with the design and construction of his model aerodromes before having a falling-out with Langley and being taken on by Chanute late in 1895 to help with his glider project.[11]

A comparison of the AEA glider with that of Chanute and Herring a decade before illustrates the new direction taken by the association, which brought it into line with conventional aeronautical practice. Both craft, for example, were biplanes, with two superposed wings separated by lightweight but strong Pratt trusses, adapted by Chanute from bridge designs and also employed by the Wrights in their gliders and airplanes. The wings on the AEA glider were 25 feet long, with chords (widths) of 6 feet, resulting in low aspect ratios of 4.2:1. (Aspect ratio is the span of the wing divided by its chord; generally speaking, a higher aspect ratio means greater aerodynamic efficiency.)

The wings had a total surface area of 270 square feet. They were spaced 5 feet apart and were divided into three 5-foot-long panels, with the lower center panel left open for the flier to suspend his body with his arms and control the glider by swinging his weight in various directions in the manner of a modern hang glider. The AEA glider's wings had a slight longitudinal curvature and had two fixed vertical triangular surfaces that were attached to the rear out-ermost connecting struts, evidently intended to mitigate side slips in flight. In contrast, the Chanute-Herring glider had wings spanning 16 feet, with 4-foot 3-inch chords and aspect ratios of 4:1. The total surface area was 136 square feet. Unlike the AEA machine, there was no cut-out on the lower wing, because the flier hung by his arms from a framework beneath the structure. Constructed of bamboo and spruce, with linen-covered wings, the AEA glider weighed 72 pounds, compared to the Chanute-Herring glider's 31 pounds. The AEA machine had a fixed flat horizontal tail without a vertical stabilizer, while the Chanute-Herring glider had a cruciform tail spring-loaded on a universal joint to compensate for wind gusts.[12]

Back in Hammondsport in January 1908, the AEA began experiments with the new Curtiss-built glider. On the afternoon of the thirteenth, after waiting for a major snowstorm to subside, the group hauled the glider to Mount Washington, an elevation on the east side of the lake. Baldwin and Selfridge went first, making glides up to three hundred feet and landing softly in nearly two feet of snow. Curtiss accomplished one short flight before the wind picked up and the team called it quits. Despite gusty winds, the flights continued the next day. Curtiss flew nearly 210 feet but found he had to swing his body a great deal to maintain control. Soon to turn sixty, Bell left the fly-ing to his younger associates, who for the next two months exercised the glider at every opportunity, changing details as needed and comparing their results to those of Chanute and other experimenters. Curtiss recalled that the experiments "made very hard work for everybody. It was a case of trudging laboriously up the steep hillsides and hauling or carrying the glider to the top by slow stages."[13] It is tempting to dismiss the AEA glider as a feeble attempt by the association to catch up to where Chanute and Herring were a decade earlier. Even worse, it was not even close to the breakthrough Wright glider of 1902, with which the brothers flew farther than six hundred feet in full three-axis control made possible by differential deflection of the wings ("wing warping"), a front elevator, and tail rudder. Yet the Hammondsport glider was an important step forward that brought the AEA into the mainstream of aeronautics—albeit belatedly—and provided Curtiss and other members of Bell's team with valuable experience that they applied to more ambitious future projects.

Evidence that the glider got the group thinking in the right direction was Selfridge's letter of 15 January to the Wrights, in which he asked the brothers about the construction of wings and the movement of centers of pressure on curved surfaces at various angles of attack. Wilbur responded promptly, writing that he and his brother had found that the center of pressure moved toward the front of a wing as the angle of attack diminished and suggested that the AEA should study the patent they had received in 1906 for their 1902 glider. He also provided details on the material and shape of their wing ribs and how they had attached the fabric to them. The Wrights were already familiar with the AEA from a late-December letter from Curtiss in which he told them about the association and its objectives and offered to supply them with one of his 50-horsepower V-8 engines. Not surprisingly, Wilbur turned down the offer. Selfridge and Curtiss harbored no ulterior motives or ill intent in their approaches to the Wrights, which were meant to open a dialogue with the brothers. For their part, the Wrights were secure in their knowledge that they were far ahead of any potential competitors and were confident that an organization headed by Bell would be focused on research and not profits.[14]

While still experimenting with the glider, the AEA moved on to its first powered machine. Selfridge was assigned to the task in consideration of the risk he had taken in trying out the *Cygnet* for the first time and his superior knowledge of the state of the art of flying. Officially named Aerodrome Number 1 in acknowledgment of Langley's contributions to flight, the machine quickly became known as the *Red Wing* for the color of the silk used as a wing covering. The top wing was 43 feet long, with a chord of 6 feet 4 inches at the center and 4 feet at the tips; the bottom wing had a span of 36 feet 8 inches with the same variation in chord. The corresponding average aspect ratios were 8.2:1 and 6.9:1, and the total surface area was 385.7 square feet. The wing ribs were laminated wood, with ash strips on the outside of the covering for additional stiffening. A pair of skids attached to the main framework constituted the landing gear. Propulsion came from one of Curtiss' 40-horsepower V-8s, now well proved in various airship applications, directly linked with a shaft to a two-blade steel pusher propeller. There was no provision for lateral (or roll) control, possibly due to concerns about infringing on the Wright patent. Instead, Selfridge hoped that the combination of dihedral on the lower wing and negative dihedral (or droop) on the upper wing, giving them a lenticular shape when viewed from head on, would impart a measure of inherent stability. A 4-foot-by-4-foot vertical tail rudder and an 8-foot-by-2-foot front elevator, both supported by struts fabricated from lightweight yet strong bamboo, provided side-to-side (yaw) and longitudinal (pitch) control. Without pilot and fuel, the 26-foot-long *Red Wing* weighed 385 pounds (also known as its tare or empty weight); with pilot and fuel the craft's total weight came to 557 pounds (its maximum takeoff weight or MTOW). In comparison, the Wright 1903 *Flyer* was larger, with 6 ½-foot-wide wings spanning 40 feet 4 inches (for an aspect ratio of 6.1:1), and a total area of 510 square feet. The empty (tare) weight of the Wright was a hefty 605 pounds, and its total weight was 756 pounds, almost 200 pounds more than the *Red Wing*.[15]

Bell rushed back to Hammondsport from Washington, where he had been attending to Mabel, who had been seriously ill for more than a month, arriving just in time for the first experiments with the *Red Wing*. On 9 March, Curtiss was first to try out the craft on the ice near the lakeshore, followed by test runs by Selfridge and Baldwin. They found that the machine had good rudder control at reduced throttle. Three days later, on the morning of the twelfth, the group hired the steamer *Springstead* to carry the airplane three miles north to a point where there were longer stretches of solid ice for the first flight tests. With some difficulty they off-loaded it onto the ice, which even at that point was starting to soften and break up. Recalled to active duty only days before, Selfridge was not present, and Casey Baldwin won the lottery to replace him as pilot. At about 10:30 AM, Curtiss fired up the engine, Baldwin took his seat, and almost immediately the machine surged forward, quickly gathering speed and lifting off the ice after traveling less than two hundred feet. Much to everyone's astonishment, a portion of the horizontal tail surface gave way while the craft was about ten feet in the air, causing it to make a 180-degree circle to the right before landing. The total distance measured was an inch less than 319 feet, attested to by twenty-five witnesses. Coming down the lakefront road, Bell saw the vessel with the *Red Wing* on board steaming back to Hammondsport and turned around to greet them at the wharf in town. He said he was much disappointed that he "had missed a great historical occasion."[16]

Curtiss remembered being elated with the results: "We had succeeded!" Then, with more enthusiasm than rational analysis, he added that "we knew now we could build a machine that would fly longer and come down at the direction of the operator with safety to both." The *New York Times* touted the event as "the first successful public flight by a heavier-than-air flying machine in America." The Wrights must have read this absurd news flash with a mix of amusement and annoyance, for it was not as if they had been experimenting with flying machines in a remote Himalayan kingdom. More than two years before, on 5 October 1905, Wilbur had flown more than twenty-four miles and stayed in the air just under forty minutes at the brothers' Huffman Prairie flying field outside Dayton. Perhaps thirty people watched, and Dayton and Cincinnati papers covered the story the next day.[17] Nevertheless, the AEA members, having come together only five months before, were overjoyed with the flight of the *Red Wing*. Limited as it was, the achievement marked an important first step that verified their hard work and commitment to getting into the air.

Bell was determined to garner as much publicity as possible for the *Red Wing* and the AEA generally. Augustus Post, secretary of the Aero Club of America, became one of the AEA's principal cheerleaders. Curtiss, Bell, Baldwin, McCurdy, and Selfridge were all in New York for the Aero Club's second annual banquet at the Hotel St. Regis on the evening of 14 March, where club president Cortlandt Field Bishop hailed Bell for his success with the *Red Wing*. Bell quickly demurred, insisting that all the credit was due to the work of his associates, especially Curtiss, "the motor expert of America," whose lightweight engine had been vital to the project. Credit was due, also, to his wife—probably the first woman, Bell said, to have "taken an active part in making an experiment in aeronautics a complete success." Bell also went out of his way to praise the accomplishments of the Wright brothers, although he did make a disapproving comment about what he considered their secrecy.[18]

Curtiss and the others returned to Hammondsport on 17 March for another try with the *Red Wing*, now slightly modified with a beefed-up two-surface tail. Warm weather had caused the ice to recede even more than it had on the twelfth, forcing them to take the *Springstead* farther down the lake. "We saw some very good samples of flying machines on the way down," Curtiss wrote to Mabel Bell, explaining that the lakeshore was "completely lined with gulls, wild duck, and wild geese." Once they wrestled the craft onto the ice, it began to snow, followed by rain, which soaked the untreated wing fabric. This added fifty pounds to the machine's weight by Curtiss' estimate. A coin toss with Selfridge, now back from active duty, put Casey Baldwin in the pilot's seat. Curtiss started the engine and advanced the spark to give it more power than it had had on the previous trial. The *Red Wing* leaped into the air after a run of less than fifty feet. Before it had flown no more than 125 feet, a sudden gust of wind pushed the right wing up, the craft tilted forty-five degrees to the left, and crashed onto the ice from a height of twenty feet, "completely demolishing the left half of the machine" according to Curtiss. "Luckily, Casey was not at all hurt by the jar, and while the experience was disastrous to the machine, it has taught us a great deal."[19]

The *Red Wing*'s flights, hardly impressive in view of the Wrights' achievements, helped to widen a growing division between the brothers and the Aerial Experiment Association. Bell, like Chanute, had vigorously defended the Wrights from those who doubted their accomplishments. But for some time he had been concerned about what he considered the excessive secrecy of the Wrights, which he believed ran counter to the open exchange of information vital to any scientific or technical endeavor. Sensitive to such criticism from an eminence like Bell, the Wrights maintained that they had not kept their early work confidential and that anyone desiring information about their airplane need only consult their 1906 patent, although they admitted at the same time that they had not gone out of their way to encourage much attention from the general public.[20]

To Bell, the principal lesson from the 17 March *Red Wing* "catastrophe" was that the team "had over-rated the automatic stability of this form of machine and brought home forcibly the advisability of directing attention to some form of control over lateral stability." Casey Baldwin, next in the AEA's sequence of designers, agreed that some form of enhanced control was essential. Drawing heavily on the basic *Red Wing* model, the new AEA machine, known as Aerodrome Number 2, was a biplane with the wings drawn together at their tips, covered with plain, undyed muslin, which earned the craft its nickname *White Wing*. A more critical change was the addition of triangular, articulated surfaces extending from the wingtips to facilitate lateral control. These were linked by cables to what Baldwin called a "tiller" with two arms cradling the operator's shoulders. When the aviator leaned to the left the system depressed the movable tips on the right wings and raised those on the left wings, increasing the lift on the right wings and decreasing the lift on the left wings, thereby banking the craft to the left. It was logical and straightforward. Bell had suggested using the surfaces, not realizing that as early as 1868 experimenters had suggested similar means of lateral balance in flying machines, and apparently ignorant of their use by French aeronautical pioneer Robert Esnault-Pelterie four years previously. Not until McCurdy and Selfridge described their control system to French aviator Henry Farman at an exhibition at Brighton Beach in late July and early August that year did they learn that they were known as ailerons (French for "little wings"). Bell further attested that although he was unaware of any of the specific details of the

Wrights' control system, he and others in the AEA did know about the brothers' wing warping and had rejected it out of worries about patent infringement and because they believed it weakened the wing structure. During extended discussions of the merits of the aileron system throughout most of April, some doubted whether the pilot would be able to cope with any additional controls. Curtiss, on the other hand, insisted that he "personally favored" the method, mostly because it mimicked the movements he was familiar with from riding motorcycles at speed.[21]

In other respects, the *White Wing* was nearly identical to the *Red Wing*. Baldwin reused the latter's engine, undamaged in the accident, and he incorporated the *Red Wing*'s biplane horizontal tail. A wheeled undercarriage—reputedly the first on an American flying machine—was used in place of the skids. Other changes included a 6-foot-diameter wood propeller and a steering wheel to control rudder movements. Unlike the *Red Wing*, both wings were the same size—43 feet 6 inches long (including ailerons), with a maximum chord of 6 feet 6 inches in their centers, tapering to 4 feet at their tips, for a total area of 408.5 square feet. At 430 pounds, minus the pilot and fuel, the *White Wing*'s tare weight exceeded that of the *Red Wing*. Construction took more than seven weeks, with the machine completed on 9 May 1908.[22]

Harry Champlin volunteered his Stony Brook Farm horse track in Pleasant Valley for the first flights of the new AEA machine. It was not an ideal venue for flight testing, but was about the best available within close proximity to Hammondsport. A tent served as a makeshift hangar. Rain and sometimes snow held up the work, yet the poor weather conditions did not deter Hammondsporters and news people from turning out to watch the proceedings. They had to wait until 13 May when conditions were finally right for the first trials, interrupted when the lower wing of the craft scraped the raised margins of the narrow race course. The team tried the grass infield, only to have the *White Wing*'s undercarriage damaged from the uneven turf. Raising the machine on its wheels and widening and smoothing the track solved the problem in time for more ground tests on 17 May with Selfridge at the controls. The next day, after the addition of a steerable nose wheel, Casey Baldwin made the first flight, only to have it cut short after 279 feet when the propeller became entangled with the trailing edge of the lower wing. Selfridge made two flights the next day, the second of which was the best at 240 feet, marred by damage to the front wheel on landing.[23]

Curtiss, who had just turned thirty the day before, was next in line when flights resumed late in the afternoon of the twenty-second. On his first attempt the *White Wing*'s engine failed to put out enough power and he landed on the track after flying a little more than three hundred feet. After adding more oil to the engine, he flew again, covering 615 feet before briefly touching down and getting airborne again. Curtiss was in "perfect control at all times" during the nineteen-second flight, which extended a total distance of 1,017 feet. It was by far the best the *White Wing* and the AEA had done with any of their machines. Curtiss later remarked about how well the control system worked: "When the machine first raised, the right side began to tilt down, which was easily corrected by the use of the adjustable tips which were operated by leaning to the high side and engaging a lever with the shoulders. This control seemed to work very well indeed." The *Hammondsport Herald* declared that Curtiss had "made the phenomenal flight of the series," while Curtiss recalled afterwards that he "felt very much elated" by the experience. Not only did the flight substantiate that Bell's team was on the right track with their aircraft design and control system, but it provided preliminary affirmation that Curtiss had an instinctive "feel" for the airplane's control system and of all the *White Wing*'s pilots had the most potential as an aviator.[24]

Unfortunately, things did not go as well the next day. This time it was McCurdy's turn with the *White Wing*. He took off with no trouble, and reached a height of about twenty feet where he encountered a stiff breeze that tipped the machine to the right. He tried to compensate with the aileron controls, but did not react quickly enough to keep the right wing from striking the ground, causing the craft to pivot and turn upside down before coming to rest 549 feet from the start. McCurdy narrowly missed being struck by the engine and came away with only a few scratches, but the *White Wing* was so badly damaged that the group determined that it was best not to effect repairs but to rebuild the machine in highly modified form. In the meantime, work began on 26 May on a third machine, for which Curtiss took primary responsibility.[25]

Aerodrome Number 3, given the tentative name *Four-Leaved Clover* by Curtiss, was nearly a *White Wing* clone, the group wisely eschewing radical changes in favor of incremental improvements to the basic design. Curtiss' V-8 engine had survived McCurdy's wreck of the *White Wing*, as did the biplane tail, but the propeller had not, to be replaced with a new, slightly smaller one. The wings of the new machine were a foot shorter than those of the previous airplane and had the same distinctive opposing dihedrals as previous AEA models. The wing chords were 6½ feet in their centers and 4 feet 5 inches at their ends, for a total area of 370 square feet. The tare weight had increased to 473 pounds.[26]

The Aero Club of America, steward for the better part of a year of a handsome silver trophy offered by the *Scientific American* magazine to the first aviator to make a straight-line flight of one kilometer (3,281 feet) in a heavier-than-air flying machine, provided added incentive to finish and try out the new machine. By the magazine's rules, the Aero Club would set more demanding objectives in each succeeding year, which if successfully accomplished would give the winner permanent possession of the trophy after three years. The zeal of Curtiss and the younger members of the AEA infected Bell, who decided to delay his summer trip to Baddeck and spend more time in Hammondsport to work on the latest project. Moreover, Augustus Post of the Aero Club had been closely following the association's work. He even attended some of its meetings and reported back to the club's headquarters in New York, where there was much enthusiasm for Bell and his team. In contrast, the Wrights, preoccupied with impending public trials of their airplane and suspicious of a group they now began to believe was infringing on their 1906 patent, rejected the club's overtures that they try for the trophy.[27]

Bell's decision to maximize publicity for the AEA and its experiments had the result of gaining the Wrights' attention. That Bell was involved impressed the Wrights with the legitimacy of the association, but the *Red Wing* flights, if anything, mostly reinforced the brothers' notion that they were comfortably ahead of any potential competitors and that the AEA was far from flying a practical airplane. The *White Wing*, on the other hand, demonstrated that Bell's team understood the problem of lateral control and had a solution that more than likely was covered in the Wrights' patent. So long as the AEA and others confined their focus to experimentation and had no intention of profiting from their work, the Wrights were unconcerned. But in June Orville had read that Bell and Curtiss planned to sell airplanes. That rumors of the AEA going into the airplane business proved unfounded mattered little, for the seeds of controversy had been planted.[28]

Inspired by the hard-shelled flying beetles that swarmed around Hammondsport in the late spring, Bell took it upon himself to name Curtiss' new machine the *June Bug*. The name was inconsistent with the prior nomenclature, but better than Curtiss' appellation. *Yellow Wing* would have been more appropriate. In any case, the airplane's first test flight on the evening of 19 June was aborted when the tail fell apart. The next day, with a new and stronger empennage and the Bells present for the occasion, Curtiss tried again, but failed to get into the air in three attempts. Conferring afterwards, the group concurred with Curtiss that the open weave of the wing fabric was too permeable, thus reducing lift. Borrowing on his and Tom Baldwin's experience with airship envelopes, the *June Bug*'s wings received a noxious coating (or "dope") of paraffin mixed in gasoline, to ensure they were airtight. The results spoke for themselves on the evening of the twenty-first. Curtiss flew 456 feet, then 417 feet, and finally made a third flight of 1,266 feet that easily surpassed his *White Wing* mark from a month before. "This last flight is the longest yet made in public in America," declared the AEA, obviously ignoring what the Wrights had done nearly three years before.[29]

That the team still had much to learn was evident the next day, 22 June, when Curtiss could not get the machine into the air. Another liberal dousing of the wings with dope, applied hot and this time with the addition of turpentine and yellow ochre (to help with photography, according to Curtiss), did the trick. Curtiss made two flights late on 24 June, both abbreviated due to excessive wind. The next morning Curtiss made a flight of 2,175 feet lasting forty-one seconds and reaching a height of forty feet. He found that the ailerons were effective in providing lateral control, but problems with pitch and yaw control led him to recommend that the size of the front elevator and the rear rudder be increased. Quickly modified, the *June Bug* was ready by that evening, by which time "several hundred spectators" had gathered at the racetrack. What they saw deserved every one of their cheers. Curtiss was up for a full minute and flew 3,420 feet, reaching the perimeter of the field at one point and making a partial circle before landing. Control was good, but longitudinal stability could still stand improvement. To fix the problem, Curtiss moved the engine slightly farther back in the frame and positioned the pilot's seat and the front elevator one foot farther forward, increasing the length of the machine to 27½ feet. Two more flights on 27 June of 1,200 and 1,620 feet confirmed the efficacy of the modifications.[30] It may not have been clear either to Curtiss or to the rest of the team, but they were involved in the classic cycle of aeronautical testing, with a self-taught engineer in the pilot's seat providing subjective data that led to increased aircraft performance.

Having already flown more than a kilometer with the *June Bug*, the AEA had no doubts that the *Scientific American* trophy was within their grasp. They contacted the Aero Club immediately following Curtiss' successful 25 June flight to advise the club that they were ready to compete for the prize. On the twenty-ninth Selfridge and Curtiss went to New York to consult with Post about the attempt. Bell and his wife, meanwhile, had left for Baddeck via Toronto, but stayed in touch through regular telegrams. Post was sympathetic, but Charles Munn of the *Scientific American* was not; he still hoped to get the Wrights involved. Once again the brothers declined, citing as a reason the club's rules stipulating that the machine had to start under its own power, which meant they would have to abandon the catapult they used to get their wheelless craft into the air. One final hurdle was deciding where to hold the event. The Aero Club thought it more appropriate to hold it in New York, where it would generate a bigger audience and more publicity, but in the end they had no choice and acceded to having the trial in Hammondsport on the Fourth of July.[31]

Curtiss made two short flights with the *June Bug* on 2 July, during which he found the machine hard to control due to the breezy conditions. "When I strike a gust of wind it's like hitting a steep grade on a motor cycle; it's as solid a reality as that," Curtiss commented later. The next morning, Curtiss lost control moments after taking off, and the machine rolled to the left and struck the ground, suffering damage to its left wing and front elevator. Following hasty repairs, the airplane was ready for Curtiss to try again in the early evening. He flew the entire length of the field and was about to attempt a turn, but he hesitated and had to land when he approached a stand of trees. The flight covered 3,900 feet in a little more than sixty-eight seconds and convinced Selfridge that they were "all ready for tomorrow."[32]

As luck would have it, the weather turned rotten on Saturday the fourth, although it did not deter a substantial crowd from gathering at Stony Brook Farm that morning. Among those who turned out were Post, Herring, Tom Baldwin, Stanley Y. Beach, representing the *Scientific American*, and Charles M. Manly. The latter had been Langley's chief engineer and had designed the superb radial engine that powered his 1903 aerodrome. Also present was David Fairchild and his wife Marian, the Bells' second daughter, who kept company with Lena Curtiss, along with a large number of reporters and photographers. Marian wrote to her father that "the air was full of the click click of shutters," and that motion picture cameramen were also present to record the event. Rain showers came and went, until finally the clouds lifted, the wind died, and Curtiss decided to give it a try at 5:45 PM. Soon after taking off he quickly soared to forty feet above the ground. Worried, Lena exclaimed: "Oh, why does he go so high?" Uncomfortable with the controls, and nearing the end of the field, Curtiss cut off the motor and descended to an easy landing, having covered 2,700 feet in the air, a "very pretty flight" according to the *Hammondsport Herald*, but some distance short of the required kilometer.[33]

Curtiss thought an adjustment to the tail would give him better control and he was right. He took off again at about 7:00 PM. With eight cylinders roaring in his ears and the *June Bug* streaming a mist of oil smoke, Curtiss exceeded not just a kilometer but a mile in less than two minutes, then made a half-turn and landed in a field well beyond the racetrack. The total distance was about six thousand feet, although in a straight line from the starting point the measurement was 5,090 feet, and the time in the air was 1 minute, 42½ seconds. Amid raucous cheers and jubilant applause, the crowd rushed through the fields to greet him, all intent on being the first to congratulate him. David Fairchild was ecstatic: "The thing is done. Man flies!" Curtiss recalled that "she flew like a real June Bug," and that because he was concentrating so hard on flying he "saw nothing except the course and the flag marking a distance of one kilometer. . . . I might have gone a great deal farther, as the motor was working beautifully and I had the machine under perfect control." Bell telegraphed from a hotel on Prince Edward Island: "[A]ccept our heartiest congratulations upon your magnificent success." Curtiss and the AEA had won the *Scientific American* trophy but they had more to accomplish before they were finished with the *June Bug*.[34]

The next day, before "nearly the entire population of Hammondsport and the surrounding country" and the Aero Club representatives who had stayed in town for another day, Curtiss flew again. The flight lasted seventy-five seconds and covered 4,500 feet, and for the first time he made a complete circle. We have his own account: "The start was made as usual and after going about half a mile in a straight line, the writer attempted the curve. To do this, I steered to the right with the rudder and inclined the right wing tip down at the same time by the movement of the shoulders. I made a rather awkward turn, either tilting the machine too much or not enough but finally got around and was headed back toward the starting point." He tried another turn but by then had bled off too much speed and had to come down, damaging the front elevator and the right wing. Repaired with a larger front elevator, the *June Bug* was in the air again on 8 July, only to have the flight cut short after about 2,700 feet when the engine cut off and Curtiss could not restart it. Upon learning of the *June Bug*'s success on the fourth, Bell had wired the Washington law firm of Mauro, Cameron, Lewis, and Massie with a request to send one of their people to Hammondsport to have a close look at the airplane. Sheldon Cameron, one of the firm's patent attorneys, showed up. After examining the machine, Cameron reported that the ailerons, shoulder control system, landing gear, and steerable front wheel might be worth patent applications.[35]

At this juncture, perceiving that Curtiss and the AEA constituted a potential serious threat to their invention, the Wrights decided it was time to intervene. On 10 July, Wilbur wrote to Orville from France, where he was demonstrating their airplane in anticipation of a contract with a local business syndicate, that the time may have come to remind Curtiss "that we have a patent covering broadly the combination with wings to right and left of the center of a flying machine which can be adjusted to different angles of incidence of vertical surfaces adjustable to correct inequalities in the horizontal resistance of the differently adjusted wings. Say that we do not believe that flyers can be made practical without using this combination, and inquire whether he would like to take a license to operate under our patent for exhibition purposes." Orville acknowledged that he "had been thinking of writing Curtiss" about the matter. He also thought they needed to inform the *Scientific American* that "we had furnished [the AEA] the information as to how our older machines were constructed, and that they have followed this construction very closely, but have failed to mention the fact in any of their writings."[36]

Orville followed up with a letter to Curtiss on 20 July in which he cautioned that he and his brother had never given him or the AEA "permission to use the patented features of our machine for exhibitions, or in a commercial way," and that they believed "it will be very difficult to develop a successful machine without the use of some of the features covered in this patent." Curtiss replied four days later from Hammondsport: "Contrary to news-paper reports, I do not expect to do anything in the way of exhibitions. My flights here have been in connection with the Aerial Experiment Association's work. I have referred the matter of the patents to the Secretary of the Association." The more Orville learned about the *June Bug*'s ailerons and system of lateral control the more convinced he became that those details were covered in their patent.[37]

Delighted with the success of the *June Bug*, Bell recommended, and his associates agreed, to build still another machine, the rationale being that they wanted to have a backup in case something happened to the *June Bug*. Next in the AEA's order of priority, Douglas McCurdy had responsibility for the new airplane, officially Aerodrome Number 4, which generally followed the *June Bug*'s design and construction. In Hammondsport Curtiss and Selfridge helped McCurdy with the project, while Baldwin assisted Bell in Baddeck with the *Cygnet II*, a second large craft based on the tetrahedral principle. Work proceeded in fits and starts through the summer of 1908 in large part because Curtiss and Selfridge were busy with other commitments. McCurdy used his spare time learning to fly the *June Bug*. He made five flights on 27 July, followed the next day by another in which he made a complete circle and landed at the point where he took off. Selfridge also honed his skills in almost daily flights in the *June Bug* in late July and early August before being called to Washington to serve on an Army aeronautical board. He was to evaluate the performance of the Wright airplane and a craft Augustus Herring had promised to deliver in time for the trials at Fort Myer, Virginia, located just across the Potomac River from Washington.[38]

In November 1907, the Army's Signal Corps had called for bids for a heavier-than-air flying machine, the specifications carefully written to favor the Wrights, who along with Herring were awarded contracts in February 1908 to provide machines for evaluation. At about the same time, a similar solicitation went out for an airship, closely adhering to performance data Tom Baldwin and Curtiss had discussed with the Army leadership in the fall of 1907. On 24 February 1908, Baldwin won the contract with a low bid of $6,750, obligated to deliver the craft within 150 days for trials at Fort Myer. To meet the Army's specifications, Baldwin's airship needed to attain a speed of eighteen miles per hour and meet various endurance and other criteria. Bonuses would be paid if the machine exceeded requirements. Twice the size of the *California Arrow*, the airship could not be controlled by having the pilot shift his weight back and forth in the framework; instead, Baldwin and Curtiss fitted the machine with a front-mounted two-surface elevator for longitudinal stability. More problematic was the two-hour endurance rule, necessitating a water-cooled motor significantly heavier than the air-cooled engines Curtiss was familiar with. With Henry Kleckler's assistance, Curtiss modified one of his 25-horsepower inline 4-cylinder engines for water cooling, adding about seventy-five pounds for the radiator, water pump, and water to the original's 110 pounds. The engine and propeller were mounted at the front of the machine in tractor configuration. A special rubberized silk fabric ensured that the airship's 96-foot-long, 20,000-cubic-foot envelope was gas-tight.[39]

Baldwin planned to dispatch his airship, now officially designated *Signal Corps 1* (*SC-1*), to Fort Myer during the week of 12 July, but was delayed while he secured a tent to house the machine on the post's drill field. Curtiss arrived on the twenty-seventh with four mechanics to expedite assembling the craft, a process that consumed the better part of a week. On 4 August, Baldwin and Curtiss took to the air for a thirty-minute flight. Other flights followed on an almost daily basis for the next ten days, during which the duo encountered remarkably few problems. Bad weather cut short one flight and another had to be postponed while Curtiss wrestled with an ignition problem in the motor, but on the seventh, things went so well that Curtiss took it upon himself to act as an observer, sketching a map of the terrain as they passed over it at altitudes up to six hundred feet. Still not entirely certain his motor was putting out as much power as would be needed for the speed tests, Curtiss raced out of town on the eighth for Hammondsport to fabricate a couple of new carburetors. He was back for another flight on the eleventh that went well enough for Baldwin to declare the airship ready for its official trials.[40]

Baldwin and Curtiss took off on the evening of the twelfth for the *SC-1*'s first speed tests, with Selfridge on the ground as the Army's official timer. Not far into the flight, an ignition wire broke, dropping out one of the engine's four cylinders, followed by a total loss of spark that killed the motor and forced the craft down in a cornfield. Curtiss effected repairs so that they could get back to Fort Myer. Interviewed afterward, he observed: "We seemed to have everything against us." Two days later, everything was for them. With the engine running perfectly, the airship averaged just under twenty miles per hour in two flights, exceeding the Army's requirement by nearly two miles per hour. Curtiss thought it could make another ten miles per hour with more flying experience and some tweaking of the motor to extract more horsepower. The endurance trial on the evening of 15 August went just as well. Baldwin and Curtiss were in the air for two hours and five minutes, flying thirty-three miles over the five-mile course, at times reaching speeds in excess of forty-five miles per hour and exciting the crowd at dusk as the airship's engine emitted bursts of fire "like a demon from the sky." Curtiss went back to Hammondsport to work on the new AEA machine and make more flights in the *June Bug* while Baldwin stayed behind at Fort Myer to instruct Selfridge, Lt. Benjamin D. Foulois, and Lt. Frank P. Lahm in the operation of his airship.[41]

With Wilbur on the other side of the Atlantic astonishing the French with the Wright airplane, Orville had responsibility for the Army demonstration flights at Fort Myer, starting on 3 September. He was not pleased that Selfridge was a member of the evaluation team, believing his connections with the brothers' potential rivals Bell and the AEA constituted a conflict of interest. He wrote to Wilbur that "I will be glad to have Selfridge out of the way. I don't trust him an inch. He is intensely interested in the subject, and plans to meet me often at dinners, etc., where he can try to pump me. He has a good education, and a clear mind. I understand that he does a good deal of knocking behind my back." On the other hand, Wilbur thought highly of Foulois and other officers at Fort Myer, one of whom was Lt. George C. Sweet, detailed by the Navy to observe the trials and anxious lest the Army secure a monopoly on the new technology.[42]

Nor was Orville especially overjoyed when Curtiss showed up at Fort Myer on 3 September to help Baldwin sort out mechanical problems with the *SC-1*'s engine. He seemed pleased that Curtiss, despite his experience with aero engines, had "not been able to make the motor on the dirigible run more than a minute or two without missing about half its explosions. Ours runs without a miss." Although wary of Curtiss and his possible hidden agenda for being at Fort Myer, Wright did not find him as offensive as Selfridge. At one point, discussing an airplane that engineering students at Cornell were building, Curtiss told Wright that he had seen it and that it closely followed the Wright design. In a letter to Bell on the seventh, Curtiss said that he had talked with Wright, although "nothing was said about his patents on adjustable surfaces. He has nothing startling about his machine and no secrets." He went on to observe that Orville's "first flight was rather short as Mr. Wright said he was unaccustomed to the machine, and the levers seemed awkward for him. He made a wrong move and headed for the tent, which necessitated immediate landing." Curtiss was not enamored of the Wrights' method of getting their machines airborne. "The launching device, which includes a derrick, and a big weight which drops the pulleys and rope to give the initial velocity, does not seem to be very well liked, and I believe that all who have seen our machine and the Wrights' prefer our method of starting on wheels to skids." And, not surprisingly, Curtiss found the Wrights' engine "rather crude and not exceptionally light."[43]

Before the month was out, fate dictated that the Wrights and the AEA would suffer a mutual tragedy at Fort Myer. As he gained more confidence in his skills, Wright made progressively longer flights in the airplane, one of which on 11 September lasted more than seventy minutes and others in which he took up various Army officers as part of their indoctrination to aviation. It was Selfridge's turn to fly with Wright on the evening of the seventeenth. The circling flight 150 feet above the drill field was uneventful until a tapping noise from the back of the airplane convinced Wright that something was amiss and that he needed to kill the motor and land immediately. But it was too late. Before he could get back on the ground, the craft began to vibrate, yawing to the right, and then falling off to the left as Wright desperately attempted to regain control. Moments before the crash, Wright heard Selfridge say something like "Oh! Oh!" Within minutes rescuers arrived at the scene, finding both fliers drenched in blood, their clothing shredded, and the pair in need of immediate medical attention. Wright was in bad shape, with a broken left leg, broken ribs, lacerations, and back injuries, but Selfridge was unconscious with a fractured skull and died hours later despite emergency surgery to save his life. He earned the dubious honor of being the first to perish in a powered airplane accident.[44]

Bell's son-in-law David Fairchild wired Bell the bad news about Selfridge's death and his guess that a broken propeller had caused the accident. Curtiss confirmed the details of the crash by phone soon after it happened. Like everyone in Hammondsport he was shocked and saddened when news came the next day that Selfridge had died. He left Hammondsport as soon as he could to attend a special meeting of the AEA in Washington on 21 September. The group passed two resolutions: the first expressed the "loss of a dear friend and valued associate," and the second, to Orville, offered the "deepest sympathy for his grief" over Selfridge's death and their best wishes for his full and speedy recovery.[45]

Agreeing with Fairchild that the cause of the accident had been a broken propeller, Bell speculated that if the brothers had somehow arranged both propellers on a single shaft, the accident would not have occurred. He also attributed the mishap to pilot error and Orville's overcorrection of the front elevator controls, which pitched the airplane up into a low-altitude stall from which recovery was impossible. Curtiss generally concurred with Bell's assessment. He understood the potential for disaster due to the differential thrust caused by the sudden failure of one of a pair of propellers: "I do not see how it would be possible to handle an aeroplane of the Wright type after one propeller had broken unless the power were shut off instantly and, even then, the momentum of the revolving parts might give force enough to the remaining propeller to cause the operator to lose control." Curtiss had also been experimenting at Hammondsport with an arrangement using two belt-driven propellers on concentric shafts, and just to be on the safe side, assured his AEA colleagues that "we have discontinued further experiments with this construction."[46]

Subsequent investigation revealed that a combination of factors, as is the case with most aircraft accidents, caused the crash that resulted in Selfridge's fatal injuries. On the sixteenth, the day before the accident, Wright had installed two new propellers on the airplane, with blades six inches longer than the old ones but with the same width. In flight the next day the right propeller for some reason had split longitudinally, causing its pitch, or the angle it struck the air, to decrease, thus losing thrust and setting up a vibration that loosened the propeller in its mounting. Thrown out of alignment, the propeller severed one of the support wires to the rudder, which rotated sideways and acted like an elevator to drive the craft downwards. There was absolutely nothing Wright could have done to control the machine or prevent the crash after the propeller failure.[47]

Business commitments in Hammondsport prevented Curtiss from attending Selfridge's funeral and burial at Arlington Cemetery, but he was back in Washington for another meeting of the AEA at Bell's home on 26 September. There the group agreed to appoint Selfridge's father as a voting member and to extend the association for another six months with Mabel Bell again covering expenses. Charles J. Bell, a banker cousin of Alexander Graham Bell, came into the AEA as a trustee with responsibility for overseeing patents and finances. Later, Bell wrote to Curtiss asking him what he thought about contacting the Army to see if it might be interested in using one of the AEA airplanes during the interval while Orville recovered and the brothers prepared another machine for evaluation. "I can say," Bell commented about the Wrights, "that we are their friends, and not their competitors, and will not do anything that would interfere with their contract with the government." Curtiss replied on 1 October: "Think well of your idea. All here with you in any action you take." Army officials declined, although they promised to dispatch a replacement officer to Hammondsport to monitor the AEA's flying experiments.[48]

Bell now believed that the association had gone far beyond its original mandate "to get into the air" and could continue only by identifying key innovations, securing patent rights to them, and offering them to businessmen as potential investment opportunities. But Bell did not think much could be derived from the Hammondsport experiments, because the "general features" of the four airplanes built and flown there duplicated work already done by others who held patent rights. "Should any patents we obtained turn out to be subordinate to other patents already granted," he warned, "the owners of these patents, not being affiliated with the Association would be liable to make trouble." Once clear of the patent hurdle, though, three alternatives were possible: the money could be distributed among the membership and the association dissolved; the money could be held by the association "indefinitely" and plowed back into continuing experiments; or the association could use the funds to establish "a permanent institution or society to promote the art of aviation." "This third plan would be my desire," he concluded. No matter what choice the group made, it was crucial over the remaining six months of the association to concentrate on the "development of practical improvements of a patentable nature" to guarantee that the AEA left a permanent legacy.[49] It was obvious to Curtiss that Bell wanted the association to pour its energy and resources into his tetrahedral designs. As a consequence he was not likely to receive much support for continuing development of the *June Bug* or for any assistance should he or other members of the AEA identify key design elements worthy of patent protection.

That said, Bell wanted the AEA to be in the best position to defend itself should it go ahead with patents derived from the Hammondsport experiments, and on 29 September he outlined for his attorneys what he thought were the key differences between the AEA's and the Wrights' machines. Foremost was the AEA's use of rigid wings as opposed to the Wrights' flexible wings and wing-warping system. It was a fundamental difference in design philosophy: "We do not twist our aeroplanes [wings], or any portion of them, for any purpose whatsoever: Indeed, we look upon this kind of action as distinctly detrimental from a structural point of view, and our form of truss is specially designed to prevent it." Another important difference was how the Wrights coordinated wing-warping to movements of the airplane's vertical tail rudder, a feature they had introduced as a result of experiments with their 1902 glider. Bell pointed out that the Hammondsport machines achieved lateral control using the ailerons, and did not necessarily require simultaneous aileron and rudder action to make a banking turn.

It was clear from Bell's reading of the Wright patent that it was broadly written to include control derived from any movement of the "lateral margins" of the wings by any flying machine. Here lay the crux of the matter should the AEA be charged with infringement. "If we do this [that is, move the wings' "lateral margins"] we infringe their patent according to their own declaration. But if we do not, do we infringe?" He was certain that "in our machine we do not move 'the lateral margins of the aeroplanes' at all; and could not move them, even if we so desired, on account of the rigid nature of the trussing employed." Yet he also predicted that the Wrights would attempt to make a case that the AEA's ailerons were in effect "the lateral margins of the aeroplane," and that when they were moved it constituted an infringement. For Bell the response to this charge was logical: the ailerons, having no airfoil curvature, were not lifting surfaces and therefore were "mere appendages" that could be placed anywhere on the craft and contributed nothing to its support in the air. "I am decidedly of the opinion that our invention is not covered by the Wright Brothers patent," Bell concluded.[50]

That fall, while Baldwin assisted Bell at Baddeck with the *Cygnet II*, and Bell wrestled with the patent implications of the association's work, the *June Bug* became in effect the AEA's principal research airplane, with Curtiss and McCurdy almost constantly modifying the machine while flying it as often as possible. Tests of the airplane without tail surfaces had demonstrated that the speed could be increased without any adverse handling effects, and fitting wings with a revised airfoil cross-section improved lift. On 10 September, Curtiss was trying out a new rudder and front elevator when a fuel line broke during the flight and he lost power on four of the eight cylinders. Instead of landing immediately, he decided to see how well the airplane performed on reduced power, completing a turn and flying another half mile before bringing the airplane down. The flights also revealed that larger ailerons were needed for better lateral stability and demonstrated the inherent shortcomings of the air-cooled engine, which quickly overheated and limited the duration they could spend in the air.[51]

The most unusual experiment with the *June Bug* came as a result of McCurdy's suggestion on 23 October to modify the machine with pontoons or floats for flights from the water. Curtiss liked the idea, having written in August that "starting a flying machine from and landing on the water has been on my mind for some time. It has many advantages, and I believe can be worked out." He imagined that providing the airplane with the capability of operating from water would make it "indispensable for war purposes" as well as enhancing its attractiveness for flying exhibitions, should the AEA decide to go in that direction. Moreover, the experiment allowed preliminary evaluation of Curtiss' new water-cooled 50-horsepower, 8-cylinder V-type motor. When completed, the *Loon*, as it was known, had two fabric-covered 20-foot-long pontoons. The first trial on 28 November ended with a broken propeller shaft, and the next on the following day showed some of the unforeseen problems associated with water flying. Despite a favorable wind and a speed of twenty-seven miles per hour, the craft refused to lift off, convincing Curtiss that "it will take a great amount of power to get these boats out of the water, as we now have perhaps twice more than would be needed to fly after getting in the air." He was optimistic that additional tests would go better, but as it turned out no one had time for more experiments with the *Loon* once McCurdy's new AEA machine was completed and ready to fly.[52]

That airplane, the association's fourth and last, not counting the *Loon*, benefitted from prior knowledge and was superbly designed and constructed. Impressed with its appearance, the *Hammondsport Herald* remarked that it was "finished like an up-to-date automobile." McCurdy named it the *Silver Dart* for the color of the wings' upper surfaces and in expectation that its performance would surpass any of its predecessors—hours, not minutes of flying. First tried out on the *Loon*, the *Silver Dart*'s engine was based on Curtiss' water-cooled inline 4-cylinder motor used in the *SC-1*. It had two banks of four cast-iron cylinders set at ninety degrees from the crankshaft and was "undersquare," with a 3¾-inch bore and 4-inch stroke. Curtiss mounted the engine on the lower wing, with a belt attached to a pulley and shaft driving the 8-foot-diameter propeller located above the motor and behind the wings. The drive belt, like those on some of his V-twin motorcycles, was built up from riveted multi-ply leather segments. The radiator was located vertically between the wings in front of the engine and behind the pilot. The wing covering was silk, treated with the same rubberized concoction used on the Baldwin airship to ensure the envelope was gas-tight.[53]

The *Silver Dart* was the biggest and heaviest machine built by the AEA. The wings spanned 49 feet, with 6 feet 4 inch chords in the center, tapering to 4 feet at their tips, for respective average aspect ratios of 8.2:1 and 12.2:1 (the highest yet for an AEA airplane), and a total surface area of 420 square feet. The wings featured the same negative and positive dihedral of the previous machines, and thus the lenticular appearance when viewed from head on. Based on the flight experience with the *June Bug*, the airplane had big ailerons and a sizeable front elevator, although the rudder was not particularly large. Without pilot and fuel, the airplane weighed 710 pounds, 237 more than the *June Bug*.[54]

Despite optimism that the *Silver Dart* would be flying before the leaves fell that autumn, a series of problems prevented its early completion. On 14 October, Curtiss revealed his frustration that "the new engine is taking more time than we have ever required to build a new motor." He thought it would be ready within a week, but he was mistaken. Another two weeks passed before the motor left the Curtiss shop and was installed in the airplane, which had been at Champlin's Stony Brook racetrack for some time. Even then, the security of the tent was not enough to prevent the *Silver Dart* from suffering damage when Champlin's forty-pound dog bounded onto the wing one evening, ripping out the lightweight fabric from one of the panels. Nagging difficulties with the engine, among them leaks in the copper water jackets encasing the cylinders and cylinders that worked loose from the crankcase, added to Curtiss' annoyance. Chronic slippage of the drive belt was less of a problem, but to satisfy McCurdy he substituted a heavier and more complex chain drive. When that, too, proved unsatisfactory, he switched back to the belt drive, thus incurring even more delays. He told Bell on 24 November that he had not written to him because he "had nothing good to report."[55]

A dusting of snow covered the fields in Pleasant Valley on 6 December when McCurdy at last took the *Silver Dart* into the air for three flights, only to have them cut short because of high winds and poor running due to condensation in the fuel tank. Still, they were encouraging enough for Curtiss to report that McCurdy "got an opportunity to get a feel for the control," which was "more sensitive" than on the *June Bug*. A flight three days later ended with a hard landing and severe damage to the undercarriage. After repairs, McCurdy took off again on the fourteenth for four more flights, followed by two more on the seventeenth, one of which covered a mile and three-quarters. On his way to Baddeck on 20 December, Bell stopped in Hammondsport to observe McCurdy in action. Joining him were two editors, James Means of the *Aeronautical Annual* and Ernest L. Jones of *Aeronautics*, along with Wilbur R. Kimball representing the Aeronautic Society of New York, an offshoot of the Aero Club of America. Adverse winds thwarted three attempts to get into the air on the twentieth, and continued bad weather the following day precluded a test of the airplane with a new propeller. After the visitors left on the twenty-second, McCurdy was "much mortified" and Curtiss apologetic that "we did not get off very good flights." Both knew that they had missed a golden opportunity to show Bell and others that they were indeed making progress toward a practical airplane.[56]

While Curtiss and Bell labored over the *Silver Dart*, Bell's patent attorneys submitted a list of potentially patentable features of the Hammondsport machines, which Bell forwarded to the AEA members for their comments on 18 November. Closely adhering to Bell's 29 September document, the list of claims began with the ailerons, referred to as "lateral balancing rudders," specifically noting that they contributed nothing to the wings' lift and therefore lay outside the Wrights' patent. That the rigid wings were not to "be constructed to be warped or flexed for the purpose of restoring lateral balance" again drew a distinction between the Hammondsport control system and that used by the Wrights. Among the other twenty-six claims were the shoulder yoke operating mechanism for the ailerons and the use of a wheeled undercarriage with a steerable front wheel. Bell was concerned about the possible confusion over the use of the word "aeroplane," and suggested using "aero-surface" or some other nomenclature, and he thought the description of the wings' opposing dihedral configuration was contradictory and unclear.[57]

After the Christmas and New Year's holidays, Curtiss had time to reflect on the momentous year that had just passed. The AEA had accomplished everything, and more, than anyone could have anticipated in the fall of 1907—save for the terrible loss of Tom Selfridge at Fort Myer. Yet it was obvious that the association and its members stood at a crossroads. Considering the possible directions the group might take, Bell had made it clear he wanted to direct it toward establishing a permanent aeronautical laboratory. Curtiss, however, had already begun to think that his future might not lie with the AEA or some successor partnership after the six-month extension expired. Nor did he feel entirely comfortable with the emphasis Bell intended to place on his tetrahedral machines following the success of the *June Bug* and the potential promised by the *Silver Dart*.

Would it not be better, Curtiss mused, to move on to manufacturing and exhibiting airplanes of his own design and construction? After all, he had done exceedingly well building and selling motorcycles and there was no reason for anyone to doubt that he would be able to transfer that experience to airplanes. He was fully aware of the Wrights' patent and the potential legal minefield it presented to those wanting to enter into aviation as a business, but he had reasonable assurance from Bell and his patent lawyers that the unique features of the AEA's airplanes would not constitute an infringement. Even more compelling was the challenge of flight. By the end of 1908, he had demonstrated his skills as a flier, not in the league of the Wrights but certainly among the most accomplished there were outside Dayton. As he packed up the *Silver Dart* on 6 January for shipment to Baddeck and looked forward to another meeting of the AEA, he could not help but wonder if the time had come to consider charting his own course in the beckoning sky.[58]

—3—

The "Flying Bug"

T he frozen Bras d'Or Lakes and the surrounding hills must have
had a beautiful bleakness to them when Glenn and Lena arrived
at Bell's Beinn Bhreagh estate on 29 January 1909. They had left
Hammondsport four days earlier with plans for Lena to stay at Baddeck for
two weeks and for Curtiss to spend as much time as needed to sort out the
Silver Dart and make sure that his motor functioned satisfactorily in Bell's
big *Cygnet II* tetrahedral machine. The Bells received the couple with their
usual hospitality, highlighted by stimulating conversation around the hearth
in the Great Hall, plenty to eat and drink, and the reassuring conviviality that
had marked the association from its inception. Lena liked the fellowship of
the association so much that she changed her mind and decided to stay until
Glenn was ready to leave.[1]

Curtiss had delayed the trip to Nova Scotia for some weeks, pleading with
Bell on 5 January that a meeting of his company's board of directors scheduled
for the fourteenth meant he would miss the association's gathering on the
eighth. In the interim, he and McCurdy had made one more attempt to get
the *Loon* off the water, this time with hydrofoils attached to the bottoms of the
pontoons in an attempt to break them loose from the water. The experiment
proved disastrous late in the day on 2 January when one of the floats sprang a
leak and the craft sank next to the dock; Curtiss and McCurdy immediately
wired Bell telling him "experiments ended." McCurdy got to Baddeck in time
for the 8 January meeting, while Curtiss remained in Hammondsport to finish
packing up the *Silver Dart* for shipment to Baddeck and to attend to "other
important business," including further modifications and tests of the *Silver
Dart*'s engine.[2]

When Curtiss arrived at Beinn Bhreagh the first order of business was
resolution of the patent question. For the most part, the original specifications from patent attorneys Mauro, Cameron remained intact, with relatively

few amendments or elisions since November. Discussions brought the total number of claims down from the original twenty-eight to twenty-five, fifteen of which were to be filed under chief engineer Casey Baldwin's name. The others, including the crucial rigid wings and ailerons, were to be held jointly by Bell, Curtiss, and the rest of the AEA membership. Bell communicated the association's changes and suggestions to his lawyers, who filed the joint application on 8 April.[3]

Whether or not to exploit the successes of the AEA financially was the other chief item for discussion at Baddeck that winter. Bell was loath to continue the association as a business, fearing that he and his wife, who had major financial interest in the organization, would likely continue to be the principal stakeholders after it launched into airplane exhibitions or other profit-making activities. He also knew that no investors would come forward without assurances of the successful outcome of the AEA's patent applications and that once the organization started making money with its flying machines the Wrights would initiate litigation. It was a classic catch-22. The AEA could engage in commercial activity, thereby inviting an infringement suit and resulting legal expenses, which in turn could only be paid for through profit-making ventures and outside investment capital unlikely to be forthcoming while patents were pending and litigation was in process. But it was possible, Bell reasoned, for the members to form their own company with the limited capital they had available, and begin small-scale exhibitions with the *June Bug* and *Silver Dart*, and perhaps one more machine built by Curtiss. He recommended that Curtiss be named to manage the new company and asked him to come up with estimates of how much money the business would need for one year's operation.[4]

Curtiss responded with some of his thoughts on 15 February. So far, no one had made any money with airplanes, other than "the winning of a few prizes." Only "government contracts and exhibition work" were likely to bring results in the near future, wrote Curtiss, and the Wrights were "in on the 'ground floor'" with their connections in Washington. Curtiss was optimistic that exhibitions and "prize chasing" could yield some income without incurring massive expenses. He estimated that not more than $10,000 would be needed to get such an enterprise off the ground and provide the capital needed to carry it through its first year. Thus encouraged, Bell recommended and the AEA informally approved on 20 February a proposal to put $100,000 of its own money into a company—tentatively called the American Aerodrome Company—that would take over all of the association's assets in the form of patents and physical property. Mabel Bell would receive $35,000 up front to reimburse her for the money she put into the AEA, payable to her in shares in the new company. The remaining $65,000 in shares were to be held in the firm's treasury, of which $10,000 worth would be sold to the Bells' and other members' friends to cover the first year's operating expenses.[5]

His entrepreneurial spirit energized, Curtiss was already thinking along similar lines about exploiting the profit potential of his and the AEA's work. In the fall of 1908, he and McCurdy had talked with the Aero Club of America about the possibility of using the *Silver Dart* to defend the *Scientific American* trophy, which now required a flight of at least twenty-five kilometers. The Aeronautic Society of New York had leased Morris Park, a racetrack in the Bronx, for the use of its members, and the club had designated it the venue for the trophy flights. On 22 October, Curtiss visited with members of the Aero Club's contest committee and checked out the Morris Park site, which he deemed "impossible" to fly from. In any case, there was no way the *Silver Dart* was flight ready at the time. More important, though, Curtiss had initiated contacts with the Aeronautic Society that would continue over the next few months and eventually mature into full-scale collaboration.[6]

Curtiss had all these things on his mind during his stay in Baddeck, and was further burdened with the technical responsibility of making sure his engine could power McCurdy's *Silver Dart* on long flights, and fulfilling his obligation to Bell to get the *Cygnet II* into the air. Facing delays in the delivery of the *Silver Dart* and its engine, Curtiss and McCurdy decided to use the extra time to experiment with propellers on a three-runner ice boat that looked dangerous just standing still. With William Bedwin, the head of Bell's aeronautical lab, operating the engine, McCurdy monitoring the propeller data, and Curtiss driving, the trio took off for a run down the bay on the afternoon of 8 February. The accident happened on the way back. Bedwin failed to cut the throttle as they neared the dock and, with no brakes, was unable to stop. The machine crashed so hard that all three men were thrown out, with Curtiss striking the steering wheel and winding up with a huge gash in his lower lip. First aid staunched the flow of blood until a doctor arrived to stitch up the wound. It took several days in bed before he recovered, and the nerve damage was such that he never regained feeling in that part of his jaw.[7]

Finally, on 11 February the engine and all the *Silver Dart* components arrived in Baddeck. At that point the group decided to accommodate Bell's wishes by using the machine's engine and propeller in the *Cygnet II*. On 22 February, McCurdy piloted Bell's craft over the ice on Baddeck Bay for about one hundred yards before shutting off the motor, which was not developing full power. The engine ran better on the second and third attempts to get the craft airborne, but the tests ended when the propeller broke loose from its shaft and was destroyed. While awaiting a new propeller, Curtiss and McCurdy transferred the engine to the *Silver Dart*. On the twenty-third, McCurdy took off from Baddeck Bay in the *Silver Dart* on what was the first airplane flight in Canada. It was "a most satisfactory trial" said Curtiss, obviously pleased. The next day, McCurdy flew more than 4½ miles around the bay. "The flight of the *Silver Dart* was the best ever made by the members of the A.E.A. Everything worked perfectly," Curtiss reported, except that there was damage to one of the wings and a wheel when McCurdy landed. The *Silver Dart*'s engine and propeller then went into the *Cygnet II* for more experiments late that same day, which ended in the breakage of some of the wires supporting the engine.[8]

With repairs to the two machines expected to take a while, Glenn and Lena left Beinn Bhreagh on the twenty-sixth. Sadly, neither ever returned to the big house in Baddeck. Lena arrived in Hammondsport on 1 March, followed by Glenn two days later after he stopped over in New York to attend to urgent business affairs. Crowded into the next two days were public revelations about new commercial ventures that Curtiss had been negotiating for weeks, if not months.[9]

On 3 March, the Aeronautic Society's president Lee S. Burridge broke the news that he had commissioned Curtiss to supply an airplane to be used by the society for flight lessons and exhibitions. Curtiss had in fact reached the understanding with the society on 21 January and had accepted an advance payment of $500, but the two parties had agreed to keep the contract secret pending final decisions on the status of the AEA. In an effort to distance himself from the AEA and its work, Curtiss stressed that the new airplane would be substantially different from the *Silver Dart* or other machines he had developed jointly with the association. It would cost $5,000 to build and was scheduled for delivery in May at Morris Park, where Curtiss would make a series of public flights.[10]

The second bombshell out of New York came from Cortlandt Field Bishop, president of the Aero Club of America, who announced at a press conference on 3 March that Curtiss and Augustus Herring had joined forces to form a new company, the first enterprise in the country dedicated exclusively to the manufacture and sale of airplanes and airships. How this happened had as many twists and turns as the plot line of a suspense novel.

From the discussions at Beinn Bhreagh earlier in the year, it is clear that Bell, Curtiss, and the other members of the AEA were moving toward the creation of a company to carry on with the association's work while engaging in the manufacture and exhibition of airplanes. Others had the same idea. At some point, probably in January before Curtiss left for Baddeck, Herring had spoken with Tom Baldwin at the Aero Club in New York about certain unspecified "devices" that he believed when adapted to the AEA's airplanes would so enhance their performance as to make them highly competitive in the "world's market." Baldwin passed this information along to Curtiss, who was open to the possibilities of collaboration. Even more tempting was Bishop's willingness to put his own money into an aviation company, and through his connections among New York's wealthy elites to entice others to make similar financial commitments.[11]

Bishop's involvement alone might have been enough for Curtiss to move forward with the scheme, but he knew that Herring himself brought important assets to the table. Herring claimed to hold patents that predated those of the Wrights and that Curtiss assumed were "fundamental and strong." Any patents, especially any covering aircraft control and stability systems, would be useful in defending against a suit brought by the Wrights for infringement. Then there was Octave Chanute. The grand old man of aviation had worked with Herring and heard that he had made a short flight in a biplane hang glider powered by a compressed-air engine in St. Joseph, Michigan, in the fall of 1898. Further enhancing Herring's legitimacy was the Army's airplane competition, where Herring was the only entry other than the Wright brothers. It did not seem to matter to Curtiss that all Herring had produced for the Army by the fall of 1908 were two suitcases and a trunk, which he claimed contained the parts for his airplane. Herring used the extra time after Orville's accident and subsequent extension of the Army's contract deadline to generate as much publicity as he could. He let it be known, for example, that he had assembled and flown his airplane in secret, had received overtures from foreign investors, and promised to make public flights with his airplane in May or June before handing it over to the Army. If Curtiss harbored any reservations about his new partner, Herring's reputation as an innovator in aeronautics, his connections within the aviation community, his pioneering patents, and his endorsement by wealthy New Yorkers were sufficient to allay any suspicions he may have had.[12]

On 12 February 1909, Herring wrote to Curtiss proposing an exchange of stock in a new company equivalent to the valuation of the inventory Curtiss held in his manufacturing company. Curtiss wired back on the seventeenth: "proposition agreeable." He elaborated in a letter the same day that the $50,000 estimated value of his company's inventory would be his contribution to the new enterprise, noting that it did not include other assets worth perhaps another $150,000, and that the company had done $120,000 in business in 1908. Curtiss stressed that his company was earning "handsome profits" and was "bound to grow" in the year to come. Its one hundred employees were working on orders for two airplanes, an unspecified number of airplane engines, and three hundred motorcycles. He emphasized to Herring "that in taking over the Curtiss Co. you would get a very *substantial* business not to mention our future prospects." When Herring inquired about Bell's interest in joining them, Curtiss answered that "I do not think Mr. Bell would consider making any connection with this company as he has a plan for a big organization and I think best not to mention this at present; however if I should come with you I think the other scheme would be given up." Even though the experiments at Baddeck were not finished, Curtiss informed Herring on 21 February that he planned to leave Baddeck and meet with him in New York to discuss more details of the proposed company.[13]

How much, if anything, Bell and other members of the AEA knew about these developments is open to some interpretation. Despite telling Herring that he thought it unwise to ask Bell if he were interested in joining the new company, Curtiss did bring the subject up with him in a general way. As expected, Bell was not interested, but he was broadly favorable to the idea of a "commercial organization" with Curtiss as manager. Curtiss biographer C. R. Roseberry contends that Curtiss had at least hinted that a deal with Herring was in the offing; otherwise Bell would have insisted on the full membership voting on his American Aerodrome Company idea before Curtiss left Baddeck. He also notes that Curtiss wired McCurdy on 4 March about the "Cup Trial" and that he had "made [the] Herring proposition," assuming that McCurdy must have been familiar with what Curtiss meant. Yet Bell's 6 March telegram asking Curtiss to "write fully concerning your arrangement with Herring and how it affects your relations with Aerial Experiment Association" strongly indicates that Bell first learned of the Herring partnership from the newspapers and that for whatever reason Curtiss had been less than candid with him or other members of the association.[14]

Curtiss immediately telegraphed that the "proposed Herring arrangement will not affect Association's plans." His more informative letter dated 5 March arrived in Baddeck a few days later. He was enthused about Herring's patents, especially those that dealt with the use of gyroscopes to achieve automatic stability: "Mr. Herring showed me a great deal, and I would not be at all surprised if his patents, backed by a strong company, would pretty well control the use of the gyroscope in obtaining automatic equilibrium." He further explained:

> If the deal goes through, I will be manager of the Company and everything will go on just as it has, except that we will have Mr. Herring's devices on the machines which we may build, which, by the way, recalls the fact that I accepted an order from the Aeronautical Society for an aeroplane to be delivered in the Spring at Morris Park, N.Y. I did this on my own responsibility with the idea that if the consolidation was made with Herring it would be turned over to the new company, or if a commercial organization succeeded the Experiment Association the order would be turned over to them. If neither of these materialized, the Curtiss Co. would endeavor to fill the order itself.

As soon as the Herring scheme was realized, Curtiss planned to go to Washington to provide Charles Bell with details. He saw no reason why Bell's proposed Aerodrome Company could not go forward "unless the members of the Association would care to come into the Herring combination. This would please Mr. Herring I am sure, and I don't know but that it would be just as well for the Association." In closing, he promised Bell he would "advise [him] of any further developments."[15]

Over the next two weeks, Curtiss, Herring, and Bishop hammered out the financial and operational details of the new company in meetings in Hammondsport and New York. Interviewed in his office in Hammondsport on 9 March, Curtiss remarked that "the possibilities of the new company in the aeroplane field are unlimited," and that work had already begun on the Aeronautic Society's machine. Herring was even less restrained in his comments. He told the press that the new company was building not one but four airplanes, and a glider, and that the first of the machines would be ready for flights in May. On the thirteenth, stockholders unanimously approved the transfer of their holdings in the G. H. Curtiss Manufacturing Company to the new, as yet unnamed, firm. The *Hammondsport Herald* believed that "this deal will mean much to the industrial growth of Hammondsport," with more capital allowing increases in the size of the Curtiss factory and an expansion of the work force.[16]

Curtiss and Herring closed the deal on 19 March and filed the papers of incorporation with the secretary of state's office in Albany that evening. Named the Herring-Curtiss Manufacturing Company and capitalized at $360,000, the new firm intended to produce airplanes as well as other motor-driven vehicles and engines at Curtiss' Hammondsport factory. The stock was divided into 1,800 shares of preferred and 1,800 shares of common stock, with each share valued at $100. The principal stockholders of the old Curtiss company stayed on, joined by Bishop, Peter Cooper Hewitt, and other wealthy New York Aero Club members. Curtiss received 160 shares of preferred and 400 shares of common stock; Herring was the majority stockholder, with more than 2,000 shares of preferred and common. Curtiss assigned all the assets of his old company, his total real estate holdings, and any patents he held as a member of the AEA to the new firm; Herring, for his part, contributed his existing and pending patents, a small amount of shop equipment, and $650 in cash. Curtiss and Herring each received $5,000 annual salaries. At a meeting on the twentieth in New York, the board of directors elected Monroe Wheeler president, Curtiss vice-president and manager, Herring second vice-president, and Lynn Masson secretary and treasurer, thereby ensuring continuity with the earlier company and partially offsetting some of the initial financial leverage Herring had in the new undertaking. Before returning to Hammondsport from New York, Curtiss attended the Aero Club's annual banquet at the Hotel St. Regis that evening, where he received the coveted *Scientific American* trophy for the *June Bug*'s flight but said nothing more about the new company's plans for the future.[17]

Without Curtiss, the rest of the AEA members went about their business in Baddeck. Bell thought that McCurdy and the *Silver Dart* should contest for the *Scientific American* trophy, but changed his mind when he realized that the Aero Club had decided to award the prize for the longest flight in excess of twenty-five kilometers made before the end of 1909. This meant that if McCurdy flew the required twenty-five kilometers within the next few weeks there was a good chance someone else—the Wrights or even Curtiss—would exceed that distance later in the year. Reluctantly, he withdrew McCurdy and the AEA from the competition. On 31 March, Bell, Baldwin, and McCurdy met for the last time, Bell recording that "the Aerial Experiment Association is now a thing of the past." McCurdy stayed on at Baddeck through the rest of the spring. In flights totaling more than a thousand miles with the *Silver Dart*, he emerged as an accomplished aviator, not in Curtiss' or the Wrights' league, but certainly among the few in the world who had logged so much time in the air. His and Curtiss' paths would intersect again in the not-too-distant future.[18]

For Curtiss and his shop foreman, Henry Kleckler, the main priority was meeting a tight deadline of 22 May for the delivery of the Aeronautic Society's machine. To verify specific elements of the airplane's design, they built a small wind tunnel, about fifteen to eighteen inches square. Unlike the better-known Wright brothers' 1901 tunnel, it employed an induced draft, meaning that the fan pulled the air through the tunnel instead of pushing it. An automobile radiator on the far end of the tunnel straightened the flow of air, and a crude manometer recorded air pressures. It is not known what other instruments might have been employed to obtain test data, although it is likely that Curtiss and Kleckler first used tobacco smoke and later silk threads to study air flows around model wings and control surfaces. Two years later, Curtiss wrote that "we have a little wind tunnel here which is very interesting and instructive. We have learned a number of things in connection with the resistance of bodies passing through the air," which he expected would be useful in making "worthwhile" advances to the design of his airplanes.[19]

When the new airplane was finished, even the most casual observer could discern its heritage, but there were important differences that marked a departure from those built by the AEA. The location of the ailerons was one. In his 29 September document differentiating the Hammondsport machines from the Wright airplane, Bell had maintained that the ailerons of the Hammondsport airplanes were not lifting surfaces integral to the wings and could, therefore, be located anywhere on the aerostructure. He argued, and Curtiss agreed, that they could not logically constitute an infringement of the Wright patent. Curtiss and Kleckler placed the ailerons on the new machine midway between the wings, attached to points on the outermost front interplane struts and extending beyond the wings. Curtiss used the same shoulder yoke control system that had worked so well on the AEA airplanes. The other notable visible difference was the absence of the negative and positive wing dihedral that had given the wings of the AEA machines their characteristic lenticular appearance. Neither Curtiss nor Kleckler believed this feature had any utility and it only complicated the wing construction. Thus the new airplane had straight wings, 28 feet 9 inches long, with a chord of 4½ feet their entire length. The resulting aspect ratio of 6.4:1 was a good deal lower than the *Silver Dart's* but generally in line with that of the other AEA machines. The total wing area was 258 square feet.[20]

Compact, simple, rugged, and incorporating intuitive controls, the Aeronautic Society's airplane displayed all the characteristics of Curtiss' subsequent designs. Weight without the pilot and fuel was about 400 pounds, a little more than the old *Red Wing*, and far less than the *Silver Dart*. For propulsion, Curtiss chose one of his well-proved 25-horsepower, 4-cylinder water-cooled in-line engines, mounted midway between the wings behind the pilot and driving a 6-foot-diameter wood propeller. A vertical rudder and fixed horizontal tail made up the empennage, a biplane front elevator provided pitch control, and a tricycle undercarriage constituted the landing gear. The wing fabric was rubberized silk, as used on the *Silver Dart*, but coated with an ochre-tinted dope similar in hue to that used on the *June Bug*. The framework, mostly made of spruce, received a yellow varnish, which, combined with the color of the fabric gave the airplane a distinctive golden appearance. It was known initially as the *Gold Bug* because of its color, even though its official designation was *Curtiss No. 1*.[21]

Curtiss finished the airplane by 26 May, having received a short extension to the Aeronautic Society's deadline for its completion, and took it out for its first trials at Hammondsport on the evening of 6 June. Curtiss made two flights, covering a mile and a half-mile respectively, without attempting any turns. The next evening he went up again for two more flights, during each of which he circled the field and landed at the point where he had taken off. The local paper believed "these were the most successful flights yet made in Hammondsport in any machine." After one more test flight, Curtiss shipped the machine to Morris Park on 12 June, where he and Kleckler spent the next six days setting it up. Herring was also present, offering not-so-useful suggestions about engine performance and busying himself by marking off various distances at the 1½-mile oval track. It was almost dark on the evening of 18 June when Curtiss made his initial flights at Morris Park. They were noteworthy as the first true controlled airplane flights in New York City, easily surpassing Farman's perfunctory straight-line hops at Brighton Beach in 1908. Curtiss was extra-cautious, making sure the controls worked satisfactorily, staying within the confines of the racetrack, and covering no more than a half-mile on each of the flights. Six more flights on 24 June convinced him that he had designed and built a good airplane for the Aeronautic Society and that with it he stood a reasonable chance of competing for the *Scientific American* trophy.[22]

Defending the trophy was not high on Curtiss' agenda until after he learned that Bell had withdrawn McCurdy's *Silver Dart* from the competition. Convinced he had a potential winner, Curtiss persuaded the Aeronautic

Society to give him more time to test the new machine and delay handing it over until he had made an attempt at the prize. Bishop and the Aero Club supported Curtiss' decision to try for the trophy and had ideas about him competing for something even more ambitious. It was an international air meet planned for that summer in France. The world's first major international aeronautical competition would be an extraordinary affair featuring, among other events, a speed contest for a trophy offered by American expatriate and aviation enthusiast James Gordon Bennett. Curtiss knew the *Gold Bug* lacked the power to be competitive, and consented to build a new eight-cylinder engine and enter the contest provided Bishop and the Aero Club covered any expenses he incurred over and above the $5,000 Gordon Bennett prize. Bishop was eager to have an American entry in the absence of the Wright brothers, who were too busy with a new Army airplane and unwilling to "compete for trophies" against aviators they suspected of violating their patent holdings. He was more than happy to submit Curtiss' name to the organizers of the event.[23]

On 26 June, a sweltering day in New York, more than five thousand paying customers packed the grandstand and infield for the Aeronautic Society's first big public event at Morris Park. Curtiss was the main attraction, and he did not disappoint the crowd. That afternoon he made a short warm-up flight of about a quarter-mile, followed by a more spectacular flight in which he started on the backstretch, followed the track around to the grandstand where he made a turn to cross the infield, and landed within yards of his starting point. The *New York Times* declared the exhibition "one of the most successful events of the kind ever held in this country," and the Curtiss machine "a real flier." Another throng, estimated at fifteen thousand, was at Morris Park on 5 July for what they hoped would be an encore performance. Adverse winds grounded Curtiss until just before dark when he took off for a two-mile flight around the track that easily exceeded Bishop's minimal requirement. Successful as he was at Morris Park, Curtiss recognized that the venue was too confined to let him stretch the *Gold Bug*'s legs and that he needed to find something more spacious if he were to challenge for the new *Scientific American* trophy.[24]

Curtiss took a short break to travel to Washington to observe the new flying machine Orville Wright was testing at Fort Myer to fulfill the terms of the brothers' Army contract. He may also have had hopes of discussing patent issues with the Wrights, knowing that they were likely to sue as soon as he completed the deal with the Aeronautic Society and the Herring-Curtiss firm began manufacturing and selling airplanes. Orville and the Army machine started off with short flights on 29 June, only to suffer a setback on 2 July when the airplane was damaged in a hard landing after the motor shut down in flight. No more flying was possible until the brothers obtained and fitted new wing fabric. Nothing indicates that Curtiss met with the Wrights while he was in town. He later wrote to them "to express my admiration for the fine exhibition of flying I witnessed at Fort Meyer [sic]" and offered suggestions about how they might want to fix their engine problems. The "small flights" he had made at Morris Park, he went on, "did not pan out well" and he was looking for a better location to make longer attempts. In closing he offered that "in regard to patent matters, I want to suggest that if you contemplate any action that the matter be taken up privately between us to save if possible annoyance and publicity of lawsuits and trials." The Wrights did not respond.[25]

Turning to the matters immediately at hand in New York, Curtiss needed a place more suitable than Morris Park for the long flights he told the Wrights he was "anxious to experiment" with. With representatives of the Aero Club, he reconnoitered an area known as Hempstead Plains on Long Island about twenty miles from Manhattan. The site, a broad, flat, treeless grassland north of the Mineola Fairgrounds, was perfect not only for flights with the *Gold Bug* but also for trials of the new airplane he was building for the international competition, now set for August in the French city of Rheims. Curtiss accompanied the *Gold Bug* to Hempstead on 10 July, and took the machine up for a two-mile flight just before dark on the thirteenth. Afterwards, with the machine back in a large tent hangar, Curtiss said "it was the easiest and most satisfactory flight I ever made with the new machine" and that "the long flat expanse of the Hempstead Plains presents ideal conditions for aviation." Early the next morning Curtiss flew twice around the field, for a distance of five miles at an average speed of about forty-five miles per hour. According to Curtiss, "things went so smoothly that if I had carried an orange with me I would have been glad to eat it." On the sixteenth, he flew ten times around the field, for a total of fifteen miles, spending more than twenty-two minutes in the air, and coming down only because he was hungry for breakfast. He knew that the airplane was more than ready to compete for the *Scientific American* contest.[26]

Curtiss was up early on the seventeenth for the attempt, as were some three thousand spectators keen to see a record-setting flight over the triangular, 1⅓-mile course that had been marked out by Charles Manly, serving again as the Aero Club's official judge. Curtiss took off at 5:15 AM, quickly logging a kilometer to win a modest prize offered by Cortlandt Bishop for the first flight to surpass the one-kilometer distance of the previous year's *Scientific American* competition. He was in the air again at 5:30. The first dozen or so laps went without any problems, but then the wind picked up, reaching twelve miles per hour during the last couple of circuits. Running low on gas and not wishing to press his luck with the wind, Curtiss cut the flight short after nineteen laps. In 52½ minutes he had officially flown 24.7 miles around the track (starting and stopping distances and Curtiss' sweeping turns well outside the course markers added an estimated five miles to the total). Interviewed afterward, Curtiss said that "the machine never responded better to the slightest change of the levers and the forward planes [elevators], while the engine was perfection itself. . . . If I had been able to start half an hour earlier I could have stayed in the air over an hour with the utmost ease." Because no one attempted a formal challenge to Curtiss' record before the end of 1909, the *Scientific American* trophy was his for a second consecutive year. If there were any doubts about Curtiss' flying abilities or his airplane, they were erased that morning in less than an hour. Only the Wrights and a handful of European aviators had stayed in the air longer or flown farther.[27]

Curtiss told reporters that he had the "flying bug in his ear" and wanted "to fly every time it is possible to do so." But he also understood that the terms of his contract with the Aeronautic Society obligated him to instruct two fliers in the operation of the new airplane, now named the *Golden Flier*. The two students were Alexander Williams, a French citizen living in New York who had designed an unsuccessful flying machine under the auspices of the Aeronautic Society, and Charles F. Willard, a twenty-eight-year-old New York engineer. Curtiss took the machine up early in the morning of 18 July, carving a figure-eight over the field, before handing it over to Willard for his first lesson. Willard demonstrated his innate abilities, flying about five hundred feet, gently touching down, and then proceeding for another two hundred feet. Curtiss was quick with his praise: "Well done. It was better than my first flight." Then it was Williams' turn. He overcompensated with the elevator control immediately after taking off, quickly reaching an altitude of fifty feet. Williams then turned sharply to the right, sending the machine into a dive that ended in a crash. Curtiss and the others rushed to the scene, where they found Williams with a broken arm and other more superficial injuries that put him in the hospital. The airplane's wings were badly damaged, the elevator destroyed, controls wrecked, and the front wheel broken, but the engine was all right. There was little Curtiss could do to effect repairs at Mineola, so he left for Hammondsport right away with the promise to return in a few days with new materials and replacement parts.[28]

Curtiss needed the time in Hammondsport, where the new airplane for the Gordon Bennett competition was under construction and there was plenty of other business to be wrapped up before he could leave for Europe. One matter was the motorcycle side of the business, which his old friend Tank Waters took over as head of the Marvel Motorcycle Company. And there was Herring. Curtiss and others in Hammondsport grew increasingly concerned about his commitment to the new company and his dilatoriness in turning over his patents and fulfilling other obligations. He had also failed to deliver an airplane to the Army and in the end had to forfeit the contract. For his part, Herring was unhappy with Curtiss' arrangement with Waters, which he believed deprived the company of its principal profit-making segment, and he even went so far as to blame Curtiss for not intervening with the Signal Corps to help secure one of the two contract extensions he had received. All was far from well with the Herring-Curtiss enterprise as Curtiss prepared to return to New York before heading across the Atlantic to take on the challenge of the international aviation meet in France.[29]

Some indication of the level of opposition he faced came on 25 July, while Curtiss was in Hammondsport working on his new machine and assembling parts for the damaged *Golden Flier*. Drawn by a prize offered by Lord Northcliffe, wealthy publisher of the *London Daily Mail* and an early aviation proponent, French aviator Louis Blériot, in a monoplane of his own design and construction, became the first to fly across the English Channel, completing the flight in just thirty-seven minutes. Asked to comment, Curtiss praised Blériot for his courage and for his "splendid performance" in spanning the Channel. He had a fine airplane, but Curtiss was quick to point out that his own machine, "without doubt could make the trip easily. I have traveled thirty miles in it without a stop, and the trip across the Channel is only twenty-one miles." Furthermore, his new airplane was lighter and more powerful than Blériot's, implying that he stood a good chance of beating him in any head-to-head competition.[30]

Glenn and Lena, along with Harry Genung and his wife, left Hammondsport for New York on the night of 2 August 1909. The next day Curtiss went out to Mineola to complete repairs to the *Golden Flier* before turning it over to the Aeronautic Society and receiving the balance of his $5,000 payment due. That evening he took the machine out for a couple of brief test flights. Curtiss planned to provide Willard with some last-minute instructions the next morning, but had to cancel due to bad weather. Willard assured him that he would spend the next few days at Hempstead Plains getting more experience with the *Flier* before embarking on an ambitious series of exhibition flights under the auspices of a new company spun off by the Aeronautic Society expressly for that purpose. Curtiss had no chance to test his new airplane before he left for France. "It has been a rush to get the machine finished," he confessed, although he was reasonably certain he would have enough time once he arrived to try it out and get it ready for the competition.[31]

At ten in the morning the next day, 5 August, Curtiss embarked on the French Line steamer *La Savoie*, bound for Le Havre. Secured in four crates in the ship's hold was the airplane he intended to fly. At the dock, Lena bade her husband farewell with advice to "be sure and bring back that cup," handing him an American flag to carry with him during the races. As the ship pulled away, he replied, "I'll do my best." With him was Tod C. ("Slim") Shriver, one of Tom Baldwin's mechanics and later an aviator in his own right, and a friend from Rochester, Ward Fisher. Cortlandt Bishop had gone over earlier to find accommodations and to make arrangements at the flying field. A day out into the Atlantic, Curtiss sent a radiogram to Lena telling her he was "well and no symptoms of sea sickness" such as he and Tank Waters had suffered on their voyage back from Ormond Beach two years previously. Imagine the sense of adventure and apprehension Curtiss must have had as he strolled the decks of the big liner. Just thirty-one, he had previously journeyed only as far as Florida's central coast. Now he was on his way across the ocean as the sole American to compete against Europe's most experienced fliers, carrying with him the responsibility of upholding his country's reputation in the air.[32]

Six days later, Curtiss was in Le Havre, where he arranged to have his airplane shipped to Rheims as "personal baggage" in order to ensure its safe and speedy arrival. The next day Bishop intercepted Curtiss while he was changing trains in Paris and introduced him to James Gordon Bennett, who added to the patriotic weight on Curtiss' shoulders by telling him he wanted an American to win his trophy. Aviation-crazed Parisians, still in wonder over Wilbur Wright's magnificent flights that past fall and winter, were ecstatic to have another American flier on their soil. "For the time, at least," read a cable from Paris, "he is quite as popular as the Wrights were, if not more so, for they declined the issue when they were invited to take part in the grand tournament, while Curtiss pluckily accepted it. . . . [T]hey warmed up to him more than ever, and it is certain that he will be one of the favorites in the Rheims tournament." Curtiss and his entourage completed the final leg of the long journey to Rheims by the end of the day on the thirteenth and took up temporary residence in the home of a local priest.[33]

Like other visitors, Curtiss was impressed with Rheims, an ancient town ninety miles northeast of Paris long associated with French educational culture and dominated by its superb twin-spired thirteenth-century High Gothic cathedral. Located in the heart of the French Champagne region, Rheims had a comforting familiarity to Curtiss, coming as he did from New York's wine country and growing up not far from a railroad stop in Pleasant Valley with the same name. The site for the meet, known as *La Grande Semaine d'Aviation de la Champagne*, was not far outside the city at a place called Bétheny, a wide, flat area, fenced off on all sides, with four huge grandstands accommodating fifty thousand people overlooking a rectangular ten-kilometer course. The authorities had even erected a temporary train station in anticipation of the crowds. Wood sheds were available for the competitors' airplanes, thirty-eight of which had been entered. All of the American machines (other than Curtiss') were Wrights flown by aviators trained by Wilbur. French models included three big Antoinette monoplanes, five of the speedy Blériot monoplanes, along with seven Voisins and a new biplane built by Henry Farman.[34]

Working feverishly, Curtiss had his machine set up at the flying field within a day. On seeing it for the first time, competitors and spectators alike remarked about its small size. Similar in configuration to the *Golden Flier*, the *Rheims Racer*, as it was popularly known, had wings clipped 2½ feet to 26 feet 3 inches, with the same 4½ foot chord as the *Golden Flier*, yielding a lower aspect ratio of 5.8:1. The total area was 236 square feet. Curtiss believed, correctly, that the smaller wings, which also had less camber or a flatter cross-section than those of the *Golden Flier*, would reduce drag and allow more speed. As with the *Golden Flier*, the ailerons were located between the wings and hinged on the forward outermost struts. The new engine, a water-cooled V-8 with a 4-inch stroke and 4-inch bore, churned out more than fifty horsepower through a 6-foot-diameter propeller. The total weight, less the pilot, was about 550 pounds; power and speed were the primary objectives.[35]

"Torrents of rain" and hail pelted the flying field on the night of 15–16 August, luckily not causing any damage to Curtiss' shed or airplane. But the next day he was not so fortunate. On his second test flight, Curtiss encountered a severe gust, which threw the airplane sideways, causing one wing to hit the ground. He was shaken and bruised as a result of the accident, and had to rely on a cane for the next few days. As he limped around the shed, Curtiss supervised repairs to the airplane, impatient to get back in the air as quickly as he could for he knew his competitors had already had more practice time and that he could not afford any delays.[36]

On 19 August, as Curtiss toiled to get his machine ready to fly, the Wrights followed through with their threats to take legal action. With the full agreement of Orville, then in Germany demonstrating their airplane, and after consultation with their patent lawyer in Washington, Wilbur had attorneys file a bill of complaint in the federal circuit court in New York City against the Aeronautic Society, requesting it be restrained from exhibitions of the *Golden Flier*, the only Curtiss machine then in operation. Two days later, on the twenty-first, the Wrights' lawyers registered a similar suit demanding an injunction against Curtiss himself and Herring-Curtiss as a company from manufacturing, selling, and exhibiting airplanes. By identifying Curtiss personally and timing the suits to coincide with the Rheims event, the Wrights had deliberately attempted to maximize the effect of the legal actions.[37]

Curtiss was not surprised when he learned of the suits, telling reporters at Rheims that he "had known for some time that something of this nature was contemplated." Before leaving for France he had asked a lawyer to look at the *Golden Flier* to see if it infringed the Wright patent and got an opinion that it apparently did not. At Rheims he explained that "there is nothing to support the charge of infringement. The best answer to this is the fact known to everybody, that we made public flights in America long before the Wrights did. This shows that there could not have been an imitation of their machine by us. All competent persons who are familiar with the two machines, and with whom I have discussed this matter, agree that they are unable to see how the charge of infringement can be supported, and I am confident that the court will uphold us." Bishop told reporters that it was impossible for the Curtiss machine to have infringed because it did not rely on wing warping for lateral control. There was "considerable bitterness" toward the Wrights, Bishop added, for having brought suit "at the moment when Mr. Curtiss is the sole representative of the United States in a foreign flying contest, especially as they declined to enter this contest themselves." After Lena Curtiss had been served with the initial papers on 27 August, Monroe Wheeler told the press that the first line of defense would be the "patents taken out by Herring and his associates" that predated those of the Wrights. Although he believed the Wrights were "acting in good faith in their allegations, the records of the patent office, which will be produced by the defense, will easily and satisfactorily adjust what at first was regarded by the public as a stupendous litigation."[38]

Neither side fully comprehended what the court actions portended. The Wrights expected Curtiss and others to realize quickly that once they started to make money in aviation it made sense to pay modest royalties rather than pursue expensive litigation that was almost certain to end in an adverse decision and after which they would have to provide compensation anyway. Curtiss and his legal advisers, on the other hand, were sure that they had a control system substantially different from that of the Wrights and had important patent holdings preceding those of the Wrights. They were confident that the courts would soon exonerate them of the infringement allegations. No one anticipated nearly a decade of legal pugilism that would transcend money and principle and devolve into personal animosity and attacks on the integrity of individuals and institutions.

For the present, Curtiss set aside any worries about the future to face the more immediate task of getting his racer ready for the Rheims events. Back in the air for more practice on the evening of the nineteenth, he had to maneuver his airplane to avoid an aerial collision with one of the Antoinettes. He made a longer test flight the following day, after which he "declared that he was ready for the races" and would not make any more flights before the contests began on the twenty-second. Curtiss believed he stood a "good chance" of winning the speed events, although Blériot in his mighty 80-horsepower monoplane was a "dangerous adversary" likely to challenge him.[39]

Wind and rain kept Curtiss on the ground during the opening day of the meet on Sunday, 22 August, although twenty other fliers took to the air while he waited for better conditions. The next day, Blériot showed that he was indeed a formidable opponent when he set an unofficial speed record of nearly forty-three miles per hour. Curtiss responded before dark with a lap around the course in a little over eight and a half minutes, averaging nearly a half-mile per hour faster than Blériot. He said he could have squeezed more speed out of his airplane had he flown a warm-up lap and laughed that the most "interesting incident" in the otherwise routine flight was observing the number of wrecked machines on the far side of the course. Curtiss completed a couple of practice flights on the twenty-fifth and twenty-sixth, while Frenchmen Louis Paulhan in a Voisin and Hubert Latham in an Antoinette traded unofficial endurance records and Blériot suffered a setback when he struck a fence on landing. He was unhurt, but his airplane needed to have its wings and propeller replaced and there was some speculation that the motor might have been damaged as well. Curtiss did not enter the premier endurance event, won by

Henry Farman covering a distance of more than 111 miles in a little more than three hours, with Latham second and Paulhan third.[40]

The Gordon Bennett race on 28 August was the climax to what some newspapers called the "Week of Miracles." It was a hot and sunny day that contrasted with the cold, wind, and rain that had prevailed for most of the Rheims meet: "Curtiss weather," according to some of the Americans in the crowd of 150,000. Curtiss flew a warm-up lap a little after 10:00 AM, then announced to the judges that he was ready for the timed event. Climbing slightly before each turn and then diving around the pylons, he gained precious fractions of a second on each of the two laps, finishing with a dive from a height of one hundred feet. The time of 15 minutes, 50⅗ seconds gave him a speed of forty-seven miles per hour. Heated by the sun, the air "seemed fairly to boil" on the backstretch, Curtiss remarked afterwards, and at times "I was almost thrown from my seat" by the turbulence. Congratulations came from "thousands" of spectators, among them ex-president Theodore Roosevelt's wife and his son Quentin, who declared his performance "bully." Curtiss had done well, but still had to wait the rest of the day before he could be declared the winner. Only minutes before the closing deadline, Blériot had his chance, making a brave effort but coming up 5⅗ seconds short of Curtiss' time, while surpassing Curtiss' fastest lap by 5⅖ seconds at a speed just under fifty miles per hour. Much to the pleasure of James Gordon Bennett, his trophy was now in the possession of the Aero Club of America and the $5,000 prize was in the hands of the "Champion Aviator of the World."[41]

As if the Gordon Bennett triumph were not enough, Curtiss had even more in store for the next day, the last of the meet. The main event was the $2,500 *Prix de la Vitesse*, a three-lap timed speed contest. Starting late in the day, Curtiss wrung all the power he could from his engine, flying higher and diving steeper through the turns, cutting closer to the pylons than ever before, and barreling across the finish line in 25 minutes, 49 seconds, for an average speed of more than forty-three miles per hour. He just missed beating Blériot's single-lap speed record set only minutes before. Blériot might well have won the event, but on his second lap, the rudder on his machine failed, he lost control and plunged to the ground, narrowly escaping serious injury when the airplane caught fire and was totally destroyed. At a ceremonial luncheon the next day Curtiss received a standing ovation when he entered the room and took a seat next to Blériot. Bishop praised Curtiss for his accomplishments in the air, noted that his roots were in a place where French immigrants had introduced viticulture, and promised to have a special gold medal struck by the Aero Club in his honor. Back in Paris the *Aero Club de France* named a new balloon after him, while people on the street pulled him aside to take his photograph.[42]

Cdr. Frederick L. Chapin, the American naval attaché in Paris and one of the official observers at Rheims, immediately recognized the importance of what he had seen on the field at Bétheny. In his 1 September report he remarked on Curtiss' achievement and concluded that the airplane had emerged as a technical reality with promising, but not yet clear, military and naval potential. "I am of the opinion," he wrote, "that the aeroplane would have a present usefulness in naval warfare, and that the limits of the field will be extended in the near future." He suggested that a battleship could be fitted with a launching device similar to the catapult used by the Wrights and that an auxiliary vessel could have a flight deck added to its superstructure. Airplanes might be used for gunnery spotting, blockade, mine detection, and scouting for the fleet, as well as offensive operations against ships, although low-level daylight attacks were likely to make them vulnerable to defensive fire.[43]

Curtiss had little time to absorb all the accolades or contemplate the wider meaning of his triumph at Rheims before he and Bishop left Paris on 4 September in Bishop's automobile for a trip through Germany and Switzerland to fulfill another flying engagement at Brescia in northern Italy. Enjoyable as the journey was, Curtiss found it more leisurely than he preferred and left Bishop in Lucerne, going ahead by train and arriving in Brescia on the seventh. Meanwhile, Shriver and Fisher accompanied Curtiss' *Rheims Racer* from Paris by rail. Located on the Lombardy plain, Brescia drew tourists from all over the world, attracted by its tenth-century duomo, Renaissance piazza, and its proximity to the northern Italian lakes and the Alps. As at Rheims, Blériot promised to be Curtiss' chief competitor, although Lt. Mario Calderara of the Italian navy, in a Wright, was considered a potential winner.[44]

On the opening day of the meet, 8 September, only Curtiss and Blériot got into the air. The rough field at Montichiari, a few miles southeast of Brescia, took its toll on the fliers, among them Blériot, who lost control of his machine on the ground and struck a tree, damaging its propeller. Although he was the crowd favorite, especially among the many Americans present, Curtiss made only a short flight to qualify for the main event, a fifty-kilometer race for the $10,000 *grand prix*. Weather delayed the contest until the eleventh. Curtiss took off just a few minutes before the 6:00 PM deadline and lapped the course five times, covering more than thirty-one miles in 49 minutes, 11 seconds. He landed amid cheers of "Long Live America!" and "Long Live Curtiss!" The following day, Henri Rougier, his nearest competitor, took nearly ten minutes longer to fly the required distance in his Voisin, although he went on to complete an additional ten-kilometer lap. Blériot did not try for the distance prize, concentrating instead on altitude and other contests. For the first time, Curtiss flew with a passenger, the playwright Gabriele d'Annunzio, who after circling the course several times remarked that the flight instilled in him "a feeling of ecstatic joy only comparable to the idealistic sensations of art and love." Curtiss left Brescia with Bishop for Milan and Paris. Some $15,000 richer from the victories at Rheims and Brescia, he planned to return to New York to participate in flights commemorating the tercentenary of Henry Hudson's voyage up the Hudson and Robert Fulton's 1807 steamboat excursion over the same route.[45]

On 15 September, Curtiss boarded the North German Lloyd liner *Kaiser Wilhelm II* in Cherbourg for the trip home. He arrived in New York on the morning of the twenty-first, where Lena, Lynn Masson, and about a dozen others greeted him when he stepped ashore. He told reporters that he had "enjoyed every minute of my trip abroad," and that he had "learned a lot about the flying game." The competitions confirmed in his mind the superiority of the biplane over the monoplane configuration, although he believed that both varieties would "undoubtedly undergo material improvement in the next few years." He met with representatives of the Hudson-Fulton celebration that afternoon, then retired to spend the night with Lena at the Hotel Astor. The next day, he attended a luncheon in his honor sponsored by the Aero Club and went out to inspect the flying field at Governors Island, located about a half mile off the southern tip of Manhattan and principally used by the Army as a drill ground. There he ran into Wilbur Wright, who had arrived on the nineteenth and was busy preparing his airplane for the Hudson-Fulton flights. Curtiss greeted him with a cordial "Hello, Wilbur." Wright instantly recognized him and paused from working on the airplane's motor. "Why, how are you Mr. Curtiss? I can't shake hands; they're too dirty. Glad you did so well." Curtiss replied that without the benefit of Wilbur's previous experience flying in France he would not have achieved so much. The two had another five minutes or so of friendly conversation before Curtiss looked over the shed that had been erected to house his airplane and briefly commented on the soft and sandy soil of the flying field. The Curtisses left on the morning of the twenty-third for Hammondsport, where welcome home preparations were being prepared for the village's international celebrity.[46]

No one in Hammondsport could recall a homecoming like the one Curtiss received. It started in Bath, where he and Lena arrived on a Lackawanna train about 5:30 on the evening of the twenty-third. Curtiss went first to the Steuben Club, where "he bowed and smiled and said a few words right to the point, which set the crowd wild." Monroe Wheeler hosted a reception for Lena at his home, then the Curtisses had dinner at the Reed House hotel. A Bath and Hammondsport special train took the couple and assorted dignitaries on the short trip to Hammondsport. There a carriage led a parade through the brightly lit and gaudily decorated village, while crowds jammed the streets and fireworks lit up the skies sodden with a cold rain. A red, white, and blue electric sign welcomed Curtiss to the factory on the hill. Accepting a gold medal from the town fathers, Curtiss gave a characteristically brief speech:

> Although I spent a number of years as a student of Hammondsport High School, I never learned words which are adequate to express my appreciation of the reception I have been accorded tonight, or to express my thanks for this medal which has just been presented to me. The last four weeks have been very eventful. I have met with considerable success and have met many notable people, but on no occasion have I experienced the happiness that I do tonight as I look upon this assemblage.[47]

Curtiss' accomplishment underscores the emergence of the airplane in 1909 as a practical reality, but even more significant was the realization that flight was the leading edge of what the historian Robert Wohl views as a new era in which flying captured the imagination of the Western world. In doing so, Curtiss ascended to the status of hero. The *Hammondsport Herald* gushed: "No hero, ancient or modern, was ever greeted with more loyalty than was Glenn H. Curtiss on this occasion. . . .The people of Hammondsport love and admire him for what he is, and for what, through great trials and much adversity, he has made of himself. . . . Honors do not spoil him," the paper went on, "the flattery of great men does not turn his head. His habits are as simple and his moral character as unsullied as when he was plodding the hard and uncertain road to his first foothold in the business world."[48] A self-made man, quiet, unassuming, small-town born and bred, Curtiss was willing to pit his native talent against the best that Europe could throw against him. He was the perfect image of the early twentieth-century American hero—a Lindbergh before Lindbergh.

Curtiss had little time to bask in the adulation, for he had to get a new airplane ready for the Hudson-Fulton celebration and his commitment to fly up the

Hudson to Grant's Tomb and return to the flying field at Governors Island. His preference would have been to fly the *Rheims Racer*, but Herring rendered that an impossibility when he engaged to show the machine in Wanamaker's department stores in Philadelphia and New York and at another exhibition at Filene's in Boston in November. Rodman Wanamaker, the son of the store's founder and an aviation enthusiast, supported the deal, which earned $5,000 for the Herring-Curtiss company but left Curtiss in the awkward position of having to build and test another airplane on short notice. The new machine was a virtual copy of the Rheims airplane, although with a much less powerful 25-horsepower 4-cylinder engine and ailerons that extended forty inches beyond the outermost interplane struts. Because he anticipated a good deal of over-water flying, Curtiss equipped the machine with a triangular rubber-sealed float attached to a wood skid extending longitudinally from between the rear wheels to just behind the front wheel.[49]

Curtiss arrived in New York early on the morning of 27 September, a day after his new airplane had been assembled in its hangar on Governors Island by Tod Shriver and three other mechanics. Two days later, Curtiss made a short flight around the flying field. Afterward he complained that the machine's propeller was not performing well and that the sandy soil prevented him from getting up as much speed as he liked for takeoff. Wilbur Wright easily upstaged him with three flights later in the day, including one across the bay and around the Statue of Liberty. High winds grounded both aviators for three days, giving Curtiss some extra time to confer with Tom Baldwin, whose airship had been damaged on the twenty-ninth when it fell into the river in an attempt to fly up the Hudson to Albany. Curtiss tried again late in the afternoon of 3 October. His airplane now had a four-blade propeller that he hoped would improve its performance, but all he accomplished was another short flight around the field—some who were there disputed even that. In any case, the results of the effort were disappointing, and Curtiss did not have time to attempt more flights before he had to leave for Hammondsport to prepare for another commitment in St. Louis. Now with the field to himself, Wright had a unique chance to best his chief aeronautical rival by making the round-trip flight to Grant's Tomb. On the morning of the fourth, he took off from Governors Island in his machine, which had a canoe strapped underneath for emergency flotation, completing a stunning twenty-mile flight up and down the river in about thirty-three minutes before perhaps a million onlookers.[50]

In Hammondsport barely long enough to reflect on the New York disaster, Curtiss was off with Lena on 5 October for a three-day aerial exhibition sponsored by the Aero Club of St. Louis in conjunction with a celebration of the centennial of the founding of the city. The aviation meet was at Forest Park, west of downtown on the site of the World's Fair five years earlier. In addition to Curtiss, the organizers attracted Georges Osmont, a French aviator flying a Farman biplane, Tom Baldwin with his airship refurbished from its ducking in the Hudson, and Baldwin disciples A. Roy Knabenshue and Lincoln Beachey, both piloting small airships. Curtiss arrived on the sixth and the next day made three short flights, the last ending when the fuel line clogged and the engine quit. On the morning of the eighth, he made a circuit of the three-quarter-mile track in a minute and a half, followed by a shorter flight that evening. Wind and rain kept Curtiss on the ground for most of the day on 9 October, but he did finally manage a modest flight early that evening, followed by another, his last in St. Louis, on the tenth, in which he completed another circle of the track. St. Louis helped Curtiss redeem himself after the Hudson-Fulton fiasco and left spectators and sponsors satisfied that they had seen a real airplane execute what at the time were regarded as the first flights west of Dayton, Ohio.[51]

From St. Louis it was on to Chicago for what Curtiss hoped was a series of flights at the mile-long Hawthorne Race Track in Cicero, one of the city's western suburbs. Bad weather prevented flights on 15 October, and winds persisted the following day. Not wishing to let down the crowd eager to see their first airplane in flight, Curtiss made a forty-second hop late in the afternoon. Two days later, he braved fifteen-mile-per-hour winds to make two flights, the first lasting less than a minute and the second circling the three-quarter-mile track in about ninety seconds. Again, his performance in Chicago was hardly up to what Curtiss knew he could achieve, but the flights were the first in the country's second largest city and did nothing to lessen his deserved reputation as one of the world's most accomplished aviators.[52]

Returning home with Lena on 20 October 1909 via Detroit and Cleveland, Curtiss faced dispiriting problems that transcended the wind and rain that he had to endure on his Midwestern jaunt. One of the most immediate was a developing schism within the Herring-Curtiss company. More than a little annoyed that Herring had sent the *Rheims Racer* off on exhibition, and by his failure to produce any of the patents he had promised, Curtiss came to the realization that he had made a serious mistake in forming a business alliance with Herring, but he was unsure exactly how he could disengage himself from the relationship. Fortunately, in Monroe Wheeler, Lynn Masson, and Tom Baldwin he had supporters on the company's board of directors who shared his negative opinions of Herring. They were willing to take action when Herring raised the point that Curtiss had no right to hold the money he had earned by his exhibition flights and from the cash prizes he had won, and should be forced to turn the proceeds from such over to the company. On 25 October, the directors met in Wheeler's offices in Bath and passed a resolution that had been drafted by Wheeler stating that Curtiss had a personal agreement with Cortlandt Bishop allowing him to keep the money, and that his successes were good advertising for the company and well worth his extra remuneration. Herring argued that the resolution jeopardized the assets of the company and that it had come about as the result of a conspiracy among the directors. He also fumed about Curtiss' sale of the motorcycle business to Tank Waters and the decision Wheeler and Curtiss had made without his assent to hire Jerome S. Fanciulli, a young Associated Press employee with an interest in aviation, to publicize Curtiss' exhibitions and handle the sale of his airplanes entirely separate from the Herring-Curtiss company.[53]

Curtiss temporarily left his troubles with Herring behind to head west for an exhibition at the Latonia racetrack in Covington, Kentucky, across the Ohio River from Cincinnati. The weather was good for the start of the meet on 12 November, which also featured Charles Willard and the *Golden Flier*. But after a couple of short flights, Curtiss' airplane was damaged and he was unable to continue. Meanwhile, the airships of Knabenshue and Beachey pleased the big crowds with their speed and maneuverability. Curtiss and Willard were in the air again on the thirteenth, although neither stayed up long enough to circle the track, and on the next and last day of the event high winds prevented anything more than brief hops along the front straightaway. Curtiss was as disappointed as the crowds and later admitted that the exhibition was "not very successful."[54]

Relations with Herring deteriorated through the rest of the year until there was no hope of reconciliation. By the middle of November, Bishop, in particular, had come to believe that Herring was a prevaricator and a liability to the company, not to mention a threat to Bishop's own investment in the Herring-Curtiss company. When Curtiss asked Herring at one point during the fall if he held any patents, Herring admitted that he had none but that he had applied for at least one. Meeting in Hammondsport on 18 December to review the situation, the company's board voted to begin legal proceedings in the state supreme court to require Herring to submit his patents, patent applications, and shop equipment to the company as he had been obligated to do under the terms of incorporation, and to secure a court injunction forbidding him from selling the stock he had received in payment for the patents and other holdings.[55]

Herring had rushed out of the room before the meeting was over and could not immediately be found in either Hammondsport or Bath. The rest of the story takes on soap-operatic tones. It seems that on leaving the meeting Herring called a third person in Bath, who hired a young man—not knowing he was Wheeler's son Rumsey—to drive him to Hammondsport to pick up Herring's attorney, J. John Hassett. The three men encountered Herring hiding in the bushes beside the road as they drove down the west side of the lake out of Hammondsport. Alarmed that he might be in the middle of a highjacking or kidnapping, Wheeler abandoned Herring and Hassett and returned with the mysterious third man to Bath. Herring and his compatriot then made their way to the home of a local man, telling him that their car had had a mechanical breakdown and that they needed a place to stay. He took them in for the night and the next day drove them to nearby Savona, the next stop east of Bath, where they took a train back to New York.[56]

Herring's strategy was to ignore the 18 December board stipulations and three days later to assume the offensive with a suit in the state supreme court against Curtiss and his allies. It is obvious that Herring and Hassett had been working on the retaliatory litigation for some time, for the allegations closely followed Herring's earlier complaints that Curtiss and the others had conspired to strip the company of its financial and other assets and to render Herring's stock worthless. The complaint specifically challenged the directors' decision allowing Curtiss to keep the earnings he had received from his airplane exhibitions, and required him to account for and reimburse the company for all the money he had received since the incorporation of the firm in March. It further enjoined him from any more flights unless the proceeds were guaranteed to the Herring-Curtiss company. On Christmas Eve, Justice Henry B. Coman issued a restraining order to that effect against Curtiss and the board, prohibiting the company from securing loans or fulfilling any contracts made before 25 October and in effect preventing the company from doing business pending a trial on the charges.[57]

At the end of the year Curtiss found himself entangled in not one but two interrelated legal snares, for the Wright suit lay at the heart of many of the problems with Herring. What Wheeler anticipated would be a simple matter to resolve became more complex when Herring failed to present his patents and then ran for cover when threatened with legal action to produce them. It was obvious to the company's directors that Herring held no patents. (Since

1896 he had filed only one patent, and that had been rejected by the Patent Office.) Absent the nonexistent Herring patents, the defense now had to fall back on the argument that the Curtiss lateral control system was substantially different from that of the Wrights. The first hearing, scheduled for 4 October before Judge John R. Hazel of the United States Circuit Court in Buffalo, was postponed until the sixteenth, and then put off again until 14 December.[58]

In the meantime, while Curtiss was in Chicago for the Hawthorne exhibition, he met with Octave Chanute to discuss the patent situation and the Wright suits. He came away reassured by Chanute that "the Wrights have little prospect of winning." Chanute further bolstered Curtiss' case in a letter to New York patent attorney Emerson R. Newell in which he stated that the Wrights' idea of wing-warping was not new and that he could not recall any specific examples of the kind of lateral control used by Curtiss airplanes. Newell had a meeting with Wilbur Wright a few days later and examined the Wright airplane at College Park, Maryland, outside Washington, where Wilbur was busy training the first Army aviators. Wilbur was polite and helpful, and Newell complimented him and his brother on their accomplishments in aviation and on their "splendid machine." After a close look at the Wright airplane, he did not believe there was any basis for the Wrights' claims of infringement. On November 1, Curtiss himself went to Washington. There he met Newell and the two of them conferred with Charles J. Bell about the status of the AEA patent application, possible royalty payments, and the Wright suit. They then went out to College Park to see Wilbur and his airplane. The first time Curtiss and Wright had been together since the Hudson-Fulton celebration, the meeting ended with Curtiss' assurances that there would be no "mud-slinging" from his side in the patent conflict. Curtiss left later that day for New York and a meeting of the Aero Club.[59]

Glenn and Lena were in Buffalo on 14 December for the first of two days of testimony on the Wright suit in Judge Hazel's court. The Wrights' attorney, Harry A. Toulmin, opened the case against Curtiss. He stressed that the brothers had introduced the first successful heavier-than-air flying machine and that Curtiss had in effect stolen his ideas for control from the Wrights and had colluded with Herring, who had been associated with the Wrights while they worked on their airplane. Speaking for the defense, Newell said the Wrights themselves had conceded that control surfaces attached to wings represented a prior art and argued that the Curtiss system was substantively different from that of the Wrights. Therefore it was not an infringement. The Curtisses returned to Hammondsport reasonably certain that they had made their case and that it was unlikely Hazel would issue an injunction, knowing that such action would have severe financial repercussions for the Herring-Curtiss company. Yet they remained on tenterhooks throughout the Christmas and New Year's holidays waiting for Hazel to make his decision.[60]

For Curtiss the end of another year brought mixed feelings of satisfaction about his aerial achievements and concern about what the future portended. The fame he had earned in France and Italy led to demands for him to demonstrate his airplane in major American cities, which in turn he believed would translate into airplane sales and profits. At the same time, his determination to establish an aviation business had brought him into partnership with Augustus Herring, who proved to be at the least uncooperative and at the most a disruptive and hostile fraud. Complicating matters was that Curtiss and others had been deluded into thinking Herring would be central to their case when the Wrights took legal action for patent infringement. If there was one surety amid the uncertainty at the end of 1909, it was that Curtiss had crossed a divide and was now fully committed to a career centered on the airplane as the basis for a new industrial enterprise.

—4—

The Exhibition Business

U nlike the Wrights, who condemned exhibition flying as a "monte-bank game" unworthy of their participation, Curtiss embraced show-manship as a vital component of the aviation business, essential to increasing public awareness of the airplane and ultimately to its manufacture and sale. "Flying exhibitions," he wrote in 1911, "have played an important part in the development of aviation because they have given the public a certain intimacy with the aeroplane and an opportunity to study its possibilities at close range. Competitive meets have had an even greater effect, because, like automobile races, they stimulate the manufacturers to greater efforts in the perfection of their machines."[1]

His first tentative steps into this new endeavor came in the late summer and early fall of 1909 with the failed Hudson-Fulton efforts and the flights in St. Louis, Chicago, and Cincinnati. While he was in Chicago, he had encountered a diminutive, intense young man with a nasty cigarette habit named Charles K. Hamilton. A twenty-four-year-old native of Connecticut, Hamilton had earned a deserved reputation as a showman and daredevil flying balloons and airships. Now he badly wanted to learn how to fly an airplane and pleaded with Curtiss to show him how. While grounded by the wind at Hawthorne, Curtiss conceded and let him sit in his machine to familiarize himself with the controls. If he were really serious about flying an airplane, Curtiss said, he should visit him in Hammondsport. That was all the encour-agement Hamilton needed; when Curtiss returned to Hammondsport from his Midwestern trip, Hamilton was there waiting for him.[2]

By accident, then, Curtiss had found his third student aviator, who, like Willard, displayed a natural talent for flying. Hamilton made his first flight at the Stony Brook track on 29 October, followed by another on the thirty-first. On 1 November, Hamilton flew Curtiss' Hudson-Fulton machine for more than twenty-five minutes, circling the valley nineteen times and nearly equaling the longest time Curtiss himself had spent in the air. Curtiss also flew at Stony Brook during the first week of November, impressing locals with figure eights and a precise landing at the point where he had taken off. Following discussions with his publicist Jerome Fanciulli, Curtiss decided to hire Hamilton to help out with the aerial exhibition business, but he did not want to give the Wrights further ammunition for their lawsuit by taking him on as an employee. Monroe Wheeler drafted a contract for Hamilton that became the blueprint for all future arrangements made between Curtiss and his aviators. Hamilton did not buy the airplane but rather leased it from Curtiss, paying him 60 percent of the returns from his exhibitions, splitting the cost of repairs and maintenance, and taking full responsibility for any damage or legal costs.[3]

While working with Hamilton, Curtiss received word from the Aero Club of California in early November that they wanted Curtiss to participate in a big aviation meet the club planned to hold in Los Angeles in early January. Curtiss did not hesitate to inform the organizers that he would be there. He knew that his French rival Louis Paulhan intended to fly there, and that he stood a good chance of being competitive now that the *Rheims Racer* had finally been released from Herring's grip. Hamilton wanted to compete in the tournament, too, as did Charlie Willard with the *Golden Flier*; the three men in effect formed the first Curtiss exhibition team. The Curtisses, along with Fanciulli and his wife, left Hammondsport on 30 December, taking a Lackawanna train from Bath to Buffalo and from there continuing on to Chicago's La Salle Street station via Cleveland and Toledo. After a layover in Chicago, they boarded the Santa Fe's exclusive *California Limited* for the journey to the coast, arriving at the La Grande terminal in Los Angeles on 5 January. Hamilton got there two days later.[4] Reliable rail transportation made it possible for Curtiss to engage aviation exhibitions in nearly all parts of the country, even from so remote a location as Hammondsport.

The day he arrived in Los Angeles, Curtiss learned that Judge Hazel had handed down a decision two days earlier upholding the Wrights' plea for a preliminary injunction and barring the Herring-Curtiss company from manufacturing, selling, or exhibiting flying machines. Hazel believed that the Wrights were "entitled to a broad and liberal construction" of their 1906 patent and that any airplane infringed that patent if it had a "supporting surface, the lateral portions of which are capable of adjustment to attain different angles of incidence, and a vertical rudder in the rear of the machine," and if it featured a "horizontal rudder [elevator], which is positioned forward of the machine and means for raising and lowering it so as to present its upper and lower side to the pressure of the wind." Hazel acknowledged that Curtiss had made improvements to the Wrights' control system, but insisted that the Wright patent was written clearly enough to preclude a court ruling on its technical details. In other words, in his opinion any flying machine with movable surfaces allowing effective three-dimensional control constituted an infringement.[5]

In Los Angeles, Curtiss said that he had talked with his attorneys about the judge's order and insisted that "it will not interfere with my flights," which he said were more experiments "in [the] Pacific coast atmosphere" than competitions for monetary gain. No one, least of all the Wrights or Judge Hazel, believed that Curtiss had traveled across the continent to experiment with his airplanes rather than vie with other aviators for cash prizes. Curtiss, moreover, vowed "to go ahead" with flights in Los Angeles to demonstrate that his machines did not depend, as did the Wrights' airplanes (and specifically mentioned in Judge Hazel's decision) on the vertical rudder for control in banking turns. To continue to fly, Curtiss posted a $10,000 bond and filed an appeal, gambling that he would not lose all his earnings in a settlement with the Wrights should the appellate court find against him. Further casting a pall over the Los Angeles meet was the Wrights' request on 4 January for an injunction preventing Paulhan from flying any of his four airplanes in the United States, although the court's restraining order did not come down until after the end of the event.[6]

Flying began on 9 January at the nearly two-mile-long course laid out on the Dominguez ranch, south of Los Angeles and not far from the town of Compton. Paulhan and his retinue brought two Blériot and two Farman machines, with which they planned to contest all the speed and altitude events. Five Curtiss airplanes were entered, including Hamilton's and Willard's, Curtiss' own *Rheims Racer*, and another machine he had sold to Long Island real estate magnate Clifford B. Harmon. Curtiss made three short practice flights late in the day in Harmon's airplane. He flew again the next day, when the competition formally opened. To "thunderous applause" from the enthusiastic crowd of twenty-five thousand, Curtiss followed his flight in Harmon's airplane with a fast lap around the field in the Rheims machine, only to descend with a broken propeller. Paulhan, in one of his Farmans, made three flights, one of which lasted nearly half an hour. Hamilton and Willard also flew, although Willard's engine quit halfway around the course and he had to land to effect repairs before he could return to the starting line.[7]

If Paulhan won the first round of the showdown at Dominguez Field on 10 January, Curtiss was victorious in the second round the next day. Paulhan was first into the air, with both a Farman and one of his Blériots, thrilling the crowd with his ability to control the craft in the face of unpredictable wind gusts. When it was Curtiss' turn, he wheeled out the *Rheims Racer* and, with Fanciulli sitting behind him, set a speed record for a flight with a passenger by rounding the course at fifty-five miles per hour. Not to be outdone, Paulhan made a three-mile flight with one of his mechanics on board, but fell well short of Curtiss' speed. Willard won a quick-start prize later in the day, while Curtiss took an award for the most precise landing. At one point four aviators—Curtiss, Paulhan, Willard, and Hamilton—were in the air at the same time, much to the spectators' delight.[8]

Curtiss made a couple of flights on the twelfth, including the fastest three-lap time of the meet, but they seemed inconsequential compared to Paulhan's record altitude of more than 4,600 feet in one of the Farmans. Paulhan was in the air for more than fifty minutes. On the thirteenth, Curtiss attempted to set new records for two, three, and ten laps around the course. He finished ten laps in a little under twenty-five minutes, not enough for a record, but still sufficient to beat Paulhan by five seconds. Hamilton and Willard flew on the thirteenth and fourteenth, Hamilton failing to complete ten laps on the thirteenth and cutting short an altitude flight the next day because of engine problems. Paulhan again won the crowd's approval for a round-trip cross-country flight to San Pedro and back on the fourteenth. Not to be upstaged, Curtiss responded with a new single-lap course record of two minutes, twelve seconds.[9]

Two days of rain and wind limited what the aviators could do until the seventeenth, when good weather and huge crowds returned to the aviation field. Paulhan fell well short of setting a record for absolute distance and could not beat Curtiss' ten-lap time, itself a two-minute improvement over Curtiss' previous twenty-five-minute posting. On the twentieth, the last day of the meet, Paulhan and Curtiss for the first time competed against one another in a ten-lap race, soaring over the grandstand "with the speed of express trains." Curtiss easily defeated his rival by more than a half lap. In the final accounting, Paulhan garnered $15,000 in prizes, compared to Curtiss' $5,000. The *New York Times* summed it up: "Curtiss made some remarkable flights," but they were all "extremely technical" and "coldly practical," and did not grab the public's attention in the same way Paulhan's more polished showmanship did.[10]

Nearly lost in the drama at Dominguez Field were flights by Curtiss and Hamilton in which they disabled the vertical rudders of their machines to demonstrate that the Curtiss airplanes did not, like the Wrights', depend on rudder movements to maintain equilibrium in banking turns. From experience, Curtiss knew how difficult it was to make coordinated turns without using the rudder, but he hoped that the Dominguez Field experiments, observed and recorded by Harmon, Augustus Post, and Army Lt. Paul Beck, would provide additional evidence that his airplanes had a control system that did not infringe on the Wright patent. At a dinner in Los Angeles, Curtiss cut through the legal clamor and engaged in some humor at the Wrights' expense. "They don't own the air, you know," he began.

> Did you hear about the conversation that was overheard between them at the Dayton plant? "Orville," cries Wilbur, running out of doors excitedly. "Look, here's another aviator using our patent!" "He certainly is," shouts Orville. "That's our simultaneous warping and steering movement to a T." "Call a cop," screams Wilbur. "Get another injunction!" But Orville, who had looked up through his binoculars, held his hand gently on his brother's arm. "Come on back to work, Wilbur," he said. "It's a duck."[11]

After the meet Hamilton left for San Diego, where he planned to make flights in the *Rheims Racer*, while Curtiss returned to Hammondsport, more than ever convinced that there was money to be made in the exhibition business. But somehow he would have to be rid of Herring if he were to succeed. Curtiss got good news about the Herring case the day after he left home for the Los Angeles meet when Justice Coman in vacating the injunction he had recently issued against the Herring-Curtiss company agreed with Monroe Wheeler that the original ruling in effect blocked the company from doing business and called on Herring to provide evidence of specific instances in which Curtiss' actions had harmed the company. Curtiss argued his case in public when he got back to Hammondsport on 27 January, pointing out that Herring had "absolutely failed to meet any of the terms of the contract made in the organization of the Herring-Curtiss company of which he was the promoter." Furthermore, Curtiss insisted, "the action of the board of directors in cancelling Herring's stock was fully justified by the fact that Mr. Herring has not in any way lived up to his agreement with the company, and has not paid one penny in money or otherwise for the large share of stock, which he, as promoter, secured for himself. . . . He has not delivered the patents mentioned in his agreement, and in fact it has been shown that he has no patents. He has never finished the aeroplane which he was to have built for the government, and on which he was to have tried out a number of his inventions with a view of adopting them, if practicable, in the machines of the Herring-Curtiss company." That Herring would claim the prize money "won by me in the various contests in which I have competed" was incomprehensible considering that as a result of the publicity accruing from those competitions the company had earned far more than that in profits, in which Herring appeared not to be interested.[12]

Over the next month, Curtiss and Herring proffered settlement terms that each found unacceptable, while the state supreme court determined that the company's board could not meet until the injunction against Herring was fully adjudicated, preventing Herring from voting his majority stock and thereby extending the impasse indefinitely. In the meantime, to provide some legal protection in light of the Wright suit, the company restricted its airplane sales to private customers who pledged to use the machines "for their own personal use." Even so, Curtiss found most potential buyers wanted guarantees against litigation. With the Wright and Herring cases so conflated, the firm's airplane business voluntarily and involuntarily restricted, and the company's board prohibited from meeting, the future was far from bright for Curtiss and his enterprise. Then he learned that Herring had unilaterally come to terms with W. Starling Burgess of Marblehead, Massachusetts, to market a biplane that closely resembled Curtiss' but featuring a control system that he believed did not infringe on the Wright patent. The deal was the last straw for Curtiss and his allies, who now saw no reason to try to effect a settlement with someone they knew to be a shameful and dishonest charlatan. At this point, Curtiss and Jerome Fanciulli met to discuss the situation. Fanciulli told Curtiss that he (Curtiss) had made a "great mistake" by joining with Herring, who had "attained a very bad reputation for himself," and that the partnership had damaged the company. He threatened that he could not be permanently associated with any organization in which Herring was involved.[13]

With Curtiss' and Monroe Wheeler's tacit assent, Fanciulli subsequently met with a lawyer in New York who suggested that bankruptcy might be the best alternative. This would allow Curtiss to buy the assets of the company from its receivers and thus be rid of Herring once and for all. The strategy was feasible because the Herring-Curtiss company had experienced genuine cash flow problems, which had led to difficulties securing parts from its suppliers that were needed to complete motors and motorcycles. Curtiss even

The house on Castle Hill in Hammondsport, where Glenn Curtiss grew up and lived most of his early life. *Glenn H. Curtiss Museum*

Curtiss (left) opened his own bicycle sales and service business, on Pulteney Street off the town square in Hammondsport, in March 1899. *Glenn H. Curtiss Museum*

From bicycles Curtiss turned to manufacturing and selling motorcycles in early 1902. Curtiss and his wife Lena (right) join his good friend from bicycling days C. Leonard("Tank") Waters and his wife on tandem motorcycles for a ride, sometime after 1904. *Glenn H. Curtiss Museum*

A staged photo showing Curtiss on his monster V-8-powered motorcycle following his record-breaking 24 January 1907 run at Ormond Beach, Florida. Curtiss reached a speed of 136.3 miles per hour over the measured mile, an unofficial record that stood until 1911. *Glenn H. Curtiss Museum*

By 1908, Curtiss was a successful young businessman whose motor-cycles were well known for their light weight, power, and reliability. Those attributes attracted builders of flying machines at the time. *Glenn H. Curtiss Museum*

In 1904, Thomas S. Baldwin ordered a motorcycle engine from Curtiss to use in one of his airships. Later, Baldwin relocated his airship operations from San Francisco to Hammondsport. Curtiss flew one of Baldwin's airships at Hammondsport in June 1907. It was his first solo flight in an aircraft of any kind. *Glenn H. Curtiss Museum*

Alexander Graham Bell provided the inspiration for the Aerial Experiment Association, formed in September 1907. From left are: Frederick W. ("Casey") Baldwin, Army Lt. Thomas E. Selfridge, Curtiss, Bell, John Alexander Douglas (J. A. D.) McCurdy. Augustus Post (right), secretary of the Aero Club of America, was not a member of the AEA. *Glenn H. Curtiss Museum*

The AEA's glider, tested in Hammondsport in the winter of 1908, placed the group in the mainstream of aeronautical development. *Glenn H. Curtiss Museum*

The *Red Wing* was the AEA's first powered machine, shown here on icy Lake Keuka in March 1908. *Glenn H. Curtiss Museum*

Curtiss, in the background with cap, white shirt, and tie, flew the AEA's *White Wing* more than one thousand feet at Hammondsport on 22 May 1908. It was his first experience in a powered heavier-than-air machine. *Glenn H. Curtiss Museum*

Curtiss designed the *June Bug* for the AEA. He flew it in Hammondsport on 4 July 1908 to win the *Scientific American* trophy for a flight of more than one kilometer. *Glenn H. Curtiss Museum*

In an early effort at water flying, Curtiss fitted the *June Bug* with floats. Tests on Lake Keuka in November 1908 were not successful. *National Archives*

Although Curtiss relied primarily on his intuitive engineering talent in designing airplanes, he used this small wind tunnel to gather aerodynamic data in the spring of 1909. *Glenn H. Curtiss Museum*

La Grande Semaine d'Aviation de la Champagne at Rheims in August 1909 established Curtiss' international reputation as an aviation hero. This is his *Rheims Racer*, the V-8-powered airplane with which he won the Gordon Bennett speed trophy at the French meet. *National Archives*

Curtiss flew the *Hudson Flier* from Albany to New York City in May 1910, setting a distance record and further enhancing his image as one of the nation's and the world's most accomplished aviators. *Glenn H. Curtiss Museum*

In an exhibition sponsored by the *New York World* Curtiss dropped dummy bombs from the *Hudson Flier* on the outline of a battleship in Lake Keuka in late June 1910. *Glenn H. Curtiss Museum*

GLENN CURTIS AND HIS BIPLANE

Curtiss flew at an international air meet at Belmont Park on Long Island in October 1910. Capt. Washington Irving Chambers was present at the event, along with two other naval officers, to observe Curtiss and other aviators. *Glenn H. Curtiss Museum*

Beginning in September 1910, Capt. Washington Irving Chambers had responsibility for aviation in his capacity as assistant to the Aide for Material in the office of the Secretary of the Navy. His collaboration with Curtiss helped shape the course of early naval aviation. *U.S.Naval Institute Photo Archives*

Eugene Ely was a member of the Curtiss exhibition team. Curtiss is on the right. Chambers and Curtiss believed Ely's skills and experience made him an ideal candidate for the first ship-flying experiments in November 1910 and January 1911. *Naval Historical Center*

Flying from Warship

Eugene Ely takes off from a platform on the scout cruiser *Birmingham*, near Hampton Roads on 14 November 1910. His four-minute flight was the first from a ship. *Naval Historical Center*

In another first, Eugene Ely lands on the armored cruiser *Pennsylvania* in San Francisco Bay on 18 January 1911. *Naval Historical Center*

In December 1910, Chambers chose Theodore C. ("Spuds") Ellyson, a 1905 Annapolis graduate, as the first naval officer to learn to fly with Curtiss at his winter training field on North Island, San Diego. *Glenn H. Curtiss Museum*

Curtiss in the air at North Island in February 1911. The ship in the background is the *Pennsylvania*, which had come down from San Francisco for more flying experiments. *National Archives*

had to take out a personal loan to meet payroll and other expenses. Although Curtiss and Wheeler denied any secret understanding to employ bankruptcy as a means of eliminating Herring from the company, it was in both men's interests to do so. Not only was Wheeler Curtiss' attorney, but he was also a director of the Bank of Hammondsport, which was the principal creditor in the Herring-Curtiss company. It is logical to assume that Wheeler was behind the bank's decision to call in a $7,500 note that it had with the company, which led the bank to file a legal claim with other Hammondsport creditors in the United States District Court in Buffalo that precipitated the firm's involuntary liquidation on 1 April 1910.[14]

Gabriel Pankhurst, formerly head of the accounting department of the Kirkham Motor Company in Bath, took over as the company's court-appointed trustee and immediately informed Curtiss and Herring that they would no longer receive their salaries. Public statements that the creditors would get their money and that the company would continue to operate helped reassure Hammondsporters and the firm's employees that the company would carry on as before and emerge from bankruptcy without too much delay. Not surprisingly, Herring did not simply go away, appealing the petition as a creditor and requesting that someone other than Pankhurst be appointed as a trustee. Hearings on the case began in July and continued through the rest of the summer. In a long letter to his fellow creditors, Herring charged Curtiss as the company's "sole manager" with a laundry list of offenses, among them theft and fraud. His claim that Curtiss had conspired with Wheeler and others to bankrupt the company so that Curtiss could buy the firm and its assets at "junk prices" came close to the mark, but his argument that he and not Curtiss, Wheeler, or the other directors of the company was best suited to bring the company out of bankruptcy and into profitability did not elicit support from any of the other creditors. During three days of testimony in July and August, Curtiss carefully refuted all of Herring's accusations, a job made considerably easier due to Herring's track record of dubious claims and general lack of credibility within the aviation community.[15]

Meanwhile, Curtiss continued to fight the Wright lawsuit with all the resources he had available. One of the most promising arguments in his defense was that his airplanes could maintain stability in the air and turn without relying on a movable rudder, which he and Hamilton had first demonstrated at Dominguez Field in January. Curtiss followed up those experiments with a more intensive round of tests in Hammondsport in February while flying from the frozen surface of Lake Keuka in his 4-cylinder machine.

He flew six times with the airplane's rudder fixed in position and the steering wheel sealed so that any movement could be verified after the flights. Augustus Post was present in his capacity as secretary of the Aero Club of America to attest to the results. He, too, flew the airplane, making three short practice flights to debut as an aviator in his own right. The results of the tests were mathematically confirmed by Dr. Albert F. Zahm, the man responsible for establishing the nation's first aeronautical laboratory at Catholic University in Washington in 1901. After reviewing the new information, Judge Hazel agreed on 14 March to another hearing on the preliminary injunction prohibiting Curtiss from manufacturing or selling airplanes.[16]

A possible divorce from the quarrelsome Herring and potential removal of Hazel's restraining order were positive developments in the late winter and early spring of 1910 but Curtiss had other things on his mind, too. In particular he was in the process of designing and constructing a new airplane specifically intended to compete for the $10,000 prize offered by Joseph Pulitzer's *New York World* for the first flight between New York and Albany. The newspaper had hoped to award the prize as part of the Hudson-Fulton celebration the previous fall, but attempts by Tom Baldwin and another airship pilot, George Tomlinson, had ended in failure, prompting an extension of the deadline until October 1910. The flight could be made in either direction, but had to be completed in twenty-four hours; only two stops were permitted. In attempting the flight, Curtiss hoped to make up for the disappointment at Governors Island, but there was another lure—the *Scientific American* trophy, now being awarded for a cross-country flight of at least fifty miles. Winning the prize for the third time meant retiring it to his permanent possession.[17]

Determined to proceed, Curtiss assigned Henry Kleckler and Damon Merrill, another of his shop workers, responsibility for an airplane capable of making the 150-mile flight over the river between the two cities. Although Curtiss, Bell, and the other members of the AEA had been highly critical of the Wrights for their secrecy, the shoe was now on the other foot. The last thing Curtiss needed was for Herring to intervene. To ensure that Herring would not learn of the new machine, Curtiss had it assembled, at his personal expense, in a temporary shop set up on Pulteney Street, and he made sure there was no publicity. Considering the possibility of a water landing, Curtiss fitted the airplane with two cylindrical metal floats fastened under the lower wing just outboard of the landing gear, and a cork-filled canvas bag placed on a keel extending forward of the main wheels to just behind the front wheel. The lower wing of the craft had a span of a little more than 30 feet, and the upper wing had 4-foot extensions on its outer ends. Both wings had 4-foot 6-inch chords, for a total area of 306 square feet. Without a pilot, the airplane weighed 855 pounds; power came from a new 50-horsepower water-cooled V-8 motor.[18]

Curtiss set off with Lena and the new airplane on the evening of 2 April for an aviation meet in Memphis, where they joined Willard, Hamilton, and one of Curtiss' latest students, James C. ("Bud") Mars, formerly a parachute jumper and assistant to Tom Baldwin. The meet opened on 7 April at the city's Tri-State Fairgrounds. That day Curtiss set a new record for a quick start in his airplane, after which he took Lena up as a passenger—the first time she flew with her husband. Mars made his first public flights in one of Curtiss' four-cylinder machines, negotiating the mile-long course at heights up to four hundred feet. An otherwise unspectacular event ended on the tenth when gusty winds caused Mars to lose control of his airplane, which plunged onto the top of a car parked in the infield, demolishing his machine. Fortunately, none of the five passengers in the automobile were injured. Mars himself came away with nothing more than a few bruises.[19]

Following the meet, the Curtisses and Charley Hamilton continued on to San Antonio, Texas, where Tom Baldwin joined them at an aviation exhibition that began on 21 April as part of the city's annual spring carnival. Now a convert to heavier-than-air flight, Baldwin brought his *Red Devil*, a biplane he had built in Hammondsport that strongly resembled Curtiss' designs. Although adverse winds limited the flying in Texas, Curtiss set another quick-start record and carried a newspaper reporter to an altitude of five hundred feet. If nothing else, the exhibitions in Memphis and San Antonio were useful in providing experience with the new airplane under a variety of conditions and helped prepare him for the considerably more ambitious New York–Albany flight.[20]

Thorough preparation was essential if Curtiss were to succeed with a flight nearly three times farther than any he had made before. After studying maps and consulting the Weather Bureau, he decided that he could better take advantage of the prevailing winds by flying south from Albany rather than north from Manhattan. For his starting point he chose Van Rensselaer Island, a low, sandy stretch along the Hudson cultivated by truck gardeners. Meanwhile, he continued tests of the new airplane in Hammondsport, including a forty-minute flight on 21 May around the valley and over the lake, ending with a gentle landing in the water to see how well the flotation equipment worked. The next day he packed and shipped the airplane to Albany, and on the twenty-third, he and Lena, accompanied by Fanciulli and his wife,

Henry Kleckler, and two mechanics, arrived in the city and took up residence in the Hotel Ten Eyck.[21]

Not long after getting to Albany, Curtiss rented a field on Van Rensselaer Island where he set up a tent to house the airplane while it was being assembled and tested for the flight. On the twenty-fourth, accompanied by Lena and the Fanciullis, he took a steamer down the Hudson to familiarize himself with the route. Curtiss carefully noted key landmarks along the way and peppered the boat's captain with questions about wind conditions at various points where the highlands dropped precipitously down to the water. He seriously debated with his wife and friends the possibility of flying under the railroad bridge at Poughkeepsie rather than over it. In New York he verified his intentions to go for the *World*'s prize with the Aero Club, which assigned Augustus Post as official observer for the flight, tentatively set for 26 May. The Curtiss party boarded a train for Albany the next day, stopping over in Poughkeepsie to scout out potential locations where he could land, refuel, and effect any necessary repairs. They found a grassy field south of town at a place known as Camelot, whose owner was delighted to have Curtiss use it and was even willing to mark the site with a red flag to make it easier to spot from the air.[22]

Back in Albany on the evening of the twenty-fifth, Curtiss began what turned out to be four days of frustrating delays, not only for him but for the *World*, its readers, and New Yorkers eagerly anticipating the flight sooner rather than later. The airplane was not fully assembled and ready to fly until the twenty-sixth. Unfavorable weather kept him on the ground until late the following day when he took off at dusk for a short practice flight, in part to mollify the many spectators who had gathered on the island. He was ready to go early the next morning but learned that the wind was picking up down the valley. He waited until he heard that the wind had abated, but it was blowing too hard in Albany by then to risk the attempt. After this discouraging setback, the *New York Times* reported that Curtiss' usual optimism had deserted him and that he was "beginning to lose faith in the feasibility of the undertaking." He awoke early the next morning, a Sunday, 29 May, to find ideal weather conditions—a clear blue sky and little or no wind. He knew "it was now or never."[23]

While Lena and the rest of the Curtiss entourage boarded a New York Central train chartered by the *New York Times*, Curtiss donned a leather jacket, rubber boots, and a makeshift lifebelt and climbed into the seat of what was now generally known as the *Hudson Flier*. A small group of perhaps a hundred saw him take off at 7:03 AM. Within a half-hour Curtiss had worked his way up to about one thousand feet near the town of Hudson. He had passed Lena's train, which had been held up on the east side of the river. The tracks soon cleared, however, and the train, accelerating to fifty miles per hour, caught up with him and kept pace with Curtiss the rest of the journey. Telegrams went out that he was on his way, and people gathered along the route to catch a glimpse of what they hoped would be an epoch-making occasion. For Curtiss, the first leg of the flight was thoroughly enjoyable. "The air was calm . . . and the motor sounded like music," he recalled, and he could relax enough to observe the boat traffic on the river and the clusters of people along the shore. He flew over the bridge at Poughkeepsie, banked left, and dropped down to a perfect landing at Camelot. The time was 8:25 AM. Curtiss had covered seventy-five miles in an hour and twenty-two minutes, easily winning the *Scientific American* trophy. The only problem was that he had to borrow gasoline and oil from local motorists because the supplier he had made arrangements with failed to show up. He was back in the air at 9:29 AM.[24]

If the first half of the flight was uneventful the same cannot be said of the second leg. About twenty miles south of Poughkeepsie Curtiss encountered some of the worst turbulence he had ever experienced, while approaching the scenic but treacherous narrows between Storm King Mountain on the west side of the river and Breakneck Ridge on the east. The first gust nearly threw him from his seat, causing the airplane to fall at least a hundred feet, and Curtiss barely regained control before hitting even rougher air a few moments later. "It was the worst plunge I ever got in an aeroplane," he related later, "and I don't want to get another one like it soon." Curtiss took the machine down to within fifty feet of the water, where he expected to find calmer winds, but only ran into more buffeting. Conditions improved once he cleared the narrows. By the time he passed West Point at about 10:00 AM the winds had eased enough so that he felt confident he would be able to complete the flight, provided he had enough oil. Much to his dismay, he had noticed that the motor had begun to emit a trail of blue smoke—characteristic of excessive oil consumption that later proved to be due to a major leak. Rather than risk a seized engine somewhere over the congested city, Curtiss decided to land at 10:35 AM on the grounds of an estate at Inwood, just across the Harlem River from Yonkers and well within the city limits. Now he could officially claim the *World*'s prize. Still determined to achieve his final destination of Governors Island, he replenished the machine's fuel and oil and made a tricky takeoff at 11:42 AM. He landed at Governors Island precisely at noon, having flown a little more than 150 miles in two hours and forty-six minutes.[25]

Now, a century later, it is nearly impossible to grasp how sensational the flight was at the time. It was the longest flight between two cities ever completed, and it linked by air the capital of the nation's most populous state with the country's largest city and chief financial center. Curtiss recalled that "it certainly looked as though half the population was along Riverside Drive or on top of the thousands of apartment houses that stretch for miles along the river" as he soared down the Hudson and around the Statue of Liberty. Officers on board the 3,750-ton scout cruiser *Salem*, anchored in the stream off Eighty-Ninth Street, said that they had "never witnessed a more wonderful sight." Just as she got off the ferry linking Governors Island to the Battery, Lena greeted him with a hug and a warm kiss. Then they were whisked away for a celebratory luncheon at the Hotel Astor, followed by the award ceremony at the Pulitzer Building. Two nights later the Curtisses attended an official banquet at the Astor. There the mayor of New York formally accepted a letter from the mayor of Albany that Curtiss had carried with him on the epic flight. To much laughter and applause, Curtiss said that in all his preparations "there was one thing which I entirely overlooked, and that was the possibility of being called on to speak." He briefly remarked on the need for municipalities to provide landing fields for the aviators of the future, thanked everyone, and stepped down from the podium amid "tremendous applause." The *Times* wrote that "man has now conquered the air." The *Birmingham News* recorded that with the flight "victory over the air has been accomplished." And the *Hammondsport Herald* proudly declared that "there never was in this country anything like Glenn Curtiss' achievement." What would he do now asked a *Times* reporter? Curtiss replied that he would "rest and go home to Hammondsport," where he planned to "continue at work on my experiments with a craft designed to start from water as well as to light on it."[26]

The next day Curtiss was back in Hammondsport, where, true to form, he did not wait long before tackling the problem of landing and taking off from the water. Possibly inspired by Wilbur Wright, who had lashed a canoe to his airplane for his flight up and down the Hudson from Governors Island the previous fall, Curtiss had fitted one of his standard 4-cylinder "school machines" with a canoe that had been reinforced and topped with a canvas cover. Small floats and planing surfaces were fixed under the tips of the lower wings to provide lateral stability in the water. Curtiss and Kleckler had begun work on the machine before the Memphis exhibition then set it aside while putting together the *Hudson Flier*. Now they had time for more experiments. The ungainly machine was incapable of flight, but Curtiss learned important lessons about hydrodynamics and balance from the experiments. He also became a convert to the single-float configuration that he carried forward to later, more intensive experiments with waterborne craft.[27]

In Hammondsport Curtiss also got good news about the Wright suit. On 14 June, a panel of judges on the United States Circuit Court of Appeals by a unanimous decision vacated Judge Hazel's injunction, arguing that "infringement was not so clearly established as to justify a preliminary injunction." The judges' decision resulted in part because neither side had been able to present conclusive data and that additional evidence had been presented since the injunction that had yet to be heard. Needless to say, Curtiss was elated with the decision. He told reporters that he had not had time to present all the evidence in his favor before Hazel had issued the injunction and that his experiments had shown that his control system did not depend on the interaction of the ailerons and rudder to effect turns or to establish balance in flight. "I am glad the decision has been made," he went on, "as it sustains the position I have maintained and clears away the clouds in the aeronautical sky." The Wrights declared that the decision was "a pity," noting that the court did not throw out the infringement case, which still had to be adjudicated. "In the end we will undoubtedly win," they asserted.[28]

Now out from under the injunction if not free of his legal problems, Curtiss concentrated on a full exhibition calendar, beginning with a demonstration of aerial bombing in Hammondsport sponsored by the *New York World*. After Curtiss' Albany-to-New York flight, the *World* had predicted that in the not-too-distant future the airplane would deliver decisive blows against modern battleships. What better way to demonstrate that potential than a series of bombing experiments, and who better to carry them out than Curtiss? The *World*, therefore, arranged for retired Rear Adm. William W. Kimball, an ordnance specialist, to organize a "scientific" experiment at Hammondsport. Army Signal Corps Maj. Samuel Reber, a member of the Aero Club of America, and infantry Lt. Vincent M. Elmore were selected as observers. To preserve the exclusiveness of its story, the *World* made sure that preparations took place quietly. No other paper's reporters were informed, and even the residents of the village were not fully aware of what was going on. In the lake not far off shore from Kingsley Flats a raft and floats demarcated the outline of a ship 500 feet long and 90 feet wide. On the evening of 29 June, piloting the *Hudson Flier*, Curtiss dropped an eight-inch-long section of lead pipe on the target from an altitude of 150 feet, missing by only ten feet. Before he could try again, damage to the propeller forced him to land in the water, once more demonstrating the effectiveness of the machine's flotation gear. At dawn the next day, the propeller repaired overnight, Curtiss was in the air again. Of his first four "shots" two hit the target and two missed. He followed with another fourteen drops. Ten of the projectiles hit home and four missed before the wind picked up and he had to land back on shore. A good-sized crowd was present that evening for still another round of experiments during which Curtiss scored three successes out of four attempts, including one hit from nine hundred feet up.[29]

Although the *World* boasted that the results of the tests "should go a long way toward proving how much the navies of the great powers have to fear from the airship in its present state of development," Kimball offered a more sober analysis. He concluded that the airplane could not operate in bad weather and that the noise from its engine and propeller would alert defenders to its approach. Bombing accuracy was likely to drop dramatically when the machine flew at heights high enough to make it relatively immune from gunfire. Curtiss, too, was cautious in his appraisal. Among other things, he "learned that it is going to be difficult to hit a target simply by throwing [the missile] by hand." During the bombing exercise he "could not see whether I had hit the target or not and therefore I was unable to correct any errors." He believed it was essential to have a second person in the airplane to release the weapons and to observe the results and recommended that more tests be conducted, preferably paid for by one or both of the armed services. If they did "not care to invest in machines for the purpose, we are willing to co-operate with them to the extent of their sending representatives here and having us work out the problem together."[30]

Curtiss had little time to ponder the deeper meaning of the bombing experiments for the future of naval warfare because he was busy preparing for a big Fourth of July event at Atlantic City sponsored by the Pennsylvania Railroad. By this time, the Wrights had reluctantly entered the exhibition business and had begun training their own aviators for the show circuit. One of their premier fliers, Walter Brookins, had signed on for the Atlantic City extravaganza, which some estimated might draw a million spectators over the course of eight days. Curtiss opened the meet with a short hop over the beach, declaring it "the most dangerous flight" he had made up to that point due to the swirling wind. On the seventh he flew some distance out over the water. He "found that the air is steadier over the ocean than in any place over land" and concluded that "there is practically no limit except the carrying of fuel on ocean flights." Brookins flew on the ninth, setting an altitude record of 6,175 feet. Two days later, Curtiss won a $5,000 prize for a fifty-mile flight over a 2½-mile closed course set up in the ocean just off the beach. On the last day of the exhibition, 12 July, Curtiss swooped low over a yacht just offshore, dropping oranges close alongside with astonishing accuracy, even splashing some of those on board. One observer concluded that a battleship off the coast would "have been completely at the mercy" of the airplane had it been armed with real explosives.[31]

Among the hundreds of thousands at Atlantic City was a young naval constructor, Lt. Holden C. ("Dick") Richardson, a 1901 Naval Academy graduate who had earned bachelor's and master's degrees in naval architecture from the Massachusetts Institute of Technology. Richardson, who had been working at the Philadelphia Navy Yard, came over specifically to see the Wright and Curtiss machines. He was impressed that Curtiss was able to take off from the beach without the assistance of the catapult that Brookins in the Wright machine had to rely on. After a close examination of both airplanes, Richardson concluded that the Wright control system was "very unnatural" in comparison to the Curtiss' shoulder yoke, which was "definitely better." Like others at the meet, Richardson was "very much worried" when Curtiss took off and then "disappeared off down the beach," not returning for an hour or so. Curtiss had decided to fly to a nearby town and visit a friend without telling anyone of his intentions. Impressed with the fliers' skills and the maneuverability of their machines, Richardson later built and tested a glider, narrowly escaping serious injury when it crashed while being towed behind a car driven by his friend and future naval aviator, Lt. Henry C. Mustin.[32]

Following flights at a five-day exhibition in Omaha, 24–28 July, Curtiss and Bud Mars returned east, where they joined Tom Baldwin on the thirty-first to prepare for a meet in gritty, industrial Pittsburgh. Sponsored by the city's new aero club, the exhibition took place at a racetrack on Brunot's Island, a short distance down the Ohio River from the city's historic Point. Mars started things off on 4 August with a flight that was cut short by high winds. The next day, Curtiss made six flights, Mars three, and Baldwin went up for a brief flight in his *Red Devil*. On the sixth, Curtiss made an impressive flight up and down the river some distance from the island, then raced Mars around the one-mile course, only to see Mars earn all the publicity for a daring flight after sundown. Over the remaining two days of the meet Curtiss and Mars both made short flights, during some of which Curtiss flew with passengers, and Augustus Post attempted but failed to make his first public flights in one of the Curtiss machines.[33]

His exhibition team now boasting a gaggle of aviators, Curtiss decided to showcase them at the Sheepshead Bay racetrack in Brooklyn, where he hoped the team's achievements would serve as a "barometer" of public interest in aviation. Joining Curtiss, Mars, Willard, McCurdy, and Post was a relative newcomer, twenty-three-year-old Eugene B. Ely, who had impressed Curtiss with his flying skills at a meet in Minneapolis in June and who had flown with Curtiss and Mars in Omaha in July. On the first day, 19 August, Curtiss, Mars, Ely, and McCurdy were all in the air at the same time, forming an aerial "parade" circling the track at about two hundred feet. Unpredictable winds for most of the day on the twentieth limited everyone to short hops around the track, much to the dismay of the ten thousand spectators. When the winds died early in the evening, the Curtiss quartet—now joined by Willard in his new V-8-powered *Banshee*, jointly designed with Curtiss specifically for the exhibition circuit— were again in the air together, flying over the track and surrounding neighborhoods in what appeared to be a coordinated aerial ballet. Curtiss had to leave for another engagement in Cleveland before the end of the meet, but Mars, Ely, McCurdy, and Post continued flights at the track until the exhibition ended on 28 August. A highlight of the show was the demonstration by McCurdy of a wireless telegraph set, which he carried aloft and from which he sent signals to a receiving unit on the roof of the spectators' grandstand. In later years he asserted that this was the first successful demonstration of air-to-ground radio communication, although it is possible another aviator conducted similar tests from a Wright airplane at Mineola earlier in the month.[34]

Before the end of August, Curtiss and his *Hudson Flier* were at Euclid Beach, an amusement park on the shores of Lake Erie about five miles northeast of downtown Cleveland, preparing for what he hoped would be a record-breaking roundtrip overwater flight to Cedar Point, nearly sixty-five miles to the west on Sandusky Bay. Following a series of warm-up flights, Curtiss took off from Euclid Beach on the thirty-first and landed on the sand near Cedar Point's Hotel Breakers after an uneventful hour and eighteen-minute flight. On the return trip the next day, he struggled against headwinds and sporadic showers, yet still managed to complete the journey in an hour and forty-two minutes, easily beating an eastbound train carrying Lena, Bud Mars, and Eugene Ely. "It was a great ride," he told reporters afterwards, pocketing the hefty $15,000 prize before leaving for Boston and a major flying exhibition organized by the Harvard Aeronautical Society at Squantum Field.[35]

The field was located on a marshy peninsula jutting out into Dorchester Bay just south of the city. There Curtiss found himself in the middle of a gathering of some of the best aviators in the world, with Englishman Claude Grahame-White and his 100-horsepower Gnome-powered Blériot monoplane promising to offer the most competition in the speed events. Others present at the opening of the tournament on 3 September were another Englishman, A. V. Roe, with a triplane of his own design, Wright fliers Walter Brookins and Ralph Johnstone, as well as Clifford Harmon and Augustus Post in Curtiss machines. Charley Willard and Curtiss teamed up to fly the *Banshee*. The main event was a two-lap race on 7 September over a course laid out from the flying field to Boston Light, totaling about thirty miles. Grahame-White easily won with a time of just over forty minutes. Curtiss refused to try for the $10,000 purse, having determined that the *Banshee* did not have the power to make a good showing and contenting himself with second place in a shorter speed event the same day.[36]

The meet's organizers were displeased with the lackluster performances of Curtiss and the other American aviators. One of them, Adams Claflin, singled out Curtiss for being "unprepared" to challenge Grahame-White and even threatened to withhold his guaranteed payments. "I do not see how I can be blamed justly for that," Curtiss angrily replied to Claflin's charges. "I did my level best to make a showing and devoted a lot of time in a vain effort to get the required amount of speed." Even with an engine swap he could not match the power of the Blériot. In an attempt to redeem himself, Curtiss challenged Grahame-White to a winner-take-all three-lap match race on 15 September, only to be further humiliated when Grahame-White beat him by nearly seventeen seconds.[37] A personal disappointment for Curtiss, the Boston–Harvard meet underscored the vicissitudes of aerial competition and served notice to Americans that the Europeans were not standing still in aviation.

Worse was still to come, as was apparent from Curtiss' performance at an exhibition at the Allentown Fair in Pennsylvania less than a week later. McCurdy was present for the start of the show on 20 September but made no flights that day or the next, after Curtiss vetoed his plan to fly to Philadelphia following a direct route that took him over thousand-foot Lehigh Mountain. The big crowd, numbering in excess of thirty thousand, was more than a little dismayed that McCurdy did not make the flight. Things continued to deteriorate the next day when engine problems kept McCurdy on the ground. Curtiss quickly came down from Hammondsport and tried to salvage the exhibition with short flights around the fairgrounds. On the twenty-third, he attempted the Philadelphia flight—over a safer route along the Delaware—but got only six miles outside the city before making a forced landing when his oil-starved engine gave out. The president of the fair association believed that Curtiss had reneged on his promises and had not fulfilled his contract: "We are through with him. He has disappointed and disgusted us and we will have nothing whatever to do with him."[38]

Adding insult to injury was a disagreement, begun earlier in the year, between Curtiss and Charley Hamilton, which escalated into another nasty legal battle. Ever since the Dominguez Field meet, Curtiss and Fanciulli had harbored doubts about Hamilton's honesty, suspecting him of not fully disclosing the amounts he was taking in and thus not returning the money owed under his personal contract with Curtiss. A letter from the organizer of an exhibition at Charlotte, North Carolina, complaining that Hamilton had "repudiated his contract" and forced cancellation of the show, did nothing to inspire Curtiss' confidence in his associate. When Hamilton refused to pay Curtiss his 60 percent royalties following a record 13 June round-trip New York-to-Philadelphia flight and attempted to abrogate his contracts, Curtiss filed suit in Steuben County to recover his share of Hamilton's $10,000 prize. Curtiss said he was "very sorry that this split came," because he liked Hamilton personally and admired his talent as a flier, but that "a little too much success has turned his head." Hamilton later charged that Curtiss had prevented him from flying at Atlantic City and Boston, in clear violation of their contract, from which he continued to demand his release. The dispute ended when Curtiss won a monetary judgment against Hamilton, who went on with his sensational career as a daredevil aviator until his death in 1914 due to complications from tuberculosis.[39]

The break with Hamilton and the proliferation of individual personal contracts with his fliers pushed Curtiss to form a company expressly for the management of the exhibition business. Incorporated as the Curtiss Exhibition Company on 30 July 1910 with $20,000 in capital (nearly all of which came from Curtiss), the firm had Curtiss, Monroe Wheeler, and Fanciulli as its only stockholders. From his office on Broadway in New York, Fanciulli as vice-president and general manager orchestrated all contracts, schedules, travel, and expenses associated with the business. Generally, the contracts with the new company followed the pattern of the arrangements Curtiss had made individually, but with some changes. For example, instead of a set 40 percent of receipts retained by the flier, there was now a sliding scale, with newcomers taking a smaller percentage, and the more experienced aviators taking more than 50 percent. It was not uncommon for the best fliers to make up to $5,000 a day. This was big money at the time for Curtiss aviators, offset understandably by the tremendous risks incurred in flying the airplanes of the day. In contrast, the Wright team, managed by A. Roy Knabenshue, paid its aviators a flat rate of $20 per week and $50 per day when they flew, and the company pocketed all the prize money except for a minimal set amount awarded the flier.[40]

Ever alert to positive publicity for the Curtiss enterprise, Fanciulli was drawn to Blanche Stuart Scott, a native of Rochester and an early devotee of the automobile. She was well known for a highly publicized six-thousand-mile transcontinental journey in the spring of 1910 sponsored by the Willys Overland Company. Fanciulli contacted her in New York to see if she might be interested in learning to fly. She was, and with a little gentle persuasion Fanciulli got Curtiss to agree to instruct her in Hammondsport. After the usual indoctrination in the basic operation of the machine, Curtiss turned her loose at Pleasant Valley for what was known as "grass-cutting." On one of her first trips down the field, she recalled, "a puff of wind caught me. It blew me into the air forty or fifty feet, and this seemed like 400. Yes, I got down all right. After that, I wasn't going to stay on the ground any more, and I never did." She made her first hop in early September 1910, followed by longer flights around the field, earning distinction as one of the first two woman pilots in the country to fly solo. Scott proved to be a natural flier and within a month flew with Eugene Ely at an exhibition in Fort Wayne, Indiana, thereafter earning a national reputation as the "Tomboy of the Air."[41]

Another newcomer to the Curtiss fold in the fall of 1910 was airship pilot Lincoln Beachey, whose introduction to heavier-than-air flight at a meet in Indianapolis in June of that year had ended in the destruction of his home-built monoplane. At one point fellow airshipman Roy Knabenshue had tried to recruit Beachey for the Wright exhibition team, but Beachey decided his future lay with Curtiss, and he began lessons at Hammondsport before the end of the year. Beachey was not a natural aviator and wrecked more than his share of equipment. Some wondered why Curtiss kept him on, but he recognized Beachey's talent for showmanship and thought he demonstrated enough promise to include him as one of his exhibition fliers early in 1911. He went on to become one of the greatest of all the early aviators, stunning crowds with his "vertical drop," a steep dive from which he pulled out just before it appeared he would strike the ground, then looping-the-loop, a maneuver that seemed to defy both gravity and description. The first American to succeed in that stunt, Beachey was also noted for other spectacular firsts, including flights around the Capitol dome in Washington, under the arch bridge below

Niagara Falls, and indoors at the Palace of Machinery during the Panama Pacific Exhibition in San Francisco.[42]

With the creation of the new exhibition company, Curtiss, who was now well past his thirty-first birthday, announced his decision to cut back on his own flying and hand most of it over to the younger and now more experienced members of his team. He may have envisaged getting out of exhibition flying entirely, but that proved impossible due in part to commitments he had already made. Curtiss also relished the limelight; he was a popular aerial virtuoso who excelled at flying and enjoyed performing in front of crowds. In an expansive mood after his Albany–New York flight, he expressed interest in a $25,000 prize offered jointly by the *New York Times* and the *Chicago Evening Post* for the first flight between Chicago and New York. The thousand-mile flight was an ambitious challenge, by far the longest distance ever flown, and the rules dictated that it had to be accomplished in no more than seven days. By the middle of July, Curtiss had officially entered the contest, scheduled to begin on 8 October as the featured event of a two-week air show at the Hawthorne track in Cicero, just outside Chicago. Hamilton, Mars, Baldwin, Willard, and McCurdy were among the other entrants; no Wright aviators committed to the contest. On 10 September, Curtiss changed his mind and announced that he would not participate in the Chicago–New York race but reassured everyone that he would still fly at Chicago and "give what aid I can" to the contestants flying Curtiss machines.[43]

Curtiss arrived in Chicago on 1 October with Lena, Ely, McCurdy, and Blanche Scott to find Hamilton, Willard, and Post already there. Hamilton had a formidable 115-horsepower monoplane, but he had been banged up in an accident at an exhibition in Sacramento on 9 September. Seriously ill, he was in no shape to fly and withdrew from the event that morning. Curtiss, McCurdy, Willard, and Post all got into the air on the evening of the first, much to the pleasure of the crowd, which had never seen that many airplanes aloft at the same time. On the evening of the second, Curtiss in his *Hudson Flier* lapped the course four times at speeds up to sixty miles per hour, joined at one point by Willard, McCurdy, and Post. Wind and rain hampered flying over the next few days, giving Curtiss a chance to travel to Cleveland to organize a repair and refueling base for his fliers entered in the Chicago–New York race. As one rival aviator after another bowed out of the competition, Curtiss and the event's promoters decided that McCurdy, Willard, and Ely would start the race from Hawthorne. After a short distance, McCurdy and Willard would land, and Ely, who had won a lottery, would continue on to New York in the most reliable of the Curtiss machines—the V-8 *Banshee* that Willard and Curtiss had flown in Boston.[44]

After a twenty-four hour delay and one final test flight by Curtiss, Ely took off from the Hawthorne track on the afternoon of the ninth, the weather cloudy and cold. McCurdy and Willard, as planned, followed him into the air, making brief flights beyond the track. Unfortunately, Ely got only as far as the south side Chicago neighborhood of Beverly Hills, where carburetor problems forced him to land. The fix—a new mixture needle—was easy, but when he attempted to take off the front wheel of his machine collapsed, grounding him for the night while Curtiss' people rushed to effect repairs. Ely's woes continued the next day. Only minutes after taking off, the fuel line broke and the engine quit, bringing him down in a nearby field where he ran into a ditch that nearly flipped the machine over and badly damaged the front elevator. Flung out of his seat, Ely was unhurt, but repairs took most of the rest of the day. He was back in the air by 5:00 PM, but within forty-five minutes he encountered more engine problems as he neared East Chicago, Indiana, making another rough landing on marshy ground that broke the front elevator again. Curtiss returned to Chicago the next day, intent on salvaging parts from Augustus Post's airplane, but it had already been crated and shipped. With no spares available, three days lost, and only thirty-two miles into the flight, Curtiss wisely decided to cancel the attempt.[45]

Even if all had gone well, it is far from certain that Ely would have succeeded in making the flight from Chicago to New York given the state of the aeronautical art in 1910. Nearly a year later in September and October 1911, Calbraith P. Rodgers, a Wright aviator, flew from New York to Chicago on one leg of his historic transcontinental flight, but it took him twenty-one days and he experienced at least seven major and minor accidents along the way. None of the Curtiss aviators could claim such a heroic achievement that year, but on the whole the Curtiss exhibition team was exceptionally active. An advertisement for the Curtiss flying schools claimed that the Curtiss squad and Curtiss airplanes were in the air an aggregate of 660 days, flew more than twenty thousand miles, and provided 85 percent of the exhibitions in 1911. Ultimately fulfilling his promise to Lena to give up the dangerous but lucrative business, Curtiss himself made what was likely his last exhibition flight at Winona Lake, Indiana, in July 1911, where he took celebrated professional baseball star and evangelist Billy Sunday up for his first airplane ride.[46]

The failure in Chicago in the fall of 1910 had been a another letdown for Curtiss, but he had little time to ruminate on this or the other vicissitudes of what so far had been for him a momentous year. He had more than enough to do to get ready for the next show at the Belmont Park racetrack on Long Island, the biggest exhibition yet for him and his team. For the meet, which included a defense of the Gordon Bennett trophy he had won the year before at Rheims, Curtiss brought an entirely new machine. Essentially a monoplane with a small surface above and behind the pilot, and powered by a 51-horsepower V-8 engine, it had a span of a little more than 26 feet and weighed about 600 pounds. Curtiss chose Ely to fly it, anticipating that he would be one of the members of the team selected by the Aero Club of America for the Gordon Bennett defense. The competition was expected to be the highlight of the event and was eagerly anticipated by the entire aviation community.[47]

The Partnership

Belmont Park was the place for the elites of New York to see and be seen in the fall of 1910. They came to this horse-racing mecca in suburban Nassau County to be part of the International Aviation Tournament, one of the biggest and most sensational air meets in the country up to that time, an event that attracted nearly thirty aviators from five countries vying for more than $72,000 in prizes for distance, altitude, speed, and endurance. When Curtiss arrived with his team on 22 September for the official start of the competition, the Wright squad was already there in force, with three machines, including the powerful new Model R *Baby Grand* flown by Ralph Johnstone. From France came a three-member Blériot team, and Englishman Grahame-White, also flying a Blériot, was certain to place high in the competition. Another Blériot aviator, the American John B. Moisant, had made a name for himself in Europe and was eager to try for the Gordon Bennett trophy. The occasion also drew three naval officers from Washington: Lt. Nathaniel H. Wright, who had recently been selected to survey aviation for the Bureau of Steam Engineering; Lt. William McEntee, who had also been chosen a few days earlier to do the same for the Bureau of Construction and Repair; and Capt. Washington Irving Chambers, recently detailed to advise the Navy Department on the potential applications of aviation. All three viewed the exhibition as an opportunity to observe in person what the airplane could do and to gather as much information on the new technology as possible.[1]

That the naval hierarchy was serious about aviation in 1910 was evident by the choice of Chambers, a senior captain assigned on 26 September to coordinate aviation matters in his capacity as assistant to the Aide for Material in the office of the Secretary of the Navy. A Naval Academy graduate in the class of 1876, Chambers had earned a reputation in the service as a reformer and as a skilled and knowledgeable engineer from his work on torpedoes, mines, submarines, and the design of all-big-gun dreadnought-type battleships. He also had considerable command experience, having come to Washington in December 1909 fresh from command of the battleship *Louisiana*. Far from an enthusiast or a dreamer, and with a clear vision of what advanced technology could bring to the service and its missions, Chambers had the full support of Adm. George Dewey, president of the Navy's General Board, who endorsed his appointment and insisted that "the value of aeroplanes for use in naval warfare should be investigated without delay."[2] If the Navy wanted someone with experience who could provide a thorough and unbiased appraisal of the present state of the art in aviation and an honest assessment of its implications for the future, the service needed to look no further. Chambers was the ideal person for the job.

Chambers arrived at Belmont on 28 October to find a veritable aeronautical bazaar, jammed with a plethora of foreign and homegrown airplanes, aviators, and manufacturers, both amateur and professional. The most impressive French machines were the Blériots, powerful and fast monoplanes, and the Antoinettes, also monoplanes, which Chambers found "the most graceful of all" and models of expert craftsmanship. Among the American airplanes, the Wrights showed mixed results. Johnstone's powerful *Baby Grand* set a new altitude record, while Walter Brookins' Wright machine suffered from chronic engine problems. The Curtisses also drew Chambers' attention, although regrettably they failed to perform up to expectations. On the twenty-fifth, McCurdy failed to complete a race out to Garden City, coming down in a field in Rockville Center not too far from Belmont. Curtiss, who had to help McCurdy secure the airplane for the night in the face of rain and high winds, remarked the next day that he was exhausted but that "it's all in an aviator's life." The new Curtiss monoplane was also a disappointment, considered too tricky and dangerous to fly. Curtiss wisely decided to withdraw from the Gordon Bennett contest, won by Grahame-White on the twenty-ninth in one of the speedy Blériots.[3]

No one would have been surprised had Chambers looked to one of Curtiss' rivals to introduce aviation to the Navy considering the poor showing of the Curtiss machines at Belmont, but that was not to be the case. Chambers attended another big air meet at Halethorpe, Maryland, a short distance southwest of Baltimore, featuring Wright, Antoinette, Blériot, and Curtiss machines. There, on 2 November, he finally met Curtiss, who was present with Eugene Ely and Charles Willard. Chambers watched the fliers drop flour-bag "bombs" on a target and saw Willard put on a show of speed over a mile-long course. Violent storms the next day destroyed Ely's and Willard's airplanes, but the program resumed after a few days' delay so that Ely was able to make a short flight in a replacement machine on the tenth. Chambers came away from the Halethorpe exhibition "deeply impressed with what he saw" and confident that the Navy leadership could be convinced of the efficacy of the new technology "demonstration by demonstration."[4]

Chambers' visits to the Belmont and Halethorpe aviation exhibitions were the catalysts that took Curtiss, his airplanes, and the Navy though a remarkable continent-wide sequence of events in the winter of 1910–1911 that offered a glimpse of the future of the airplane at sea. Although he had already begun a friendship with Curtiss, Chambers considered it politic to approach the Wrights first about collaboration on future experiments involving taking off and landing on board ships. But when he contacted Wilbur Wright to see if the brothers were willing and able to carry out such demonstrations he received a polite but firm refusal. They were even opposed to lending one of their exhibition fliers for a scheme they considered little short of preposterous.[5]

With the Wrights out of the picture, Chambers next turned to Curtiss, who was immediately receptive to the idea of working with the Navy on an experiment showing the feasibility of flying an airplane from a ship. In fact, Curtiss and McCurdy were already involved in just such a project. Following the Belmont exhibition, Curtiss arranged with the Hamburg-American Line to have McCurdy try for a $5,000 prize offered by the *New York World* by flying from a liner fifty miles at sea and landing in Manhattan with a bag of mail from the ship. Curtiss rushed from Halethorpe to New York on 4 November to oversee completion of a sloping eighty-foot-long fan-shaped wood platform over the bow of the big Hamburg-American liner *Kaiserin Auguste Victoria*. He told the press that he was "confident of the success of the experiment," which he speculated would lead to regular flights carrying letters between ships and shore, saving a day each way on priority mail deliveries. McCurdy arrived the same morning with the airplane he had flown at Halethorpe. He predicted that the demonstration would "show the world that the aeroplane has some practical use." Secretary of the Navy George von L. Meyer was reluctant to provide official sanction for a such an obviously commercial enterprise but nevertheless made available two torpedo boat destroyers to accompany the liner out to sea and closely follow McCurdy on his flight. Chambers was to be an official observer. The officer in charge of the torpedo boat unit, Cdr. George C. Day, remarked that the experiment, "if successful will cause a lot of thinking in naval circles the world over."[6]

Originally set for 5 November, the flight had to be postponed due to two days of bad weather in New York. Curtiss and Hamburg-American officials agreed to dismantle the platform on the *Kaiserin*, reinstall it over the stern of the smaller *Pennsylvania*, and aim for a flight a week later. Work was finished on the platform by 9 November and plans made for the flight, now scheduled for the eleventh. When the ship was ten miles off Fire Island, it would reverse engines and steam astern at about ten knots, providing enough wind over the deck for McCurdy to take off. He planned to fly the fifty miles back to Governors Island in about an hour. Curtiss, Bud Mars, and some of the team's mechanics would trail him in a steam yacht, along with the Navy ships. "Nothing less than a twenty-mile wind" would prevent McCurdy from pulling off the flight, Curtiss said.[7]

But even the best-laid plans often do not succeed. The airplane was lifted into place on the platform the afternoon of 10 November and positioned for takeoff. Early the next morning, though, came the surprise that Mars had replaced McCurdy, who was otherwise occupied at the Halethorpe meet. Everything with the airplane looked good, and the weather, for a change that fall, was cooperating. Then, with only minutes to go before the ship was to sail at noon, disaster struck. As Curtiss ran the engine up, a piece of hard rubber tubing left on a wing flew into the airplane's structure and broke off part of a bamboo strut, which in turn struck and fractured the propeller. One of the ship's complement was hit by the propeller fragment but was not seriously injured. With no replacement propeller available, the only option was to offload the airplane and let the ship sail after about an hour's delay.[8]

It was impossible not to be discouraged that the ship flight failed, for it would have been a spectacular demonstration of the airplane at sea, but there was some consolation in that Chambers now had the opportunity to pursue his own plans for a takeoff from the deck of a ship—this time with the full support of the Navy and its leadership. Chambers contacted Capt. Frank F. Fletcher, Aide for Material to the Secretary of the Navy, to borrow the 2,750-ton scout cruiser *Birmingham* for the experiments. Chambers also secured the use of Curtiss' *Hudson Flier* and the services of Ely for the planned tests as soon as Ely finished up at Halethorpe. On 9 November 1910 workers under Lieutenant McEntee's direction at the Norfolk Navy Yard began erecting a wood deck over the *Birmingham*'s bow. Generally resembling the Hamburg-American platform, although not widening as it extended forward over the ship's forecastle, the structure was 83 feet long and 24 feet wide, with a slope of five degrees. It was 37 feet above the water at its extreme end.[9]

As soon as the Halethorpe exhibition ended on the twelfth, Ely headed for Norfolk, arriving with the airplane the next day. Chambers' plan bore a striking resemblance to McCurdy's abortive Hamburg-American flight. The *Birmingham* was to stand out into Chesapeake Bay and at some distance offshore launch Ely while making about ten knots. Four torpedo boat destroyers—the *Bailey*, *Roe*, *Stringham*, and *Terry*—would be stationed along the fifty-mile flight path back to the Norfolk Navy Yard. On the morning of 14 November, sailors safely lifted Ely's airplane onto the platform while Ely and Chambers closely followed the operation. The *Birmingham* got underway about 11:30 AM. As the ship pulled up off Old Point Comfort, the big question was the weather. The wind was light, it was chilly, and there were fog, a few rain showers, and even some hail in the area. Because the forecast was for even worse conditions, the consensus was to go ahead with the demonstration as soon as possible, but heavy rain through the early afternoon held things up until about 3:00 PM, when it finally let up. Ely quickly got into the machine, started it up, and decided to make the attempt even though the ship was still at anchor. Sixteen minutes later, Ely rolled down the deck and off the forward edge of the platform without the benefit of the cruiser's forward motion. As he dove to gain as much flying speed as possible, his wheels and propeller touched the water before he climbed to a safe altitude. It was a near thing, because the impact damaged the propeller and Ely was partially blinded by the salt water spray.[10]

Ely was experienced enough to know his limits; he would not attempt the flight to Norfolk with a potentially crippled airplane and under such poor weather conditions. Nearly getting lost as the rain "beat into his face," Ely first turned out into the bay, and then back toward the shore. He spotted the beach on the north side of Willoughby Spit, not far from Fort Monroe, and landed without further damage to the airplane. A launch from the *Roe* quickly picked him up. The flight lasted only about four minutes and covered two and a half miles, nothing close to the original ambitious objectives.[11]

Chambers was relieved that Ely did not try for Norfolk, expressing "grave doubts about [Ely's] ability to get his bearings in thick weather, over a landscape with which he was unfamiliar." Pronouncing the experiment a success, he immediately declared to the press that Ely's flight "was more than he had anticipated" and expressed confidence "that the time is near when all scout cruisers will be equipped with a number of aeroplanes." He was especially encouraged that Ely had succeeded in flying off the ship while it was anchored. The experiment, he told reporters, "showed beyond doubt that his task would have been much simpler if the Birmingham had been moving." Secretary of the Navy von L. Meyer thanked Ely a few days later "for the service you have performed, gratuitously, in demonstrating the possibility of using an aeroplane, from a ship, in connection with the problem of naval scouting. . . .Your achievement, which was actuated by purely zealous and patriotic motives, is much appreciated."[12]

In his report on the flight, Chambers expressed concern that had the ship been underway and the airplane not been launched safely, it and the aviator might have been run over. He thought it more practical to have the flying-off platform located at the stern of the ship, where it could be lengthened and integrated with the ship's structure without interfering with the guns or other aspects of the ship's operations. Takeoffs, even with underpowered and older airplanes such as Ely's, were possible while the vessel was stationary, and landings would be easier with the ship steaming ahead to create wind over the deck. Added safety could come from nets strung along the sides of the platform. If conditions made a landing impossible, the aviator could always ditch alongside the ship and be recovered by one of the ship's boats.[13] The next phase was logical—both launch and land an airplane from a ship.

The ship experiments were only one dimension of Curtiss' plans to bring aviation into the Navy. On 29 November, he wrote to Secretary von L. Meyer: "My own experiences and the results attained by several of the aviators operating machines for me justify me in venturing to prophesy that the military branches of the government, in the very near future, will find an aeroplane equipment absolutely essential." Curtiss explained that he was "prepared to instruct an officer of the navy in the operation and construction of the Curtiss aeroplane." Acknowledging that the service lacked the money to pay for such training, he added that "I am making this offer with the understanding that it involves no expense for the Navy Department" other than what it would cost to assign such an officer to aviation duty. The Navy accepted the offer on 13 December.[14]

The Navy's quick and positive response to Curtiss' proposal was not surprising. Less than two weeks earlier, Lieutenant Wright had proposed that the Navy buy two airplanes each from the principal American manufacturers, and Chambers had made it known that he wanted to have officers trained by Wright and Curtiss before the Navy took possession of its first airplanes. The deal with the Navy was fortuitous. With the Herring-Curtiss company in receivership, airplane and motor orders dwindled and the Hammondsport factory closed before the end of the year, idling more than a hundred employees. Furthermore, the uncertainties caused by the Wright patent suit had deterred potential buyers of Curtiss airplanes. In an attempt to end the legal impasse,

Curtiss had met with the Wrights at least once during 1910, but they could not reach an agreement. Another chance to settle the suit out of court came and went in November when Curtiss rejected Wilbur Wright's suggestion that he pay a license fee for each airplane manufactured and for each day one of his machines appeared in an exhibition. Eager to do whatever he could to salvage his business, Curtiss knew that his offer to the Navy was likely to be well received. In the long run it would more than pay for itself by familiarizing naval officers with the construction and operation of his airplanes and most likely lead to a contract to supply one or more of them to the service. Moreover, the proposal echoed the February 1908 contract for an airship that he and Baldwin had signed with the Army, and the similar agreement the Wrights had reached at the same time with the War Department, both of which included flight instruction for at least two officers.[15]

Chambers' choice for flight instruction with Curtiss was Theodore C. ("Spuds") Ellyson, a 1905 Annapolis graduate who was just entering the submarine service. Kenneth Whiting, a friend and fellow Academy classmate who had watched the Curtiss team perform at Sheepshead Bay that summer, and a convert to flying, had sounded him out on aviation earlier in December when the two got together in Norfolk. Discouraged by delays in completing the sub he was slated to command and figuring he had nothing to lose at that stage of his career, Ellyson put in for aviation duty on the sixteenth of the month.[16]

Meanwhile, Chambers was looking for an officer who was young, technically inclined, energetic (preferably with athletic ability), and who was both enthusiastic and mature. He also wanted someone who would help establish the legitimacy of aviation. "I remind you," he wrote to Ellyson in early 1911, "that you were selected because you were not regarded as a crank but as a well balanced man who would be able to assist in building up a system of aviation training in the Navy. I've no doubt you see the importance of avoiding the hippodrome part of the business and will not do stunts just for the sake of notoriety or to thrill the crowd." Finally, he needed someone who could get to the West Coast to join Curtiss as soon as possible. Ellyson met all the criteria and received his orders on 27 December at the same time he learned he had been promoted to lieutenant.[17]

Ellyson used the time on the long train ride to California to do his homework on aviation and read as much as he could about Curtiss and his accomplishments. He arrived in Los Angeles on 2 January 1911 and went straight to Dominguez Field, where a second big aviation meet was under way, and there met Curtiss for the first time. Curtiss, Lena, his mother Lua, and her son Carl

Adams (Curtiss' half-brother), had been in the city since before Christmas, and just the day before he and Lena had been in the Rose Parade in Pasadena. The immediate reason for the Curtisses' presence on the West Coast was Curtiss and his team's participation in the Los Angeles exhibition and another to follow shortly thereafter in San Francisco, but he was also interested in locating a site with a more salubrious climate than wintertime Hammondsport for flight experiments and instruction. The arrangement worked out well for Ellyson, too, who liked Curtiss from the start and relished the opportunity to gain firsthand knowledge of airplane construction and operation.[18]

Dominguez Field was another triumph for Curtiss. He was at the top of his game during the meet, dazzling the crowd with throttled-back descending spirals and low passes over the field. At one point he and his airplane achieved an unofficial timed speed of more than sixty miles per hour. Generally the Curtiss machines outperformed the Wrights. In one event Phil Parmalee in the Wright *Baby Grand* went head-to-head with Eugene Ely, who won the contest "with several seconds to spare" in his Curtiss racer. But the dangers of the exhibition business came home to everyone on a cold, blustery New Year's Eve when Arch Hoxsey's Wright flipped over as he was coming down from an altitude record attempt. The airplane crumpled and tumbled to earth, instantly killing Hoxsey. Curtiss said he was "shocked" by the accident, and that Hoxsey "should meet his end so suddenly and before our very eyes has been a great blow" to him and the other aviators at Los Angeles, who knew Hoxsey well and had immense respect for his flying abilities.[19]

Curtiss did not have much time to dwell on the obvious risks of his profession, and needed to scout southern California for places to continue his flying instruction and airplane experiments. He had learned about the advantages of the area in January 1910 when he participated in the first Los Angeles aviation meet, but he was also familiar with Florida from his "hell-rider" days. The Sunshine State had the climate he desired and it was considerably closer to Hammondsport than was California, but weather and distance were not the only factors in his decision. Like the Wrights a decade earlier, Curtiss sought a relatively isolated place where he could leave the press of day-to-day business affairs and carry out his experiments without constantly having to deal with the public. In the end, Chambers may have been singularly influential in tipping the scales to the west, where the Navy since the previous century had found good harbors, favorable weather, and a welcoming populace.[20]

Of the choices available in California, San Diego came out on top. The city had sponsored a "San Diego Day" at the 1910 Dominguez Field meet, where Curtiss had discussed the possibility of making the first flight from Los Angeles to San Diego, but the arrangements fell through for undisclosed reasons. A burgeoning city with just under forty thousand people in 1910, San Diego was trying to emerge from the shadows of its more glamorous, populous, and economically powerful neighbors to the north. Over the years the city had flirted with the Navy, viewing the service and its people as a stimulus for growth and each time losing out to San Francisco and the Los Angeles port of San Pedro when it came to major fleet support installations. By 1910 the city had appeared to turn the corner. Through the efforts of the chamber of commerce and friends in Congress, San Diego got its first permanent naval facility—a coaling depot—in 1904. A wireless station on the heights of Point Loma followed two years later. Not until 1909, though, did the Navy begin to consider San Diego seriously, starting with the establishment of a permanent base for the Pacific Torpedo Fleet.[21] To many people aviation exuded twentieth-century modernity, and the community's movers and shakers believed that luring Curtiss and his Navy fliers to San Diego would yield long-term economic benefits to their city.

One of the city's most enthusiastic aviation boosters was David Charles ("Charlie") Collier, a prominent lawyer and real estate developer. As founder and president of the San Diego chapter of the Aero Club of America, which had sponsored the first Dominguez Field meet, Collier had met with Curtiss soon after his arrival in California in December 1910 and had made a preliminary offer of support for his flight school and experimental work. Collier put Curtiss in touch with John D. Spreckels of the Coronado Beach Company, which owned North Island, then a flat, sandy, undeveloped, six-mile-long expanse across the bay from San Diego. A half-mile stretch of water known as Spanish Bight separated the island from the beach community of Coronado. On 2 January, the same day Ellyson arrived in Los Angeles, he and Curtiss left for San Diego. The next morning they inspected North Island, which Ellyson said Curtiss found "ideal for the instruction of beginners," and Spanish Bight, shallow and calm enough for experiments with water flying. To local newspaper reporters Curtiss proclaimed: "This is my first visit here, and I cannot say too much of the city. So far as the aviation facilities are concerned, there is no better place on the coast." Curtiss agreed to begin flying at North Island as soon as practicable, and promised to put on a two-day public aviation exhibition starting on the twenty-first.[22]

North Island, which could only be reached by boat from San Diego or Coronado, promised a combination of privacy and propinquity to a city with most of the resources Curtiss and his fliers would need. For accommodations, Curtiss and his wife rented a cottage in Coronado adjacent to the fashionable Spreckels-owned Hotel del Coronado, where they were joined by Lua and Carl Adams. Later, when he had a chance to catch his breath from the almost incessant activity in the first months of 1911, Curtiss described what the place was like for readers of the *Hammondsport Herald*. After dispelling a local rumor that he had bought North Island, which was far beyond his or any other potential buyer's means, Curtiss went on to explain that San Diego had little industry other than "selling lots to Easterners," and, like Hammondsport, had only one rail connection. "Aside from our camp, there is nothing on the island but some sage brush and a million jack rabbits," he continued. "Rabbits are so numerous that they get in the way of starting and alighting our aeroplanes." In fact, only recently one of his aviators had run into a rabbit while landing, which "ruined the propeller as well as the rabbit." Those back home waiting to dig out at the end of another Hammondsport winter must have envied him: "The mornings are almost always calm and excellent for practice work. It is claimed that the climate is the least variable in the world, and there is less than 10 degrees difference between summer and winter. We have a delightful combination of sunshine, flowers, ants, and lizards."[23] It is possible that Hammondsporters would not have found year-round ants and lizards as "delightful" as did Curtiss.

By the middle of January, a Curtiss mechanic was at the island assembling one of the airplanes Curtiss had flown at Dominguez Field, and Aero Club members had cleared brush and leveled an area on the south end of the island and were working on opening up two other fields for flying. A barn served as a temporary hangar while the club erected two canvas and tarpaper structures to house Curtiss' airplanes. Curtiss himself set up a hangar on the shore of Spanish Bight and installed a pier on the northeast corner of the island for boats going back and forth to San Diego and Coronado. According to the terms of the lease signed on 4 February, Curtiss had exclusive use of the property for three years at no cost. Spreckels, who had been trying for more than two decades to drum up military interest in North Island to stimulate its development, insisted that Curtiss bring in Army and Navy aviators for flight instruction, and that periodically he hold public aviation exhibitions. If the land were sold in the interim or the company wanted to improve it in anticipation of its sale, Curtiss would be required to vacate the premises.[24]

While Curtiss was making arrangements for the aviation camp at San Diego he also began collaborating with Chambers on another dramatic Navy ship-flying experiment, to be held at the same time as the San Francisco air meet, which began on 7 January at the Tanforan racetrack south of the city. Curtiss and Chambers understood that for the airplane to prove itself in naval warfare not only did it have to take off from a ship at sea but it also had to be recovered in some manner. There were two alternatives. The first, and the most hazardous, was to land back on board the ship, which involved expert flying and a specially constructed platform. The second was easier: land on the water next to the ship and be hauled aboard. This required a craft—later known as a hydroairplane—that was capable of taking off from and landing on the water. Curtiss was hard at work on a hydroairplane in San Diego, but it was far from perfected. So both he and Chambers agreed that, despite the risk, the first experiment should be to land on a ship with a conventional airplane. Because Curtiss and Ely had committed to perform at the San Francisco exhibition and Ellyson was there, too, reporting to Chambers on the various events, it made sense to plan a ship flight at the same time. Ely, the only aviator in the world to have flown off a ship, was the natural choice for the challenging new assignment, which Curtiss realistically saw "as most difficult of accomplishment."[25]

The ship this time was the *Pennsylvania*, a five-year-old, 13,400-ton armored cruiser commanded by Capt. Charles F. ("Frog") Pond. Pond put the ship into the Mare Island Navy Yard in Vallejo on San Francisco Bay on 4 January, where workers began erecting a wood platform over the cruiser's stern. Ellyson inspected the installation with Ely the following day. The 31½-foot-wide deck was gently inclined towards the stern and stretched more than 119 feet from the superstructure to the fantail. It fully covered the aft 8-inch gun turret and had a 14-foot extension angled at thirty degrees that overhung the stern. One-foot-high rails and awnings, stretched from the sides of the platform to the boat davits, provided some protection from going overboard. The slope of the deck was intended to help slow the airplane, and canvas screens at the end of the platform ensured against the possibility of colliding with the ship's superstructure. Still, Curtiss, Ely, and others were uncertain about bringing the airplane safely to a halt. Ellyson may have suggested a method that bore a striking resemblance to later carrier arresting gear—twenty-two lines, stretched between pairs of sand-filled seabags and held a few inches above the deck by longitudinal wood runners spaced twelve feet apart, were to engage hooks attached to a skid on the bottom of the airplane. Pond vetoed the idea of having his ship under way for the test, fearing a collision in the crowded anchorage.[26]

Poor weather delayed the attempt until 18 January, by which time Curtiss and Ellyson had left for San Diego to get experiments and flight instruction under way at North Island. That morning was cloudy and misty with light winds, and there was an iciness in the air that Ely found "uncomfortable." Donning a pair of bicycle inner tubes as a substitute for the pneumatic life preserver Chambers had lent him for the *Birmingham* flight, and with "never a doubt" that he could pull off the dangerous feat, Ely took off from Tanforan at 10:45 AM. He found a "good stiff breeze" at an altitude of about 1,500 feet and some haze obscuring the *Pennsylvania* and other ships in the bay as he sped along at about sixty miles per hour. A half mile or so from the ship, he reduced his speed and dropped down as he soared over the armored cruiser *Maryland*. Ely then wheeled toward the *Pennsylvania* and lined up with the deck when he was about a hundred yards out. As he cleared the end of the platform at about forty miles per hour, Ely encountered a wind gust that tipped the airplane slightly, but he quickly adjusted, cut the engine, and touched down, the hooks seizing the eleventh athwartships line and bringing the machine to a rest in about thirty feet. The time was 11:01 AM. Ely had made the whole evolution look easy, but Chambers knew better. In his follow-up report, he remarked on the "marvelous skill, accuracy of judgment, and quickness of brain" the aviator needed to pull off the landing.[27]

Sailors, officers, and civilians alike applauded and cheered, and the ships let out blasts from their sirens as Ely triumphantly set foot on the deck. His wife Mabel was the first to congratulate him, telling him that she "knew he could do it." Captain Pond remarked that Ely was the "coolest man on board" his vessel. Following a round of interviews and photographs, Ely and his wife dined with Pond in his cabin, then he climbed back into his airplane and took off just before noon on the return flight to the Tanforan field, landing at 12:13 PM. Ely told reporters that the flight had been "easy enough. . . . I think the trick could be successfully turned nine times out of ten." Curtiss sent a letter to Ely to "congratulate you on your success with the flights to and from the PENNSYLVANIA and regret very much I was unable to be there to grasp your hand and that of Mrs. Ely on that occasion." Later, reflecting on Ely's feat, Curtiss wrote: "I don't think there has ever been so remarkable a landing made with an aeroplane as Ely's. . . . [A] few feet either way, a sudden puff of wind . . . or any one of a dozen other things, might have spelled disaster for the whole undertaking, deprived the daring aviator of a well earned success, and the world of a remarkable, spectacular demonstration of practical aviation."[28]

Ely's *Birmingham* and *Pennsylvania* flights, though obvious successes, were in reality little more than stunts and did not presage the integration of aviation into the fleet in any realistic near term. Superficially resembling modern carrier takeoffs and landings, Ely's flights took place under circumstances unlikely to occur in wartime or even in peacetime maneuvers. Moreover, the platforms were rudimentary affairs that interfered with the vessels' armament and would have been at minimum nuisances during routine operations at sea. No one understood this better than Chambers. He acknowledged that the *Pennsylvania* experiment was enough for him "to place myself on record as positively assured of the importance of the aeroplane in future naval warfare, certainly for scouting purposes." Yet "if aeroplanes are to be of real service they must be kept in more or less constant use for instruction, training, and maneuvers. We must be as familiar with them as we are with guns and boats." And he was not in favor of committing to a dedicated aviation ship, which he derided as a "garage vessel" that would add an unnecessary auxiliary to the fleet. Much better, to Chambers, was "utilizing nature's aerodrome, the water," with a hydroairplane capable of landing and taking off at sea and being serviced as needed on existing warships without impairing their offensive capability.[29]

On the opposite side of the country, J. A. D. McCurdy had been working closely with the Navy on another demonstration that in some ways had more implications for the immediate future of naval aviation than Ely's flights. Even though Curtiss had made some notable overwater flights in 1910, no one had yet flown a long distance out of sight of land, an essential requirement for the operation of aircraft at sea. In early January 1911, the *Havana Post* offered a prize for the first person to make the hundred-mile flight from Key West to Havana as part of a major aviation meet being held in the city. When it was confirmed that McCurdy and other Curtiss aviators had committed to the Havana event and that McCurdy himself was willing to make the distance flight, Chambers jumped at the opportunity to cooperate. Each flight involving the Navy, he said, "adds a little more to our information on the subject of aviation." As planning for the flight matured, Chambers directed the naval station at Key West to make a destroyer division available to assist McCurdy, functioning both as lifeguards and as directional aids.[30]

Chambers outlined the scheme to Cdr. Yates Stirling, who had responsibility for the destroyer division assigned to the project. Stirling's ships would steam out of Key West at intervals and take up stations ten to fifteen miles apart so that at altitude McCurdy could see both the ship ahead of him and the one behind him. The vessels were to stay in radio contact with one another, and possibly with the airplane too, since McCurdy had previously had a successful experiment with ground-to-air wireless communication. Left to work out the details, Stirling sailed on 21 January 1911 with McCurdy in the destroyer *Paulding* to reconnoiter the route. After the ship returned to Key West, the Curtiss company supplied a wood platform that seamen erected over the *Paulding*'s stern. The deck was hinged in such a way that part of it could be inclined into the water, allowing the airplane to be winched aboard should McCurdy have to land prematurely. If necessary, repairs could be made to the airplane and it could be refueled and launched to continue the flight. McCurdy's airplane was not equipped with a radio, although it did have a compass and small pontoons under the wings for emergency flotation. All was ready by 23 January; it was simply a matter of waiting for good weather and favorable sea conditions.[31]

Nearly a week passed before the winds died, the skies cleared, and the seas were calm enough for the attempt. Four ships from the destroyer division joined a lighthouse tender and a revenue cutter on the route. With all in readiness, at 7:22 on the morning of the thirtieth, McCurdy took off from the field at Key West, circled the island twice, thrilling the crowds that had gathered for the occasion, and headed toward the first station ship at about 1,500 feet. The flight went as planned for about two hours. McCurdy found the sensation of being suspended between the sky and sea to be "glorious." Wireless messages flashed from ship to ship as McCurdy passed overhead, each in succession getting up steam to chase behind him. At about 9:30 AM, just as McCurdy flew over the destroyer *Terry*, the next-to-last ship on the route, the airplane's engine ran out of oil, destroying the main bearings. McCurdy cut the ignition and swiftly glided to a smooth water landing about six miles from the Cuban coast. The *Terry* and the *Paulding*, the last ship in line, both sped to the rescue. Arriving on the scene within minutes, they found McCurdy unharmed but the airplane was floating at an angle with its engine submerged and tail planes broken. Because waves had damaged the platform on the *Paulding* the airplane could not be hauled on board as originally planned and the crew had to man-handle the machine over the side of the ship. With no prospect of continuing the flight, the *Terry* and the *Paulding* proceeded to Havana.[32]

Vast swarms of people cheered as the American ships entered the harbor about twenty minutes after noon. McCurdy was in good spirits, despite the frustration of having the flight cut short while he was literally within sight of the Cuban coastline, taking heart that he had accomplished the longest over-water flight on record. He wired Secretary of the Navy von L. Meyer to thank him for the Navy's backing, then told newspaper reporters that the Navy had supported him magnificently and that the flight was one more demonstration that the Navy was not, as some had alleged, indifferent to aviation.[33] McCurdy's feat presaged long-distance ocean flights to come later, all of which featured Navy ships stationed at intervals along the flight paths to provide support and radio communication coordinating the sea and air components.

McCurdy's flight reinforced Curtiss' ideas about the hydroairplane as the solution to practical water flying and his conviction that under the circumstances a machine with floats would have allowed McCurdy to land in the water, effect repairs, and continue on to Havana. Back at North Island on 18 January with Ellyson, Curtiss and the rest of the team put nearly all their effort into the hydro. Their methodology was an exercise in empiricism rather than science, with a sequence of failures before they achieved success. Curtiss began by modifying a standard 60-horsepower V-8 D-model shipped out from Hammondsport with a tandem-float arrangement. Constructed of tin-covered wood, the main float was nearly square, 5 feet wide and 6 feet long, spanning the space between the two main wheels. A 30-inch-long float replaced the front wheel, and motorcycle inner tubes provided flotation at the wingtips. Within a couple of days the pontoons had been fitted and the hydro was ready for its first trials.[34]

Initial experiments with the tandem-float configuration in Spanish Bight were disappointing. As the airplane accelerated through the water, the forward pontoon submerged, while the turbulent wake from the main pontoon swamped its after end, preventing the machine from lifting from the water. To make matters worse, excessive spray knocked splinters from the wood pusher propeller. Adjusting the angle of the main float to the structure of the airplane and adding a two-foot canvas extension to its forward end did nothing to correct the problems, nor did changes to the front elevator. In vain, too, was the addition of small hydrodynamic and aerodynamic surfaces ahead of the forward pontoon in an attempt to lift the front of the craft and achieve a more favorable angle of attack on takeoff. Discomfort added to the discouragement. "We were in the water almost all day long," Curtiss recalled. "No thought was given to wet clothing and cold feet. We virtually lived in our bathing suits." Despite warm, sunny days, the water of Spanish Bight in the winter could be bone-chilling.[35]

Regardless of their exertions, the best the group could coax out of the hydro were a few short hops, which did not please Curtiss in the least. Nor did it satisfy the appetites of local reporters, eager for any information about the experiments at North Island and not entirely happy with Curtiss' appeal for them to be patient or his explanation that he did not "expect to accomplish great things in a few days." Some time before the third week of the month, content with neither the appearance nor the performance of the machine, Curtiss retired to his cottage in Coronado and roughed out a design for a single, narrow pontoon with a flat bottom. Robert H. Baker, who ran a local machine shop, fabricated the 12-foot-by-2-foot pontoon in a matter of a few days. More the result of trial-and-error, experience, and intuition than putting abstract hydrodynamic theory into practice, the float was carefully contoured so that as the airplane gained speed it planed in such a way as to give the machine the right attitude for takeoff. It was also finely crafted, built up of spruce strips over a spruce frame and weighing less than half that of the tandem floats of the earlier configuration.[36]

By 24 January, the hydro with the new pontoon and Curtiss at the controls got up to forty-five miles per hour and made some short "skipping" flights, according to Ellyson. Curtiss was now sure that the airplane would fly, but wanted, as Ellyson said, "to get the feel of the machine before attempting too much." With experience, Curtiss found he needed to get the craft quickly up to planing speed, where he could then maintain its attitude with the elevator and stay in the air for up to 150 feet. "This I did a number of times, and to all practical purposes that was a flight," Curtiss recalled, but he knew a public demonstration was necessary before he could unequivocally proclaim success.[37]

The payoff for all of the team's hard work came early in the afternoon of 26 January. With only a handful of spectators present, Curtiss taxied out from the beach and headed into a light northwest breeze and calm waters in Spanish Bight. He opened the throttle and gained speed until the float barely skimmed the surface of the water before pulling back on the elevator control to lift the craft free of the water and into the air. "So suddenly did it rise that it quite took me by surprise," he wrote, in spite of his considerable experience with the hydro's handling. He made three more flights that day, the longest covering about half a mile at a height of about 150 feet. The next day, Curtiss made a five-mile flight, passing over ships in the harbor and flying along the waterfront, followed by two more flights on 1 February. To reporters on the scene for the 26 January flights he remarked that "for a long time I have believed that I ought to make the aeroplane a practicable machine for the use of the navy, and for that purpose it must be able to fly from the water and land on the water." He exulted later that "a page was added to aviation history," and that the airplane "was no more a land bird, but a water fowl as well." Ellyson was more restrained. He reported that the hydro could not "rise from the water except under perfect weather conditions," and that the spray had seriously damaged the propeller. On the other hand, "with stronger construction, perfection of details, and substitution of metal for wooden propeller, I am confident that the aeroplane can be operated from the water under any weather conditions that it could be operated from [on] land."[38]

Confident that he had solved most of the problems of the hydroairplane, Curtiss took time out to fulfill the obligations of his lease at North Island with a two-day public flying exhibition in Coronado, held on 28 and 29 January under the sponsorship of the San Diego Aero Club. To kick off the event, Curtiss flew over from North Island and landed in front of the grandstands set up on the polo grounds of the Coronado Country Club. Curtiss thrilled a crowd estimated at 1,500 the next day by chasing a balloon around the field, banking so sharply that his wings nearly touched the ground. Lena, Lua and Carl Adams, and Curtiss' mother-in-law Jennie Neff were among the spectators; Lena was less than thrilled by the aerial display and urged her husband to promise never again to do any stunt flying. Ely and Curtiss exhibition aviator Hugh Robinson were also participants. According to Ellyson, Ely put on "the prettiest exhibition of flying that I have ever seen," although he took unnecessary risks that Ellyson thought were bound to catch up with him.[39]

On the second day of the Coronado meet, Ellyson demonstrated Curtiss' flight training methods in a way that turned out to be more exciting than any of the ten thousand people present could have anticipated. Ellyson intended to taxi back and forth on the field, showing how a novice aviator familiarized himself with the controls and handling of the airplane. A wood block limited the travel of the foot throttle so that the airplane could not achieve enough speed to take off. His first trip down the field went well, but after he turned the airplane around and headed back, he hit a bump, the block shook loose, and as the machine surged ahead he fell back in his seat, pulling the elevator control with him. The airplane jumped fifteen feet into the air, then fell off to one side and came to an abrupt halt with a damaged wing. Ellyson's pride was hurt more than anything else. He apologized to Curtiss, who told him it was all part of the learning experience and that the airplane could be easily repaired.[40]

Following the Coronado interlude, Curtiss returned to his hydroairplane experiments in anticipation that they might result in the Navy buying one of his machines. He agreed with Ellyson that the next phase of their work was to demonstrate that the airplane could be landed next to a ship and lifted on board then placed back in the water for takeoff so that it could return to its starting point. If they were successful the tests would yield a clearer picture of the utility of the hydroairplane at sea. In an attempt to mitigate the spray damage to the pusher propeller, Curtiss turned the engine and propeller around and fitted them to the front of the airplane, with him sitting behind the radiator and wings. Meanwhile, the *Pennsylvania* had come down from San Francisco after the Ely flights. Captain Pond, her commanding officer, was enthusiastic about participating in more aviation experiments in San Diego. When Curtiss informed Pond that he was ready to fly out to the cruiser, which lay at anchor off North Island, Pond quickly responded: "[C]ome on over." At about 8:00 AM on 17 February, Curtiss took off from Spanish Bight, arriving at the ship a few minutes later and landing just off its starboard quarter. Sailors threw a line and pulled the airplane in to the vessel, where a boat crane brought it and Curtiss on board. Ten minutes later, the crane hoisted Curtiss and the airplane back into the water and he returned to North Island, taxiing all the way and never getting airborne. Curtiss was elated, exclaiming that the experiment had been "made without any preparation," and that it had "demonstrated to the navy department that the use of the aeroplane, or rather the hydroplane, for warships at sea is practical . . . without the use of a specially fitted up deck." Although the test provided convincing evidence that the hydro could operate from a ship, many improvements were needed before it would be useful for naval operations. For example, wind and water conditions had to be perfect, and the airplane was incapable of carrying more than one person. Furthermore, Curtiss was displeased with the tractor configuration, which upset the craft's balance and handling characteristics and possibly was the reason why he did not attempt to fly the machine back to shore.[41]

Another round of experiments and one more version of the hydro were needed before Chambers and Ellyson felt confident about recommending acquisition of an airplane from Curtiss. To get more lift to carry a second person, Curtiss first tested a triplane configuration, but then decided that adding an extra panel to the wings yielded the same results. On 23 February he flew the craft with Ellyson as a passenger. Next he added a set of retractable wheels and on the twenty-sixth made a striking demonstration of the airplane's flexibility. From the waters of Spanish Bight he flew to a sand spit off North Island, took off again from the water, landed on the beach near the Hotel del Coronado, and from there flew back and landed in Spanish Bight. The airplane, which was most likely the world's first amphibian, was known as the Triad for its ability to operate on land, in the sea, and in the air.[42]

Flight instruction, involving would-be Army and Navy aviators as well as civilians determined to learn how to master the air, paralleled Curtiss' experiments with the hydroairplane that winter. When Ellyson got to North Island he found an eclectic group of airplanes—Curtisses, obviously, but also a Wright, Antoinette and Blériot monoplanes, and a few designed and built by amateurs. The collection gave Ellyson an ideal opportunity to compare and contrast the various types in anticipation of the Navy's ordering a service machine. Ellyson found the Wright machine to be well-built and capable of flying in almost all weather conditions, but he worried that a broken control wire would render the wing-warping mechanism inoperable. The Curtiss he thought was the better of the two. It flew as often as the Wright and could maintain lateral control even if for some reason one of the ailerons malfunctioned. He did not think much of the French machines, which were hard to fly even under ideal weather conditions. To Chambers he wrote that "I don't think there is a place in the country that can compare with this place for instructional purposes," and he urged him to exercise whatever influence he had to have the Navy set up a permanent flying station at North Island.[43]

Because there were no two-seat airplanes, students were generally on their own once Curtiss had introduced them to the airplane and its controls and briefed them on how the airplane and its engine had been designed and constructed. Using a 4-cylinder machine with limited power, which the students referred to as the "Lizzie," Curtiss restricted movement of the throttle, substituting metal pins for the wood blocks following Ellyson's mishap at Coronado. Students ran the airplane along the ground to familiarize themselves with how it responded to control inputs as it gained speed, usually making about twenty-five passes before Curtiss was satisfied that his protégés were ready to take to the air. There was a lot to learn, especially in coordinating the throttle openings with the elevator, aileron, and rudder movements. Believing that students were more proficient in the air if they understood how an airplane worked, Curtiss also insisted that they do most of their own repair work, including in Ellyson's case taking a V-8 engine apart and putting it back together. Ellyson kept a diary of each day's accomplishments, which he referred to as he gained more experience, and he reported regularly to both Chambers and the secretary of the Navy.[44]

Safety was the primary consideration, for everyone knew that a serious accident or death would be a blow to the effort to demonstrate the viability of the airplane as a naval technology. Army aviators at North Island derided the Curtiss training method as too slow, alleging that Lt. Benjamin Foulois had learned to fly with the Wrights in only three weeks. Ellyson was sensitive to such criticism, both in terms of the traditional interservice rivalry and the Curtiss-Wright controversy. He countered that Foulois had been the Wrights' only student, and that he had never made a flight of more than ten minutes' duration. "The only way to become a successful aviator," Ellyson told Chambers, "is to remain under a capable instructor, and practice constantly until he decides that you are capable to try it alone." Chambers noted that 1910 had seen the deaths of thirty-two aviators—an appalling toll—but not one of those killed had been in a Curtiss airplane. Later he warned Ellyson about the possible consequences if he or any other naval aviators were hurt or killed at an air meet: "If you should meet with an accident we would all be blamed. . . . [I]n the present stage of the game we will have to go very carefully to convince Congress that we are in earnest and not making aviation for the sake of publicity."[45]

With only one airplane and six avid students, it was hard for everyone to get in the requisite experience before Curtiss considered them ready for their first flights. By the middle of January, Paul W. Beck, John C. Walker, and G. E. M. Kelly, all Army lieutenants, had arrived at North Island, in addition to two civilians, Robert St. Henry and Charles C. Witmer. Ellyson and Witmer became friends, both sharing an interest with Curtiss in the hydro. Curtiss installed an 8-cylinder engine in the trainer and gave Ellyson, Witmer, and Beck the go-ahead to fly as soon as they felt comfortable with the more powerful machine. Curtiss was pleased that Ellyson, especially, was "progressing satisfactorily," and by the middle of February thought he would "very soon be quite capable of taking care of operating an aeroplane and instructing others." For Ellyson the big day finally came on 5 March when he made his "first real flights" in the "Lizzie." He covered about six miles, but refrained from making any turns and stayed within twenty-five feet of the ground.[46]

Within another ten days Ellyson advanced from the "Lizzie" to the hydro, now rebuilt with wheels and an 8-cylinder engine. After a rough first takeoff and landing, Ellyson gained more confidence with what he conceded was a "damned tricky crate" until Curtiss thought he was ready to attempt his first turns. Curtiss took Ellyson up as a passenger to demonstrate then handed the machine over to him for his first solo flights, which Ellyson completed by the third week of March. Ellyson honed his flying skills with each flight, impressing Curtiss with his ability to handle the machine under even the windiest conditions. On 11 April, Curtiss reported to Secretary von L. Meyer that he considered Ellyson's training completed, and the Navy for all intents and purposes had its first aviator.[47]

Not only did the Navy get its first aviator through the Curtiss-Ellyson collaboration but it also led to the Navy's first airplane. Chambers alerted Ellyson in late January that Congress soon planned to authorize money for the acquisition of an airplane or airplanes, and that he and Curtiss should be ready with a design so that they could move ahead as expeditiously as possible. Ellyson believed that one airplane could not meet the Navy's needs and suggested that the Navy buy two. One would be a 4-cylinder machine like the "Lizzie," to be used for initial training, and the second a more powerful, two-seat craft that could be used on both land and water. The total price he estimated at $11,000. Over the next couple of months, following general guidelines from Chambers and with the assistance of Ellyson, Curtiss worked up specifications for an airplane suitable for service use. It was a 60-horsepower, 8-cylinder model, seating two aviators, and had a top speed of sixty-five miles per hour with one aboard, and forty-five miles per hour with two. The control system was typical Curtiss, with the steering wheel mounted on a column controlling the rudder and elevators located both at the front and rear of the airplane. A shoulder yoke operated the ailerons. Most important, it was a Triad, capable of flying from both land and water. The $10,000 estimated cost included the airplane, spare parts, and the instruction of two aviators.[48]

Chambers moved quickly once he learned on 14 April that $25,000 had been earmarked from the annual naval appropriation act to buy aircraft. He bypassed the competitive bidding process and, relying on nothing more than verbal agreements, arranged for the Wright company to build a land machine and for Curtiss to deliver an 8-cylinder amphibian similar to the Triad as well as a less powerful 4-cylinder trainer like the old "Lizzie." The Wrights were to train an aviator and a mechanic, and Curtiss agreed to train another flier and three mechanics.[49]

By this time Curtiss was ready to wrap up his work at North Island and looked forward to getting back to Hammondsport. Before leaving, he took the hydro out on 31 March for a last spin around the bay and arranged with the aero club for another exhibition at Coronado on 2 April. Before a small crowd, Hugh Robinson, a member of Curtiss' exhibition team, flew mock attacks against a "fort" laid out on the polo grounds, while Ellyson and Witmer demonstrated how Curtiss instructed students in the "Lizzie." Curtiss left San Diego that day with Lena to attend to business interests in San Francisco, leaving Lua and Carl behind in Coronado. On the long train trip east, Curtiss stopped off in Salt Lake City. He, Ely, and Willard participated in a ten-day aviation carnival held in conjunction with the Mormons' Church Conference

Week, at Bonneville Park on the south shore of the Great Salt Lake about fifteen miles west of the city. Some twelve thousand people saw Curtiss fly the Triad twice from the lake, on 8 and 9 April, a remarkable achievement considering the high density altitude at more than 4,200 feet above sea level.[50]

On the fifteenth, two days before the Curtisses arrived back in Hammondsport, Curtiss bought his Hammondsport factory from the trustee handling the assets of the bankrupt Herring-Curtiss company, finally ending the long-running dispute with Augustus Herring. He assured anxious Hammondsporters that he wanted to get the factory going as soon as he could and that he would resume the experimental program and continue the collaboration with the Navy that had proved so fruitful at North Island.[51] As Curtiss and his team broke up and left San Diego that spring, they were excited about the prospects for aviation in the Navy while at the same time being fully aware of the dangers inherent in their work. Chambers, more than anyone, knew that a bad accident or even worse a death would not only be tragic but it would jeopardize their whole enterprise. Nevertheless, all those involved, not least Curtiss himself, were pleased with the accomplishments that had come from the partnership he had forged with the Navy and looked forward to even more promising results on the shores of Lake Keuka.

—6—

High above Keuka's Waters

Curtiss returned to Hammondsport with Lena on 17 April 1911 eager to get on with his hydroairplane and other experiments, but first he had to get his factory back up and running "as speedily as possible," according to the local newspaper. It was no simple task. During the months the place had lain idle workmen had dispersed and would have to be lured back, and Curtiss could only hope that the plant's machinery had not deteriorated during the shutdown. He had more than enough motivation, for at last he felt in charge of his own destiny, and the Hammondsport community was counting on him to revitalize the enterprise. To demonstrate his sincerity and commitment to his hometown, Curtiss took to the air again, making two flights the next week that were well received by the local populace. Nevertheless, another eight months would pass before the new Curtiss Motor Company—incorporated on 19 December 1911—formally assumed the assets of the bankrupt Herring-Curtiss firm. Curtiss was president and general manager of the new business, which included the Curtiss Aeroplane Company as a subsidiary, and he held half of the $600,000 in capital. Monroe Wheeler, Jerome Fanciulli, and G. Ray Hall were among the directors and major stockholders.[1]

That spring Curtiss sought to continue his collaboration with the Navy on airplane development and he hoped the service would agree to establish a permanent flying school close to him and his factory in Hammondsport. In March Curtiss asked Ellyson to follow him home for additional instruction in the 8-cylinder machine and to get experience with the hydroairplane and the Triad. Ellyson was delighted at the prospect, writing to Chambers on the fifth that "I would like very much to do this, and honestly believe that it would be the best thing to do. . . . There is no doubt" he went on, "but that I will become a better flier by sticking to him for a while longer than I will ever become if I have to learn the rest of it alone." Nothing sounded better to

Chambers. He wrote back instructing Ellyson to stop first in Washington to help out with the acquisition of the Navy's first airplanes and assist in planning for a permanent training facility somewhere in the East. "Then," he continued, "you can be ordered to Hammondsport, N.Y., at such a time as you think suitable to continue in the good work, and the shop experience will probably be of use to you." Naturally, Curtiss was pleased with Chambers' decision, telling Ellyson that he would have an airplane ready for him to fly as soon as he arrived in Hammondsport and providing further enticement with a promise to instruct him in the operation of the hydro.[2]

After observing the Curtiss flights in Salt Lake City, Ellyson made his way to Washington, arriving there on the same day the Curtisses got back home to Hammondsport. Upon his arrival, Ellyson met with Chambers, who introduced him to other officers in hopes that his experience and enthusiasm for aviation would rub off. Ellyson found that the last month had seen major developments regarding the administration and structure of naval aviation and was pleased to see that steps had been taken to procure the Navy's first airplanes. On 13 March, Chambers was exclusively assigned to aviation duty and placed in charge of a new Office of Naval Aeronautics. He had no staff or budget, but at this juncture those deficiencies were less important than the broad authority he had to make decisions affecting the initial direction and acceptance of the new technology. Although the aeronautics office transferred from the General Board to the Bureau of Navigation in the middle of April, Chambers still reported directly to the Secretary of the Navy. Before the reorganization, he had informed Secretary von L. Meyer that in the last six months remarkable progress had been made in demonstrating the operation of airplanes from ships, flying from land and water, long-distance and duration flights, observation and photography from airplanes, wireless communications between an airplane and a ground station, and—perhaps most important—the training of aviators.[3]

High on Chambers' priority list was the acquisition of the two airplanes from Curtiss. Chambers had persuaded von L. Meyer to recommend inserting $25,000 for the purchase of aircraft in the naval appropriations bill for 1912. Congress passed the act on 4 March 1911, making the money available to the Navy to buy the airplanes as soon as the new fiscal year began on 1 July. Ellyson estimated their cost would be something less than $10,000. Chambers also understood that having Ellyson stay close to Curtiss would not only enhance Ellyson's flying skills but would also allow him to monitor the construction and testing of the two machines—in effect serving as the Navy's first inspector of naval aircraft. In Washington the pair worked together to refine the specifications for the two airplanes, one an 8-cylinder, two-seat Triad capable of both land and water operations, and the other a 4-cylinder, single-seat training airplane with limited flight capability. Chambers completed requisitions for the two Curtiss airplanes on 8 May, the date later chosen by the Navy, for some obscure reason, to mark the official founding of naval aviation.[4]

The records are sketchy on which airplane received which designation, and even the most authoritative secondary sources are confusing. What is clear is that the first of the airplanes received the designation A-1, which may have initially been a 4-cylinder machine, but at some stage during its construction became a 50-horsepower 8-cylinder Triad. The second airplane, designated A-2, was originally a 4-cylinder land machine, but later was modified as a hydro. "A" was for Curtiss; airplanes from the Wright company received the "B" designation.[5]

Of nearly equal urgency was establishing a permanent aviation station and training facility somewhere on the East Coast. For a time Chambers believed Charleston, South Carolina, was an option, provided there was enough smooth water there to facilitate hydroairplane operations. Ellyson had recently spent more than a month in Charleston, during which time there had only been one good flying day, so he favored something farther up the coast and closer to Curtiss' Hammondsport factory. By the beginning of May, Charleston had dropped out of consideration and a new site, Greenbury Point, on the north shore of the Severn River across from the Naval Academy in Annapolis, had emerged as the favorite. The government owned sixty acres there that Chambers thought was "almost ideal." Its only drawbacks were the proximity of some rifle ranges and the tract's potential use as part of the Academy's dairy farm. Neither of these Chambers thought were obstacles to the tract's summer use for aviation purposes. Yet if either Chambers or Ellyson thought that the Greenbury Point station would be ready soon, they were badly mistaken. Building a wooden hangar, filling and draining low-lying areas, and other work associated with establishing a flying field took longer than expected, with the result that for the time being Hammondsport remained the Navy's principal locus for aviation experiments and flight training.[6]

Ellyson finally arrived in Hammondsport on 1 May and found a room at Mrs. Lulu Mott's boardinghouse on the corner of Main and Shethar streets a block from the town square. He was mildly disappointed that Curtiss had more than he could handle "reorganizing and getting things in running shape" at the factory and had little time to attend to his or the Navy's needs. The flying field, conveniently located at Kingsley Flats, was a half mile long and ended at the lake on one end—adequate but smaller than what Ellyson and Chambers were looking for in a permanent training facility. For the time being, Baldwin's airship hangar and sheds near the water's edge were available to house the airplanes and other equipment, and a new hangar would be finished before the end of the month. At first there was nothing for Ellyson to fly: the hydro was there but not set up, and a 4-cylinder trainer would not be ready for another couple of days. Would-be fliers trickled into town, drawn to the new Curtiss flying school and seeking to learn the art from the master. Ellyson pleaded with Chambers to do what he could to expedite acquisition of the Navy's two airplanes so that they could be test flown as soon as possible.[7]

With little else to do, Ellyson traveled to Bridgeport, Connecticut, for a four-day exhibition Curtiss had scheduled to begin on 11 May. McCurdy and Beachey did all the flying. While McCurdy made only short hops around the field, Beachey was at his best. He started with a long flight over the city on the opening day of the meet and followed up with two days of spectacular stunt and altitude flying that culminated in a fast flight from Bridgeport to New Haven on the last day of the exhibition. Ellyson observed that Bridgeport was not satisfactory for flying because of all the trees that surrounded it, but he had taken time to look over the field at Mineola, where Curtiss had flown two years earlier, and found it "nearly ideal" for aviation purposes.[8]

Once everyone had returned from the Bridgeport exhibition and things settled into a routine at Hammondsport, Curtiss turned his attention to working with Ellyson and the Navy projects. Curtiss had more time, in part, because he had enough confidence in Ellyson to turn over to him some of the preliminary student instruction. For a week or so, Ellyson rounded up the would-be aviators staying at Mrs. Mott's place and watched over them as they spent most of their mornings running the 4-cylinder machine back and forth on the Kingsley Flats field, familiarizing themselves with its controls and handling before the wind came up. In the meantime Ellyson and Curtiss worked on the new hydroairplane, which was set up as a Triad with retractable wheels. The first test flight on 16 May was a failure, when the hydro failed to become airborne due to engine problems and a leaky float. Curtiss tried again the next day, but found that the machine's balance was too far forward to get into the air.[9]

Nothing haunted early aviation as much as the specter of injury and death from accident, and no one knew this more than Curtiss who, despite his popular image of derring-do, was resolutely safety-conscious. Even so, accidents, as they say, happen, which on the eighteenth became apparent to everyone in Hammondsport. That day Curtiss took the hydro up for a five-minute flight. On landing the stabilizing float under the right wing struck something in the water, causing the machine to slew sharply to the right. Inspection revealed that the float had a leak, but it was drained and repaired, and Curtiss went back out a few minutes later for another brief flight. Despite gusty winds, the machine handled well, but as he began his landing approach, the hydro suddenly pitched over, the tip of the main float dug in, and the craft somersaulted, landing upside down in the water. Catapulted by the impact headlong through the forward elevator and into four feet of water, Curtiss sustained only a cut above one eye and a bruised and strained leg. The hydro came out in worse shape, its pontoon smashed, both lower wings broken, and various struts and control surfaces badly damaged.[10]

Curtiss downplayed the mishap in the local paper, which noted it as a "slight accident" not worthy of the sensational coverage it had received elsewhere. Curtiss was embarrassed that he had wrecked the airplane, especially because he had made many successful landings in both land and water machines without any problems. As with many aircraft accidents, this one was the result of a combination of factors, notably a sudden shift in weight when water that had leaked into the central float surged forward at the same time a gust of wind struck the tail. Curtiss wrote to Chambers that the crash had "taught us a good lesson." In repairing the damage, he modified the float design to include individual compartments divided by watertight bulkheads to prevent sudden weight transfers, and moved the front elevator to the top of the float so that it would not be an obstacle if the aviator were pitched forward from the seat. Relieved that Curtiss had not been seriously hurt, Chambers stressed that he had "the utmost confidence in your ability to work out the naval aeroplane problem to our entire satisfaction."[11]

The accident also pointed up the shortcomings of Curtiss' trial-and-error approach to engineering, which historian Louis Casey described as "heavy-handed"— meaning that Curtiss relied too much on experimentation and not enough on design.[12] Had he had formal training as an engineer Curtiss would have been aware of the possibility of changes in an airplane's center of gravity caused by a leaky pontoon and would have taken steps to improve its design and construction. Moving the location of the front elevator so that it would not be hit by the flier in an accident was at best an ad hoc afterthought. At worst it was a tacit acknowledgment that improved aerodynamic controls were safety considerations secondary to ensuring an unimpeded trajectory for a hapless aviator ejected from an airplane. Still, the design changes were another step forward in a long and difficult process leading to a relatively safe and reliable hydroairplane.

Ellyson had to bide his time waiting for the hydro to be repaired and for Curtiss to complete a second one before he made his first flights in Hammondsport. Both craft had their elevators mounted forward on the pontoon, "so in case a bad landing is made and I should be thrown out," Ellyson noted, "I will go clear over everything." Yet he was confident that "flying over the water with this rig is the safest proposition that I know of in the aviation line, and if a man is only a good swimmer and takes ordinary precautions I do not see how he can possibly come to grief." Ellyson flew as a passenger with Curtiss on 3 June, then on the eighth took the second hydro out for the first time by himself. Nearly ecstatic about his solo flight in the hydro, he telegraphed Chambers that he "made three flights alone in Hydroplane today she handles beautifully have waited a long time but it was well worth it."[13]

In mid-June, Ellyson accompanied Curtiss to aviation meets at Akron, Ohio, and Fall River, Massachusetts, interrupting his training with the hydro. Ellyson used the trip to Akron on 13 June as an excuse to meet with Goodyear people about their rubberized fabric, which offered potential advantages as a waterproof covering for airplanes. While in Akron he was impressed with how well the 8-cylinder hydro took off and landed from the restricted confines of a small lake. At Fall River Ellyson flew as a passenger with Curtiss, observing that the machine performed well despite adverse wind and wave conditions, and that it generated only a little more spray than usual.[14]

The long-awaited arrival in Hammondsport of Lt. (jg) John H. Towers on the evening of 27 June delighted Ellyson almost as much as flying the hydro. A twenty-five-year-old gunnery officer with a strong technical bent, Towers had followed Ellyson out of the Academy by a year but preceded him in applying for aviation duty. Chambers liked the qualities he saw in the young officer, but Towers was in Europe serving on the battleship *Michigan* when Chambers got his request for aviation duty. Needing someone who could go right away to North Island for flight training, Chambers picked Ellyson for the assignment first. When the *Michigan* got back to the East Coast it was convenient for Chambers to ask for Towers' transfer to aviation training at Hammondsport. Keen to have a fellow officer join him, Ellyson had nagged Chambers for weeks about the status of Towers' orders, each time learning that one bureaucratic obstacle or another had held them up and worrying that delays would make it harder for him to catch up with flight training. Not until 20 June did the orders come through, formally detaching Towers from the *Michigan* and sending him to Hammondsport to join Curtiss and Ellyson.[15]

Ellyson met Towers at the Bath and Hammondsport train station down near the lake and escorted him back to Mrs. Mott's boardinghouse. Adverse winds precluded flying the next morning, so Ellyson decided to take Towers to see Curtiss who, when not at Kingsley Flats, was usually hard at work in the factory. Towers recalled much later that he had followed Curtiss' career through the newspapers and that he had been particularly impressed by his triumph in winning the Gordon Bennett prize at Rheims in 1909. Expecting "to meet a human dynamo of heroic stature," Towers instead encountered a "modest, retiring man" whose demeanor belied his reputation as a former motorcycle "hell-rider" and one of the world's most accomplished aviators. The factory mirrored Curtiss' personality—modest in capacity and informal in organization. Following the shop tour, Curtiss took Towers next door to his house, introduced him to Lena, and offered him a drink. Thinking that he would get a chance to sample some of the region's sparkling wines, Towers instead accepted a big glass of buttermilk, which he politely drank even though he found it intensely distasteful. Towers recalled: "I didn't believe I could swallow the stuff, but I thought I had to try. . . . Fortunately, I made the porch rail just barely in time." Curtiss could not help but laugh and asked, "Why didn't you say you didn't *like* buttermilk?" Potentially embarrassing, the incident instead was an overture to a long-lasting friendship between the two men.[16]

Ellyson, and not Curtiss, assumed primary responsibility for Towers' flight training. The arrangement made sense, for it freed up Curtiss to concentrate on the design and construction of airplanes, while simultaneously creating the nucleus for a potentially self-perpetuating system of naval officers instructing each other in aviation. Early on the morning of the twenty-ninth, Ellyson rolled Towers out of bed and hauled him down to Kingsley Flats where he briefed him on the 4-cylinder "Lizzie's" controls and how the machine responded to them. After he ran the craft up and down the field to make sure all was in order, he turned it over to Towers. Thinking more throttle rather than less was in order, Towers quickly found himself airborne and heading for the trees at the far end of the field, at which point one wing dipped and struck the ground and the machine somersaulted into what Towers called a "mass of bamboo, wire, and linen." Shaken, bruised, and sustaining torn ankle ligaments, Towers was out of commission for a while—as was the "Lizzie." What had gone wrong was obvious: Towers weighed about twenty pounds less than Ellyson, which was just enough to allow the "Lizzie" to lift off, despite Ellyson's usual precaution of placing a wedge under the throttle to restrict its movement.[17]

While Towers recovered from his injuries, Ellyson spent most of his time working with Curtiss on completing and setting up the A-1 Triad. According to Curtiss, the 75-horsepower, 8-cylinder engine for the Triad "exceeded our expectations" upon completion of tests on the twenty-seventh. Ellyson crowed that "the new engine is a beauty." As the work neared an end, Curtiss wrote to Chambers that "it is my wish to push the manufacture of aeroplanes, and, if possible, secure a large part of the Navy business. We are the best equipped from every point of view to produce the most practical and up-to-date aeroplanes at as low a cost as they can be made." He invited Chambers to come up to Hammondsport at his earliest convenience to tour the factory, see the new Navy airplanes, and to watch Ellyson go for his aviator's license.[18]

Curtiss and Ellyson were overly sanguine about the 8-cylinder engine, for in subsequent trials it developed leaky water jackets and lubrication problems that required it to be torn down and rebuilt. Rather than wait and risk disappointing Chambers, who had accepted Curtiss' invitation and was due to arrive in Bath on the morning of 1 July, Ellyson and Curtiss completed assembly of the machine with a standard 50-horsepower engine. Chambers was present, along with Albert Zahm, serving as official recorder of aviation licensees for the Aero Club of America, when Curtiss took the hydro out for its maiden flight on the evening of the first. Happy with the balance of the airplane, Curtiss landed and took Ellyson up as a passenger for another short hop. Ellyson came after with two flights to try for his license. He carefully followed the flight regimen, which included a prescribed distance and a series of figure-eight maneuvers, but failed the test because he had not been told that he needed to turn off the motor before descending for a landing. The next day Ellyson again flew twice, this time adhering to the new instructions and winning the coveted license.[19]

After Ellyson's flights, Curtiss gave Chambers a ten-minute ride in the A-1, then took Charles Witmer and Zahm up as passengers before dusk on the second. Then someone—most likely Curtiss and Ellyson together—had a brainstorm: Why not fly Chambers down the lake to Penn Yan, where he could make his train connections back to Washington the next day? A little after six o'clock on the evening of the third, Ellyson taxied out into the lake with Chambers in the seat next to him. It did not take long before he discovered that his and Chambers' combined weight, together with calm wind conditions, meant the craft lacked enough power to get airborne. Ellyson piloted the craft so that it just skimmed the surface of the water at about forty-five miles per hour until they reached Keuka eight miles down the lake. There they met Curtiss and had dinner before they climbed back aboard the A-1 to complete the journey to Penn Yan. Ellyson's flight back to Hammondsport went smoothly, except that he failed on his first attempt to land when he found it hard to judge where the surface of the water was in the dark.[20]

Curtiss was happy to accommodate the fliers at Hammondsport for as long as necessary pending completion of the facilities at Greenbury Point, finding it more convenient to work with them and the new Navy airplanes at home rather than at a distance. By 7 July the newly rebuilt 75-horsepower engine had been installed in the A-1 and test flown for the first time, Ellyson declaring it "a wonder" and capable of speeds up to sixty miles per hour without a passenger. On the ninth, Curtiss flew the A-1 from land, raising the wheels after he took off, and landing in the water. Two days later, he and Ellyson flew the machine as a landplane with the pontoon removed. Meanwhile, the A-2 with the 4-cylinder engine was finished. Curtiss took it for its first test flight on the evening of 13 July, followed a few minutes later by a short hop with Ellyson at the controls.[21]

Towers had recovered enough to fly with Curtiss in the A-1 on 6 July and with Ellyson six days later, before getting back in the "Lizzie" to resume his interrupted flight instruction. He proved to be an apt pupil, soon making passes over the length of the flying field and advancing to the A-2 for more ambitious hops up to forty feet above the ground. By early August, he was making turns with Curtiss' "Lizzie," and even venturing out over the lake before making a full turn back to the field. Problems plagued the 8-cylinder engine through much of the month. On 21 August, while Ellyson was flying with Towers in the A-1 in the landplane configuration, the motor suddenly quit and Ellyson made a forced landing in the lake. Towers was thrown from the machine on impact, but Ellyson remained in his seat as the craft turned upside down. Both had to wriggle their way through the interplane wires and struts to the surface, and they clung to the airplane for two and a half hours in the chilly water before a boat arrived to tow them and the machine to shore. Neither they nor the machine was seriously damaged, but the accident served as another reminder of the inherent dangers of flying. Ultimately the problems with the 8-cylinder engine accumulated to the point where Curtiss had to rebuild it at his own expense. On a more positive note, Curtiss introduced a new control system in the A-1 that allowed the steering wheel and column to be pivoted from the pilot's seat to the passenger seat, both of which now had shoulder yokes for operating the ailerons. The setup presaged later full dual control systems in Curtiss aircraft that transformed pilot instruction.[22]

Of particular interest to Chambers and the Navy were the experiments at Hammondsport in the summer of 1911 on means of launching hydroairplanes from ships. Ely's flights had shown that it was possible to launch and land airplanes using platforms on ships, but these were landplanes and the platforms were large and interfered with the ships' armament and operations. Both Curtiss and Ellyson thought something simpler and adaptable to hydros would be more practical. After Ely's landing and takeoff from the *Pennsylvania* in San Francisco, Captain Pond suggested that an airplane could be launched from a ship using a wire cable stretched taut from the ship's superstructure to the bow. Pursuing the idea, Curtiss first proposed removing the wheels from one of his standard land machines, fitting a small planing surface in place of the front wheels, and substituting two small metal pontoons for the rear wheels so that the craft would remain afloat long enough after landing to be hauled back on board the ship. With so many other things going on that summer, it was not until August that Curtiss and Ellyson had time to devote to ship-launching experiments.[23]

To get things going, Ellyson asked Chambers on 17 August if he could have a suitable length of ¾-inch wire cable sent to Hammondsport from the Washington Navy Yard. Two days later he described the plans for the launching device. The cable would be strung from a pile sunk in the water just offshore to two angled sheer legs, or poles, about twenty feet high located on land three hundred feet back from the lake. Two smaller cables would parallel the main cable to provide balance under the wings, and a metal groove in the center of the bottom of the main float would help guide the craft before it lifted off from the cable. The idea was to run a series of tests in sequence to determine the shortest distance needed for the hydro to become airborne. Although the hope was to carry out the experiments within a matter of days, nothing had been accomplished by the end of the month. Ellyson complained that "everything seems to be working against us, though I suppose that it is always that way when new things are tried out for the first time. We have been ready to try out the wire for several days now but the weather here for the past week has been very bad, rain every day with heavy winds and extremely cold for this time of the year." Curtiss added: "This scheme of sliding down the wire seems simple but when you come to do it there are many obstacles and problems to work out. Still looks feasible, however."[24]

Not until 7 September was the device ready for testing, at which point they had to use one of Curtiss' hydros because the A-1 was down for repairs once again. Curtiss generally followed the cable setup per Ellyson's outline to Chambers earlier in the summer, although the cable was only 250 feet long and the height sixteen rather than twenty feet. Worried about preserving lateral control and stability of the airplane as it started down the wire, Curtiss insisted that two men run alongside holding on to lines attached to the braces under each wing, which they could slip off once the machine gained sufficient speed. Ellyson volunteered as pilot despite Curtiss' reservations. Ellyson ran the engine up to full speed, the machine started down the wire into a ten-mile-per-hour wind, and got away in about 150 feet. "Everything happened so quickly and went off so smoothly that I hardly know what happened," Ellyson told Chambers, adding that the men holding the lines had to release them almost immediately. He also guessed that with a little more wind the takeoff could have been made in about one hundred feet. Despite the success of the experiment, it was not repeated, and it was clear to Chambers and others that such a wire-launching device would not work well if the vessel were rolling and pitching at sea. Nevertheless, the experiments at Hammondsport had set in motion other ideas for launching aircraft from ships.[25]

Recently promoted to lieutenant, Towers made rapid progress in flight instruction in August and early September, proving himself to be one of those gifted with a natural "feel" for the air. When Ellyson was confident that Towers had mastered the A-2, which flew well so long as the 4-cylinder engine was properly tuned, he persuaded Curtiss to let him equip it with one of his 8-cylinder engines so that Towers could get experience with a faster and more powerful machine while the A-1 was being repaired. With Zahm present for the Aero Club of America, Towers tried for his license on 11 September in the A-2, which had been modified with the 8-cylinder motor and fitted with wheels. He flew well but flubbed one of his landings and failed the test. Even so, Ellyson could not help but be impressed, wiring Chambers that day that Towers "is [a] wonder." Towers went out again two days later on the afternoon of the thirteenth. This time he performed flawlessly, earning his license and joining Ellyson as the Navy's second Curtiss-trained aviator.[26]

Within a week, Ellyson and Towers, along with the two Navy airplanes, left Hammondsport for Annapolis. It had been a busy summer, with noteworthy accomplishments by Curtiss and the Navy's fliers, and yet there had still been plenty of spare time for the young men to enjoy themselves away from the often stultifying Navy routine. The company of attractive young women, concerts at the lakeside pavilion, loafing along the lakeshore, swimming, boating, movies, and the occasional motorcycle tour in the hills around town (both Ellyson and Towers bought Curtiss machines) provided off-duty enjoyment. Towers drank in moderation, but Ellyson did so to excess; shop foreman Henry Kleckler remembered Ellyson as "a boozer and more than once tee-totally blotto." Sometimes, after more than a few whiskeys, Ellyson hopped on his motorcycle and took off, leaving his friends worrying about the consequences of an accident, but Towers usually found him not far out of town "snoring away peacefully in a ditch." Possibly as a result of his more moderate habits, Towers was the better aviator, while Ellyson's flying was "erratic," Kleckler recalled many years later.[27]

Towers got to Greenbury Point before the end of the month. There he found that the facility's hangar had been completed, but the grounds themselves still had not yet been completely cleared, the area available for the landing field was marginal, and the water off the beach along the Severn was shallower than he would have liked. Stray bullets from the nearby Academy rifle range were also a problem, requiring a hiatus in flying on days when the range was in use. On the other hand, Capt. Thomas W. Kinkaid, in charge of the Naval Experiment Station next door, was interested in aviation and offered his help as needed, especially with engine repairs and testing. Ellyson arrived in Annapolis on 4 October, after attending an aviation meet on Long Island. For his part, he worried that the A-2, which had performed adequately as a land machine and was all right for practice flights even on a small field, would not do well when set up as a hydro unless it had an 8-cylinder motor. Towers took the A-1 up for a ten-minute flight on 30 September to inaugurate the new facility, and on 3 October made a few longer flights. Ellyson flew the A-1 at Annapolis for the first time on the seventh.[28]

Lt. John Rodgers also reported for duty at Annapolis that fall. During the summer, Rodgers had become the Navy's second aviator when he completed flight instruction at the Wrights' historic Huffman Prairie outside Dayton. Rodgers was an Academy graduate, class of 1903, and the scion of a naval family going back to the previous century. Following him in early November was Ens. Victor D. Herbster, a 1908 Academy graduate who had been assigned to Greenbury Point for instruction under Rodgers. A Wright airplane, with the Navy designation B-1, accompanied Rodgers from Dayton to Greenbury Point; later it was equipped with twin floats for comparative trials with the two Curtiss machines.[29]

Despite mechanical problems and the occasional accidents that served as reminders of the perils of aviation, confidence in both the airplanes and the aviators' flying skills grew to the point where Ellyson and Chambers considered the possibility of making an endurance flight with the A-1. The idea was Ellyson's. On 7 September, while he was still in Hammondsport, he wrote to Chambers that the A-1's engine was running for up to ten hours without any problems. "As soon as we reach Annapolis," he went on, "we will be ready to fly to Washington if you so desire, either across country or by following the Bay and Potomac." The longer route down the Chesapeake Bay was preferable, "for I think that it would establish the world's record, certainly the American record for over water flight, and will call attention to the hydroplane safety features. Of course Towers will make the flight with me."[30]

From an Annapolis-to-Washington flight the project evolved into something more ambitious, eventually maturing into a round-trip down the Chesapeake to Hampton Roads, an effort Ellyson considered essential to demonstrating the capabilities of the Navy's new hydroairplane and the skill and training of the Navy's first aviators. Ellyson and Towers left the naval station about noon on 10 October. They covered only about thirty miles before they had to land near a beach on the west shore of the bay to make minor repairs before taking off again. After another twenty minutes in the air they were down once more due to another mechanical problem. Back in the air, and after traveling only seventy-nine miles in about two hours total flying time, disaster struck when the engine's crankshaft bearings gave out. The pair and their machine had to be picked up by a torpedo boat and taken back to Annapolis.[31]

Curtiss, who was at a loss as to why there had been so much trouble with the A-1's engine, explained to Chambers that its construction differed from his other 8-cylinder motors only in ways that should make it more reliable, and not less so. Equally puzzling was that Ellyson knew as much as anyone about the maintenance routine for the motor. Just in case, Curtiss immediately dispatched another motor to Ellyson so that he would have two of them in preparation for the next attempt at the distance flight. In general, Curtiss had doubts about the wisdom of the exercise, which he considered a "big undertaking at this time of the year," when there was a strong likelihood of bad weather. Would it not be preferable, he asked Chambers, for Ellyson and Towers to go back to Ellyson's original idea of making a round-trip between Annapolis and Washington, which in itself would be far from easy? Looking ahead and changing the subject, Curtiss agreed with Chambers that it was a good idea to have Ellyson, along with any other officers who might be interested in aviation, join him in San Diego, where he planned to continue flight instruction and experimentation for another winter.[32]

Rather than take a chance with the old motor, Ellyson fitted the A-1 with the new one sent by Curtiss. Completing other repairs and modifications to the airplane, he set out on the afternoon of 25 October for Hampton Roads with Towers in the right seat, where at times he spelled Ellyson in flying the aircraft and fixed minor problems in flight. After 112 miles and more than two hours in the air, an overheating engine due to a leaky radiator brought them down near Milford Haven, where they made temporary repairs and refueled before resuming their journey. They got as far as Buckroe Beach, only a few miles from their destination, before they were again forced to land. Water from the radiator had gotten into the magneto ignition and caused the engine to misfire. The next afternoon, after fixing the radiator and patching the float, which had been damaged in running the craft onto the beach, Towers had the controls for the short, five-minute hop to Fort Monroe to complete the first half of their odyssey.[33]

And an odyssey it was, for the return to Annapolis proved even more difficult than the flight down the Chesapeake. Having replaced the A-1's pontoon and radiator, and taking advantage of a break in the weather after a day of high wind and rain, Ellyson and Towers left Hampton Roads on the morning of the thirtieth. They got only as far as the York River before an overheating engine brought them down. Temporary fixes sufficed to get them a little farther up the bay until a broken shaft in the water pump, coupled with recurring radiator leaks, ended that day's flying. They lost another two days making repairs and waiting for the weather to improve before they got back in the air on the morning of 2 November. When a carburetor brace fractured as a result of engine vibrations, the duo decided to land to make emergency repairs before something more serious broke, only to have weather ground them for the rest of the day. They did not get back to the flying field at Annapolis until late in the afternoon of the third.[34]

As far as lessons learned the experience was a mixed bag. Curtiss was right about attempting the flight so late in the season, although more days were lost to mechanical difficulties than were lost to bad weather. But Ellyson and Chambers were right that there was no better time to demonstrate to the public and their fellow officers how good the Navy's airplanes and aviators were. Those who argued for the inherent safety of the hydroairplane were vindicated, because the craft could land and take off just about anywhere under a variety of wind and water conditions, and it was clear that if everything worked just right, the hydro had excellent endurance. At the same time, it was also obvious that a good deal more development was needed before the Navy had a reliable, high-powered engine from Curtiss.[35] Most encouraging, though, was the human factor: Ellyson and Towers displayed teamwork, persistence, skill, and resourcefulness throughout what was one of the year's most remarkable aviation accomplishments.

Steadily worsening weather and the deteriorating mechanical condition of the airplanes at Annapolis made flying increasingly difficult through the rest of the year. Towers gave everyone a scare on 15 November when he took the A-1 up for a flight over the bay. He was in the middle of a turn a few minutes after taking off when a gust of wind upset the airplane, sending it plummeting into the water from a height of about 150 feet. Towers was thrown out of the seat when the airplane struck the water, and he got tangled in the wreckage as it turned over and sank. Luck was again on his side as he was able to free himself and climb onto the upside-down pontoon, where he remained for three-quarters of an hour before a rescue boat arrived. Towers spent a few days in the hospital with bruises and a sprained ankle, while the airplane had to have major structural repairs and a complete engine rebuild. In the meantime, the miserable weather kept people from working more than about three hours a day in the hangar, although they were able to do some testing in the small wind tunnel at the Experimental Station. Towers also managed to carve out time in the busy flight schedule to experiment with an aircraft radio telegraph set developed by Ens. Charles H. Maddox. The apparatus used a wire antenna deployed from the airplane after it left the ground, and which repeatedly broke in the airstream during flight.[36]

Faced with the prospects of continued poor weather at Annapolis, Chambers had two choices about where to send his fledgling aviation detachment for the winter: the fliers could go to the big Navy base at Guantánamo, Cuba; or they could head back to North Island in San Diego. Guantánamo was attractive because it would allow the aviators to work with the fleet on a day-to-day basis, demonstrating how the airplane could be useful for scouting and gunfire spotting and affording non-flying officers the opportunity to get to know and work with their flying counterparts. Chambers also considered splitting the team up, sending half to Cuba and half to California. Ellyson objected both to Guantánamo and to dividing up the detachment. "I think all the aviators should go to San Diego," he told Chambers. "We can work with the ships there, and they always have the time, and have shown interest in the work, whereas the Atlantic Fleet is always busy and rushed." Moreover, he pointed out, there was no source of aircraft spares and supplies at Guantánamo and that it would take weeks to ship them in case there was an accident and damage to the airplanes. Ellyson also opposed breaking up the teams that had bonded over the summer. "Any aeroplane for effective work must be a two man machine. Again it takes some little time and experience to work up a two man team. Towers and I both have confidence in each other, and that is something I fear I would not have in four out of five men in the air. . . . It seems to me that San Diego is the logical place for all machines."[37]

Chambers rightly concluded that the men and their equipment were not yet ready for extensive practical operations with the fleet. Rather than risk embarrassment or failure for everyone to see, he acceded to Ellyson's importunities to send the aviators to North Island. He telegraphed Curtiss on 23 December to tell him that he was authorizing that all of the personnel be sent to San Diego, where he expected them to arrive sometime after the first of the year. Curtiss immediately replied that "I am delighted to receive your message today that the Navy Detachment will start for North Island January 1st. We will make all necessary arrangements to receive them and render any assistance within our power." Curtiss had been on the West Coast for nearly a month. He and Lena had left Hammondsport on the night of 24 November, a little earlier than expected after he had been notified that San Diego was planning aviation events at North Island as part of a celebration in association with the groundbreaking for the city's grand Panama-California Exposition. Upon arriving in San Diego a few days later he took up residence on Fourth Street in the city. His mother, Lua, was already there, having stayed behind in Coronado with her son Carl Adams when Curtiss had returned to Hammondsport in the spring.[38]

Curtiss could not help but be pleased with the accomplishments of the past year, not the least being his success with "water flying" and the hydroairplane. Believing that the machine had practical appeal beyond the Navy and that it might generate sales among private aviation enthusiasts, Curtiss had applied for a patent on the hydro in August. Emerson Newell, whom Curtiss had taken on as his counsel in the patent dispute with the Wrights, drafted the application in such a way that it encompassed not only the appearance and function of the machine at the time, but any changes that might be made by Curtiss or others in the future. Publicity—and potential profits—came when his friends in New York recognized Curtiss for his work with the hydroairplane by presenting him with the first Aero Club of America Trophy, donated by the club's president, publishing magnate Robert J. Collier, in the expectation that it be awarded annually for the "greatest achievement in aviation in America."[39]

The hydro was as much a result of the collaboration between Curtiss and the Navy as it was an individual achievement, symbolizing as it did a formal commitment by Chambers and the service to the airplane and aviation. For his part, Chambers was satisfied with the year's accomplishments. Among them were the Navy's first aviation appropriation, the acquisition of three airplanes (including two new-design hydros from Curtiss), four aviators (two trained by Curtiss and two by the Wrights), establishing a more or less permanent airfield and training facility at Annapolis, launching airplanes from ships and landing them back on board, and demonstrating by record flights that the airplane had potential for use with the fleet.[40] As for Curtiss, he had regained control of his business and had seen the partnership between him and the Navy mature into a cooperative venture that would benefit both parties and over the next few years lay a foundation for the continued development of naval aviation.

—7—

The Navy's Wings

Aviation was not the fast track to promotion for young officers in the battleship Navy in the early part of the last century. On the other hand, summers in New York's alluring Finger Lakes and winters in sunny southern California while participating in an exciting and potentially important new technology scarcely warranted griping. And none came from Ellyson, Towers, and the others as they made their way back across the country in January 1912 to join Curtiss and his flying operations at North Island. Over the next year their association with Curtiss expanded to include projects specifically intended to enhance the viability of the airplane and aviation as potential components of the fleet.

With San Diego's Panama-California ceremonies postponed until the spring of 1913, Curtiss turned his attention to his commitments to the Navy and the experimental work that he thrived on, especially the design and development of the so-called flying boat, which promised better all-around performance than previous hydroairplanes. Chambers believed that Curtiss had been contemplating something like a flying boat as early as 1908, but he probably meant the failed *Loon* or the hydro and not what finally evolved over the next three years. It is likely that Curtiss came up with the concept in the summer of 1911. He surmised that substituting a boat-like displacement hull for the awkward and drag-inducing pontoon of the hydro would strengthen the airplane's construction and increase its hydrodynamic and aerodynamic performance. That September Curtiss asked Ellyson and others in the aviation detachment at Annapolis what they thought could be done to improve the hydro. They recommended adding an enclosure for the pilot and instruments to make the machine more usable in such marginal weather as they had encountered on the Chesapeake. Ellyson recalled: "It was at this time that [Curtiss] outlined to us his idea of the 'Flying Boat,' and although we listened with respect and enthusiasm, we feared that for once he was attempting the impossible. . . . As a matter of fact we were so skeptical that I am afraid that we did not give the matter serious thought."[1] Despite Ellyson's doubts, Curtiss was confident he had a design that would overcome the operational and other limitations inherent in the hydro.

Toward the end of November 1911, Curtiss wrote to Chambers to bring him up to date on progress on the flying boat, which he hoped would be ready for tests in San Diego over the winter. He also sent Chambers a rough drawing of the craft, on condition that Chambers keep it confidential until he was ready to reveal it to the public. Chambers encouraged him to pursue the concept in hopes that it would be finished some time the following summer so that he could recommend its purchase by the Navy in the next fiscal year. He also promised to make the model basin at the Washington Navy Yard available for experiments with various hull designs.[2]

In a departure from the usual configurations of Curtiss airplanes, the flying boat featured two tractor propellers rather than the single pusher propeller typical of his land machines and hydros. The propellers were driven by a chain connected to a 60-horsepower V-8 mounted forward in the hull beneath a protective cover. The pilot and passenger sat low and well behind the wings. Curtiss deviated from his usual direct-drive pusher arrangement in an effort to gear down the propellers, gaining more power from them at lower speeds while achieving a lower center of gravity and better accessibility to the engine as the craft sat on the water. Yet as the machine neared completion, Curtiss had doubts. He wrote to Chambers that "the chain transmission and complications do not look good to me. I like the direct drive for its simplicity and reliability."[3]

Tests of the flying boat in San Diego on 10 January 1912 revealed some of the problems Curtiss anticipated, particularly the unreliability of the chain drive, as well as nose-heaviness in the water. Over several days, Curtiss ran the craft through the water and made some brief hops, but never succeeded in getting the craft truly airborne.[4] The failure of Curtiss' first flying boat is another example of the consequences of his engineering methodology, rooted in native instincts rather than careful analysis. Standard engineering practice demands that one design change be made at a time, so that the cause of a failure can be immediately determined; multiple changes, such as those Curtiss made with his first flying boat, introduce so many variables that it is virtually impossible to isolate the reason or reasons why something did not work. More often than not Curtiss got it right—with sometimes spectacular results—but in this instance the result was a disappointment indicating that he needed to rethink the concept.

Not long after the flying boat trials, the Navy contingent began to filter in to North Island. Both Ellyson and Towers were back by 15 January and together rented a cottage in Coronado. Ten days later the railcar carrying the Navy's equipment arrived in San Diego. With the help of crew members and a lighter from the supply and repair ship *Iris*, the A-1 and A-2 hydros were unloaded and with the rest of the equipment were hauled across the bay to North Island. Rodgers and his wife arrived on the twentieth and also rented a cottage, while Herbster for the time being camped out in a tent on North Island. The Wright B-1 arrived on 1 February. The Curtiss and Wright aviators occupied separate tent hangars on the bay about a mile north of the Curtiss flying field, with a wood ramp facilitating access to the water. Displaying a wry sense of humor, the Curtiss aviators nicknamed their place "Camp Trouble."[5]

Among Chambers' objectives for the winter season was comparing the performance of the Curtiss and Wright machines. He also wanted to know how the aviators adapted to the idiosyncratic control systems of the two airplanes, which were so different that aviators who had learned to fly on one system were reluctant to try the other. Chambers recognized that Curtiss had done more than the Wrights to prove that the airplane could be routinely operated from ships and that Curtiss had a more promising control arrangement, but the Curtiss system would have to demonstrate its superiority "or else it won't suit us." For flight instruction and for the airplane to become fully integrated with the fleet, the Navy would have to choose one or the other system as standard. Curtiss' innovation of dual controls with two steering wheels and a foot throttle that could be actuated from either seat made his system even more attractive, because it permitted the instructor to fly with the student, something Curtiss believed essential to the success of training aviators in hydroairplanes, where over the water the old method of solo instruction was impractical and dangerous.[6]

Continuing mechanical troubles bedeviled the A-1 and frustrated the Curtiss aviators at North Island. On its first flight on 30 January, the airplane came down with an overheated engine, necessitating modifications to the water pump and the fitting of a new propeller in hopes that the lower revolutions per minute would reduce the stress on the motor. After repairs, the machine saw almost daily use for the first two weeks of February, during which Ellyson and Towers took some of the Navy enlisted men and students from the Curtiss school for their first airplane flights. Flights ended on 14 February. When Ellyson took the airplane out with a passenger to demonstrate the Curtiss dual control system installed only two days before, the engine kept misfiring and he was unable to get the craft airborne. Further investigation revealed major internal problems in the motor that required its complete rebuilding. With the A-1 down, and the A-2 unavailable while it was being set up as a replacement, Ellyson and Towers shared flying time with Rodgers and Curtiss in the B-1. They found it underpowered and difficult to land and take off safely due to its poorly designed twin floats. But the Wright machine, for all its faults, proved rugged and reliable, testimony to the brothers' careful attention to detail in the construction of their airplanes. On 28 February, Herbster flew the B-1 to earn his license and officially become the Navy's fourth aviator.[7]

Chambers admired Curtiss and respected his innate engineering ability but he harbored reservations about his empirical methodology and worried that it might impede progress toward ensuring that Curtiss' airplanes met the Navy's requirements. He also understood the fundamental tenet that it was easier to train an engineer as an aviator than it was to educate an aviator in engineering. Accordingly, Chambers assigned Lt. Dick Richardson to North Island to work with Curtiss on technical matters relating to the hydro and flying boat and at the same time learn to fly, in effect making him the Navy's pioneer engineering test pilot. Richardson had been focused for some time on the design and performance of hydroairplane pontoons and floats, and had just completed a brief tour at the Washington Navy Yard's model basin, where he worked with fellow constructor William McIntee to refine his ideas and data.[8]

Richardson did not get to San Diego until 3 March, following delays in his orders and the customary long transcontinental train ride. Not long after Richardson arrived, Curtiss wrote to Chambers that "I have met him and like him very much." Ellyson and Towers had the responsibility for teaching the burly Richardson to fly, which Towers likened to "teaching Gargantua to dance." But after a couple of days of running back and forth on the ground in one of the Curtiss "Lizzies," Richardson accomplished his first short hop, exulting that "I found the machine off the ground, and was delighted to discover that I had it under control." He was disappointed that he was unable to work with a hydro, but expected he would be able to within a matter of days and was keen to try out his ideas regarding pontoons with sharp bows and V-shaped bottoms.[9]

Then disaster struck. On the ninth a windstorm swept over North Island, destroying one of the Navy's tent hangars and damaging the A-2, which took a few days to repair. Despite gusty winds, Ellyson flew the machine from the

Navy camp over to the Curtiss field on the morning of the fourteenth. About noon, as the swirling winds seemed to abate, Ellyson went up one more time to make sure the conditions were safe enough to let Richardson take one of the "Lizzies" out. Shortly after taking off, and at a height of about twenty-five feet, the airplane suddenly dropped, taking Ellyson completely by surprise. He regained control, but seconds later the machine went into another dive, from which there was no hope of recovering. Upon striking the ground, and digging "an awful hole in the field," according to Towers, the airplane tumbled onto its back, trapping the unconscious Ellyson between the two wings. Towers raced to the scene on his motorcycle and pulled Ellyson from the wreckage. He was badly bruised, temporarily blinded from the sand in his eyes, and had a sprained back and a concussion. In considerable pain, Ellyson spent a week in bed doped up with painkillers, and another month passed before he felt well enough to resume his duties.[10]

While Ellyson was laid up, Richardson turned his attention to a new pontoon built by the Navy according to specifications based on data from his model basin experiments. The Richardson-inspired float was long and narrow, with a sharp bow and a V-bottom. Curtiss thought it had possibilities, but Towers derided the float as "useless" and looked like its design had been "evolved by expanding the dimensions of a toothpick." The first trial of the Richardson pontoon was less than a success. Herbster flew the B-1, fitted with two of the new floats, on 1 March, only to experience control problems and crash while attempting a landing. He was unhurt but the airplane was badly damaged. Richardson believed the accident had been caused by water leaking into one of the pontoons, which led to an uneven weight distribution, and was not due to any faults in the float design. The mishap, though, was further proof in his mind that a single pontoon was a superior configuration to twin floats.[11]

To settle the matter once and for all, Towers took the A-1 out with the Richardson-designed float in early April. He found that the bow of the float tended to submerge at speed, and that he could not get the airplane to lift off the water. "I am disappointed with the result," Richardson wrote to Chambers, "and find it hard to account for the failure," which he attributed to uneven propeller thrust and odd shifts in the airplane's center of gravity. Later he recalled that he had come to San Diego thinking that his floats were "beauties," but the tests led Curtiss to conclude that Richardson "was too much of a boat builder and not enough [of] a flier." Still, Richardson was not about to give up. He recommended that towing tests at the Washington Navy Yard be done with quarter-size models complete with wings and tail surfaces in order to sort out what was obviously a more complex balance of aerodynamics and hydrodynamics than he had anticipated.[12]

The aviation unit—minus Ellyson—was busy for the remainder of its stay at North Island, despite interruptions caused by unusually bad weather. Back on its original Curtiss float, the A-1 belied its reputation for unreliability, with nearly thirty flights from late March to late April, most of them with Towers at the controls. Richardson went up with Towers for a short flight in the A-1 for the first time on 25 March. Longer flights followed through the first week of April. Richardson soloed in the A-1 on 22 April, but on a second flight the next day the airplane yawed to the right as he came in for a landing, the wing on that side submerged, and the craft overturned, with major damage to the wing and the tail. Richardson blamed himself for the accident, caused when he attempted a turn at too low an altitude and speed, thus inducing a classic stall. "I regret the resulting damage to the machine exceedingly, but hope I have learned my lesson from it, and that the net result will be better judgment and more confidence in the future," he told Chambers. The A-2, back in commission as a hydro on 15 April, had to suffice for Towers and Richardson for the next two weeks while the damaged A-1 was crated for shipment back to Annapolis.[13]

There was also a lot of activity across the way at the Curtiss flying field, where the concentration was on civilian flight instruction. Because Curtiss was preoccupied with experimental work, he delegated most of the training to John W. ("Mac") McClaskey, a retired Marine lieutenant who had learned to fly at Hammondsport the previous summer. It was a big class, and a diverse one. For the first time, the school took on an international tone with the arrival of Mohan M. Singh from India, Motohisa Kondo and Takeishi Kono from Japan, and Greek army Capt. George Capistini. Julia Clark from Denver, who was Curtiss' second female student, was there, too, along with two married couples.[14]

Another member of the Curtiss group was John Lansing ("Lanny") Callan. An Albany, New York, resident determined to become an aviator, Callan was the perfect example of the virtues of persistence, presence, and hard work. He had first approached Jerome Fanciulli in December 1910 asking him how "to obtain a personal interview with Mr. Curtiss in regard to getting a position with him as an operator of one of his machines." Fanciulli informed him that Curtiss was in San Diego and wisely counseled twenty-four-year-old Callan that he might first want to learn to fly, suggesting that the Curtiss school might be an excellent choice. But Callan's father, a prominent real estate broker, was not enthusiastic about his son going into aviation and refused to lend him the $500 needed for lessons. Not willing to take "no" for an answer, Callan met Curtiss in Hammondsport in the summer of 1911 and secured from him an understanding that he could join him in San Diego at the end of the year if he could put $250 up front and guarantee the remainder after completing half of the course. Callan arrived in San Diego before the end of the year, got a room in the "club house" on North Island, and launched into the course before the rest of the students arrived. Advancing quickly, he completed his instruction and received his aviator's license before the beginning of March.[15]

Meanwhile, on 18 April, Curtiss and Lena—now seven months pregnant with their second child—had returned home to Hammondsport. The aviation unit left North Island on 1 May with orders to report back to the camp in Annapolis. The canvas hangars that lent Annapolis such an aspect of impermanency were something Chambers insisted on because he wanted to ensure that aviation could move with the fleet as needed. For Richardson it was literally back to the drawing board as he headed to the Washington Navy Yard for more research on float designs. After leaving North Island, Ellyson also went to Washington, where he worked with Chambers on matters relating to airplane specifications and procurement, before joining Towers and the others at Annapolis.[16]

A little less than two months after getting back to Hammondsport, the Curtisses celebrated the birth of a son on Sunday morning, 16 June. As overjoyed as they had been overwrought a decade earlier with the death of Carlton, the couple named the healthy 8½-pound newborn Glenn Hammond Jr. Curtiss wrote to his mother Lua that "the baby is all right and Lena doing well." Friends and acquaintances throughout the country sent their congratulations on the arrival of the family's "new aviator."[17]

Through the remainder of the spring and early summer of 1912 at Hammondsport Curtiss was determined to solve the problems that had been so evident with his abortive flying boat design, while taking care to keep the work under wraps until he was ready to announce success. He went back to basics, reverting to the pusher configuration with a 75-horsepower V-8 engine mounted between the two wings, and following the general design and specifications of the successful 1911 hydroairplane. The flying boat featured a hull that was 26 feet long and flat-bottomed like the hydro's central pontoon, with similar watertight compartments. Small metal floats under the lower wings provided balance in the water. The aviators sat side by side operating the usual shoulder yoke and wheel controls. At first, Curtiss fitted the machine with a front elevator, but he soon discarded it, confirming Towers' and Ellyson's discovery with the Navy airplanes that the rear elevator provided more than adequate pitch control. The protective hood over the bow and the elongated vertical fin gave the craft a sleek appearance that contrasted with that of the ungainly looking hydros.[18]

Initial flight tests ended in failure when the craft would not under any circumstances lift off the water, forcing Curtiss to rethink the hull design. Curtiss knew about some of the fundamentals of hydroplaning from his experiences with the AEA and understood that the trouble with his flying boat was a result of the hull becoming "sealed" to the surface of the water, but he was unsure how to solve the problem. He quizzed everyone about it and even closely observed the action of the hull in the water from a speedboat, hoping to see something that would lead to an answer. Hydrodynamic drag caused by the longer hull was the likely culprit, but less obvious was how to mitigate it so that the hull attained what later engineers referred to as the "hump," where the craft transitioned to planing, hydrodynamic resistance dropped off dramatically, and aerodynamics started to take over. At last, in what is sometimes referred to by historians as a "Eureka moment," Curtiss visualized a separation or "jog" in the bottom of the hull that would disrupt the flow sufficiently to break the hull loose. It was similar in principle to the spoilers commonly fitted to the top surface of airplane wings to disrupt the airflow over them. Curtiss instructed his shop foreman Henry Kleckler to cut out blocks of wood that he fixed transversely to the hull to create what later became known as a "step" that allowed the forward part of the hull to plane while lifting the rear of the hull clear of the water, thereby lessening drag. The results were instantaneously positive. On the next test flight, according to Kleckler, "they found they could rise on top of the water and take off like a flying dog."[19]

Due to Curtiss' extreme secrecy, it is unclear exactly when he carried out experiments with the flying boat modified with the "step." Ellyson must have observed some of the testing during a visit to Hammondsport in the first week of July, for he wired Chambers on the fifth that he had "tried out new flying boat tonight and it has many fine points." He stayed in Hammondsport to help Curtiss with additional testing. Curtiss informed Chambers on 9 July that "I am glad to report that after making a slight change in the angle point of the bottom of our new flying boat, it left the water as easily with two persons as with one the day before, and we had no trouble at all in getting up in a calm [sic]. The more we use it, the better we like it." A little more than a week later he wrote to Chambers: "The flying boat No. 2 is a weight carrier. I made a flight the other day with two passengers in the regular seats and a man lying on the boat between the main surfaces and the tail. There was no trouble whatever in getting out of the water."[20]

By the middle of July, Curtiss was confident enough in the new flying boat to encourage publicity. The *New York Times* reported that the flying boat was in daily use and praised the machine as "stronger, more compact, and simpler than anything thus far designed by Curtiss." The hometown *Hammondsport Herald* stressed the safety of the flying boat and Curtiss' expectations that it would generate a clientele of wealthy sportsmen interested in "aerial yachting." Curtiss accepted the Aero Club of America's 1912 Collier Trophy for his work on the flying boat—the second year in a row that he won the honor—and three years later, on 8 June 1915, received a comprehensive patent, which specifically cited the step on or near the center of gravity that allowed the craft to "readily break from the water and rise into the air."[21]

For the present, though, Curtiss kept the Navy in sharp focus. Seeking expert opinion and advice, he told Chambers that "I wish Mr. Richardson could come up to Hammondsport and see the machine. We would like to exchange ideas with him. Can you not send him up to inspect it?" More than pleased to have a chance to escape the Washington heat and humidity for the Finger Lakes and to see the flying boat in person, Richardson was ready for a change of scenery when Chambers obliged Curtiss' request. As soon as Richardson reached Hammondsport on 9 August he met with Curtiss, who wrote to Chambers: "We have had a very pleasant—and I trust profitable—conference. We are not having good weather just now, but as soon as the stormy conditions subside I want to take Mr. Richardson out in the flying boat and it will be interesting to learn his opinion of it." The bad weather was not unwelcome, for it gave Richardson the opportunity to spend time in the factory and closely examine the flying boat. Flight tests impressed him. With the step the flying boat "gets away so very easily that you cannot detect the instant" when it became airborne. There were still problems with slow acceleration to planing speed and excessive spray, however; Richardson solved these by making slight changes to the shape of the bow and incorporating air vents in the hull behind the step. While at Hammondsport, Richardson finally earned his flying license while checking out in the hydro. He later officially became naval aviator number thirteen.[22]

Toward the end of August, Curtiss dropped his experimental work in Hammondsport to travel to Europe for the first time since his momentous

The first Curtiss hydroairplane, tested by Curtiss and Ellyson at North Island in mid-January 1911. With tandem floats, or pontoons, the craft did not perform well. *National Archives*

The hydro with the single pontoon was a success in late January 1911. *National Naval Aviation Museum. Courtesy of David Burke*

In another experiment, Curtiss fitted the hydro with retractable wheels, creating what may have been the first amphibian. It was known as the Triad because it could operate on land, the water, and the air. On 26 February 1911, he flew the machine from North Island and landed on the beach at the Hotel del Coronado. *National Naval Aviation Museum. Courtesy of David Burke*

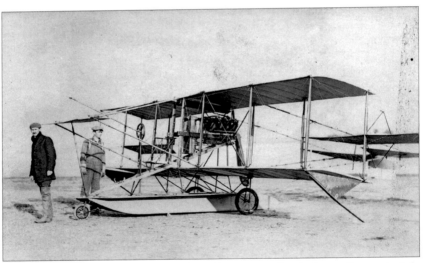

The Triad on the beach at North Island in February 1911. Curtiss is standing on the left. Note the wheeled undercarriage. *Glenn H. Curtiss Museum*

At the end of January 1911, Curtiss, Ely, and Ellyson took part in a flying exhibition at the polo grounds at the Coronado Country Club, across Spanish Bight from North Island. Here Ellyson prepares to demonstrate the Curtiss airplane. He had planned to taxi across the field but inadvertently took off and made a short flight. *National Naval Aviation Museum. Courtesy of David Burke*

Curtiss turned the hydroairplane's engine and propeller around to the tractor configuration, possibly to reduce spray damage to the propeller. Although he was not happy with its performance, he flew it out to the *Pennsylvania* from North Island and landed it next to the ship on 17 February 1911. Here Curtiss is standing next to the hydro after it had been hoisted aboard the ship—another first in naval aviation. *National Archives*

The hydro in its single-float configuration at Hammondsport ready for more flights in the spring of 1911. *National Archives*

Lt. (jg) John H. Towers joined Ellyson and Curtiss at Hammondsport in June 1911. Towers (left) flew with Ellyson in the A-1, the Navy's first airplane, in July 1911. Note that the airplane has a wheel and control column that can be swung from the pilot's seat to the passenger's seat. *National Archives*

The Navy's A-1 at Hammondsport in early July 1911. Albert Zahm is in the straw hat, third from the left; Curtiss is on the left, with his hand on the wheel and control column; Ellyson is next, to the right, with Chambers (in cap) and Towers next to him on the right. *National Archives*

Chambers and Ellyson in the A-1 before their attempted flight to Penn Yan from Hammondsport in July 1911. *National Archives*

Hammondsport in 1911 or 1912. The "X" marks Curtiss' house on the hill, with the factory nearly surrounding it. In the distance is the flying field with hangars just visible to the extreme left. *Glenn H. Curtiss Museum*

Curtiss and Ellyson believed that hydros could be launched from small warships using a wire apparatus. They tested it with one of Curtiss' hydros at Hammondsport in September 1911. Although the launch was successful, the device was impractical due to the rolling and pitching of a vessel at sea. *National Archives*

The flying boat was one of Curtiss' most important contributions to naval aviation. After his first design failed, Curtiss succeeded with this machine at Hammondsport in the early summer of 1912. The key was the introduction of the "step," a transverse break in the hull that allowed the flying boat to plane and lift free of the water. *National Archives*

Ellyson clings to the rear of the flying boat in this demonstration of the airplane's weight-carrying capacity at Hammondsport in July 1912. *Glenn H. Curtiss Museum*

Hammondsport was busy in the late summer of 1912. Three landplanes and two hydros share space with the flying boat, on the water in the background. *National Archives*

Tests of the Navy's first flying boat, the C-1, began in Hammondsport in October 1912. *National Archives*

The Curtiss Navy A-2 hydro reconfigured in October 1913 as the OWL (Over Water and Land) amphibian. With the cowl over the pilot's and passenger's seats it superficially resembles a flying boat. *Glenn H. Curtiss Museum*

The Navy's Curtiss C-2 flying boat was equipped with Lawrence Sperry's gyroscopic stabilizer in the late summer and fall of 1913. Lt. Patrick N. L. Bellinger and Sperry flew the C-2 at Hammondsport in October of that year. *National Archives*

One of Curtiss' most ambitious projects was the *America* transatlantic flying boat, developed with funding from Rodman Wanamaker. It is shown here at Hammondsport in late June 1914. Note the extensions on the hull, intended to improve the flying boat's hydrodynamics. *National Archives*

Curtiss substantially rebuilt Samuel P. Langley's 1903 aerodrome and flew it a short distance on Lake Keuka in May 1914. He hoped the flight would demonstrate that Langley had a machine capable of flight before the Wright brothers and thereby strengthen his case in the patent litigation with the Wright interests. *Glenn H. Curtiss Museum*

In December 1917, the Curtiss Engineering Corporation opened a large experimental facility in Garden City, New York. Representative of the continuing partnership between the Navy and Curtiss, it served as a research and development center for the Navy in the late 1910s and early 1920s. *Glenn H. Curtiss Museum*

The *NC-4* on the Tagus River, Lisbon, Portugal, after completing the flight from Newfoundland in May 1919. The NC project was another example of the collaboration between Curtiss and the Navy and the culmination of Curtiss' dreams of achieving a flight across the Atlantic. *National Archives*

Like many aircraft manufacturers, Curtiss believed that racing "improved the breed." The Navy saw air racing as a means of developing and testing high-performance fighter aircraft. Bert Acosta won the 1921 Pulitzer race in the Curtiss-Navy CR-2 at Omaha in November 1921. *National Archives*

John Towers was an honorary pallbearer at Curtiss' funeral in Hammondsport on 24 July 1930. On the right is Army Air Service Lt. Col. Frank M. Andrews, an early air power advocate. *Glenn H. Curtiss Museum*

triumph in the Gordon Bennett competition in Rheims three years earlier. The purpose of the trip was customer relations, meant to follow up on current overseas airplane orders and drum up new sales to private and government buyers. Curtiss left home on 21 August, taking one of the big liners out of New York for France. In Paris he secured an order for a hydro from Louis Paulhan, and in Berlin he met Russian officials who committed to buying three hydros and two extra motors. Soon after his return to Hammondsport on 3 October the local paper crowed that Curtiss had done "a thriving business" while he was in Europe and the additional airplane orders would "keep the Curtiss works here busy for some time to come."[23]

Ellyson spent most of the rest of July and nearly all of August in Hammondsport working with Curtiss on the flying boat, while Towers handled nearly all of the flight instruction and experimentation at Annapolis. Towers nevertheless got away from Annapolis twice to fly the new Curtiss machine at Hammondsport, confirming the reports of Ellyson and Richardson that the flying boat had excellent performance. If the reports coming out of Hammondsport that summer and fall were only half true, Chambers was encouraged that he had in the flying boat an airplane that had the potential to realize his goal of fleet aviation. With a new aircraft appropriation for fiscal year 1913 available in July, Chambers ordered a flying boat and another Triad from Curtiss, along with a second flying boat from W. Starling Burgess, a Marblehead, Massachusetts, yacht builder. Chambers especially wanted to compare the Curtiss and Burgess machines in operations with the fleet during the winter of 1913, although late delivery of the Burgess rendered that impossible.[24]

Ely's flights in 1910 and 1911 conclusively proved that airplanes could fly from and land on ships, provided they were equipped with suitable platforms, but it was clear that such structures would hinder normal ship operations. Curtiss' Hammondsport experiments in September 1911 with the wire-cable apparatus pointed the way to a means of launching hydroairplanes from ships without using cumbersome and expensive platforms, but the device would not work under real-world sea conditions. Again, Chambers took the initiative. Borrowing from torpedo technology, which used compressed air to launch the missiles from surface ships and submarines, Chambers suggested to Curtiss in December 1911 that an old 18-inch-diameter torpedo tube could be used as the basis for a catapult to accelerate an airplane to flying speed in a short distance. Curtiss liked the idea. In January 1912, he wrote to Chambers that a "small single passenger machine" would be "easy to set up, easy to stow away . . . easy to launch and easy to operate," and that he was more than happy to design and build such an airplane for the Navy. Before heading to North Island, Richardson did some "back of the envelope" calculations that showed a considerable force would be needed to launch an airplane within a distance of thirty feet, and recommended a step-by-step series of experiments with a land machine to prove the concept.[25]

By the middle of June, Richardson and Chambers had completed the compressed-air catapult at the Washington Navy Yard and shipped it to Annapolis, where it was set up at the Santee Dock for trials. Ellyson volunteered for the first attempts. On the afternoon of 31 July he climbed aboard the A-1, took the controls, and brought the big V-8 up to full power before signaling Richardson to fire the catapult by opening the air release valve. The sudden jolt slammed Ellyson back into the seat and his hands pulled the control wheel back as far as it would go. As the front of the hydro leapt off the launching car, the machine careened to the left, stalled, and fell upside down in the river, sustaining considerable damage but fortunately not injuring Ellyson. It was immediately obvious to Richardson that it would be necessary to secure the airplane to the launching car through the entire length of its travel, and that the release valve would have to be redesigned to moderate the explosive force of the compressed air.[26]

Richardson, who was also occupied with the Curtiss flying boat, could not complete redesigning the catapult until November. He moved the project back to the Washington Navy Yard, mounting the catapult on a barge that was towed out into the Anacostia River for tests using the Curtiss hydro with the designation A-3. Once more, Ellyson volunteered for the first launch, scheduled for 12 November. Curtiss was present for the experiment that day, which in comparison to the one at Annapolis in July went off without a hitch. Exulting that "I have never seen anything prettier in my life than the getting away of Lieutenant Ellyson this afternoon," Curtiss proclaimed the catapult "the greatest aviation advance since wheels replaced skids for aeroplane landing gear" and praised Chambers for his "brilliant achievement." Chambers quickly corrected the last part of Curtiss' remarks to stress that the catapult was a "joint cooperative effort."[27]

Largely as a result of that cooperation, Chambers was rightly satisfied with the progress that had been made in naval aviation by the fall of 1912. In a report to the secretary of the Navy on 21 September, Chambers optimistically claimed that "although the aeroplane has not yet arrived at the state of perfection required by all the work contemplated for it in naval warfare," enough had been done that the technology stood on the brink of becoming a determining factor in future conflicts. In the immediate future, airplanes carried by "all large ships" or flying from advanced bases would be used to scout enemy fleets, reconnoiter advanced bases, provide communication, and strike submarines, docks, ships in harbor, hangars, and ammunition storehouses. These realities, Chambers believed, had come about because aviation had transcended its nascent phase, where it had been dominated by the "crude efforts of the pioneer aviators" to the "domain of engineering" where "scientific engineers" prevailed.[28]

Appropriations for aviation in the Navy had been meager at best. In addition to the $25,000 set aside in the fiscal year 1912 budget, another $65,000 was forthcoming in fiscal year 1913—a substantial increase but much less than what Chambers requested and trifling in comparison to the European powers and Japan. Nevertheless, much had been accomplished over the past year and a half. Noteworthy were the acquisition of airplanes, the training of aviators, and the establishment of bases of operations, flight instruction, and experimentation at Hammondsport, North Island, and Greenbury Point. By the late summer of 1912, the Navy's first four aviators had accumulated more than 126 hours of flight time in three airplanes, with Ellyson and Towers leading the way with nearly eighty hours between them. On 6 October Towers had set a record with a flight of more than six hours in the A-2 at Annapolis. Experimentation and research had resulted in the development of the hydroairplane, the flying boat, lightweight and reliable aircraft engines, the catapult, and aeronautical instruments. More needed to be done, particularly with engine self-starters for hydros and flying boats and the development of a practical means of automatic stability to increase safety and lessen pilot fatigue on long flights, but nothing was more important than funding. Chambers could see no reason why a spending ceiling had been placed on airplanes, which were then categorized as "ship's equipment," when no such limits had been set for ship's boats, steering machinery, boilers, or other examples of ship's gear. The policy did not save any money and limited his and other aviation officers' flexibility to direct money where it was most needed. Chambers concluded his report with a recommendation for the establishment of a national aeronautical laboratory where systematic and well-funded research would secure American technological leadership and enhance the theoretical and practical understanding of aviation.[29]

Meanwhile, Curtiss had returned to Hammondsport on 3 October 1912 from his European trip, and was eager to get back to his work with the Navy, which included the new hydro (A-3) and another flying boat, designated C-1, the first of five such machines ordered by the service. A few days later

Chambers arrived in town to observe Curtiss and Ellyson put the C-1 through its paces. He liked what he saw, but insisted that the flying boat needed to be able to operate in adverse weather conditions if it were to find acceptance with the fleet. Curtiss agreed and arranged with Ellyson to have the flying boat shipped to Rochester, where he expected they could find wind and wave conditions on Lake Ontario to test the craft's all-weather capabilities.[30]

Ellyson went ahead to Rochester with one of Curtiss' mechanics. He arrived on 8 October and set up the flying boat in the armory in Summerville, on the lake just north of the city. In contrast to the usual airplane demonstrations, which more often than not were postponed or cancelled by bad weather, Ellyson said that "for the first time I prayed for wind and rough water before flying." He had to wait five days before a "northeaster" generated four-foot swells and a twelve to fifteen mile per hour wind offshore. Curtiss got the word while he was on business in New York and hurried to Rochester, arriving with Lena on the morning of the thirteenth. Also present for the tests were Henry Kleckler, Curtiss fliers Hugh Robinson and Beckwith Havens, and Lincoln Beachey. Rather than risk a change in the weather by waiting to make the flights in the afternoon as planned, Curtiss and Beachey hopped into the machine at about 11:00 AM, taxied down the Genesee River into the lake, and took off without any difficulty. They flew east, circled back to land in the water just off the end of Charlotte Boulevard, and brought the craft onto the beach, where Kleckler climbed on board for another flight out over the lake and back. Because he did not get word about the change in plans, Ellyson missed the flights, but he agreed with Curtiss that the trials proved beyond doubt the robustness and practicality of the flying boat.[31]

More testing of the C-1 followed that month and early the next in Hammondsport. Only one day after his marriage on 15 November, Ellyson got his orders to report to Hammondsport for the C-1's acceptance trials. The flights began with preliminary speed runs on the twentieth with Francis Wildman, one of Curtiss' factory pilots, at the controls. Richardson arrived on the twenty-sixth to lend a hand, which Ellyson much appreciated, because snow and below-freezing temperatures meant there was some urgency to complete the exercise. On a flight on the twenty-eighth, Ellyson found the flying boat's controls difficult to operate as a result of spray that had frozen on the cables. Two days later the machine passed its final tests, climbing to more than 1,500 feet in less than fifteen minutes and achieving nearly sixty miles per hour fully loaded over a measured-mile course. The prospect of more bad weather caused endurance flights to be waived, and the machine was packed up for shipment to Washington for further trials. Satisfied that the flying boat exceeded his and the Navy's expectations, Ellyson left for Washington on 1 December, the same day Curtiss closed up the house on the hill and set out across the country to spend another winter in San Diego.[32]

Among the Navy people drawn to Hammondsport that fall was Lt. Jerome C. Hunsaker, a Construction Corps officer specializing in aeronautics who wanted to observe firsthand what Curtiss was doing with hydros and flying boats. Like so many other visitors, Hunsaker found Curtiss to be a "genial and considerate host," and the pair shared a common interest in hunting and fishing and the outdoors in general. He stayed on a few more days after concluding his official business to join Curtiss in shooting pheasants among the vineyards along the lakeshore. As their professional relationship intersected numerous times over the next decade, their acquaintance grew into a personal friendship that lasted through the remainder of Curtiss' life.[33]

With Curtiss in San Diego there was nothing to keep the Navy in Hammondsport, so the aviation contingent moved back to Washington and Annapolis for the few weeks remaining in 1912. Chambers, Richardson, and Ellyson were primarily interested in the catapult, which they rightly saw as one of the keys to the success of aviation with the fleet, and they wanted to see how it worked with the new Curtiss flying boat. Ellyson was at the controls of the C-1 for the catapult test from the barge at the Washington Navy Yard on 17 December, which like the demonstration the month before was a complete success; Ellyson nonchalantly called it "routine." Noteworthy as it was, the achievement was only another step forward, for more development and improvements would be needed before the mechanism was ready to go to sea. In the interval, Chambers considered that enough progress had been made that it was time to send the fliers and their airplanes to Guantánamo, where they would finally have the opportunity to show the fleet what aviation could do, rather than follow Curtiss to North Island as had been done the previous two winters.[34]

The 1912–1913 season was Curtiss' last at North Island. When he learned that the Navy was headed for Guantánamo, he approached the Army to see if it was interested in using North Island, where he still had one more year remaining on his lease. With its fledgling aviation detachment divided in 1912 between the field at College Park, Maryland, and Augusta, Georgia, the Army's Signal Corps jumped at the opportunity to consolidate operations at North Island, where a number of early Army aviators had learned to fly with Curtiss in the winter and early spring of 1911. The first contingent arrived in November to stake a claim to the former Navy camp next to Spanish Bight, with the first airplanes—Curtisses—following by the middle of December. Later named Rockwell Field in memory of a young officer killed in an airplane accident, the site became the Army's first permanent aviation training facility.[35]

In contrast to the past two stays on the West Coast, the winter of 1912–1913 was nearly a four-month holiday for Curtiss and his family. He had no direct responsibility for instruction at the civilian school, having turned that over to another of his former students, John D. Cooper, and his obligations to the Army amounted to little more than ensuring that the North Island unit received the aircraft ordered from Hammondsport. Lt. Harold Geiger was in charge of the Army training school, which included three other officers and sixteen enlisted men. Lured by an eighteen-hole course at the Coronado Country Club within a stone's throw of his bungalow, Curtiss took up golf, which he enjoyed to the point where he fretted that it might become a "temptation" that took too much of his spare time. He flew when he wanted to fly, often taking up wealthy guests at the Hotel del Coronado on sightseeing flights, hoping that the experience would turn them into customers for one of his flying boats. And he retained some of his Navy connections by helping arrange a baseball series in March between the Army fliers at North Island and the submarine crews based at San Diego.[36]

Yet life was hardly carefree on the West Coast. Toward the end of February 1913 Curtiss learned that Judge Hazel in Buffalo had for a second time ruled against him in the patent case with the Wrights. Attempts to reconcile the differences between the two parties since Hazel's initial 1910 ruling had all come to naught. Moreover, following Wilbur's untimely death in May 1912, Orville had become increasingly preoccupied with the dispute, to the extent of blaming Curtiss for adding to the stress his brother had endured in the months leading up to his death. For Orville the fight with Curtiss transcended the legal to the personal, and there was no compromising with the man he now despised. Although Curtiss appealed Hazel's decision in the United States Circuit Court of Appeals and could temporarily continue to manufacture and sell airplanes, he knew from experience that he had little expectation of success in the long term.[37]

At North Island Curtiss continued to pursue experimental work, which included flights of a new airplane designed to meet Army specifications for a machine that could be used both as a scout and as a trainer. Curtiss began work on the project in the fall of 1912, but did not complete it before he left Hammondsport, entrusting shop foreman Henry Kleckler to finish the airplane and ship it to San Diego, where it arrived on 4 February. Unlike his pusher designs, the new airplane featured a tractor engine, which Curtiss expected would eliminate the risk of the engine breaking loose and slamming into the pilot in an accident. The wings, ailerons, tail surfaces, 8-cylinder engine, and control system were borrowed from those used on Curtiss flying boats, but there the similarities ended. The Model G tractor scout, as it was known, had the engine mounted in a cowling low in front of the pilot, with a three-blade chain-driven propeller, tricycle landing gear, and wings that could be neatly folded to allow easy railcar transportation or storage below decks on a ship. Test flights began on 11 February, only to end prematurely when one of the Army aviators damaged the machine in an accident a week later. Repairs took until the middle of March, when the more experienced John Cooper took over testing of the machine, which continued through the spring. The Army accepted the airplane following trials in June.[38]

Curtiss did not lack Navy projects either. One of them was a variant of the Triad known as the OWL (Over Water and Land), in which Chambers had taken a personal interest by the end of 1912. Based on preliminary specifications of the OWL sent to him by Chambers, Curtiss responded with a design proposal in early January 1913. With more than enough other work to occupy him, Curtiss did not accord the OWL a high priority, although he did test some aspects of the design in September of that year by modifying the A-2 with a new pontoon, tricycle landing gear that retracted into metal-lined pockets on the bottom and sides of the pontoon, lowered seats, and a wood-and-fabric hood over the front of the craft. Tests at Hammondsport in October revealed weight and hydrodynamic problems with the OWL that were never completely solved. Towers disliked the airplane, finding it inferior to both the hydro and the flying boat, although Chambers remained enthusiastic enough to authorize Curtiss to go ahead with an improved version, which the factory completed in late 1913.[39]

Despite lukewarm enthusiasm for the OWL, Chambers liked its potential flexibility and continued to champion it as an airplane that could accompany the fleet, then once ashore operate in conjunction with the Marines' advanced base force. The concept, involving the seizure of a chain of temporary support facilities, was integral to the movement of the American fleet across the Pacific in a war against Japan. Marine aircraft would help defend these bases as well as serve in reconnaissance and scouting roles. Chambers arranged to have two Marines, Lt. Bernard L. ("Barney") Smith and 2nd Lt. William M. McIlvain, train with the aviators at Annapolis in the fall of 1912. Smith was among those who flew the first OWL. The new OWL, larger and more substantially constructed than the first example, underwent further evaluation with the Marines during exercises in early 1914 off the island of Culebra in Puerto Rico, but apparently it never entered the Navy's aircraft inventory.[40]

Another project that greatly interested Chambers and the Navy in 1912 and 1913 was the development of a mechanism to enhance aircraft stability, one of the most elusive goals of early airplane builders and fliers. Many proposals had been put forward over the years to achieve stability in airplanes, generally breaking down into two categories: the first being instruments to enable the aviator to establish equilibrium under adverse weather and visibility conditions; and the second the use of mechanisms to achieve such equilibrium without pilot input. For the latter, as early as 1905–1906, the Wrights had begun to explore means of automatic stability, and in February 1908 had applied for a patent for a pendulum-and-vane "feedback" device to provide three-axis control. Curtiss, too, was interested in automatic stability, but believed the gyroscope, which had already been demonstrated as an effective means of ship stabilization, was the answer. In October 1908, Curtiss responded to a newspaper reporter's questions about Orville Wright's accident at Fort Myer the month before. Even though the investigation had revealed that a defective propeller had broken and severed the control wires of the Wright machine, Curtiss blamed "pilot error" and asserted that the cause was a "loss of equilibrium." "It is possible that the gyroscope will be brought in to play to overcome this [problem]," he concluded. In June 1910, following his historic Albany-to-New York flight, Curtiss met Elmer A. Sperry, an engineer well known for his work with the Navy on gyroscopic stabilization of ships and the development of the gyrocompass, who thought the gyroscope could be adapted for use in airplanes. Concurrently, Chambers understood that some means of automatic stability was crucial to his objective of aviation with the fleet. He was pleased to share his ideas with Curtiss, who had followed up his contact with Sperry to propose in early 1911 a scaled-down "entirely automatic" gyroscopically-controlled airplane that could be used by the Navy as a gunnery target.[41]

Sperry had given up on efforts to achieve automatic stability in airplanes after an abortive attempt in 1909–1910 to develop a stabilizer for a monoplane built by Stanley Beach, the aviation editor for the *Scientific American*. But Sperry changed his mind in the spring of 1912 when his son Lawrence decided to learn to fly and pursue a career as an aeronautical engineer. Finding Lawrence adamant about his decision, the elder Sperry reasoned that he might as well combine his interest in airplanes with a project to develop an automatic stabilizer using one gyroscope to provide longitudinal control and a second gyroscope for lateral control, each linked by compressed-air-driven servomotors to the flight surfaces. Fortuitously, Sperry's renewed interest in the technology coincided with Chambers' commitment to see the Navy take the lead in the development of a safe and stable airplane. Grasping the potential of Sperry's device, Chambers wrote to a junior officer in June 1912 that "I have been hammering at the aeroplane builders for some time, trying to get them interested in automatic or semi-automatic stabilizing mechanism" and that at last he seemed "on the verge of success." Curtiss also saw the possibilities. In July, he wrote to Elmer Sperry that recent airplane accidents might have been averted had his stabilizer been available, and that "this is the psychological moment to demonstrate such a device." Not long afterward, Chambers met with Sperry to discuss tests of a gyroscopic control mechanism fitted to the Curtiss C-1 flying boat when it was ready for flights at Hammondsport. Curtiss agreed to make the Navy machine available for the experiments.[42]

Shortly after Curtiss returned from Europe in early October 1912, Lawrence delivered a version of the control device to Hammondsport for preliminary testing. Because the C-1 was still not completed, the mechanism was installed on Curtiss' first flying boat. For Lawrence, not yet twenty in the fall of 1912, Hammondsport was a treat. He stayed at Lulu Mott's place, where he met one aviator after another, befriending them all, especially Ellyson, who affectionately nicknamed him "Gyro." He went up with Curtiss in the flying boat on Thanksgiving to test the stabilizer, which provided excellent lateral control despite "puffy winds." In another flight in late November to test lateral stability, Ellyson verified that Sperry's device "seemed to function perfectly." The elder Sperry was also happy with the results and told Ellyson before he left Hammondsport that he hoped the device could be demonstrated in the C-1 at Guantánamo and that he was "anxious that the Navy get the credit for developing the stabilizer." Chambers, however, preferred more tests before he was ready to exhibit the mechanism to the fleet. With snow and cold weather hampering further work in Hammondsport, Sperry decided to accept Curtiss' offer to continue experiments with him in San Diego for the remainder of the winter.[43]

Before the end of January, Sperry equipped a flying boat Curtiss had supplied to the Army with the stabilizer and began a series of trials at North Island to perfect the longitudinal control mechanism. All did not go well. An accident in February destroyed the stabilizer-equipped airplane and badly injured the Army aviator. While waiting for a new flying boat, Sperry temporarily fitted the device to one of the Curtiss landplanes, which he and Lieutenant

Geiger used to test the longitudinal control apparatus in a series of flights in late March and early April. During one demonstration, Geiger maneuvered over and around the Navy ships in the bay, impressing everyone with the way the stabilizer-equipped machine held steady in banking turns. But another crash on 8 April killed one of the Army pilots and wrecked the new flying boat, effectively ending Sperry's experiments and serving as another sobering reminder of the dangers inherent in aviation. Neither flying boat accident had been caused by the control mechanism, but the experiments at North Island showed that perfection of the Sperry stabilizer would need a good deal more time and verified the reservations Chambers had about the control system. Despite mounting expenses and nagging technical obstacles, Chambers assured Sperry that he and Curtiss remained committed to the project.[44]

Curtiss returned to Hammondsport in April 1913. Sperry joined him a month later, intending to install an improved and simplified version of the stabilizer in the C-2, the second of the Navy flying boats. Still supportive of the project, Chambers was mindful that while Sperry "claimed that satisfactory progress" had been made with the stabilizer at San Diego, "as yet no Navy Aviator has had an opportunity to test it in any of the Navy machines." Chambers wanted to see results as soon as possible, but he had to wait until July, when Marine Barney Smith and Navy Lt. Patrick N. L. Bellinger, who had learned to fly with Towers at Annapolis and Guantánamo the previous fall and winter, were in Hammondsport to try out Sperry's apparatus. Officially retired at the end of June, but still actively in charge of aviation, Chambers traveled to Hammondsport with his wife Isabella in the middle of July to combine a short vacation with an up-close look at the stabilizer-equipped flying boat.[45]

Dick Richardson was also in Hammondsport to provide an engineer's perspective on the stabilizer and verify that adequate progress was being made. His investigations revealed that while in theory the three-axis control worked well, in reality it was unable to make the subtle adjustments needed as aircraft attitude, load, speed, altitude, propeller thrust, and other factors entered the equation. He concluded that although the device was useful and even necessary, automatic control was not a substitute for a skilled and experienced aviator. Bellinger and Sperry confirmed Richardson's positive appraisal of the project with scores of flights in the summer and fall. On one round-trip from Hammondsport to Penn Yan, a distance of more than forty miles in "squally weather," Bellinger did not once touch the airplane's controls. Despite such progress, Chambers had to cancel a demonstration scheduled for members of the House Naval Affairs Committee in October because he had no assurances that the device would function adequately and he did not want to risk a public failure.[46]

Following the experiments in San Diego and Hammondsport in 1913, the Sperrys acknowledged that the control mechanism required more development and before the end of the year concentrated on an improved version using a single stabilized platform on which the controlling gyros were mounted, in place of the separate mechanisms used previously. In January 1914, confident that the new stabilizer would work, Lawrence entered a "safe airplane" contest sponsored by the French and arranged with Curtiss to use one of his flying boats in the competition. With his aviator's license from the Curtiss school in hand, Lawrence put the machine through a rigorous series of tests before the French judges and his anxious parents, beating the European competition to win a substantial prize for the best airplane control mechanism.[47] A result of a three-way collaboration among Curtiss, the Sperrys, and the Navy, the automatic stabilizer was one of the significant achievements in early aviation history, earning Elmer Sperry the coveted Collier Trophy in 1914, and pointing the way toward safer and more stable aircraft of the future.

Curtiss had been more than pleased to let Sperry use one of his airplanes in the French safe-flying contest, viewing it as another opportunity to demonstrate the safety and reliability of his flying boat to overseas customers. In fact, one of the reasons why Curtiss had not been able to observe many of the stabilizer experiments in Hammondsport in the early fall of 1913 was because he had been in Europe on a sales trip. He embarked in New York on the new Hamburg-American liner *Imperator* on 30 August, bound for England, France, and other European countries on a whirlwind tour to sell flying boats and hydroairplanes. He met with particular success in Russia, where Charlie Witmer had been training naval aviators at Sevastopol in Curtiss hydros, and where there was interest in setting up a factory in St. Petersburg to manufacture Curtiss airplanes free from patent restrictions. Curtiss himself demonstrated his new Model F flying boat on the south coast of England, hoping that it would garner orders from wealthy sportsman fliers. The Model F was successful in part due to its 90-horsepower OX engine, one in a series of engines that had evolved after 1911 largely as a result of Navy demands for more power in its Curtiss hydros and flying boats. Though not without its faults, the engine by the end of 1913 was widely respected for its combination of power and dependability. Curtiss returned on the North German Lloyd liner *George Washington* from Bremen, reaching New York on 26 October.[48]

With the expiration of his three-year lease at North Island limiting his warm-weather options in the late fall of 1913, Curtiss decided to return to Europe, where he could combine relaxation with his family and follow up on the business contacts he had made on his earlier trip. "The business of aeroplane building abroad, where the governments are taking [an] active interest in aviation, is too good to lose," he told reporters. "Here, on the contrary, there is not enough work to make my Hammondsport factory pay. . . . For a long time I have been sending a major part of our output abroad." With Lena, Glenn Jr., and the family's nurse Miss Minnie Hendershott, he left New York on the French liner *Lorraine* on 3 December, planning to attend an aeronautics show in Paris before heading to the south of France where he had rented a villa on the Mediterranean in Nice. It was almost idyllic, but it did not last. On 13 January word came that the federal appeals court had upheld Judge Hazel's decision on the Wright patent case. Leaving his family in Naples where he was to demonstrate the flying boat for the Italian government, Curtiss cut short his stay, sailing from Cherbourg on 1 February and arriving ten days later in New York to review his options with his legal brain trust. Another compelling reason to come home was that preliminary negotiations on an ambitious project to design and build a big new flying boat were about to come to fruition.[49]

—8—

Headwinds

As he stepped off the North German Lloyd liner *Prinz Friedrich Wilhelm* in New York on 10 February 1914, Curtiss confronted a calendar jammed with details needing his immediate attention—starting with decisions about the next legal step following the United States Circuit Court of Appeals decision upholding Judge Hazel's prior ruling in favor of the Wrights.[1] It was clear to Curtiss and his legal team that the appellate opinion meant that the Wrights did not hold a patent on merely the means for lateral control of an airplane but that for all practical purposes they owned monopoly rights to the airplane itself.

Content with having won a personal victory over Curtiss, Orville Wright opposed his own company's board of directors, who wanted to take swift action to put Curtiss and other manufacturers out of business. This left the door open for Curtiss and his legal advisers to consider a fresh strategy in their battle with Wright. Curtiss received timely legal assistance from W. Benton Crisp, a lawyer notable for advising Henry Ford in his struggle to break the notorious automobile patent held by George Selden. Written defensively so as to cover all self-propelled "road engines" and upheld in various infringement suits, the patent demanded royalty payments from all automobile manufacturers. Ford refused to do so, and after eight years of legal battles won a favorable court decision in 1911. Even though Selden, a lawyer, had not invented anything, while the Wrights, obviously, had introduced one of the most important technologies of the twentieth century, Ford believed that Curtiss' case was similar to his own. He met Curtiss in Hammondsport and promised Crisp's legal help if he wanted it.[2]

With Crisp at the helm, Curtiss' high-powered legal team devised a clever plan of action to force the Wright interests back to court in a fresh round of infringement suits. If the heart of the Wright patent covered the simultaneous manipulation of wing warping or ailerons to achieve lateral control, why not introduce a system to decouple the ailerons and ensure that only one on each wing functioned at the same time? Subsequently, Curtiss announced that a careful reading of the appellate decision showed that the validity of the Wright patent rested not on claims for the originality of any individual element of the airplane's design, but rather on a control system based on a novel "combination" of systems allowing three-axis stability. Henceforth, so as not to be in violation of the Wright patent, his airplanes would no longer be capable of simultaneous aileron movements. Sure enough, the strategy worked. When the Wright company once more sued for infringement in federal court in Buffalo, the judge ordered the injunction against Curtiss lifted, which allowed his company to manufacture airplanes unimpeded for the time being.[3]

Far more attractive to Curtiss as aviator and innovator than the tedious legal confrontation with Wright was an ambitious project to design and build an airplane capable of crossing the Atlantic. For nearly a century the Atlantic had beckoned. First to pick up the challenge were nineteenth-century American aeronauts, some of whom died in their attempts to cross the ocean by balloon and others who saw their ambitions crushed in the face of technological and financial realities. Airships, particularly large ones with rigid structures such as those designed and built by the German Zeppelin company, promised long range and excellent load-carrying capacity and seemed a good bet to be the first across.[4] In contrast, the airplane in the second decade of the century seemed incapable of long-duration flights, but the development of the flying boat by Curtiss in 1912 and 1913 appeared to offer at least some chance of success. As for Curtiss personally, he found it impossible to resist the lure of the Atlantic, which stirred his competitive and creative soul, while in Washington a project of such magnitude resonated well with Chambers, still looking for ways to demonstrate further the potential of the airplane at sea.

Curtiss seems to have been inspired about a transatlantic flight as early as 1912, when he suggested that the flying boat had the potential to leap the ocean between Nova Scotia and Ireland. Yet Curtiss' imagination far outdistanced the technical realities of 1912 or even 1913, although the six-plus-hour endurance flight of Towers at Annapolis in October 1912 and the big, four-passenger flying boat built for Chicago millionaire and aviation enthusiast Harold F. McCormick in 1913 pointed tantalizingly to the possibility. Chambers, too, had such a flight in mind. In May, Chambers responded to an inquiry from a Pennsylvania man who had proposed building a transatlantic airplane with a polite admission that his "conception of the requisites is correct [but] that it will require more time than you anticipate to develop the right machine." Curtiss first broached the idea to Chambers in a letter of 26 November 1913: "The latest thing in aviation is a proposition for trans-Atlantic flight. I do not know as yet whether it will materialize, but it is assuming a very interesting aspect."[5]

Presumably, Curtiss was alluding to discussions he had with Lewis Rodman Wanamaker, scion of the Philadelphia department store family, about underwriting a transatlantic flight. While heading his father's department store operations in Paris, Wanamaker had avidly followed Louis Blériot's Channel flight, and had become a devout convert to aviation. He had bought a Blériot type XI monoplane that he took back to Philadelphia in the fall of 1909. When, where, and how Curtiss met Wanamaker is not known. Possibly it was at a meeting of the Aero Club of America in New York as early as June 1913. Regardless, they were both intrigued by the announcement that had been made on 31 March 1913 by the *London Daily Mail's* Lord Northcliffe of a $50,000 prize for the first successful flight across the Atlantic. Asked by Wanamaker about the prospects for such a flight, Curtiss responded that "it was only a question of money and mathematics and the building of a stronger motor." Before Curtiss left for Europe in August on his sales tour, he went over rough sketches of a transatlantic airplane with Wanamaker and got the go-ahead to design and build a big flying boat specifically for the Atlantic crossing.[6]

While Curtiss was in England demonstrating his Model F flying boat that fall, he met with members of the Royal Aero Club and others to discuss his ideas for a transatlantic flight. There he ran into John Cyril Porte, a former Royal Navy lieutenant who was working as a test pilot for the White and Thompson Company, Curtiss' sales agents in Britain. Porte's enthusiasm for the project, his flying experience, and his comprehensive navigation skills led Curtiss to short-list him as someone to keep in mind for the transatlantic flight.[7]

Initially the idea was to follow Curtiss' earlier suggestion about a nonstop flight to Ireland, leaving from Newfoundland instead of Nova Scotia and using a relatively small flying boat with the new 200-horsepower Model V-2 liquid-cooled V-8 engine driving a tractor propeller. Curtiss believed, and Wanamaker concurred, that the flight should be made at ten thousand feet, where the west-to-east winds would boost the airplane's average speed to more than seventy-five miles per hour and allow the 1,800-mile crossing to be made in less than twenty-four hours. Two pilots—one British and one American, to underscore the solidarity between the two nations—would spell each other during the flight. These schemes remained strictly confidential through the fall of 1913, with no "leaks" until December, when the *Hammondsport Herald* ran a piece on Lt. Hermann Wahl, a German naval constructor who was in town to accept a flying boat for the German navy. On his arrival in New York, Wahl had told reporters that he was in the country to gather information on the rumored transatlantic airplane, then hastily backpedaled and said that what he really meant was that he was interested in the shipment of flying boats across the ocean. In early January Curtiss dodged British reporters' questions about competing for the *Daily Mail* prize by telling them that he had not signed any formal contracts with anyone for a transatlantic airplane.[8]

All the speculation about the transatlantic flight was at last confirmed as Curtiss was on his way back from Europe in early 1914. On 4 February, Wanamaker wrote to Alan R. Hawley, president of the Aero Club of America, of his "intention of crossing the Atlantic by one flight, if possible. . . . I sincerely hope," he continued, "that the operators and navigators may be from the Navy of the United States and of Great Britain, because naval aeronauts have the qualifications to navigate this uncharted journey in the air. . . . The transatlantic flyer to be used in the journey is now being constructed by Mr. Glenn H. Curtiss, from plans that we have been studying for a long time. . . . The crossing of the Atlantic Ocean in one flight of an aircraft is, to my mind, as important to aerial navigation as was the voyage of Columbus to transportation by water." Upon his arrival in New York on the tenth, Curtiss told the press that he was "full of confidence" that the flying boat he was building in Hammondsport would be a success, adding that "if the weather conditions are right there will be nothing to hinder the flight," which two experienced naval aviators would attempt toward the end of July.[9]

On 17 February, Capt. Mark L. Bristol, Chambers' relief in charge of aviation, confirmed the Navy's interest in the endeavor and his trust in Curtiss. Writing to the chief of the Bureau of Navigation, Bristol requested orders to send John Towers to New York City "to confer with Mr. Glenn Curtiss in regard to the design and flying of an aeroplane across the Atlantic." Bristol was certain that the project was not "a wild cat scheme," but if it turned out not to be practicable he trusted Towers as "the best man to represent us" in making an accurate assessment of its chances of success. There was a bonus, too. Towers could take the opportunity to debrief Curtiss on the latest European developments in aeronautics. Two days later, Towers received his orders to temporary duty, leaving the new permanent aeronautics station at Pensacola, in the panhandle of Florida, and arriving in New York on 23 February.[10]

In New York Towers met Curtiss, Wanamaker, and Porte, now confirmed as one of the pilots for the flight, in the Aero Club of America offices to discuss plans for the project. Towers concurred with the others on making the flight nonstop, if possible, but disagreed with Curtiss about his idea to cruise at ten thousand feet or more to take advantage of the prevailing winds. Rather, he suggested, it was best to stay at one thousand feet or less, where the aviators could spot station ships more easily and better plot their angle of drift by observing wave action. Towers' recommendation—based on his considerable experience in overwater flights—was to "stick close to the water, to study the compass, to watch the course of ships, and be ready to alight and make repairs if necessary." Towers then followed Curtiss to Hammondsport to go over specifics of the project, especially the flying boat plans. Curtiss cautioned him and the Navy that "at present, the details of construction be kept secret, as this machine will embody several features which are not yet patented." Towers returned to Pensacola "with the idea I'd come back north in May, as both Curtiss and Wanamaker wanted me to be the American pilot."[11]

A potential legal stumbling block to the project came at the end of February when Orville Wright announced that due to the recent circuit court decision Curtiss "would not be allowed to build a transatlantic aeroplane in the United States." He could, Wright surmised, construct the airplane in Canada, "the only civilized country in which our patents are not recognized," but there would be no place to land on the other side of the Atlantic where the patents did not obtain. He repeated his argument that no one could manufacture and fly airplanes without securing a license to do so from the Wright company, which could be arranged for a reasonable fee. The sole exception was Curtiss, who would never be granted a license to manufacture airplanes under any circumstances. Wanamaker's lawyer asserted that the arrangements with Curtiss for the transatlantic airplane had been made well before the court's decision and that the project could go ahead as planned. Curtiss had no comment other than a brief statement that he would receive no money for the flying boat until after it had been successfully tested. Perhaps because he did not take the transatlantic project seriously, Wright did not pursue further legal action against either Curtiss or Wanamaker.[12]

Wright's doubts about the probability of success seemed to be warranted when the V-2 motor was destroyed in bench tests in early March, forcing Curtiss to rethink the whole project. Scrapping the design for a small, fast airplane, Curtiss turned his attention to a larger flying boat, powered by a pair of his 90-horsepower water-cooled OX V-8 engines mounted between the wings and driving two pusher propellers. Towers reported to Bristol on 10 March that the new design was "fairly well worked out" and that the flying boat would probably be ready for flight tests in late May or early June.[13]

Construction of the flying boat, designated the Model H Transatlantic Flyer, occupied most of Curtiss' time in the spring of 1914. In addition to Porte, Curtiss had help on the ambitious project from George E. A. Hallett, a skilled and experienced engine mechanic who had been with Curtiss since his early North Island days. Those who saw the machine came away with an overwhelming impression of size—it was big, one of the largest airplanes in the world at the time. The airplane was more than 37 feet long, with an upper wing spanning 74 feet and a lower wing 46 feet long. It had a 4-foot-wide hull built up of cedar planking on an ash and oak frame, doubled in thickness on the V-shaped bottom to cope with the stress of landings and takeoffs. A single step was built into the hull just forward of the trailing edge of the lower wing. The wings themselves were of conventional wood construction, covered in lightweight but not very durable silk. Sitting side-by-side in a fully enclosed cabin with celluloid windows, the pilots were so close to one another that Curtiss used foot bars instead of the usual shoulder yokes to operate the ailerons, which were not interconnected and functioned independently of one another in accordance with the quest to find a loophole in the Wright patent.[14]

Anxious about the deliberate pace of the work on the big flying boat, Porte pointed out that the French and Germans had already made sixteen-hour endurance flights. He urged Curtiss to accelerate the project and aim for an attempt in June. Before leaving Hammondsport to return to England in early March, he told reporters that "naturally I want to be the first one to make the Trans-Atlantic flight, and don't think we should take the chance of letting someone beat us." More cautious, Curtiss thought the weather would be better later in the summer, and he also wanted more time for testing, but Porte continued to agitate for an earlier rather than later deadline. By the middle of April the hull had been framed in, the wings largely completed, and the engines nearly ready for testing.[15]

As the Model H project moved forward, diplomatic relations between the United States and Mexico's revolutionary government deteriorated, reaching a crisis after a minor incident involving American sailors and Mexican officials in Tampico on 9 April. Determined to use naval force to block illegal arms shipments to the Mexican regime, President Woodrow Wilson ordered the Navy to prepare to occupy the east coast port city of Veracruz. Towers and two other naval aviators received orders to take a Curtiss hydro and a Curtiss flying boat to Tampico in the cruiser *Birmingham*, while Bellinger and three other officers were dispatched to Veracruz in the battleship *Mississippi* along with another Curtiss hydro and flying boat. On 22 April, Navy ships bombarded key installations in Veracruz a day after American bluejackets had stormed ashore to occupy the city.[16]

Towers and the *Birmingham* aviators were idle in Tampico, but Bellinger and the other fliers took their airplanes ashore to carry out spotting and reconnaissance missions in support of the Veracruz operation—the first time Americans flew in combat. Towers and his group arrived later to assist Bellinger's *Mississippi* contingent with scouting and other duties, which continued on and off until the unit pulled out in the second week of June. With the transatlantic flight looming and uncertain when Towers would be relieved of his duties in Mexico, Curtiss reluctantly decided to scratch Towers from the crew. He wrote to Towers that "I fear that this Mexican affair will interfere with any plan for your engaging in the trans-Atlantic enterprise," although he wanted Towers to stay close to the project in case Porte dropped out for some reason. As Towers' replacement, Curtiss chose Hallett, whose talents might well come in handy should there be any mechanical snags during the flight.[17]

While he was in England, Porte met Capt. F. Creagh-Osborne of the Royal Navy, an expert in navigation and instruments who convinced Porte that making the flight in stages was preferable to nonstop. The first leg from Newfoundland to the Azores was about 1,100 miles, compared to 1,800 miles direct to Ireland, and it would take about twenty hours. The second stage of the flight would be from the Azores to Vigo in Spain (960 miles), and the third and last leg could hug the coast north past France to Plymouth in England. The two major disadvantages were that the route was south of the usual sea lanes, which meant not being able to rely on ships for guidance or rescue, and that hitting the Azores, nine tiny islands aggregating less than nine hundred square miles spread out over thirty-six thousand square miles, demanded expert navigation and superior instruments. Creagh-Osborne assured Porte that the compasses he had developed would be more than adequate for the task and that he would assist him and Curtiss in their installation and use. Apprehensive that potential competitors would highjack the scheme, Porte kept it to himself until he returned to Hammondsport, where he found Curtiss amenable to the new flight plan.[18]

Wanamaker's people found a good starting point for the adventure in a sheltered bay south of St. John's, Newfoundland. To scout out locations for the first intermediate stop, Curtiss dispatched Lanny Callan, one of the

North Island gang, to the Azores. Callan exemplified Curtiss' continuing Navy connections. After learning to fly at North Island in the winter of 1911–1912, Callan had signed on as an instructor at Hammondsport in the summer of 1913, during which he became friends with Bellinger, Richardson, Ens. Godfrey de Courcelles ("Chevy") Chevalier, and other naval aviators posted to Hammondsport or passing through on temporary duty. Given the rapport Callan had with these men, it made sense for Curtiss to assign him the job of helping assemble and service flying boats and hydros when the Navy moved from Annapolis to Pensacola, Florida, in January 1914. During a two-month stay in Pensacola, Callan bunked with Towers and other aviators in the battleship *Mississippi*, and flew from tent hangars on the beach, earning respect as a member of that tightly-knit, elite group of pioneer fliers.[19]

Fulfilling his responsibilities for the transatlantic project, Callan arranged for the fliers to land at Ponta Delgada, on the island of Sao Miguel about two hundred miles farther east from Newfoundland than locations in the center of the archipelago but as the largest city in the islands offering superior port facilities to any of the other locales. Callan's preparations included emergency supplies on the island of Fayal to the west in case the flying boat had to put down prematurely, and a ship at Ponta Delgada where the fliers could rest while their craft underwent repairs and refueling. He remained in the islands ready to act if necessary as a relief pilot for the second leg to Spain. Wanamaker in the meantime sailed for Europe to handle details of the last stage of the flight from Spain to England.[20]

It was obvious to Curtiss and everyone else involved with the design of the big transatlantic flying boat that they needed to come to grips with the problem of maximizing the airplane's disposable lift, or useful load. A common yardstick employed by aeronautical engineers to gauge an airplane's load-carrying efficiency is the load-to-tare ratio—that is, the ratio between the airplane's total load capacity and its empty weight. Ideally an airplane should be able to carry something close to its empty weight, but before World War II a load-to-tare ratio exceeding 40:60 was good. Not much could be done with the tare weight of the Model H given its wood and fabric construction and the weight of its engines and accessories, so within the ratio the only variables that could realistically be traded off against each other were payload and fuel. For example, payload can be increased on a short flight that does not require much fuel, or on a longer flight payload will have to shrink to accommodate more fuel. From much experience, Curtiss knew he could increase the weight of fuel and decrease the payload (or conversely, decrease the weight of fuel and increase the payload) within the airplane's total disposable lift, and he understood that these numbers were immutable—the "magic" figures that dictated the success or failure of the entire venture. To fly nonstop to the Azores from Newfoundland, the craft would have to carry a minimum of three hundred gallons of gasoline, weighing roughly 1,800 pounds. With an empty (tare) weight of about three thousand pounds, and a maximum takeoff weight (MTOW) exceeding five thousand pounds, the craft's useful load was two thousand pounds, yielding an outstanding load-to-tare ratio of 44:56—comparable to that of flying boats a generation later. The 1,800 pounds of fuel, however, took up nearly all of the airplane's useful load and might not even be enough for the Newfoundland–Azores flight.[21]

A quick business trip to New York kept Curtiss from finishing assembly of the flying boat until Sunday, 21 June, only one day before the scheduled ceremonial launch of the craft, which Wanamaker had patriotically named *America*. Over the weekend a substantial crowd had converged on Hammondsport in anticipation of the event, including a large contingent from the press. Present, too, was Towers, back from service in Mexico and assigned to monitor the project for Rear Adm. Bradley Fiske, aide for operations in the office of the secretary of the Navy. As one of the Navy's most technically and politically savvy officers, Fiske had considerable interest in determining how best to integrate aviation with the fleet. Not until early evening on the twenty-second was the flying boat ready, painted bright red for visibility and sitting on its two-wheel beaching gear at the Curtiss flying field a short distance from the edge of the lake. Joining Curtiss on the platform in front of the *America* were Porte, Hallett, and sixteen-year-old Katherine Masson, the daughter of Leon J. Masson of the Pleasant Valley Wine Company, who had the honor of christening the new machine. After reciting a short and badly-written poem by Albert Zahm, there representing the Smithsonian Institution, Masson swung a bottle of Great Western champagne against the craft's bow, only to have it fail to break. Once more she tried and once more the bottle remained intact. Much to the amusement of the more than five hundred spectators who had gathered for the event, Porte took over, fastening the bottle to the hull, whacking it with a hammer, and for his gallantry getting soaked with Hammondsport's best. By this time it was well after 6:30 PM and too late for any test flights, which were put off until the following day.[22]

The *America* took off for the first time on the afternoon of 23 June for a short flight, with Curtiss at the controls and Porte and Hallett on board. A second trial followed, this time with Porte doing the flying and Curtiss as passenger. Both extolled the airplane's performance. Porte said "it was the finest flying craft he was ever in" and was "steady as a rock." Curtiss remarked that "I can say that this boat is built to meet every condition of a transatlantic flight. I am more than satisfied with the America. I am convinced that it can do its work. The trial flight has shown us that a few minor changes are necessary but that the America is, as it stands nearly as perfect as it can be made."[23]

Anticipating difficulties getting the craft to lift from the water with the 1,800-pound fuel load, Curtiss had fixed small fins on each side of the hull, but they did not have much effect. On the twenty-seventh, fitted with a set of larger hull extensions, the America took off with seven people on board and ballast totaling nearly 1,500 pounds. All seemed well. Observing the airplane from a trailing motorboat, Curtiss predicted that "it can fly easily with the load it must take when it leaves Newfoundland." Three days later, the craft made three flights, on one of which—with ten reporters on board and ballast—the load was close to the 1,800-pound objective. Curtiss was pleased with the results, although now the airplane exhibited some longitudinal hydrodynamic instability, or "porpoising." As before, Curtiss remained optimistic—perhaps overly so—repeating his earlier assertion that "only a few minor details have to be changed" before the America was "ready for its long flight."[24]

Further tests, however, showed that far more than "minor details" would need to be taken care of before the big flying boat was ready to cross the Atlantic, or for that matter even to fly the length of Lake Keuka. On the morning of 1 July, Porte took the America out twice, returning to pronounce that the "performance was not satisfactory and that it would be impossible" to meet the planned 11 July departure date set for the transatlantic flight. Then he abruptly left Hammondsport for New York that evening. The next day Curtiss made a short flight at more than the maximum load, implying that the airplane was not the problem but that Porte's flying skills were. At the same time, Porte denied any rift with Curtiss and reassured the press that the transatlantic flight, though set back a week, was still on. Curtiss successfully flew the airplane on one engine on 5 July, but Porte found subsequent tests to be "discouraging" despite more adjustments to the hydrodynamic surfaces, forcing another week's postponement of the transatlantic departure. Keeping the best face on what was obviously becoming a major setback, Curtiss insisted that only a "few days" more work would solve the problems, although knowledgeable observers thought solutions would take weeks, thereby jeopardizing the entire venture.[25]

Richardson joined Towers in Hammondsport in the middle of July, ostensibly to observe test flights of a new Navy hydro but more important to lend his professional engineering analysis to the problems afflicting the big Curtiss flying boat. He was on the scene for tests of what was known as the "Viper" sea sled, a V-shaped surface that was reputed to offer much-reduced hydrodynamic resistance. Grafted to the bottom of the hull and tested on the eighteenth, the "Viper" did nothing more than cause so much drag that the airplane "churned" through the water far short of the speed needed for planing, let alone taking off.[26]

Immediately after the failure of the "Viper" experiment, Curtiss called a summit conference with Porte, Hallett, Towers, Richardson, and Wanamaker's representative William D. Gash to review the situation and come up with a new course of action. The next day Richardson wrote to Bristol that the "Viper" bottom and other modifications to the *America*'s hull had thrown off the center of gravity, causing the machine to "stall" at a relatively low speed under full power and placing the hull at an attitude where it could not plane. Curtiss had resisted rebuilding the hull to a different configuration for fear of exacerbating the porpoising problem and incurring further delays. Richardson later argued that another reason why the *America* had encountered hydrodynamic problems was because of changes Curtiss had made to the rear of the hull that increased water resistance and pulled the tail of the aircraft down. Rather than a recommendation for further time-consuming modifications to the hull, the consensus from the meeting was to take what Curtiss called a "short cut" and fit a third OX engine to the airplane in order to increase power on takeoff, after which the power plant could be shut down to decrease fuel consumption.[27]

Working day and night against the 1 August deadline to ship the flying boat from Hammondsport, the Curtiss people completed the modifications before dark on 23 July. The third engine was mounted on top of the upper wing, with a three-blade tractor propeller. The installation looked clumsy and weighed more than five hundred pounds, but Curtiss estimated it would yield another 1,600 pounds of disposable lift, plenty to ensure enough fuel for the ocean crossing. Once more his engineering instincts seemed right, for the *America* lifted off with a load of more than 2,600 pounds, leading Curtiss to call for more ballast and exult that "this is what we have been looking for for a long time. . . . I can't hold her down." Sadly, his optimism evaporated less than forty-eight hours later. When Porte and Hallett took the big flying boat on a flight to Penn Yan and back on the twenty-fourth they found that fuel consumption was "considerably greater than estimated" with a light load and not running the third engine. Curtiss guessed that the reason for the poor numbers was the drag caused by the windmilling propeller on the third engine and thought that operating that engine at reduced throttle would solve the problem. Tests the next day verified Curtiss' hypothesis about the drag induced by the stationary propeller and inert engine but also confirmed that no fewer than four hundred gallons (nearly 2,500 pounds) of fuel would be needed to make the Azores with any margin of safety. There was no question that the airplane would have to be substantially rebuilt, requiring at least two weeks, and that the flight would have to be postponed until 1 October.[28]

Porte declared that the decision to delay the flight was a "great disappointment to all of us" and boarded a train for New York to wait until the *America* was again ready for testing. Curtiss said that they had "nothing to lose and everything to gain" by waiting and predicted that an early fall flight might find even better weather than expected in the summer. Almost immediately workers started disassembling the big flying boat, while Curtiss considered changes to the hull to overcome the hydrodynamic woes that had plagued the airplane from its inception. The result by the end of August was a vastly improved airplane, featuring tapered sponsons on each side of the forward part of the hull to augment buoyancy and add more planing surface. Other changes reduced the weight of the hull, which, coupled with rebuilt engines with more displacement and 15 percent more power, allowed the third engine to be removed, cut fuel consumption, and brought the endurance up to where the Newfoundland–Azores leg was again possible. But by then it was too late. Germany had invaded neutral Belgium on 4 August, plunging France, Britain, and nearly all of Europe into the terrifying abyss of World War I. Within days, Porte gave up his Atlantic dream to return to England to go on active aviation duty with the Royal Navy, and the Aero Club announced that the transatlantic flight was off until the end of hostilities.[29]

The travails of the *America* and the failure of the transatlantic project in the summer of 1914 provide further evidence of the deficiencies of Curtiss' empirical approach to aeronautical engineering. For the most part, his intuition had served him well, resulting in such breakthroughs as his control system, the hydroairplane, and most dramatically the flying boat. But even with the hydro and flying boat, it had taken a painstaking process of trial and error before Curtiss had devised float and hull configurations that overcame serious hydrodynamic obstacles. With the *America*, more than twice the size and weight of even his biggest previous airplanes, Curtiss had strayed into new territory, where prior experience did not obtain and where mathematical theory and systematic experimentation were essential. Exacerbating the technical challenges Curtiss faced in 1914 was a tight deadline to get the transatlantic flying boat ready before the narrow weather window closed at the end of the summer. Without knowing it, Curtiss had crossed a technological threshold where old cut-and-try methodologies gave way to new research and development realities that were to define the future trajectory of aeronautics.

Where aviation was headed in the United States had for years also been bound by the seemingly never-ending patent dispute between the Wrights and Curtiss. In a peculiar juxtaposition, Curtiss' 1914 quest to defend himself and his company against the Wright claims meshed with efforts by the Smithsonian Institution to revive the reputation of former secretary Samuel P. Langley, by rebuilding his old aerodrome and proving that it indeed was capable of flight. The idea had been mooted not too long after Langley's death in 1906, gaining traction through the advocacy of Bell and Chanute, as well as Charles D. Walcott, the current secretary of the Smithsonian and a staunch supporter of Langley's aeronautical experiments. Added momentum came with the creation of the Smithsonian's Langley Aerodynamical Laboratory in 1913, headed by Albert Zahm. A witness for Curtiss in the patent case, Zahm averred scientific impartiality, arguing that his interest was to demonstrate whether or not the Langley machine was flight-worthy and to explore "more fully the advantages of the tandem wing type of aeroplane." As for Curtiss, a successful demonstration of the Langley aerodrome would provide evidence of prior practice and help to undermine Wright's case as the litigation entered a new phase following the appellate court's ruling.[30] From its inception, the Langley aerodrome project had behind it an abundance of motives far beyond simply a demonstration of a historical aviation artifact.

Curtiss exhibition pilot Lincoln Beachey was most likely first in taking the step from sentiment to reality when he asked on 21 January 1914 that he be permitted to reconstruct and fly the Langley machine using a new motor. As a member of the Smithsonian Board of Regents, Bell argued against the proposal, and Walcott declined Beachey's request, while still holding open the possibility of building and flying an exact copy. Once he heard of Beachey's idea, Curtiss sought out Bell's advice. On 16 February, he wrote to Bell: "There has been some talk of reproducing the old Langley machine and having it flown. I should like to know what you think of this plan, as it would be an easy thing to do, provided it is worthwhile." Faced with Orville Wright's fierce determination to prohibit him from manufacturing airplanes even under license, Curtiss made no secret of the possible legal benefits that would accrue should someone demonstrate that Langley's aerodrome was capable of flight. He wrote to Beachey in March that a demonstration of the machine "would go a long way toward showing that the Wrights did not invent the flying machine as a whole but only a balancing device," and that in the next round of litigation "we would get a better decision."[31]

Not surprisingly, given his close association with the Smithsonian and Curtiss, Bell served as intermediary in bringing the two together on the Langley project. Walcott phoned Bell on 25 March to tell him that Curtiss was enthusiastic about building a replica of the Langley aerodrome and that he thought it could be completed within a little more than a month at a cost of about $2,000. When Bell told him that he did not think it wise for the Smithsonian to use its own funds for the experiment, Walcott offered to put up half of the money himself, and Bell agreed to "chip in" the other half. The next day, Bell talked to Walcott again. Believing that his connections with the AEA and its patents might compromise the project, Bell reasoned that "it may be well for me to be careful about endorsing the proposition that Smithsonian funds should be expended upon this experiment" and said that he would not vote on the matter should it be taken up by the institution's regents. Further to insulate himself from possible conflicts of interest, Bell suggested that the Aero Club of America might act as sponsor and that the experiment could be justified as a technical exercise to demonstrate how the tandem wing configuration might enhance aircraft stability and safety. Nevertheless, he deferred to Walcott and told him he was amenable to doing "whatever he decided was best to be done."[32]

Curtiss and Walcott met with Bell in his home in Washington on 30 March to discuss the situation with J. A. D. McCurdy and a patent attorney. Walcott upped the ante with a proposal to rebuild and fly the original Langley machine instead of a reproduction, with Bell countering that it was a priceless artifact that should not be hazarded in flight tests. All concurred that, regardless, the experiment should be carried out as quietly as possible. In the end, Walcott decided unilaterally to have the aerodrome rebuilt and retained Curtiss to do the work. He also brought in Charles M. Manly, Langley's engine builder and chief engineer, to supervise the entire project and appointed Zahm as the Smithsonian's official representative during the reconstruction and testing. The battered and broken aerodrome was shipped to Hammondsport sometime in early April.[33]

In accordance with the understanding among Walcott, Bell, and Curtiss, work on the Langley machine was kept confidential and was carried out in a corner of the Curtiss factory. The *Hammondsport Herald*, which rarely missed any news about Curtiss, did not mention the project until 20 May. Nor was there anything in the *New York Times*, possibly because the paper considered the *America* project of more interest to their readers than rebuilding a nearly forgotten aviation relic. Given the condition of the aerodrome and Curtiss' preoccupation with the transatlantic project, restoration took longer than anticipated. The engine—an innovative 52-horsepower water-cooled 5-cylinder radial built by Manly—was in such bad shape that it could put out only about thirty-five horsepower despite upgrades to its ignition and fuel systems. Slight, nearly indiscernible, changes were also made to the twin, shaft-driven pusher propellers to accommodate the reduced engine power. All four wings were extensively rebuilt, with most of the original hollow wing ribs replaced with new ones fabricated from laminated wood, the wood spars beefed up, leading-edge extensions removed, and the covering replaced entirely with varnished cotton. Curtiss considerably modified the system of wire trusses to reinforce the wings and moved the kingposts supporting the truss assemblies to positions closer to the wings' centers of pressure. Only brief consideration was given to replicating Langley's expensive and complicated catapult launch mechanism, thought by most to have been responsible for the failure in the first place; instead Curtiss fitted the machine with three pontoons, two forward and one aft, to allow takeoffs and landings on the water. Langley had given about as much thought to control as he did to getting his machine safely back to earth. Curtiss faithfully omitted any means of lateral stability other than the pronounced dihedral of the wings, with minimal control in yaw provided by a vertical rudder under the machine and the big cruciform tail connected through cables to a steering wheel on a column in front of the pilot. The tail was fixed on its vertical axis to provide inherent longitudinal stability.[34]

The public and the press got their first look at the Langley machine when it was assembled at the Curtiss flying field on the morning of 28 May. Zahm and Walcott were both present. Curtiss took the craft out for its first test, which was intended only to see if everything worked satisfactorily. He headed into the light breeze drifting across the lake and lifted into the air for a five-second hop of about 150 feet. It was hardly what anyone would consider a flight, yet the demonstration was enough for Walcott to declare he was "well pleased" and for the *New York Times* to proclaim that the aerodrome "vindicated itself and its inventor." The paper added that it was now clear that Langley's "fatal mistake was in his method of launching the machine" and not in any fundamental flaws in the machine's design or construction. Bell was effusive in a telegram congratulating Curtiss for his "successful vindication of Langley's drome. This is really the crowning achievement of your career at least so far. My best wishes for your continued success."[35]

Orville Wright, to say the least, did not see things the same way as did those on the scene in Hammondsport. Far from a "vindication" of Langley, Wright believed the experiments only proved the mendacity of Curtiss and his Smithsonian accomplices in a conspiracy to undermine his and his brother's airplane patents. Obviously Orville himself could not go to Hammondsport to see what was going on, but he persuaded Griffith Brewer, who was in Dayton at the time gathering information on the Wrights for a book on early aviation history, to investigate the aerodrome project. Brewer had been an ally of the Wrights since 1908 when he flew with Wilbur at Le Mans, and had been instrumental in establishing the British Wright Company in 1913. By the time Brewer arrived in Hammondsport during the second week of June, Curtiss had demonstrated the machine a few more times, more to generate publicity than to provide additional data on the aerodrome's construction and performance. Then he took the machine apart and began more extensive modifications, allegedly to conduct additional experiments intended to explore the tandem-wing configuration.[36]

Brewer's report and attached photos of the Langley machine confirmed Orville's suspicions. In a letter to the *New York Times* on 21 June, Brewer itemized the fundamental shortcomings of the Langley machine that rendered it unflyable, among them structural deficiencies, inefficient propellers, a complete lack of means of controlling it in flight, and no reliable way to launch or land it. He followed with two rhetorical questions: Why had the aerodrome been "altered from its original historical state to try to make it fly?" and why had there been no "impartial, unprejudiced" experts present to observe or carry out the tests? In an editorial two days later, the *Times* concluded that the results of the trials did not warrant the conclusion that Langley's aerodrome could have flown in 1903, and that the "experiment, no matter how successful, was of little or no importance as bearing on the questions of priority" for the invention of the airplane.[37] The public relations front of the patent war, which up to then had seemed to be going Curtiss' way, had now turned in the Wrights' favor.

Nevertheless, momentum and the persistence of Walcott, Zahm, and the Smithsonian carried the Langley project forward, with diminishing returns for Curtiss personally and professionally. Sensing that there was not much more to be gained and immersed with other concerns, particularly setting up a new factory in Buffalo, Curtiss distanced himself from the experiments and let his subordinates and Zahm proceed with even more modifications to the aerodrome, including an 80-horsepower Curtiss engine, a single tractor propeller, wings with much less camber, a relocated pilot's seat, and so many other changes that the machine only superficially resembled Langley's original. One of Curtiss' students, Elwood ("Gink") Doherty, flew the machine in September 1914 for distances of more than a half mile at up to thirty feet above the lake. Doherty and Walter E. Johnson, a mechanic and instructor at the Curtiss school in Hammondsport, flew from the ice near Keuka in April and followed with longer flights later that spring and summer, including one by Doherty to Keuka and back that covered twenty miles. None of the fliers succeeded in getting the aerodrome to complete a turn. Regardless, the *Hammondsport Herald* boasted that these and previous tests showed that "Langley gave us a new science and Glenn Curtiss has redeemed his name."[38]

By June 1915, Orville was so furious with the Langley experiments and the attendant publicity that he imposed on his older brother Lorin to make the trip to Hammondsport in June 1915 and report on the most recent activities. To add to the intrigue (or perhaps by now the absurdity) enmeshing the aerodrome project, Lorin used the name "W. L. Oren" and stayed in Bath rather than Hammondsport to protect his anonymity. He wandered around the Curtiss hangars, photographing the aerodrome and a few of the flying boats and dispatching the information to Orville by special delivery letters from Bath. One morning, as he watched Walter Johnson attempt a takeoff, he saw the aerodrome's rear wings fold upward and collapse in a manner startlingly reminiscent of the December 1903 accident that ended Langley's quest for flight. Lorin's espionage was unveiled when workers spotted him taking pictures as the craft was dragged back to shore. The Curtiss people commandeered his camera and film, but the damage had been done, for now Orville had dramatic proof of the aerodrome's inherent structural weakness despite the many changes made by Curtiss to render it airworthy.[39]

At the same time, there was not much more Orville could do legally. He had no direct interest in the patent litigation following the reorganization and sale of the Wright Aeronautical Company in October 1915, and he knew he had to be careful not to appear to be attacking the memory of Langley, whose work had inspired him and his brother to take up the challenge of inventing the airplane. All that remained in the aftermath of the episode was a festering controversy with the Smithsonian over the public display of the restored Langley machine and its misidentification as "the first man-carrying aeroplane in the history of the world capable of sustained free flight." Unable to reach a settlement with the Smithsonian leadership, Orville refused to let them have the Wright 1903 flyer, which in 1928 went to the Science Museum in London, where it remained for two decades. The airplane finally returned to the United States in 1948, only after the Smithsonian acknowledged in print that the Wrights and not Langley were first to succeed in sustained heavier-than-air flight.[40]

The Langley project was only one chapter in the saga of Curtiss' continued efforts to show that the Wrights did not enjoy primacy in their invention and that their patent therefore did not give his rivals universal rights to the manufacture of airplanes. In 1883, a French inventor, Alexandre Goupil, had designed, tested, and patented a flying machine incorporating movable surfaces on each side of the fuselage that acted much like the elevons found in modern delta-wing aircraft in providing control in both pitch and roll. Curtiss understood that this was an important precedent of a machine that potentially had full three-axis control, and that if he demonstrated that an accurate reconstruction of Goupil's machine could fly he would further bolster his legal case against the Wright interests. The result was one of the strangest of all Curtiss aircraft, known as the Duck for its peculiar appearance. Powered by a 100-horsepower Curtiss OXX V-8 engine driving a tractor propeller and fitted with the Langley aerodrome floats, the Duck made some short hops off the water at Hammondsport in 1916. It was later equipped with a wheeled undercarriage and flown at the Curtiss field at Newport News, Virginia.[41]

Neither the Langley nor the Goupil projects did anything to further the course of aviation technology, nor did they enhance Curtiss' reputation as an aircraft designer and builder. Commenting on the Langley affair, the historian Richard K. Smith went so far as to blame Curtiss for participating in a "wholly fraudulent demonstration" that contributed only to a "smug, self-serving bureaucracy's refusal to admit error." Some latter-day Curtiss apologists insist that Curtiss, Kleckler, Zahm, Manly, and Walcott should be taken at their word that they did everything they could to rebuild the Langley machine exactly as it was in 1903, and that the 1914 tests proved that Langley must be given credit at least for introducing a "working prototype" of the airplane. Quite the opposite is true. The evidence is incontrovertible that the 1914 iteration of the aerodrome was substantially different, and that by 1915 it had been so altered as to have virtually nothing in common with the original other than its tandem-wing configuration. It is also reasonable to surmise that had the patent litigation continued beyond 1917, Curtiss would not have hesitated to enter into the record as evidence against the Wrights his experiments with the aerodrome and the Goupil Duck.[42]

In truth, the 1914–1915 Langley experiments proved only that the modified aerodrome could under some circumstances make brief hops and that when much more extensively reconstructed was marginally capable of flight—nothing more and nothing less. To maintain that the experiments meant more is a gross distortion of the facts and intellectually dishonest. On the other hand, one cannot blame Curtiss for doing everything in his power to seek allies or devise new strategies to defend himself in the face of a threat to his company and his livelihood, or that by 1914 Orville's motives had transcended any reasonable business interests and had devolved into what amounted to a blood feud. In the final analysis, the reconstructed Langley and Goupil flying machines damaged both Curtiss' stature as an aeronautical innovator and his case against the Wright patent in the court of public opinion. More important, the demonstrations were an unwelcome distraction from the more important and immediate need to cultivate his Navy connections and ensure his enterprise was ready to face the harsh realities of the global conflict that in a few years would engulf the country and bring unprecedented demands on his company for aircraft and engines.

On 4 August 1914, German forces drove across the frontier into Belgium, and the comfortable European-dominated global order of the early twentieth century fell to pieces. That day, Curtiss was at the Aero Club in New York. In reply to questions from the press about what the outbreak of war meant for aviation, Curtiss was unusually voluble. "When general fighting begins," he said, "you will see aeroplanes rising as from the dark corners of the earth and the European sky will be literally dotted with them. Their value for reconnoitering and for dropping bombs will be enormous." The European powers had "thousands" of airplanes "ready for immediate service." France, to no one's surprise, was the leader, with 1,200 airplanes, followed by Germany with six hundred and Britain with three hundred. Often overlooked, Russia had built up an air arm that was at least the size of Britain's. Curtiss forecast great battles of attrition in the air, where the opponents would lose aircraft at about equal rates, and that would mean the nation most able to organize aircraft production and field the most airplanes would be victorious.[43]

Yet the stark reality was that the United States, with only a handful of military aircraft, none of which could match the quality of those in Europe, was in no position to fight an air war. In his report to the secretary of the Navy in September 1914 Bristol emphasized the importance of airplanes "as a part of the fleet," warning that the Navy was "woefully deficient" and that "the development of aircraft manufacture in this country is behind that of the principal countries in Europe." The United States had perhaps twenty airplane manufacturers in 1914, with annual sales of only forty-nine airplanes, most of which came from the Curtiss and Wright companies. Of those two, Curtiss had more production experience and the better "mix" of airplanes to meet the anticipated demand from overseas and from the military at home. Of the approximately forty airplanes Curtiss delivered to the Navy, Army, and foreign governments in 1912–1913, the Navy's total was eight, with five Curtisses in the service's tiny inventory in September 1914.[44]

As things stood that fall, it was all the Curtiss company could do to keep up with its foreign orders, most of them from Britain, Italy, and Russia. Much in demand was the standardized and improved single-engine Model F flying boat, which Curtiss had demonstrated in Europe in 1913–1914 and that was widely used as a trainer. One variant had extra wing panels to provide more lift and could accommodate four people; another, built especially for the Italian navy in 1913, had a narrow hull, tandem seating, an enclosed cockpit, and ailerons on the trailing edge of the upper wing. Through the influence of John Porte, the British acquired the *America* and a sister ship in the fall of 1914, their range and payload capacity deemed useful for scouting and antisubmarine missions in the waters around the British Isles. Curtiss workers labored overtime to get the two craft ready for delivery to the British by the end of September. Three similar airplanes, designated H-2s, followed in 1915, with an order for an additional twelve—known as H-4s, or Small Americas—by the middle of the year. The H-2 and H-4 aircraft initially had Curtiss OX engines, but the British found those power plants inadequate and substituted more powerful Anzani radial and Clerget rotary engines with tractor propellers.[45]

Accelerated aircraft production, and the inevitable strains that came with it, were only one dimension of the new realities facing Curtiss and his company in 1914. It was also becoming obvious to the Navy that Curtiss' design and engineering methods were no longer adequate to meeting either the company's or the Navy's requirements. The *America*'s hydrodynamic shortcomings were one symptom of the problem, which again manifested itself in connection with the designs submitted by Curtiss for two new Navy hydroairplanes in the summer of 1914. When Bristol received the blueprints, he immediately found a number of discrepancies, chief among them being the estimated locations of the centers of pressure and gravity for the wings, which appeared to him likely to cause serious longitudinal instability in the airplanes. He was unhappy with the company's "reluctance" to provide all the necessary data to resolve the problem, adding: "You are apparently using cut and try methods, the time for which is past, and exact information is wanted or else an acknowledgment of [your] inability to give such information. Incorrect and insufficient information is worse than useless."[46] It was not quite an ultimatum, but the message was still clear: Curtiss had to make sure he had an engineering and design staff that was able to incorporate the latest aerodynamic theories and data into "real world" aircraft designs if his company were to continue to do business with the Navy.

It did not take long for Curtiss and such close associates as Harry Genung, now the company's general manager, to realize that they had to make major changes to the way things were done and that they had to do so quickly. The Hammondsport factory, Curtiss' old "shop," had been expanded haphazardly over the last five years and was crowded, inefficient, and not up to the task of meeting current—let alone future—aircraft and engine orders. By November 1914, the factory was working two shifts and had erected tents to provide additional storage space. Put simply, it had outgrown Hammondsport. Although Curtiss was far from eager to leave his hometown, he understood that it was necessary for both the short- and the long-term well-being of the company. Almost from the start, Buffalo was the front-runner. An important commercial and industrial center, Buffalo was one of the nation's largest cities, with more than 420,000 people in 1910. The city had grown in the mid and late nineteenth century as a transshipment point for grain and other commodities, and its development was accelerated as a result of superb rail and water connections to the East and Midwest; at one time it was second only to Chicago as a railroad hub. By the turn of the twentieth century, the city's diverse manufacturing base, skilled work force, ready access to electrical power from nearby Niagara Falls, and large financial institutions also made it attractive to investors and entrepreneurs. If all that were not enough, Buffalo's proximity—only one hundred miles or so northwest of Hammondsport—was a major reason for Curtiss to put the city high on his short list of potential sites for a new factory.[47]

Curtiss' need to expand and relocate coincided with the efforts of the Buffalo Chamber of Commerce to bring in new industries in the wake of a short business downturn in 1914. Briefly returning from Coronado, where he and his family had again taken up residence for the winter of 1914–1915, Curtiss accepted the chamber's offer to lease the disused factory of the E. R. Thomas

Motor Company at 1200 Niagara Street. The facility had ample room, was close to Lake Erie for trials of flying boats and hydros, and was near enough to Hammondsport that Curtiss and others could commute weekly if they so desired. The announcement of the acquisition of the Buffalo factory on 5 December 1914 caused "considerable excitement" in Hammondsport, where the worry had been that Curtiss intended to abandon his plant entirely. There was an understandable sigh of relief when reassurances came that the Curtiss Motor Company would remain in Hammondsport and increase output while the Curtiss Aeroplane Company would transfer to Buffalo, with Harry Genung in charge. In May 1915, the Curtisses moved from Hammondsport to Buffalo, first renting an apartment in one of the city's hotels and then, by 1916, moving to a house on fashionable, tree-lined Lincoln Parkway.[48]

Because it soon became apparent that even more space was needed than was available at the leased Niagara Street plant, the company on 10 March 1915 began renovating and expanding an old factory at the end of Churchill Street on the north side of the city. Completed in a little more than two months at a cost of $2 million, the new facility included 110,000 square feet of open space that was ideal for the construction of the big H-4 flying boats. Later in the year Curtiss acquired the Century Telephone Construction Company building at 1750 Elmwood Avenue and converted it for engine manufacture and parts production. Construction of two new buildings in Hammondsport accommodated additional engine production. A subsidiary firm, Curtiss Aeroplanes and Motors, Ltd., was organized in Canada in February 1915 primarily to supply airplanes and parts for the British from a new factory in Toronto. J. A. D. McCurdy, Curtiss' friend going back to the AEA years, became the company's managing director.[49]

In addition to the need for more space, Curtiss also had to strengthen his company's engineering staff to meet present and future demands for more and better airplanes. To that end, he brought in as the company's chief engineer Albert Zahm. Chambers had worked with Zahm on a commission that drew up a proposal in 1913 to create a national aeronautical laboratory, only to have the recommendation fail due to bureaucratic infighting and congressional indifference. In lieu of a national research facility, the Smithsonian went ahead on its own in 1913 to reestablish the Langley laboratory with Zahm in charge. At the request of Chambers, Zahm had toured Europe in 1913 with Jerome Hunsaker and coauthored with him a 1914 report on European aeronautical developments. Zahm's credentials as an aerodynamicist and his close ties with the Navy made him the perfect choice to head Curtiss' engineering program as the company strove to meet the challenges of expansion.[50]

Equally important for the future of the company's aircraft design and engineering programs was B. Douglas Thomas, formerly of Britain's Sopwith company, who had been recruited by Curtiss in the spring of 1914 to help develop new Army trainers with tractor instead of pusher engines. The first of these, the Model J—completed by the middle of May 1914 and test flown at Hammondsport as a single-float hydro—had a 90-horsepower OX engine mounted behind a front-mounted radiator. Unlike other Curtiss aircraft, the J had tandem rather than side-by-side seats. After it had been fitted with wheels and substantially modified in other respects, this airplane and a second similar example underwent further evaluation by the Army at North Island that autumn. Bristol observed the San Diego tests, remarking that the new airplane "did not show up well," particularly in its rate of climb. A third airplane, the Model N, with a 100-horsepower OXX engine, revised wings, and relocated ailerons, met the service requirements and was accepted by the Army before the end of the year. Based on the experience with the J and N, the Curtiss company introduced an improved version of the J model in 1915. This airplane evolved into the JN series, culminating by the middle of 1916 in the famous JN-4 "Jenny," built in great numbers in Buffalo and Toronto and used extensively by the Army as a trainer.[51]

These developments were of more than academic interest to the Navy, which by early 1915 had concluded that the Curtiss hydros and flying boats used for training at Pensacola were no longer acceptable for service. The main reason was that their engines, located behind the pilot's seat, commonly smashed into accident-prone neophyte aviators. This problem, coupled with the Navy's experience that Curtiss flying boats did not have the anticipated rough-water capabilities, convinced Bristol and others that tractor-configured airplanes with floats would be safer and more usable in a variety of conditions. Curtiss' friend Jerome Hunsaker—who had taken over as head of the Aircraft Division in the Navy's Bureau of Construction and Repair in July 1916 with responsibility for all aspects of aircraft design, development, and procurement—assisted Curtiss engineers in modifying the JN-4B Army trainer for Navy service. They added a central float, larger vertical stabilizer, and effected other changes to improve the airplane's control and takeoff and landing characteristics. Designated the Model N-9, the airplane proved entirely satisfactory, and the Navy ordered thirty from Curtiss, only to have the company fall behind on its delivery schedule.[52]

A torrent of orders for aircraft, nearly all of them from overseas, and big contracts from the Navy as a consequence of the March 1915 congressional appropriation of $1 million for naval aviation strained the Curtiss company to its limits. Lt. Cdr. Henry C. Mustin, an aviator and commander of the naval air station at Pensacola, surveyed aircraft manufacturers in September and October 1915 to determine their capabilities and capacity for expansion. In Buffalo he met and talked with Curtiss, who assured him that the company, then turning out five airplanes and ten engines per day, was well organized to handle more production. "The quality of workmanship in this company at the Buffalo plant is excellent, and compares favorably with that of any of the aeroplane and motor factories I visited," Mustin reported. The Hammondsport plant was in the process of a reorganization and expansion that would "put it upon the same high grade basis as the Buffalo branch" of the company. Up to 1 October, Curtiss had dispatched 125 JN trainers and forty H-4s to Europe, and had completed another three hundred trainer types and fifty more of the H-4 type. Other contemporary sources indicated that the company by September had orders for one hundred H-4 types and four hundred orders for the new Model R, an improvement of the ubiquitous JN.[53]

To Curtiss' credit, he understood that production of this magnitude went far beyond his or his company's limited management capacity, and that future expansion would demand access to capital resources ordinarily available only to the largest industrial corporations. Negotiations with potential investors culminated on 13 January 1916 with the acquisition of the Curtiss companies by a Wall Street combine headed by the New York investment firm William Morris Imbrie and Company. The deal folded the Curtiss Aeroplane Company, the Curtiss Motor Company, the Canadian Curtiss Aeroplanes and Motors, and the Curtiss Exhibition Company, which for some time had been operating flying schools at various sites around the country, into the new Curtiss Aeroplane and Motor Company, capitalized at $9 million. Curtiss was appointed president of the new company and received $5 million in cash and $3.5 million in preferred stock as a result of the reorganization. The board of directors included Curtiss and his old friends and business associates Monroe Wheeler, Harry Genung, and G. Ray Hall, along with newcomers from Wall Street James Imbrie, Murray W. Dodge, and George Palmer. In another reorganization at the end of 1916, Hall resigned as the company's treasurer and Clement M. Keys came on board as vice-president with broad executive authority over financial operations.[54] Not only did the strains of the rapid expansion in 1915–1916 reveal deficiencies in Curtiss' design and engineering structure but they also resulted in quality-control problems. In early 1915, Curtiss delivered more than fifty Model K flying boats to the Russian navy, fulfilling an order received in the fall of 1914. A derivative of the Model F, which had been in service in Russia as a trainer since 1913, the Model K was larger, accommodating three aviators instead of two, and with a 150-horsepower V-X engine instead of the 100-horsepower OXX. Not long after Curtiss test pilots began flying the machines in Sevastopol on the Black Sea, they encountered hull cracks and engine problems that left most of the aircraft useless. When efforts by Curtiss representatives to fix the problems dragged out through 1916, the Russians canceled the contract and demanded their money back, which Curtiss refused to do, arguing that the Russians' "lack of experience and bad conditions in launching and handling machines" were to blame for the trouble. The Russian government dragged Curtiss into court, but the 1917 revolutions brought an end to the legal process. Nevertheless, the litigation in 1916 and 1917 proved that the Model K's troubles began when the design and production work shifted to Buffalo, exacerbated by defective parts and inadequate testing of the new engine at the Hammondsport factory.[55] Bristol and bureau officers involved in aviation procurement could not help but view the Russian order as further evidence of the shortcomings of the Curtiss organization, demanding that the service keep a close eye on things in Buffalo and Hammondsport.

That task became even more difficult as the tempo of aircraft and engine manufacturing in Buffalo and Hammondsport increased following American entry into the war in April 1917. Surveying the aviation scene in May 1917, Jerome Hunsaker reported to his boss, Rear Adm. David W. Taylor, chief of the Bureau of Construction and Repair, that regardless of its shortcomings the Curtiss company had developed aircraft types that had been found to be "fairly acceptable," and as a result had received major production contracts. "No other company," he added, "has developed equally acceptable types, and hence the other companies cannot be given orders of any magnitude." With the establishment of the Naval Aircraft Factory in Philadelphia later in 1917, the Navy had an alternative source of aircraft production, but for the immediate future the service would have to rely primarily on Curtiss. To ensure the Navy got what it wanted from Curtiss, Hunsaker recommended and got the assignment of Cdr. George C. Westervelt to Buffalo as superintending constructor of aircraft. Westervelt was a Construction Corps officer who had graduated in the same 1901 Naval Academy class as Dick Richardson and who had hands-on experience in aviation from his work in Seattle with pioneer aircraft designer and builder William E. Boeing.[56]

Not long after settling into his new job, Westervelt reported to Hunsaker on the situation in Buffalo. In comparison to other aircraft manufacturers, whom he thought were "absolutely marking time" in anticipation of military orders, the Curtiss people were "filled with optimism" and eager to go ahead "on any quantity of orders and filling them within the required times." Westervelt was not nearly so sure, especially given some of the problems Curtiss had had with its foreign business in recent years and in delays with the N-9 contract. "They are, of course," he elaborated, "in a class by themselves, but have limitations nevertheless. Their present organization is decidedly loose jointed, and will require very material modifications before they can expect to make a favorable start on the work they contemplate doing." Exacerbating the "loose jointed" organization was that Keys and Curtiss were frequently out of town and that Genung was not providing the level of leadership needed in Buffalo.[57]

Under these circumstances, reorganization was essential. It came on 14 July 1917 with the appointment of John N. Willys to succeed Curtiss as president of the company. Willys, president of the Willys-Overland Automobile Company and a friend of Curtiss, sought to apply automotive mass production expertise and efficiency to the burgeoning Curtiss enterprises, an expectation consistent with the government's goal of bringing order out of chaos in the aircraft and engine industry. In the new arrangement, Curtiss became chairman of the board of directors, a figurehead position but one he welcomed because it freed him to concentrate on experimentation and on research and development as head of a subsidiary, the Curtiss Engineering Corporation, created a month later. Hunsaker saw it as a good move, for he believed the business had become more complex than Curtiss was comfortable with and that Curtiss was unable fully to comprehend what went on in the inner sanctums on Wall Street.[58]

By this time, too, Curtiss had other interests far from Buffalo. Continuing his quest for a more salubrious climate for winter flying, Curtiss looked first to California, with which he was familiar from his San Diego days. Yet as convenient as passenger rail travel was early in the last century, the long cross-country journey by train was a major deterrent to locating permanently on the West Coast. In the east, Miami was less than half the distance away by train and with its subtropical climate deserved serious consideration. As early as February 1911, Curtiss had considered establishing an airfield and school at Palm Beach, a resort north of Miami where he thought the wealthy northerners who habituated the place would be interested in learning to fly his hydroairplanes. The following winter, he sent one of his aviators, Charles C. Witmer, to Miami to give exhibition flights and set up a flight school. By 1915, Miami was little more than a whistle-stop on oil baron Henry M. Flagler's Florida East Coast Railway, had none of the exclusive appeal of posh Palm Beach, and had far to go to match other Florida cities like Jacksonville and Tampa, either in population or economic vitality. Still, with more than 5,500 people in 1916 the city was attracting permanent residents and sun-seeking tourists at an accelerating rate.[59]

Following a tour of the area with real estate developer Carl Fisher and representatives of Miami's chamber of commerce for several days in late October 1916, Curtiss chose a site on Miami Beach, on the other side of Biscayne Bay, where new hangars and other facilities were made ready before the end of the year for ten airplanes transferred from Buffalo. Miami Beach was a work in progress. Not even incorporated as a town until 1915, the palmetto-matted peninsula had perhaps five hundred residents, so capturing Curtiss and the flying business was a major coup for Fisher, who anticipated that the operation would stimulate development of the area. In early January 1917, the Curtiss family, including Lena's mother Jennie, moved into a rented house in Miramar, north of Miami. The next winter, 1917–1918, they took up accommodations in Flagler's elegant Royal Palm Hotel on the Miami waterfront, with its magnificent veranda and panoramic views of Biscayne Bay.[60]

Once in charge of the new Curtiss company, Willys initiated construction of the gigantic $4 million North Elmwood plant in Buffalo, which when finished by the end of 1917 had nearly 1.2 million square feet of space and was reputed to be the largest aircraft manufacturing facility in the world. By January 1918, according to one estimate, the company employed about 11,500 workers, of whom about 25 percent were women. By the end of 1917, the Curtiss company had received contracts from the Navy for eighty-four H-16 flying boats (10,900-pound aircraft powered by two of the new 12-cylinder Liberty engines and intended for long-range antisubmarine patrols), 675 HS-1 and HS-2 flying boats with single Liberty engines for short-range patrol duties, 162 R-6 floatplane trainers; thirty more N-9 trainers, and nine other aircraft. Estimates of the total production orders the company had on hand in 1917 ran as high as $20 million. To meet the demand for twin-engine flying boats in 1917, the Curtiss company took over the buildings of the Buffalo Smelting Works at the foot of Austin Street, where the company also housed its experimental engineering department.[61]

Expansion brought turmoil and change to the Curtiss company as well as the rest of the American aircraft industry in the years leading up to the American entry into World War I. In 1915, Orville had sold the Wright company to New York financial interests, and a year later they merged the reorganized company with the Glenn L. Martin Company and the Simplex Automobile Company to form the new Wright-Martin Aircraft Corporation. That firm announced in December 1916 that all aircraft manufacturers henceforth must pay a hefty annual royalty or risk violating the Wright patents. In the meantime, Curtiss had secured potentially valuable patents for his airplane control system and his hydroairplane and flying boat designs. Although he took the moral high ground in proclaiming he did not want to sue infringers, he had gone to court to protect his interests against Albert Janin, who had filed for a patent for an airplane presumably capable of landing and taking off from the water and who had claimed priority over Curtiss' hydroairplane and flying boat designs. A "tribunal" of patent attorneys in September 1915 ruled against Janin and gave Curtiss "complete control of the commercial hydroaeroplane and flying boat business which he had built up in this country and abroad." If Curtiss personally was hesitant about pursuing legal action in defense of his patents, Curtiss Aeroplane and Motor was not. In response to the Wright-Martin declaration, the company informed its competitors that it, too, would require licenses and royalty payments from all manufacturers of hydros and flying boats. Orville might have believed that the January 1914 court of appeals decision upholding the Wright patent was definitive recognition of his and his brother's claims, but Curtiss, according to Wright biographer Tom Crouch, had the last word, for by 1917 he "ruled the industry of which the Wright brothers were no longer a part."[62]

With the likelihood that the bitter, nearly eight-year-long patent feud between Curtiss and the Wright interests would smother the industry at a time when it desperately needed to meet the needs of the Army and the Navy, neither aircraft manufacturers nor the government saw any benefit in an escalation of the patent wars. In July 1917, the National Advisory Committee for Aeronautics, which had been formed in 1915 to coordinate the country's aeronautical research and development, intervened to broker a settlement whereby a new organization known as the Manufacturers Aircraft Association took over the Wright and Curtiss patents and administered a cross-licensing agreement that applied to all members of the association. In return, the Wright and Curtiss interests each received $2 million in royalty payments.[63] The patent dispute had come to an end with a settlement that recognized the equality of interests of both parties but did nothing to effect a final decision about the primacy of either the Wright or the Curtiss claims.

Historians concur that the patent fight between Curtiss and the Wrights was a factor in the United States falling behind other nations in aviation technology, but how much so is open to interpretation. Richard P. Hallion, for instance, blames "the industry's own self-inflicted wounds from the Wright patent controversy" for the damage done to American aviation. Crouch, on the other hand, acknowledges that while the quarrel caused "serious divisions within the American aeronautical community," credit must be given to the Europeans for taking the initiative, particularly in providing timely government support for aeronautics.[64] That Curtiss was responsible for the development of large multiengine aircraft and for major improvements to power plant technology indicates that the patent controversy may not have retarded American aviation after 1914. What is certain, though, is that the cost of the patent war was more personal than it was professional or financial, leaving both parties embittered and resentful and masking the important contributions each made to the development of aeronautics in the years before World War I.

Of more concern to the Navy than the final resolution of the patent fight between Curtiss and the Wrights were the occasional misunderstandings that marred the generally cordial relationship between the Curtiss company and the Navy through the remainder of the war years.

In January 1918, Hunsaker ordered a detailed survey of the company and its operations, which found, for example, that the initial slow pace of production in Buffalo had been caused in part by the failure to produce complete sets of blueprints, and by a lack of communication between the company and its subcontractors and parts suppliers. Company executives reassured him that they had resolved most, if not all, of the problems and were on pace to meet the Navy's requirements. Another report in April concluded that there were still problems in Buffalo, especially at the Churchill Street plant, which was "badly crowded" and where Curtiss' shop floor supervision was "lax." Unionized machinists and machine tool makers threatened a strike in June 1918. Had it not been averted by a wage increase, the strike would have virtually shut down all airplane and engine manufacturing in Buffalo and jeopardized completion of an order for 350 F-5L twin-engine flying boats to be built at the North Elmwood plant.[65]

Wartime difficulties with naval aircraft procurement paled in comparison to those that afflicted the Curtiss company as a consequence of its orders from the Army. Because the Army's requirements were orders of magnitude greater than those of the Navy, and the service lacked a clear picture of the types and numbers of aircraft it needed, the problems brought military production to a near-standstill by January 1918. The company approached bankruptcy as it fell behind in aircraft deliveries, was unable to convince the Army to make cash advances on its contracts, and failed to pay its subcontractors for parts and materials. Only the comparatively efficiently conceived and executed Navy trainer and flying boat programs sustained the company during those difficult months. Both services blamed Willys for waste, poor management, inadequate accounting procedures, and lack of cooperation with aircraft inspectors. The public blamed a conspiracy by big business to defraud the government and the people, and Congress determined to investigate why so much money had bought so few airplanes suitable for combat.[66]

Statistics vary on the numbers and types of aircraft and engines Curtiss produced during the war. There is, however, general agreement that between July 1917 and March 1919 the company's six American factories (Niagara Street, Churchill Street, Elmwood Avenue, Austin Street, North Elmwood, and Hammondsport) delivered 5,221 airplanes and about five thousand engines. The lion's share went to the Army, mostly JN-4s, but none of the aircraft Curtiss produced for the Army saw combat. On the other hand, the Navy received 205 big H-12, H-16, and F-5L twin-engine flying boats, numbers of which got to overseas bases in Ireland, England, and France. Curtiss produced an additional 822 HS and Model F single-engine flying boats, which also saw Navy service overseas as short-range patrol aircraft. Another 569 N-9 land-planes and hydros went to the Navy as training aircraft. At its peak, wartime employment reached more than eighteen thousand at all of the Curtiss factories, with more than two thousand employed in Hammondsport alone.[67] The problems and controversies associated with wartime production notwith-standing, Curtiss and the Curtiss company could look back on their wartime record with a justifiable sense of achievement. At the same time, the man and the industry he helped to found faced a future filled with challenges as well as opportunities for both them and the Navy.

—9—

Challenges Old and New

F ree of day-to-day managerial responsibilities in Buffalo, Curtiss spent most of his time in his "shop" in the Austin Street plant courting his first love, experimenting, which, he confessed at the time, "is never work—it is plain fun." One experimental project—the transatlantic airplane— continued to occupy much of his attention. Despite having to abandon the *America* project in the summer of 1914, Curtiss clung to his dream of accomplishing the flight at the earliest opportunity. In March 1915, he wrote to Porte that although "war orders have prevented our actually starting construction on a new Trans-Atlantic . . . we keep working at the plans upon every opportunity and will have every facility for quick work when the time comes to commence construction." The opportunity seemed at hand in September 1915 when Curtiss and Rodman Wanamaker signed a contract to have the Curtiss company design and build a "Trans-Atlantic Flyer" at a cost of $55,000. By the end of March 1916, Wanamaker had formed the America Trans Oceanic Company and had superseded his earlier agreement with Curtiss with a new and more lucrative $100,000 contract to design and build a triplane with the range and payload capacity to cross the ocean.[1]

The flying boat, known as the Model T, or the Model 3 Wanamaker Triplane, was truly a monster. The world's largest seaplane, it had a wingspan of 134 feet, a total wing area of 2,812 square feet, and a length of nearly 59 feet. An empty weight of 15,645 pounds and MTOW of 22,000 pounds gave it a load-to-tare ratio of 28:72, mediocre by later standards, but providing enough disposable lift to make the flight from Newfoundland to the Azores. Power was originally to come from four 250-horsepower Curtiss Model V-4 liquid-cooled V-12 tractor engines in individual nacelles attached to the center wing. The airplane was completed at the Buffalo factory by July 1916 and shipped in pieces to Newport News, where Curtiss had established a flying school, but it was not flown and may not even have been reassembled when it became apparent that the V-4 engines were seriously overweight. Subsequently bought by the British, the big airplane was shipped to England where it flew with four 240-horsepower Renault engines. By then, the United States was in the war, and events had moved quickly beyond the original Wanamaker transatlantic project to a new but even more ambitious concept for flying the ocean.[2]

In late August 1917 there arose another chance for the transatlantic flight, not from the son of a multimillionaire department store magnate, but from the United States Navy. Rear Adm. David W. Taylor determined that the Navy needed a new flying boat with transatlantic range, reasoning that an airplane with that capability would in effect be "self-ferrying" and thus obviate the need to use scarce and vulnerable merchant shipping to get to the war theater. Taylor met with Jerome Hunsaker, head of the bureau's Aircraft Division, and with Commander Westervelt to thrash out the fundamental design parameters of an airplane to fulfill Taylor's requirement.[3]

As the outlines of the project matured in Washington, there was consensus that Curtiss had to be brought in, if only as a courtesy, given his prior experience with the *America* flying boat and his company's involvement with the design and production of flying boats for the Navy. At the same time, Taylor, Hunsaker, and Westervelt recognized that to ensure the success of a project of this magnitude they needed the resources of the Curtiss company in what from the start they conceived to be a cooperative endeavor. More than happy to oblige, Curtiss arrived in Washington on 9 September with Henry Kleckler and William L. ("Bill") Gilmore, one of the company's best engineers. Following a conference with Taylor, Hunsaker, and Westervelt where they learned more about what the Navy wanted, Curtiss and his associates returned to Buffalo to sketch preliminary designs for a three-engine machine and a much larger five-engine craft. Both featured a short, wide hull, with the biplane empennage located high and to the rear on longitudinal wire-braced spars.[4]

Almost certainly the design was an extrapolation of the BT-1 "Flying Lifeboat," an airplane that had its origins in a meeting between Curtiss and Coast Guard officers where they discussed the hazards of effecting rescues through heavy surf. Inshore lifesaving would be safer, and the Coast Guard's rescue capabilities extended well out to sea if a flying boat could be designed to land in heavy seas or surf. Intrigued by the concept, Curtiss got together with Gilmore in Buffalo to complete an airplane with a startlingly novel design— a triplane incorporating a hull just under 25 feet long with the rear vertical stabilizer, rudder, and elevators affixed to a 15-foot boom. In a rescue mission, the craft would land at sea, jettison its wings and tail group, and make its way to shore using a small auxiliary motor. Power came from a 200-horsepower engine mounted low in the hull linked to twin shaft-driven tractor propellers; later modifications placed the engine and a single propeller on the center wing above the hull. After completing tests with the flying boat at Hampton Roads sometime in early 1918, the Navy concluded that no more information could be learned about its hydrodynamic characteristics, and the airplane was retired from service.[5]

Taylor liked Curtiss' plans for the bigger airplane but conceded that Curtiss and the Navy faced enough obstacles with the smaller design, and believed that the V-12 Liberty engine, then undergoing tests, would provide sufficient power for the trimotor alternative. Hunsaker's team proceeded as directed. In developing the preliminary design, Albert Zahm was responsible for tests of a three-foot scale model in the wind tunnel at the Washington Navy Yard, confirming the basic configuration of the tail group. Hunsaker's theoretical stability data was also useful in the design process. As with the 1914 *America*, disposable lift was the key variable. Extrapolating from the notion that the range would be the equivalent of Newfoundland to Ireland nonstop, or Newfoundland to Portugal via the Azores, the airplane would need at least eight hundred gallons of gasoline, weighing 4,800 pounds. As the plans went forward, the resulting "paper" airplane's weight went up from twenty thousand pounds to twenty-five thousand pounds, with a total wing area of 3,370 square feet.[6]

At the same time it became apparent that keeping all the work in house for such an ambitious project would overwhelm the Aircraft Division's limited staff and hold up other, higher-priority, aircraft programs. Taylor held Curtiss in high regard, considering him "one of the best friends that Naval Aviation has ever had, and [he] has done more than any other man in making Naval Aviation possible." Yet turning everything over to Curtiss, whose slack and inefficient "shop" organization had been a source of frustration for Mark Bristol three years earlier, was unwise. The compromise was to have the design, development, and initial production done by Curtiss in Buffalo, with naval officers in supervisory positions closely monitoring all dimensions of the project.[7]

To oversee work on the big flying boat, generally referred to as the TH-1 (for Taylor-Hunsaker and consistent with the Curtiss company's alphabetical designation system), the Navy assigned Westervelt to Buffalo as superintending constructor of aircraft, soon joined in September by Curtiss' old Navy friend Dick Richardson, now a lieutenant commander. Ens. Charles J. McCarthy, a 1916 MIT graduate and engineering draftsman in Hunsaker's office, arrived in Buffalo before the end of the month, responsible for stress calculations and the big flying boat's structural design details. It did not take Richardson long to realize that the trimotor was overweight, a problem soon confirmed by Hunsaker's lift and drag calculations. Richardson plunged into a redesign of the airplane, drastically cutting its MTOW to nineteen thousand pounds, with a 106-foot wingspan and a wing area of 2,375 square feet. Further revisions to the airplane's design before the end of the year brought its MTOW up to more than twenty-one thousand pounds, increased its wingspan to 126 feet, and brought the total wing area to 2,380 square feet, for a wing loading of 8.8 pounds per square foot. The hull measured 45 feet long, and with the empennage the length of the aircraft came to 68½ feet. With an empty weight of thirteen thousand pounds, the TH-1 had a respectable load-to-tare ratio of 38:62. The prospect of squeezing an additional one hundred horsepower from the 300-horsepower Liberty engine further encouraged Richardson and others that the airplane—easily the biggest yet conceived in the United States—would meet all the anticipated performance criteria.[8]

On 24 November, the Navy contracted with Curtiss Aeroplane and Motor for the design and drafting work on the airplane, under the direction of the Navy. Curtiss' total costs were to be paid by the Navy, which also contributed a generous 15 percent profit. In return the company had to relinquish to the Navy all proprietary design rights, which Curtiss found objectionable but did not feel he was in a position to dispute. At about the same time, the airplane became known as the NC, for Navy Curtiss, reflecting the cooperative nature of the project; Westervelt's suggestion that it be renamed the DWT, honoring Admiral Taylor, had found little support in the bureau, least of all from Taylor himself, who later joked that if the project failed NC would stand for "Nobody's Child."[9]

In December 1917, in the midst of the design and development phase of the NC project, Curtiss Engineering Corporation moved from Buffalo to a new site off Clinton Road next door to the Army's Hazelhurst Field in Garden City, Long Island. More or less a reincarnation of Curtiss' old Hammondsport and Buffalo "shop" organization, only with more resources and vastly more space, the Garden City establishment was essentially a corporate aeronautical research laboratory viewed by the Navy as a welcome addition to its own limited experimental facilities. Completed at a cost of $500,000 on thirty acres of property, the 60,000-square foot, three-story steel and reinforced-concrete building housed a model shop, drafting rooms, an assembly shop, and engine and propeller test facilities. A state-of-the-art 7-foot-diameter, 400-horsepower open-circuit wind tunnel, reputed to be the largest in the world at the time, occupied a separate structure. Nearby, the Curtisses spent $200,000 on a large house on Stewart Avenue and Nassau Boulevard, which with its landscaping, big garage, expansive garden, and swimming pool was considered at the time to be "one of the most attractive places in Nassau County." The Curtisses' Garden City location had many attractions, not the least of which was that it was so close to the engineering plant that on many days Glenn, forty years old and still lean and in superb physical condition, often bicycled to work.[10]

At the same time Curtiss Engineering moved to Garden City in December 1917, Taylor and Adm. Robert S. Griffin, chief of the Bureau of Steam Engineering (which had responsibility for aircraft power plants) recommended to Secretary of the Navy Josephus Daniels that the Navy proceed with construction of the NC boats. On 8 January, Daniels authorized issuing a cost-plus contract for four of the NCs to Curtiss Engineering. Curtiss was to build the first NC hull in Garden City and thereafter planned to use subcontractors for the other three because of the limited size of the plant facilities. When the Curtiss Garden City plant proved too small even for such limited manufacturing, the Navy undertook construction of an assembly building adjacent to the existing factory large enough to accommodate two of the huge airplanes. Subcontractors for the hull were boat builders Lawley and Sons in Boston and Herreshoffs in Bristol, Rhode Island; more than seven manufacturers supplied other major airframe components.[11]

Once the NC project moved from concept to production it ran into a myriad of problems, most of them connected with what Westervelt considered the "hopeless state of disorganization" in Garden City. Curtiss, who according to Hunsaker was "not a nine-to-five man," did not exercise close managerial control of the factory yet wielded veto powers over who ran things on the shop floor, adding to the confusion. Nor was Keys much help in keeping the project on schedule. Not all the delays were caused by Curtiss or management. Some were the result of material shortages, and the complex logistics of getting the NC components to Garden City for assembly. The Locke Body Company, for example, had to transport the airplane's wings and tail assembly from its factory through the narrow streets of Manhattan to Garden City on large horse-drawn wagons, escorted at night by naval officers in automobiles.[12]

Taylor wrote to Curtiss on 9 July to complain that he was "disappointed" with the slow progress, which he attributed to the company's relative lack of interest in a project originated by the Navy and not by themselves. In an attempt to move things along, Taylor threatened Curtiss with "developing an experimental and designing organization inside the Navy, and discontinuing such work with your company" and urged Curtiss "to impress upon the members of your organization that this is the most important single piece of work which has been intrusted to them, and I am expecting you to stand behind this work and bring it to a successful conclusion." Once again, responsible naval officers found shortcomings in Curtiss' organization and considered it necessary to remind him that the Navy's interests in their partnership always took precedence, especially in wartime. Curtiss' response to Taylor's letter is not known, but the ultimatum had the desired effect. Westervelt reported shortly thereafter that despite the "remarkable ineptness of the Curtiss Company . . . things are looking up and I am hopeful of getting the first boat out in a comparatively short time." Within six weeks the *NC-1* was completed.[13]

The next problem was to deliver the seven-ton airplane to the air station at Rockaway on Jamaica Bay for flight testing. Much too big to ship as a whole, the airplane had to be broken down into large components and transported by wagon some twenty miles from Garden City to the station, where the Navy had erected a hangar large enough for two of the NCs and a marine railway for getting them in and out of the water. The process took more than ten days, during which one wing was damaged by an inebriated motorist, but by 22 September all the parts had been delivered and by the end of the month the *NC-1* had been assembled and was ready for its first flights.[14]

Curtiss was present at Rockaway on Jamaica Bay for the *NC-1*'s maiden flight on 4 October. Dick Richardson was chief test pilot, joined in the cockpit by Lt. David McCulloch, an enlisted Navy machinist, and two Curtiss engineers. That afternoon, the huge flying boat slipped down the marine railway, then, following a brief high-speed test run across the calm waters of the bay, Richardson gunned the three Libertys and the *NC-1* lifted off for a brief, thirty-second flight. Five more flights followed that day, after which Richardson reported that the airplane was a little tail-heavy but otherwise flew remarkably well.[15] Completing such a large and complex airplane as well as putting in place the infrastructure for its production in a little more than a year was an accomplishment of major proportions, and a tribute to the Navy's considerable ability to mold and manage such partnerships with private aircraft manufacturers.

Longer flights at progressively heavier weights followed before the end of the year as Richardson and others explored the dimensions of the *NC-1*'s performance envelope. Fitted with three new 400-horsepower high-compression Libertys and more efficient propellers, the *NC-1* flew at an MTOW of 24,700 pounds. On November 7–9, the airplane accomplished a round-trip flight from Rockaway to Hampton Roads, with an overnight stop at Anacostia on the way down. Following this was a record flight on the twenty-fifth with fifty-one people, including a stowaway who had sneaked aboard an hour before takeoff. Further studies showed that fitting a fourth engine to the airplane would bring its MTOW up to twenty-eight thousand pounds, with a corresponding increase in disposable lift that provided more than enough range to make the Azores from Newfoundland. But with the unexpected yet welcome end of the war on 11 November Admiral Taylor's requirement for the big flying boat lost its urgency, and there loomed the prospect that the *NC-1* and her sisters would spend the rest of their days languishing in a hangar.[16]

Even before the armistice, John Towers, who had been slated to make the *America*'s aborted transatlantic flight in 1914, saw another opportunity to accomplish the mission using the big NC boats. In a memo to Chief of Naval Operations (CNO) Adm. William S. Benson on 31 October, Towers wrote that the flight meshed with the Navy's efforts to develop means of getting flying boats across the ocean directly by air, and was an opportunity for the Navy to accomplish a historic "epoch-making event" that would enhance the prestige of American aviation. He suggested that the four NCs be allocated for the flight as soon as possible after the end of the war. Benson appointed a board to study the matter, chaired by Capt. John T. Tompkins, with Towers and naval aviator Godfrey Chevalier (now a lieutenant commander) as its members. Unsurprisingly, the board recommended on 4 February 1919 that the NC boats be assigned to the flight, to take place in May, with the first leg from Newfoundland to Ponta Delgada in the Azores, and the second from the Azores to Lisbon, essentially the same route planned for the *America* in 1914. From Lisbon, the airplanes would proceed to Plymouth, England, where they would be taken apart at the Navy's wartime flying-boat base at Killingholme and crated for transport back across the Atlantic. A fleet of sixty destroyers would range every fifty miles to mark the route, and another forty or so ships would provide logistical support. Daniels approved the report and assigned Towers to head a new transatlantic (TA) section in the CNO's office. Towers assembled the best and brightest naval aviation could offer as his planning staff, including Richardson, Chevalier, and Lt. Cdr. Richard E. Byrd, scion of the famous Byrd family of Virginia and an eager new flier. Together with aviators and technical experts in operations and the various bureaus, Towers' group tackled demanding navigation, weather, instrumentation, communication, and other challenges associated with the ambitious undertaking.[17]

Hampered by tardy material deliveries and labor difficulties, work on the NCs went ahead in fits and starts at Garden City and Rockaway. Nor were things much better on the engineering side, where the decision to add a fourth engine to the boats raised the question of how to determine the optimum configuration of the power plants. The answer came largely by trial and error. The *NC-2*, which was completed and first flew at Rockaway on 3 February 1919, originally had its engines arranged like those of the *NC-1*—that is, three engines in nacelles between the wings, with the pilots sitting in the center nacelle above the hull. In an attempt to improve pilot visibility, the center engine was relocated behind the fliers, driving a pusher propeller. After a number of test flights in this configuration, the airplane was rebuilt with the engines placed in tandem in two nacelles outboard between the wings, and the aviators sitting side-by-side in the hull well forward of the propellers. With the extra power, the airplane flew at an MTOW of twenty-eight thousand pounds, but the tandem arrangement led to another problem. If one of the forward engines quit, the aft engine's pusher propeller lost most of its efficiency, throwing the entire airplane out of balance. Moreover, the aft propellers suffered from spray damage on takeoffs and landings.[18]

As a result of the experience with the *NC-2*, the Navy and Curtiss engineers compromised on the *NC-3* and *NC-4*, configuring them with two engines paired back-to-back in a center nacelle, with the aft engine linked to a two-blade pusher propeller. The remaining two engines drove two-blade tractor propellers in nacelles outboard between the upper and lower wings. The pilots sat in an open cockpit in the hull, as they had in the *NC-2*. The *NC-3* flew on 23 April, and the *NC-4* on 1 May, perilously close to the date when the transatlantic flight was to begin. Because the hangar at Rockaway had room only for the *NC-3* and the *NC-4*, the *NC-1* stayed outside where it suffered severe damage from a storm on March 27. Because no spares were available to replace its damaged lower wing, the *NC-1* was rebuilt with wings taken from the *NC-2* and converted to four engines in the same center tandem configuration as the *NC-3* and *NC-4*. This put the *NC-2* out of commission and left only three of the four boats available for the transatlantic flight.[19]

It is revealing to compare the *NC-4* in the spring of 1919 to the *NC-1* as it was completed and flown in October 1918. MTOW was up from twenty-one thousand pounds to twenty-eight thousand pounds, with the same wing area and an increased wing loading of 11.8 pounds per square foot—heavy for the time. The *NC-1*'s load-to-tare ratio of 38:62 was good, but the *NC-4*'s was an impressive 45:57 at an empty weight of 15,874 pounds, with more than eleven thousand pounds of disposable lift taken up by 1,800 gallons of fuel. At 1,420 nautical miles, the NC's range was more than enough to reach the Azores.[20]

Towers was commanding officer of the newly constituted NC Seaplane Division One assembled at Rockaway on 3 May. He wore another hat as commanding officer and navigator of the *NC-3*. There were some familiar faces among the flight crews, all of whom knew that the Navy's prestige was on the line and rested in their hands. Richardson was the *NC-3*'s pilot, and McCulloch was its copilot. Lt. Cdr. Albert C. ("Putty") Read commanded the *NC-4*, with Coast Guard Lt. Elmer Stone as pilot and Lt. Walter Hinton as copilot. *NC-1* had Pat Bellinger, now a lieutenant commander, as its commanding officer, with Lt. Cdr. Marc A. Mitscher as pilot and Lt. Louis T. Barrin as copilot.[21]

A fire that damaged the *NC-1* on 5 May, followed by bad weather, caused a five-day delay. Despite a forecast for marginal weather at their first stop—Halifax, Nova Scotia—Towers decided they could wait no longer and ordered the three aircraft to get underway on the eighth. The *NC-1* and the *NC-3* arrived in Halifax without incident, but Read's *NC-4* lost both of its centerline tandem engines and was forced down off Cape Cod. Read taxied overnight into the naval air station at Chatham, where repairs stranded the airplane until the fourteenth. In the interim, on 10 May, the other two aircraft had continued on to Trepassey Harbor, Newfoundland, the jumping-off point for the flight to the Azores. The *NC-4* arrived at Trepassey on the evening of the fifteenth following an overnight stop in Halifax.[22]

With two of the NCs on their way from Halifax to Newfoundland, Curtiss drew on his considerable knowledge of aircraft performance and oceanic weather patterns to provide the press with his appraisal of the Navy's transatlantic effort. He stressed that the design of the NCs provided the aviators with "the largest possible factor of safety. . . . The NC boats, if forced to descend, can ride a fairly high sea. . . . Repairs made, they can ascend again," he added, although the likelihood of a forced landing in mid-Atlantic was in his estimation "remote." He said that the Navy had been wise to choose the route from Newfoundland to the Azores. That leg of the journey would take about twenty hours aided by favorable winds, or no more than thirty hours if the NCs ran into adverse weather. The airplanes would fly at their most economical cruising speed, usually about seventy miles per hour to begin with, but then decreasing as the fuel was consumed and the fliers cut back the throttles or perhaps even shut down one of the engines. Between nine and fifteen hours into the flight, the aviators could make slight course changes so that they could pick up tailwinds and increase their speed to more than ninety miles per hour and arrive at Ponta Delgada as planned. If for some reason they did not get any help from the weather they could land at the westernmost island of Flores, although doing so would add another three hundred miles or so to the next leg of the flight from the Azores to Portugal.[23]

After additional repairs were made and final preparations finished, the three NCs lifted off from Trepassey on the evening of the sixteenth for the twenty-hour flight to the Azores. All went well overnight, even though the fliers ran into rough air and their craft fell out of formation and became separated. Just after dawn they ran into low overcast and fog that prevented them from visually sighting the station ships. Aboard the NC-1 Bellinger and his crew had trouble keeping on course using instruments alone. Concluding that they were lost somewhere in the vicinity of the Azores, they decided to put the airplane down so they could take radio bearings without the nagging interference caused by the engines. They made a rough landing in heavy swells that left the NC-1 undamaged but unable to take off as the wind and waves quickly worsened. A passing freighter rescued the crew and took the flying boat in tow until the tow line broke. One of the Navy destroyers arrived on the scene and attempted to rig another tow line to the derelict craft, but the rough seas thwarted the efforts, and the now-battered hulk of the NC-1 sank on the evening of the twentieth.[24]

Towers, Richardson, and the NC-3 fared no better. Through the rain and fog the crew sighted what they thought to be one of the station ships, but that in reality was an American cruiser on a parallel course well to the south of the NCs' flight path. Convinced they were well to the north of their route, the NC-3 fliers turned south, taking them even farther off course and away from the station ships and their objective in the Azores. A break in the gloom finally allowed Towers to get a sextant reading. After determining their approximate position, he ordered a turn to the north, which put them back on course toward the islands. Like Bellinger, Towers decided to land in the sea and attempt a definitive radio fix before continuing the flight, and like the NC-1, once down the NC-3 could not take off again, in part due to the rough seas but also because the impact of the landing had damaged the struts supporting the center engine nacelle. With the station ships far to the north and west of their position and no indication that their radioed distress calls had been received, the crew of the NC-3 decided their best option was to "sail" their sturdy but unflyable craft in the direction of Ponta Delgada. The extraordinary two-hundred-mile ocean odyssey in vicious weather lasted more than two days, culminating when the NC-3's elated but exhausted crew limped the badly damaged flying boat into the harbor on three engines.[25]

The *NC-3* had made it to Ponta Delgada, but the craft was beyond quick or easy repair and would not be able to complete the next stage to Portugal. Now the success of the mission lay with Read and the *NC-4*. First light on the morning of the seventeenth found the *NC-4* enshrouded in fog like the other flying boats, but deft handling of the radio gave them the bearings needed to stay on course. As the weather grew worse and the prospect of running out of fuel became not a possibility but a certainty, Read decided to land at Horta and not risk trying to make Ponta Delgada. Only minutes before the fog rolled in, the *NC-4* landed safely and was tied up next to the Navy's emergency support ship in the harbor. And there the flying boat and her crew remained for the next three days until the skies cleared. They took off again on the afternoon of the twentieth for the relatively short hop to Ponta Delgada. Weather and mechanical problems delayed the start of the flight to Portugal until the morning of the twenty-seventh. Nine and a half hours later, the *NC-4* was on the Tagus River in Lisbon after a flight noteworthy for its lack of drama. Towers, Bellinger, and the crews of the *NC-1* and *NC-3*, having arrived in Lisbon by ship some days earlier, were among the first to congratulate Read and his men on their accomplishment—the first aerial crossing of the Atlantic.[26]

The *NC-4* and her crew still faced the final leg of the flight, more than eight hundred miles north from Lisbon to Plymouth, before the Navy could declare the venture an unqualified success. Early on the morning of 30 May the big flying boat was back in the air, but did not get far before having to put down in the calm waters of an estuary to repair a fuel leak before continuing on to an overnight stop at Ferrol, Spain. Then it was an uneventful flight across the Bay of Biscay on the morning of the thirty-first, aided by another string of station ships, and into the harbor at Plymouth and a grand welcome early that afternoon. Ceremonies in Plymouth and London followed, as did a visit to Paris and a meeting with President Wilson, who was in the city for the Versailles peace negotiations, then a week's leave and the voyage back to New York on board the former German liner and now American troopship USS *Zeppelin*. As the ship entered New York's upper harbor on the afternoon of 27 June, Curtiss joined naval officers and other dignitaries on the tug *Manhattan* in greeting the aviators as the *Zeppelin* made its way through New York's upper harbor to one of the piers in Hoboken.[27]

In New York on the evening of 10 July, Curtiss hosted a welcome-home banquet at the Hotel Commodore for the intrepid transatlantic fliers. Imaginatively decorated like the interior of a giant transatlantic seaplane, the hall featured windows through which the guests could see land, the ocean, and the sky pass beneath them as searchlights illuminated the panorama. Among the speakers were David Taylor, who emphasized that the name finally given to the airplanes demonstrated the cooperative nature of the project, and John Towers, who related how quickly the Curtiss company had responded to the 5 May fire, getting the parts and people to Rockaway to repair the *NC-1* and *NC-4* in a matter of hours. Then it was Curtiss' turn: "This seems to be developing into a sort of race to see who can make the shortest speech," he remarked; "I want to say right here that I am going to be the winner." When the laughter subsided, he said that he was "more than glad to have you all here" and went on to bestow a four-foot, gold-plated model of the NC craft to the Navy and award each of the aviators commemorative medallions. In return he received an oil painting showing the three airplanes winging their way across the ocean.[28] For Curtiss the occasion must have been bittersweet, a satisfying punctuation to his dream of flying the Atlantic five years before while bringing with it the realization that not he but a squadron of naval aviators backed by an armada of ships had accomplished what was then acknowledged as the greatest achievement of the postwar air age. The NCs also marked the start of a new phase in Curtiss' aviation career. He would no longer be in the forefront of airplane design and construction and would increasingly recede into the aviation background, yet his and his company's commitment to flight remained undiminished, now focusing more on speed than endurance in the immediate postwar years.

From his earliest years Curtiss had had a strong competitive urge, manifested in his bicycle and motorcycle racing and in his own flying career. Moreover, he truly believed that racing "improved the breed" and stimulated sales, needed more than ever by the Curtiss companies in the greatly restricted aviation market of the early 1920s. To generate enthusiasm for water flying and to promote sales of his hydros and flying boats, Curtiss in 1915 had created the Marine Flying Trophy, an elaborate silver globe topped by a model flying boat, and $5,000 in cash to be awarded in $1,000 annual increments. Loosely administered by the Aero Club of America, the prize in its first year attracted a dozen competitors, one of whom, Oscar A. Brindley, a Wright aviator, won with a flight of 554 miles in less than ten hours along the Pacific Coast. The following August, Victor Carlstrom took home the trophy with a flight of 661 miles in a float-equipped Curtiss twin-engine JN, over a closed course near the Curtiss Newport News airfield. Hoping to stimulate more competitive interest in aviation, Curtiss had also suggested in early 1915 that the Navy challenge the

Army to a series of races overseen by the Aero Club of America and for which he would offer prizes to the winners. Secretary of the Navy Daniels politely declined the overture, citing the Navy's limited engineering staff and the need for them to devote their time to other, more pressing needs as the service struggled to define its aviation requirements on the eve of World War I.[29]

Following that conflict, and facing what he knew would be lean years for aircraft manufacturers, Curtiss did not hesitate to use his personal connections with naval officers in an attempt to join with them in developing new and more powerful service aircraft. In April 1920, he reminded his friend Jerome Hunsaker that regardless of what aircraft procurement decisions were made in Washington, the company and its leadership "are very desirous of renewing Navy work, feel they are entitled to it and intend to get busy at once" on any Navy aircraft orders they received. He also dropped the word that he and his people at Garden City were busy working on an airplane to enter in the international James Gordon Bennett races to be held in France later that year following a wartime hiatus.[30]

The machine Curtiss referred to was a monoplane fitted with one of Curtiss' new 427-horsepower water-cooled Model C-12 V-12 engines that was to attain the then-phenomenal speed of two hundred miles per hour. Texas oilman Seymour Cox and his wife had just provided Curtiss with what amounted to a blank check for the airplane, known as the *Texas Wildcat*, and a second example, the *Cactus Kitten*, for the sole purpose of participating in the Gordon Bennett competition. Following shakedown flights in Buffalo, Curtiss sent Roland Rohlfs, the company's chief test pilot, and the *Texas Wildcat* off to France on 5 September with the American flag he had taken to Rheims for the first Gordon Bennett competition eleven years earlier. Although Rohlfs wrecked the Curtiss entry and the other American airplanes did not finish in the races—won by the French, whose third victory retired the Gordon Bennett trophy—the effort anticipated a highly successful collaboration with the Navy in developing and building state-of-the art, high-performance racing airplanes.[31] When the opportunity came, Curtiss enthusiastically turned Garden City into the Navy's primary source for machines that competed in some of the most exciting air races the country had ever witnessed.

In cooperation with Curtiss and other manufacturers, the Navy sought to acquire a new generation of fighter aircraft based in part on the experience gained in racing. Soon after the December 1917 move to Garden City, Curtiss put his team to work on high-performance airplanes, relying on the expertise of Bill Gilmore in designing new aerostructures that incorporated the latest wind tunnel data and on Charles Kirkham, son of the Bath machinist who had supplied Curtiss with castings for his first motorcycles, for engines with dramatically increased output. One of the first fruits of their efforts was a Navy order in March 1918 for two Model 18T fighters, known in Garden City as the *Wasp*. The fighter was a two-seat triplane with a sleek laminated wood fuselage and Kirkham's new 400-horsepower water-cooled K-12, widely considered the most advanced American aero engine of the time. It flew for the first time in July with Roland Rohlfs at the controls. A month later Richardson and other naval officers were present when the airplane reached 163 miles per hour, smashing all previous world speed records. In September 1919, Rohlfs took the 18T to a world altitude record of more than thirty-four thousand feet. Fitted with a central float, the airplane, again with Rohlfs as pilot, attained 138 miles per hour at Rockaway in April 1920.[32]

Experience with the 18T translated into a major commitment by Curtiss and the Navy to cooperate on entries in the 1920 Pulitzer race. It was to be held on Thanksgiving Day, 25 November, under the auspices of the Aero Club of America at Mitchel Field, an Army facility that had been established adjacent to Hazelhurst Field on Long Island in 1917. Joseph Pulitzer's sons Joseph Jr., Ralph, and Herbert, assumed not only their father's newspaper empire on his death in 1911 but also his interest in fostering aviation through competition. After the war they offered a $5,000 prize to the winners of the Pulitzer speed contests. The Army's powerful Verville VCP racer took top honors in the 1920 race, but it could not sustain high speeds without damaging its engine. The Curtiss 18Ts were fast, one of them setting a lap record, but they, too, suffered from engine problems and did not finish the race, much to Curtiss' dismay. In contrast, Curtiss-built DH-4s and Navy Vought VE-7s generally performed well. To Jerome Hunsaker, who oversaw the Navy's Pulitzer entries, the 18Ts were "a good effort," but the race also taught an important lesson about reliability and the need for thorough testing to assure long-term success in air racing. Curtiss missed seeing Hunsaker at the airfield and invited him to a Thanksgiving lunch at his home in Garden City, which Hunsaker had to decline due to his commitments at the Pulitzer.[33]

Clement Keys, who viewed air racing as a means of demonstrating the Curtiss company's strong commitment to both commercial and military aeronautics, fully supported the Navy-Curtiss collaboration. The end of the war had brought almost immediate retrenchment of the American aircraft industry, with the cancellation of military contracts not yet completed and massive layoffs of aircraft and engine workers. Within months, Curtiss Aeroplane and Motor lost up to $75 million in production orders. The company quickly responded to the situation by selling the big North Elmwood plant and terminating its leases on its other Buffalo facilities. Only the Churchill Street factory remained, which by December 1919 was operating at barely 50 percent capacity with a handful of orders for small commercial aircraft. In what had to be a heartrending decision for Curtiss personally, for he knew what the economic consequences would be for his hometown, the company shut down the Hammondsport engine plant at the end of December 1918 and transferred all the tools and machinery to Churchill Street. Even before the armistice, aircraft and engine orders had declined, causing employment at the factory to fall below one thousand, with another four hundred or so workers laid off before the end of November. Had shutting down the Curtiss plant been the only bad news, the community would have been reasonably well off, but within a month came ratification of the Prohibition amendment, which presaged the imminent closure of the area's wine cellars.[34]

In December 1919, for what he said were more "sentimental rather than financial reasons," Curtiss helped organize a new company, Keuka Industries, in order to get the Hammondsport plant back in operation producing specialized machine parts and "high-grade" automobile engines. Former Curtiss sales manager and friend Lyman J. Seely was president, and J. H. McNamara, who had been responsible for engine production at Hammondsport, was one of the directors and the new manager of the enterprise, which in a depressed market never got off the ground. Later his old associates Beckwith Havens, Charles Witmer, and Lanny Callan ran another company, Airships Inc., out of the old factory, providing parts and components for the Navy's rigid airships. But for all practical purposes Hammondsport's years were over as a center of the aeronautical industry.[35]

Curtiss Aeroplane and Motor was in trouble by the middle of 1920. Experimental contracts, many from the Navy, had buoyed the firm's revenues, as had the sale of surplus Navy flying boats, income from its flying schools, and the disposal of the Buffalo and Hammondsport plants, but military and commercial production contracts were not sufficient to ensure financial health. In August, Keys learned that the company had only a few days to make good on $650,000 in debts and that Willys-Overland, itself suffering from poor vehicle sales in a weak national economy, would not pay them. Believing that the company had the potential to prosper in the long term and with a plan to reinvigorate production and sales, Keys convinced the boards of both companies to sell their stock holdings in Curtiss Aeroplane and Motor to him for the amount of the outstanding debts. Curtiss did not join Keys in the new ownership, taking instead an unpaid position as chairman of the company's engineering committee and retaining nominal authority over operations at Garden City. Although the changes removed Curtiss even farther from the financial and management side of the business, he was still an important part of the management team, responsible both for the cozy relationship between Garden City and the Navy and for, as Keys said, his experience and wise "engineering counsel."[36]

The Navy connection remained strong with an order for two new racers from Curtiss Engineering in June 1921. Gilmore had general responsibility for their design. To best the Army entries in the Pulitzer that year, the Navy looked for durability, reliability, and predictable handling characteristics over outright speed. Known as the Model 23 in Garden City and designated CR (Curtiss Racer) by the Navy, the biplanes had streamlined wood fuselages and 400-horsepower Model CD-12 V-12 engines and were expected to reach speeds up to 185 miles per hour. The CR-2 was completed before the CR-1 and was test flown at Garden City in August. When by mutual consent the Navy and the Army withdrew from the Pulitzer that year, Curtiss "borrowed" the CR-2 and entered it in the Pulitzer competition at Omaha that November. Flown over a closed-circuit course by Curtiss test pilot Bert Acosta, who had been with Curtiss since the old North Island days, the racer defeated the Curtiss *Cactus Kitten* with a record speed of nearly 177 miles per hour.[37]

Due in part to the success of the CRs, the Navy decided to return to racing in 1922, beginning with the Curtiss Marine Flying Trophy competition to be held in Detroit under the sponsorship of the Detroit Aviation Society. For the race, Curtiss fitted the two 18T triplanes with single floats and replaced the Kirkham engines with CD-12s. Eight Navy and Marine aviators entered the race, which began on 8 October after delays caused by bad weather. The modified 18Ts were easily the fastest over the closed twenty-mile course laid out along the Detroit River, but one of the airplanes was forced down as a result of damage to one of the wing floats, and the other was leading the race when it ran out of fuel. The winner was Navy flier Lt. Adolphus W. ("Jake") Gorton, in a TR-1 racer based on the Hunsaker-designed TS-1 biplane fighter.[38]

As he had been for the Marine Trophy competition, Curtiss was present for the Pulitzer race, which began on 14 October 1922 at the Army's Selfridge Field north of Detroit. This time both services agreed to compete, with the Navy making a two-front assault on the trophy by entering the veteran CRs rebuilt and modified by Curtiss as CR-2s, along with two new NW (Navy-

Wright) "mystery" racers. Orville Wright was there to watch the competition, too. Both of the old rivals had to be thinking not only of the still-simmering enmity between them but also of the coincidence that the race venue had been named for Tom Selfridge, Curtiss' AEA associate who had died in Orville's Fort Myer accident twelve years before. The Army entered two 375-horsepower Curtiss R-6s in the race, which came in first and second, the winner setting a new closed-course speed record of 206 miles per hour and the second-place airplane completing a lap at more than 216 miles per hour. The CRs finished third and fourth, disappointing for the Navy team, but hardly for Curtiss, who saw his airplanes totally dominate the competition and vanquish the Wrights, only one of which was raced, and it suffered an engine breakdown and did not finish.[39]

Some satisfaction for the Navy came the following September at the Schneider Cup races, a prestigious international competition for seaplanes. In preparation for the contests, Curtiss updated the CRs, now designated CR-3s, with new 485-horsepower D-12 engines, aluminum propellers, ultra-low-drag wing-surface radiators, and twin pontoons. The two Curtiss entries finished one-two, well ahead of the third-place British finisher. The swan song for the Navy-Curtiss partnership came with the Pulitzer races in St. Louis on 6 October 1923, where Curtiss was again on hand to watch two new Navy Curtiss R2C-1s, with 500-horsepower D-12s, compete alongside two Navy Wright F2W-1s. One of the R2C-1s, flown by Lt. Alford J. ("Al") Williams Jr., won, storming around the pylons at an average speed more than ten miles per hour faster than the second-place Wright machine. Intoxicated by the results, Curtiss forecast that "airplanes with a speed of 500 miles an hour would be seen in the sky in a few years."[40]

By then, Curtiss had ceased his direct involvement in the company's air racing operations, although he continued to display an undiminished spirit of innovation. Like many observers, he had been intrigued by the ability of many seabirds to stay aloft almost indefinitely without flapping their wings. To try out his ideas, Curtiss designed and built a flying-boat glider, which he completed at Garden City in early September 1922. Possibly the last airplane design for which he can be given full credit, the little 145-pound biplane featured an aluminum hull and wood and fabric wings totaling 280 square feet for a wing loading of less than a pound per square foot. Because Curtiss intended to fly the craft himself, it had the old shoulder yoke control for the ailerons and a wheel for the rudder. Curtiss first tested the glider at Manhasset Bay on Long

Island Sound on 8 September. The craft generally flew well, with one glide lasting seventeen seconds, but it was not capable of staying in the air for the extended periods he had anticipated and it was difficult to control when towed behind a high-speed motorboat.[41]

Hunsaker observed some of the glider trials. He thought the little craft might be capable of reaching altitudes of "several thousand feet" but wondered how safe it was because of its lightweight construction and the control problems it encountered when being towed. He saw no naval applications for the craft either in instructing novice seaplane pilots or as a substitute for the kite balloon in spotting gunfire from ships. In any case, he believed Curtiss had built the glider as an experiment and that it might be useful in exploring the "ground effect" phenomenon close to the surface of the sea, but its chief appeal would mostly be to the wealthy "sporting" pilot who would fly it only under conditions where its fragility would not be a concern.[42] Perhaps Curtiss was discouraged that the Navy was not more interested in the glider. More likely he was pleased his officer friends still thought enough of his talents to take the time to evaluate his airplane designs and consider their practical uses, even if they did not mesh with any of the Navy's immediate requirements. Or perhaps it did not matter, for by 1923 Curtiss' personal and business interests had drifted far from Garden City and the waters of Long Island Sound to what were rapidly emerging as new and exciting opportunities in Florida a thousand miles to the south.

Epilogue

Although the Curtisses retained their spacious home in Garden City, after 1922 the family spent more time in Miami, where Lena, Glenn Jr., and Lena's mother more or less lived permanently and where Curtiss plunged into what became a feverish speculative boom in real estate. In July 1918, Curtiss had joined with James H. Bright, a cattle rancher, to buy five thousand acres on the fringe of the Everglades west of Miami, where they planned to engage in large-scale scientific farming and ranching—essentially an agribusiness. In the meantime, when Curtiss sought a new site for his airfield and flying school, Bright offered part of his holdings in the area as a gift, seeing Curtiss' business as a down payment of sorts to encourage further development of the area. In April 1918, aviators from the First Marine Aviation Force occupied the Curtiss flying school, which the unit used as its training facility until sent overseas later in the year.[1]

The Bright connection led directly to Curtiss' involvement in the south Florida land rush. His first move was to buy out the shares in Bright's ranch owned by James' brother Charles, eventually joining Bright as part owner of his 17,000-acre cattle ranch and dairy farm. Over several years they added to their property until they held more than one hundred and twenty thousand acres of the flat Florida scrubland. Part of these holdings, north of the Miami Canal, they named Hialeah, Seminole for "upland prairie," and it was subsequently incorporated as a city in 1925. The partners formed the Curtiss-Bright Company specifically to take advantage of the real estate bonanza that enveloped Miami and south Florida, quickly earning more than $1 million from the sale of parcels in Hialeah. By November 1923, the Curtisses had completed a new pueblo-style house in the rapidly growing community. Over the next few years Curtiss persuaded his friends and family to join him, one of whom, his half-brother Carl Adams, became an associate in the Curtiss-Bright real estate enterprises. Another big holding was Brighton, a 48,000-acre tract north of

Miami and adjacent to Lake Okeechobee that Curtiss and Bright first used as a hunting preserve and on which they built a hotel intended to draw tourists and potential property owners.[2] Hialeah, meanwhile, took off as a summer resort and recreational community. In 1925, the Miami Jockey Club opened the 220-acre Hialeah Park Racetrack, one of the most lavish thoroughbred-racing venues in the state. The track also had a jai alai fronton, which brought in fans attracted by the speed and grace of the sport as well as the lure of gambling on the outcome of the matches. And the city became the site of the Miami Movie Studios, where, among others, D. W. Griffith directed and produced films. On the southern fringe of the city, Curtiss built a new airfield, home to the flying school relocated from Miami Beach.[3]

Curtiss and Bright established another community on the south side of the Miami Canal called Country Club Estates, which was later incorporated as Miami Springs. Conceived as a middle- and upper-class residential counterpoint to the chic playground of Hialeah, and featuring broad parkway-like avenues encircling a golf course and spring-fed lake, the development flourished, like everything else at the time in south Florida. The focal point was a large hotel, designed in keeping with Curtiss' preference for the pueblo-style architecture, complete with thunderbird designs and authentic Native American furnishings. Curtiss built a spacious house for his mother Lua, who moved to Country Club Estates from Coronado in 1924, and two years later, in February 1926, the Curtisses themselves settled into a big two-story house on nine acres next to the golf course. Completed at a cost of $150,000, not including another $80,000 for interior decorating, the house was planned by Curtiss himself, again following the southwestern architectural style. At the end of a winding road on the west end of the development Curtiss built a log house that he used as a hunting lodge.[4]

One of the joys of Curtiss' life at Country Club Estates was hosting visitors, who came to Florida seeking respite from the harsh northern winters. Friends golfed at his course and joined him on hunting and fishing expeditions, which were his real passion. His old friend Tank Waters was among those who spent time with him at Country Club Estates and eventually moved there from Hammondsport. Waters recalled that Curtiss was "an exceptional shot in hunting, either with a bow and arrow or gun," and that he greatly enjoyed showing off his driving skills on the narrow sandy roads around Brighton. Jerome Hunsaker's parents visited the place when they came to the Miami area on vacation in January 1928, and his father played golf with Hunsaker's old Navy buddy George Westervelt, who had come to

Country Club Estates as a permanent resident after his 1927 retirement from the service.[5]

In 1926, Curtiss created still a third south Florida community six miles north of Hialeah, which he named Opa-locka—a corruption of another Native American word roughly translated as "high dry hummock." What Curtiss initially had in mind for the new town was unclear—maybe even to him at the time. Curtiss biographer C. R. Roseberry believes that he wanted a community for people of modest income who could buy enough land to plant gardens and grow crops, but that he also foresaw the town as a home for light industry. This was not what Curtiss finally settled on. The final plans for the community envisioned a fantasy "Baghdad" based on the tales of the Arabian Nights. As construction progressed, city hall arose like a mosque with minarets and domes arranged around a central atrium. On streets named Ali Baba, Sinbad, Sesame, Caliph, and Sultan, residents and visitors found the railroad station, stores, offices, a hotel, a bank, and private homes, all expressing faux arabesque architectural themes. Dismissed by one writer as the "wackiest real estate scheme of all time," and an architectural "fraud," Opa-locka was, in the context of the real estate frenzy of the time, not so outlandish compared to other developments in the area that adopted Spanish, Mediterranean, Chinese, and other international motifs. Today, many of Opa-locka's buildings are protected on the National Register of Historic Places in part because of their unusual architecture.[6]

The frenetic Florida land boom reached a crescendo in late 1925 and early 1926. Miami, with a population of about thirty thousand in 1920, soared to an estimated seventy thousand by the middle of the decade as new high-rise buildings gave the "Magic City" its first skyline. Developers, Curtiss included, had to do little more than sketch out street plans for their new communities and watch the 10 percent down payment checks arrive from all over the Northeast and Midwest. But, as with all booms, there came the inevitable bust. By the spring of 1926 it appeared that there were fewer buyers than there had been a year before, then there was a trickle of defaults on payments, which left speculators owning land or options that they had hoped to resell at a profit, followed that summer by a massive collapse in real estate prices. As if that were not enough, a terrible hurricane struck Miami and south Florida on 18 September. When the floodwaters receded and the winds calmed, more than three hundred were dead, another four thousand injured, and eighteen thousand homeless. During the worst of the storm and for two days afterwards, Curtiss' friends in Garden City could not get in touch with him and feared the worst, finally receiving word that he and his family were safe. Exhibiting faith in the long-term prosperity and growth of the area and financially secure from his other business enterprises, Curtiss helped Hialeah and other communities rebuild in the wake of the tragedy and continued to seek other potential investment opportunities.[7]

Not surprisingly, aviation was one of them. Curtiss moved his airfield and flying school from Miami Beach to a more spacious site adjacent to Opa-locka, hoping to stimulate the development of commercial aviation, an industry that he and others believed had considerable profit potential. Known as the East Coast Aviation Camp by the end of 1926, part of the field became Miami's municipal airport, where an air express service operated in the summer of 1927. Miami accepted Curtiss' offer of additional acreage in July 1929 in return for paying to move the Navy's small airship hangar from Key West to Opa-locka. Goodyear used the hangar to house its non-rigid commercial airships or blimps, and the Navy later established an aviation reserve base with a large mooring mast and other facilities to handle its big rigid airships during winter operations. In July 1928—in a shrewd move, considering that much of his holdings had become next to worthless in the land bust—Curtiss donated 135 acres on 36th Street immediately south of Miami Springs to Miami for development as a commercial airfield, which Pan American Airways used for its airmail and passenger connections to the Caribbean and Latin America. Curtiss was among the many present for the air show dedicating the airport and the new Pan American terminal facilities on 7 January 1929. Pan American's inaugural flights to Nassau in the Bahamas began two days later.[8]

Regardless of where he lived during the 1920s Curtiss always made the effort to return to Hammondsport as often as possible. After the Curtisses had moved to Buffalo in 1915, Lena's aunt and uncle, the Osbornes, took over the Curtiss house on the hill, tending to it as the meeting place for the local women's club and making it available to the family during their visits to the village. On 4 July 1928, Curtiss returned to Hammondsport for a twentieth anniversary celebration of his *June Bug* flight. The event brought in his friends Dick Richardson and Augustus Post and perhaps ten thousand more people eager to be a part of the commemoration of the historic achievement. Asked if he was going to move back to Hammondsport, Curtiss answered: "Well, I never really moved away."[9]

A middle-aged man with time, energy, and money, and hardly ready for retirement, Curtiss actively sought ways to keep himself busy in Florida. The

America of the 1920s was increasingly a mobile society with more disposable income than ever before. As highways improved with large infusions of state, local, and federal funds, Americans took to the road in increasing numbers, where they often found an infrastructure not keeping up with their needs, especially for overnight accommodations. Few travelers were interested in hotels near downtown railroad stations. Curtiss understood this, and from his own inveterate devotion to the outdoors and hunting he also knew that a solution was some form of motor home that could provide the amenities he and others came to desire while on the move. Trailers or caravans were not new, but those available in the early 1920s were heavy, ill-handling, and crudely built. Why not, he theorized, apply aerodynamics and modern aircraft construction techniques and materials to a new generation of such vehicles?

From that concept emerged the Aerocar, "modern transportation" for a new generation of Americans on the move. Curtiss incorporated the Aerocar Corporation in September 1928 with Carl Adams as president and main offices in Opa-locka. Each example was custom built, but all had a wire-braced semi-monocoque structure that did away with the heavy chassis common to most travel trailers, a streamlined lightweight fabric-covered exterior, and a sophisticated fifth-wheel attachment to the rear of the car (preferably a coupe) that minimized dangerous horizontal and vertical motions. Luxury and safety, though, came at a cost, with Aerocars selling at the time for $2,600, not exactly in the price range for most Americans but consistent with what Curtiss sometimes called "land yachting." The company did well, exploiting a market that included not only wealthy private buyers but also companies that took their salespeople, products, and advertising displays on the road.[10]

The same year Curtiss formed his Aerocar company he faced another in what by then must have seemed to him like a recurring nightmare of expensive, time-consuming, and soul-wrenching legal woes. This time the litigation sprang from an entirely unexpected source: his old nemesis Augustus Herring, from whom he had thought he had shaken loose with the 1910 bankruptcy of the Herring-Curtiss company. The trouble was that the company, even though its stock was worthless, had never had its incorporation legally annulled. In October 1918, Herring revived the company, appointing a new board of directors that elected him president and bringing suit in the New York Supreme Court in Rochester against Curtiss, Monroe Wheeler, and others for $5 million in lost revenues and damages from the alleged fraud Curtiss and his associates perpetrated in conspiring to ensure the company's insolvency. In a deposition, Curtiss and Wheeler insisted that the Herring-Curtiss company had been in legitimate financial distress and that they had exhausted all means of avoiding bankruptcy. Curtiss admitted that he was "the poorest bookkeeper in the world," and as the person responsible for the company's financial records he had not kept an accurate accounting of receipts from flying exhibitions but that he had not been involved in any fraud. Although it is clear that Jerome Fanciulli had come up with the bankruptcy idea, and that Curtiss and Wheeler had accepted it—at least in principle—Curtiss and Wheeler denied any conspiracy in separating Herring from the company.[11]

The trial began in July 1921 and dragged out through the rest of the summer and fall, with extensive testimony from those on both sides of the suit. Finally, the presiding judge, Samuel N. Sawyer, handed down his decision at the end of April 1923. He ruled that although there had been accounting problems with the company, they had not been the result of wrongdoing, that no conspiracy had led to the firm's insolvency, and that Curtiss personally had done all he could to save the company and had not in any way sabotaged its finances to wrest control from Herring. Herring appealed the court's decision, but died on 17 July 1926 before the matter reached adjudication. His heirs took up the fight, winning a decision in appellate court in Buffalo in 1928 that determined Curtiss and Wheeler had acted against the best interests of the company's stockholders and had removed Herring without providing payment commensurate with his contributions to the firm. Outraged by the judgment, Curtiss resolved to continue litigation rather than give in on what his biographer says had become "a matter of stubborn principle."[12]

If the Curtiss-Herring dispute remained unresolved after nearly two decades, the rift between the Wrights and Curtiss came to an end in a way none of the principals ever would have dreamed when the controversy began in 1909. The 1917 cross-licensing agreement and equal payments to the Wright and Curtiss interests had brought an end to the legal struggle, and by 1921 neither Orville Wright nor Curtiss had direct financial stakes in the firms carrying their names. Under Clement Keys the Curtiss company turned the corner to profitability and went on to become the centerpiece of a massive holding company that included not only aircraft and engine manufacturing but also air transport operations and a network of airfields and flying schools. Meanwhile, Richard F. Hoyt of the investment firm Hayden, Stone and Company had constructed a similar aviation giant around the Wright Aeronautical Corporation, formed in 1919 as a successor to the Wright-Martin Corporation, and like Curtiss controlling aircraft and engine factories, airlines, and other aviation-related enterprises by 1928.

Cognizant of how much their respective companies had in common, Keys and Hoyt joined forces on 27 June 1929 to create the Curtiss-Wright Corporation, the nation's largest aviation company with holdings worth more than $75 million and a dozen subsidiaries occupying every niche of the aeronautical firmament. Curtiss agreed to join the new company's technical committee, bringing with him a sense of historical continuity if not the most current engineering expertise.[13]

An offspring of the speculative boom in aviation in the late 1920s, Curtiss-Wright became one of the many victims of the stock market crash in the fall of 1929 and suffered through a fierce decrement of sales and assets during the early 1930s. To a certain extent, the air transport industry, bolstered by lucrative federal airmail contracts, avoided the immediate effects of the crisis. In May 1930, to demonstrate its continuing involvement in commercial aviation and to show how much the industry had changed in so little time, Curtiss-Wright staged a commemoration of the twentieth anniversary of Curtiss' epic Albany–New York City flight. To reenact the flight, the company brought out one of its new eighteen-passenger Condor airliners. Big and comfortable, the Condor stood in stark contrast to the old *Hudson Flier*, yet with its internally braced fuselage and fabric-covered wings, the biplane was a relic of antiquated aeronautical technologies superseded less than three years later by the thoroughly modern Boeing 247.[14]

The flight was scheduled to coincide with Memorial Day, 30 May. After lunch at the Hotel Ten Eyck, where he had stayed in 1910, Curtiss boarded the airplane, along with Lena, Glenn Jr., Henry Kleckler, and Augustus Post. Frank Courtney, one of the company's most experienced pilots, handled the airplane on takeoff from Albany's new airport, but sitting in the left seat Curtiss had the controls for much of the flight, during which there was some of the same rough air over Storm King Mountain that Curtiss had encountered two decades earlier. Passing over Manhattan, Curtiss took the airplane around Governors Island and then turned the controls back to Courtney for the landing at Curtiss Field in Valley Stream, a few miles east of Garden City. Speaking to reporters afterwards, Curtiss remarked about what he saw as the inevitable technological future, where speedy automobiles and even speedier airplanes would whisk Americans from city to city. After dinner in New York, Curtiss and his family took a train to Washington, where he planned to watch the Marine Flying Trophy race, now in its sixteenth year of competition. It had been a special occasion for everyone, bringing back warm memories of one of Curtiss' and aviation's most outstanding early accomplishments.[15]

As was their custom since moving to Florida, the Curtisses spent the summer of 1930 in Hammondsport. This time, their stay was interrupted by trips to nearby Rochester for court appearances in an adjudication of the Herring suit by former New York Supreme Court justice William S. Andrews. For most of his life, Curtiss had been blessed with good health, marred only by a few scrapes and bruises from minor motorcycle and airplane mishaps and the strange iceboat accident at Baddeck in the winter of 1909. He had recently experienced painful bouts of appendicitis, but they had been transitory and were not considered serious enough to warrant surgery. That changed for the worse in the midst of the Herring proceedings. While spending the Independence Day holiday in Hammondsport, Curtiss experienced abdominal pain so severe that he notified Judge Andrews that he would not be able to continue his testimony in Rochester. When Herring's lawyers accused Curtiss of fakery when court reconvened on Monday, 7 July, Andrews immediately dispatched a team of physicians to Hammondsport to confirm the illness. Their diagnosis was acute appendicitis, and their recommended therapy was straightforward: immediate surgery. Andrews adjourned the case and allowed Curtiss to forgo further appearances pending his recovery. After further consultation with his family doctor, Curtiss decided to have the operation at the Buffalo General Hospital, where the surgery took place on 11 July. Any invasive medical procedure, let alone an appendectomy, was risky, yet the operation went smoothly, and in the days immediately following Curtiss was in good spirits and appeared to be convalescing normally. Towers wired on the twelfth to tell him that he was "pleased to learn you are progressing so favorably," and hoped to see him in Buffalo in a week or so. By 22 July, Curtiss was ready to return to Hammondsport, but early on the morning of the twenty-third he fell into a coma, could not be revived despite the immediate ministrations from one of the attending nurses, and died from what was later determined to be a pulmonary embolism. He was fifty-two years old.[16]

In Hammondsport on the twenty-fourth, hundreds of mourners paid their respects during visitation at the old house on Castle Hill. The next day the rector of the local Episcopal church presided over brief funeral services at the Curtiss home. Burial followed in the family plot at the Pleasant Valley cemetery. John Towers (then assistant chief of the Bureau of Aeronautics), Lanny Callan, Bill Gilmore, Henry Kleckler, Harry Genung, Tank Waters, and Rumsey Wheeler were among the many actual and honorary pallbearers. Ten airplanes circled overhead, dropping flowers on and around the gravesite as the casket was lowered into the ground. Deeply saddened, Towers could not help but recall the days in the summer of 1911 when he and Curtiss had flown the Navy's hydro over Lake Keuka and reflected that "as the planes of tomorrow roar down eternal airpaths, the gleam of their wings in sunlight, the sound of their motors at night will forever remain the symbols of that man's greatness."[17]

Chambers was among the many who expressed their condolences in the days following Curtiss' death. "I read with amazement, shock, and sorrow of the death of your dear husband and my friend," he wrote to Lena. "I understand better than any other person in the Navy how much we owe to him for progress in Naval Aviation through his generous and kindly cooperation with us in the pioneer development of that which is destined to be one of the greatest factors in national defense and future peace. But it was his personal characteristics, his personality and understanding more than his remarkable foresight and skill that endeared him to me in a bond of friendship that is one of the most cherished memories of my life."[18]

A decade after Curtiss' death, the Navy honored his memory with the commissioning in 1940 of the USS *Curtiss* (AV-4), the lead ship of a new class of 8,700-ton seaplane tenders. Lena christened the ship at the New York Shipbuilding Corporation's yards in Camden, New Jersey. The vessel survived a bomb hit during the 1941 Japanese attack on Pearl Harbor, went on to serve with American forces in the South West and Central Pacific theaters of operation during World War II, and supported seaplane operations in the Korean War. Further, though indirect, recognition came in December 1941 when the Navy commissioned the USS *Hammondsport* (AKV-2), second in a class of 4,000-ton converted aircraft transports that were critical to the supply of airplanes and equipment in the Pacific.[19]

It was impossible for anyone who had been close to Curtiss or was cognizant and appreciative of his contributions to aviation not to sense that with his death there also passed a heroic era of pioneering in aeronautics. Unquestionably Curtiss was, like most Americans in the two decades after the turn of the twentieth century, optimistic about aviation technology and its seemingly boundless promise. That optimism was unwarranted to a degree, for we know that by the end of the 1920s the airplane was far from a mature technology. Nevertheless, Curtiss must receive a large measure of credit for nurturing the airplane through its infancy. He turned his native technical abilities, physical talents, courage, and energy to flight in its crucial early stages, in the process transforming the airplane into a profitable business for him as well as his competitors. When it became obvious that the aviation industry in the early 1920s had changed from the shop culture Curtiss grew up with, he had the good sense to walk away, admittedly with a fortune that allowed him to indulge his wide-ranging interests and curiosity.

Curtiss never wavered in his belief in the potential of aviation as a vital component of the United States Navy, even though by the end of the 1920s the airplane had not yet reached the point where it constituted a fully fledged striking arm of the fleet. Most important, in a partnership forged with Chambers, Ellyson, Towers, Taylor, Hunsaker, Westervelt, and scores of other engineers and fliers in a widening technological community, Curtiss established aviation within the Navy and shaped its development between 1910 and 1920. His enthusiasm and initiative gave the Navy its first airplanes and aviators, aircraft that could take off and land from the water and operate with the fleet, flying boats with the range and payload capacity to span oceans, a research and development base, and design and manufacturing facilities capable of producing airplanes and engines in the tens of thousands. By the end of the next decade, the United States Navy had all the elements of the air power that ultimately fought and helped win World War II. Through character, force of personality, and leadership by example, Glenn Curtiss inspired others to dedicate themselves to the further development of the airplane, which by the time of his death had added a new dimension to warfare at sea. His enduring legacy was a powerful naval weapon that today constitutes a major component of the nation's defense.

Notes

Introduction: The Aviator

1. *New York World*, 30, 31 May 1910.

2. *New York Times*, 30 May 1910; Clara Studer, *Sky Storming Yankee: The Life of Glenn Curtiss* (New York: Stackpole Sons, 1937), p. 243.

3. See, for example, Jack Carpenter, *Pendulum: The Story of America's Three Aviation Pioneers* (San Juan Capistrano, CA: Arsdalen, Bosch & Co., 2003), pp. v–x; see also Seth Shulman, *Unlocking the Sky: Glenn Hammond Curtiss and the Race to Invent the Airplane* (New York: HarperCollins Publishers, 2002), pp. 28–29, 50–59, 219–22.

4. Kirk W. House, *Hell-Rider to King of the Air: Glenn Curtiss's Life of Innovation* (Warrendale, PA.: SAE International, 2003), pp. 110–11.

5. Bill Robie, *For the Greatest Achievement: A History of the Aero Club of America and the National Aeronautic Association* (Washington, DC and London: Smithsonian Institution Press, 1993), p. 68; Peter L. Jakab and Rick Young, *The Published Writings of Wilbur and Orville Wright* (Washington, DC and London: Smithsonian Institution Press, 2000), pp. 196–97.

6. Grover Loening, *Our Wings Grow Faster* (Garden City, NY: Doubleday, Doran & Co., 1935), p. 11; John H. Towers, Biographical manuscript, undated, folder 2, Biographical Notebooks File, Chronological 1910, box 5, John H. Towers Papers, Manuscript Division, Library of Congress (hereafter cited as Towers Papers,

MDLC); Richard K. Smith, *First Across! The U.S. Navy's Transatlantic Flight of 1919* (Annapolis, MD: Naval Institute Press, 1973), p. 19; Constantinos C. Markides and Paul A. Geroski, *Fast Second: How Smart Companies Bypass Radical Innovation to Enter and Dominate New Markets* (San Francisco: Jossey-Bass, 2005).

7. Tom D. Crouch, *The Bishop's Boys: A Life of Wilbur and Orville Wright* (New York: W. W. Norton & Company, 1989), pp. 417–18, 463; *Aeronautics* (London) 5 (January 1912): p. 25; Tom D. Crouch, *Wings: A History of Aviation from Kites to the Space Age* (New York: W. W. Norton & Company, 2003), pp. 147–48.

8. Ronald H. Spector, *At War at Sea: Sailors and Naval Combat in the Twentieth Century* (New York: Viking Press, 2001), pp. 137, 397.

9. William F. Trimble, "The Narrow and Pitching Deck: The Navy's Special Requirements for Aircraft," in *1998 National Aerospace Conference Proceedings* (Dayton, OH: Wright State University, 1999), pp. 215–19.

10. Crouch, *Bishop's Boys*, pp. 65, 74–76, 95, 313; Peter L. Jakab, *Visions of a Flying Machine: The Wright Brothers and the Process of Invention* (Washington, DC: Smithsonian Institution Press, 1990), pp. 1–2.

Chapter 1. Young and Restless

1. Charles Champlin, *Back There Where the Past Was: A Small-Town Boyhood* (Syracuse, NY: Syracuse University Press, 1988), pp. 17–19.

2. Ibid., pp. 19–21, 54, 56; C. R. Roseberry, *Glenn Curtiss: Pioneer of Flight* (1972; reprint, Syracuse, NY: Syracuse University Press, 1991), p. 4.

3. Roseberry, *Glenn Curtiss*, pp. 4–7; Rutha's typed remembrances, no date, Curtiss Family History, folder no. 568, Glenn Hammond Curtiss Museum, Hammondsport, New York (hereafter cited as GHCM).

4. Roseberry, *Glenn Curtiss*, pp. 6–10.

5. Glenn H. Curtiss and Augustus Post, *The Curtiss Aviation Book* (New York: Frederick A. Stokes Company, 1912), pp. 9–11; *New York Times*, 19 September 1909.

6. Roseberry, *Glenn Curtiss*, pp. 9–10; Blake McKelvey, *Rochester on the Genesee: The Growth of a City* (2d ed., Syracuse, NY: Syracuse University Press, 1993), especially pp. 99–108, 124–25; Elizabeth Brayer, *George Eastman: A Biography* (Baltimore and London: The Johns Hopkins University Press, 1996), pp. 75–76, 80–82, 91.

7. Rutha's typed remembrances, no date, Curtiss Family History, folder no. 568, GHCM; A. F. Sulzer to F. C. Ellis, 7 November 1930, Glenn H. Curtiss Collection (Clara Studer), Archives and Library, National Air and Space Museum, Washington, DC (hereafter cited as Curtiss Coll., NASM); Roseberry, *Glenn Curtiss*, pp. 10–11; Brayer, *George Eastman*, pp. 80–82, 297–98.

8. Roseberry, *Glenn Curtiss*, pp. 11, 15.

9. Roseberry, *Glenn Curtiss*, pp. 11–12; *Hammondsport Herald*, 8 May 1895, 2 June, 7 July 1897; "Curtiss Characteristics," San Diego Aerospace Museum (courtesy of George Cully).

10. Robert A Smith, *A Social History of the Bicycle: Its Early Life and Times in America* (New York: American Heritage Press, 1972), pp. 17–21, 31–33, 143–71; Tom D.

Crouch, "How the Bicycle Took Wing," *American Heritage of Invention and Technology* 2 (Summer 1986): pp. 10–16.

11. Mrs. George Osborne (brief typed reminiscence, no date), file CC-840000-05, Curtiss, Glenn H., Biographical file, Archives and Library, National Air and Space Museum, Washington, DC (hereafter cited as Curtiss file, Archives and Library, NASM); *Hammondsport Herald*, 25 July 1894, 3 June 1896, 13 October 1897; Roseberry, *Glenn Curtiss*, pp. 15, 19; James Sullivan, ed., "The History of New York State Biographies, Part 3," http://www.usgennet.org/usa/ny/state/his/bio/pt3.html (accessed 30 April 2007).

12. *Hammondsport Herald*, 16 March 1898; Surrogate's Court, Steuben County, New York, in the Matter of the Probate of the Last Will and Testament of Glenn H. Curtiss, no date (probably 1931), file CC-840000-05, Curtiss file, Archives and Library, NASM; Roseberry, *Glenn Curtiss*, pp. 15–16.

13. *Hammondsport Herald*, 4 May, 21 June 1898, 22 March 1899, 7 February, 28 March 1900, 3 April 1918; Roseberry, *Glenn Curtiss*, pp. 16–17; Merrill Stickler, "The Bicycles," undated manuscript, folder no. 608, GHCM.

14. *Hammondsport Herald*, 13 March, 14 August 1901, 12 February 1902; Roseberry, *Glenn Curtiss*, p. 17.

15. Richard Hough and L. J. K. Setright, *A History of the World's Motorcycles* (New York: Harper & Row Publishers, 1966), pp. 7, 11–14, 27–30.

16. Ibid., p. 36; Roseberry, *Glenn Curtiss*, pp. 18–19; Curtiss and Post, *Curtiss Aviation Book*, pp. 19–20.

17. Roseberry, *Glenn Curtiss*, pp. 2–3, 16, 19–20; House, *Hell-Rider*, pp. 26–27.

18. Roseberry, *Glenn Curtiss*, p. 20.

19. *Hammondsport Herald*, 22 January, 30 April, 18 June 1902; House, *Hell-Rider*, pp. 27–28, 45, 52; Roseberry, *Glenn Curtiss*, pp. 21–22.

20. Hough and Setright, *History of the World's Motorcycles*, pp. 44, 46; *New York Times*, 1, 2 September 1902; Roseberry, *Glenn Curtiss*, p. 22.

21. *Hammondsport Herald*, 15 October 1902, 25 February, 18 March, 1 April, 6 May 1903; Roseberry, *Glenn Curtiss*, p. 22; House, *Hell-Rider*, pp. 31, 45–47, 52.

22. *New York Herald*, 31 May 1903; *New York Times*, 31 May 1903; *Hammondsport Herald*, 3 June, 13, 30 September 1903.

23. Roseberry, *Glenn Curtiss*, p. 31; *Hammondsport Herald*, 10 February 1904; *New York Times*, 28 March 1903, 29, 30, 31 January 1904.

24. *New York Times*, 31 May 1904; *Hammondsport Herald*, 13 July 1904.

25. *Hammondsport Herald*, 7 September, 26 October, 2 November 1904; Roseberry, *Glenn Curtiss*, pp. 24, 31–32; House, *Hell-Rider*, pp. 52–53.

26. *Hammondsport Herald*, 3 August 1904; Tom D. Crouch, *The Eagle Aloft: Two Centuries of the Balloon in America* (Washington, DC: Smithsonian Institution Press, 1983), pp. 503–18.

27. Crouch, *Eagle Aloft*, p. 528; Roseberry, *Glenn Curtiss*, pp. 35, 460–61.

28. Roseberry, *Glenn Curtiss*, pp. 40–43.

29. *Hammondsport Herald*, 16 August, 20 September 1905; Roseberry, *Glenn Curtiss*, p. 33.

30. *Hammondsport Herald*, 4, 25 October, 22 November 1905; G. H. Curtiss Mfg. Co. incorporation, 17 October 1905, folder 10, box 1, Curtiss Coll., NASM.

31. Merrill Stickler, "G. H. Curtiss and his Motorcycles," undated manuscript; *Bicycling World* clipping, 20 January 1906; both in folder no. 610, GHCM; *New York Times*, 13, 14 January 1906; *Hammondsport Herald*, 31 January, 14 February, 7 March, 27 June 1906.

32. Roseberry, *Glenn Curtiss*, pp. 51–52; *Hammondsport Herald*, 10, 24 May 1905, 30 May 1906.

33. *Hammondsport Herald*, 1 February, 29 March, 26 April, 23 August 1905, 23 May, 8 August 1906; Roseberry, *Glenn Curtiss*, pp. 49–50.

34. *Hammondsport Herald*, 12 September 1906; Roseberry, *Glenn Curtiss*, pp. 53–54.

35. Roseberry, *Glenn Curtiss*, pp. 54–55; House, *Hell-Rider*, pp. 60–62.

36. *Hammondsport Herald*, 16 January 1907; *New York Times*, 24 January 1907; *Scientific American* 96 (9 February 1907): p. 128; Roseberry, *Glenn Curtiss*, pp. 56–57; House, *Hell-Rider*, pp. 40–41; T. A. Hodgdon to Clara Studer, 12 January 1931, (Studer) Curtiss Coll., NASM.

37. *Hammondsport Herald*, 30 January, 6 February 1907.

38. Ibid., 29 May, 12 June, 10, 31 July, 7 August 1907; *New York Times*, 1, 2 August 1907.

39. *Hammondsport Herald*, 7 November 1906, 30 October, 6, 13 November, 25 December 1907; *Herring-Curtiss Company v. Glenn Curtiss, et al.*, State of New York Supreme Court (May 1922), vol. 7, pp. 4402, 4724, folder 3, box 4, Curtiss Coll., NASM; Roseberry, *Glenn Curtiss*, pp. 46–47, 77.

40. *Herring-Curtiss Company v. Glenn Curtiss, et al.*, State of New York Supreme Court (May 1922), vol. 7, pp. 4670–71, folder 3, box 4, Curtiss Coll., NASM; *Hammondsport Herald*, 20 January, 14 April, 4 August, 3 November 1909; Roseberry, *Glenn Curtiss*, p. 179.

Chapter 2. Bell's Lab

1. Robert V. Bruce, *Bell: Alexander Graham Bell and the Conquest of Solitude* (Boston: Little, Brown and Company, 1973), pp. 355–68, 430–41; Tom D. Crouch, *A Dream of Wings: Americans and the Airplane, 1875–1905* (New York and London: W. W. Norton & Company, 1981), pp. 151–54.

2. Journal by Alexander Graham Bell, 7 June–11 December 1902, Kites and Other Aeronautical Subjects, June–December 1902; Bell to Chanute, 29 September 1903, Aviation subject file; Bell, "Aerial Locomotion," *Proceedings of the Washington Academy of Sciences* 8 (4 March 1907): pp. 421–22; all in Alexander Graham Bell Family Papers, Manuscript Division, Library of Congress (hereafter cited as Bell Papers, MDLC), http://memory.loc.gov/ammem/bellhtml/bellhome.html (accessed 11 December 2002–21 March 2007); Crouch, *Dream of Wings*, pp. 20–26, 36–41, 61–100; Roseberry, *Glenn Curtiss*, p. 69.

3. Roseberry, *Glenn Curtiss*, pp. 48–49, 56, 70; *New York Times*, 13, 19 January, 1 December 1906; Bell, "Aerial Locomotion," pp. 426–27; Bell to Mrs. David G. Fairchild, 25 July 1906, 16 October 1906, Family Correspondence, 1885–1909;

both in Bell Papers, MDLC; *Hammondsport Herald*, 7 November, 12 December 1906.

4. *Hammondsport Herald*, 15, 29 May, 19 June, 10 July 1907; G. H. Curtiss, "An Airship Chauffeur," *The American Aeronaut* 1 (January 1908): pp. 27–28.

5. Deposition of J. A. D. McCurdy, 9 April 1920, Aviation subject file; Bell to William Bedwin, 28 May 1907, Gen. Corresp., Letterbooks, 1906–1907, box 119; both in Bell Papers, MDLC; Roseberry, *Glenn Curtiss*, pp. 70-71; Crouch, *Bishop's Boys*, p. 351.

6. *Hammondsport Herald*, 17, 24 July 1907; Curtiss to Lena Curtiss, 17 July 1907, folder no. 585, GHCM; Roseberry, *Glenn Curtiss*, pp. 72–73.

7. Roseberry, *Glenn Curtiss*, pp. 74–75; F. W. Baldwin to Bell, 28 July 1907, Frederick W. Baldwin, 1906–1917, Bell Papers, MDLC.

8. *Hammondsport Herald*, 4 September 1907; Roseberry, *Glenn Curtiss*, pp. 77–78.

9. *Hammondsport Herald*, 9 October 1907; Roseberry, *Glenn Curtiss*, pp. 78–80. The full text of the AEA's charter is in Roseberry, *Glenn Curtiss*, pp. 462–64.

10. *Hammondsport Herald*, 9, 16, 30 October 1907; *New York Times*, 20, 24 October 1907; Roseberry, *Glenn Curtiss*, pp. 80–81, 84–85; Notes by Thomas E. Selfridge, 24 September 1907–24 July 1908, Aviation subject file, *Aerial Experiment Association v. Myers*, 1908–1912, Bell Papers, MDLC.

11. Minutes of meeting, 23 December 1907, Aerial Experiment Association Meetings, 1907–1909, Bell Papers, MDLC; Crouch, *Dream of Wings*, pp. 145–50, 190–98.

12. Crouch, *Dream of Wings*, pp. 190–92; Notes by Thomas E. Selfridge, September 24, 1907–July 24, 1908, Aviation subject file, *Aerial Experiment Association v. Myers*, 1908–1912, Bell Papers, MDLC.

13. Notes by Thomas E. Selfridge, September 24, 1907–July 24, 1908, Aviation subject file, *Aerial Experiment Association v. Myers*, 1908–1912, Bell Papers, MDLC; Roseberry, *Glenn Curtiss*, pp. 85–86; Curtiss and Post, *Curtiss Aviation Book*, p. 40.

14. Roseberry, *Glenn Curtiss*, pp. 81–82; Crouch, *Bishop's Boys*, p. 352.

15. Roseberry, *Glenn Curtiss*, p. 85; Louis S. Casey, *Curtiss: The Hammondsport Era, 1907–1915* (New York: Crown Publishers, 1981), pp. 8–11. For specifications of the Wright *Flyer*, see Jakab, *Visions of a Flying Machine*, p. 207.

16. Roseberry, *Glenn Curtiss*, pp. 88, 92–93; Notes by Alexander Graham Bell, 12 March 1908; McCurdy to Bell, 12 March 1908; both in General Correspondence, Frederick W. Baldwin, 1906–1917, Bell Papers, MDLC.

17. Curtiss and Post, *Curtiss Aviation Book*, p. 43; *New York Times*, 13 March 1908; Crouch, *Bishop's Boys*, pp. 297–300.

18. Roseberry, *Glenn Curtiss*, pp. 88, 93–94.

19. Curtiss to Mabel Bell, 19 March 1908, Aviation subject file, Aerial Experiment Association, 1907–1914, Bell Papers, MDLC.

20. Roseberry, *Glenn Curtiss*, pp. 86, 94; Crouch, *Bishop's Boys*, pp. 276, 326.

21. Deposition by Alexander Graham Bell, 15 January 1915, Aviation subject file, *Aerial Experiment Association v. Myers*, 1915, Bell Papers, MDLC; Roseberry, *Glenn Curtiss*, pp. 86, 96–97. See also Tom D. Crouch, "Some Notes on the History of the Aileron," undated manuscript courtesy of Tom D. Crouch.

22. Casey, *Curtiss: The Hammondsport Era*, pp. 12–15; Richard K. Smith, "The Weight Envelope: An Airplane's Fourth Dimension," *Aerospace Historian* 33 (Spring/ March 1986): p. 32.

23. Bell to Mabel Bell, 11 May 1908, Family Correspondence 1885–1909; Bulletin No. 1, July 13, 1908, Bulletins of the Aerial Experiment Association, Aviation subject file, Aerial Experiment Association; both in Bell Papers, MDLC; Roseberry, *Glenn Curtiss*, p. 99.

24. Roseberry, *Glenn Curtiss*, pp. 100–101; House, *Hell-Rider*, p. 77; G. H. Curtiss, "Ideas on Aviation," Bulletin No. 5, August 10, 1908, Bulletins of the Aerial Experiment Association, Aviation subject file, Aerial Experiment Association, Bell Papers, MDLC. There is a discrepancy on the date of Curtiss' *White Wing* flight. Roseberry has it on the twenty-first, as do Casey, *Curtiss: The Hammondsport Era*, p. 15, House, *Hell-Rider*, p. 79, and other sources, presumably relying on Bulletin No. 1, July 13, 1908, Bulletins of the Aerial Experiment Association, Aviation subject file, Aerial Experiment Association, Bell Papers, MDLC. However, Notes by Thomas E. Selfridge, September 24, 1907– July 24, 1908, Aviation subject file, *Aerial Experiment Association v. Myers*, 1908–1912; and Journal by Alexander Graham Bell, June 18, 1908–July 7, 1908, Aviation subject file, Aerial Experiment Association; both in Bell Papers, MDLC; the *Hammondsport Herald*, 27 May 1908, and the *New York Times*, 23 May 1908, confirm the flight was on the twenty-second.

25. Notes by Thomas E. Selfridge, September 24, 1907–July 24, 1908, Aviation subject file, *Aerial Experiment Association v. Myers*, 1908–1912, Bell Papers, MDLC.

26. Bell to Helen Keller, 5 June 1908, General Correspondence, Bell Papers, MDLC; Casey, *Curtiss: The Hammondsport Era*, pp. 17, 20–21; Smith, "Weight Envelope," p. 32.

27. Roseberry, *Glenn Curtiss*, pp. 102–3; Crouch, *Bishop's Boys*, p. 363.

28. Roseberry, *Glenn Curtiss*, p. 101.

29. Notes by Thomas E. Selfridge, September 24, 1907–July 24, 1908, Aviation subject file, *Aerial Experiment Association v. Myers*, 1908–1912, Bell Papers, MDLC; Roseberry, *Glenn Curtiss*, p. 105.

30. *New York Times*, 26 June 1908; Notes by Thomas E. Selfridge, September 24, 1907–July 24, 1908, Aviation subject file, *Aerial Experiment Association v. Myers*, 1908–1912, Bell Papers, MDLC.

31. Notes by Thomas E. Selfridge, September 24, 1907–July 24, 1908, Aviation subject file, *Aerial Experiment Association v. Myers*, 1908–1912, Bell Papers, MDLC; Roseberry, *Glenn Curtis*, p. 107.

32. Notes by Thomas E. Selfridge, September 24, 1907–July 24, 1908, Aviation subject file, *Aerial Experiment Association v. Myers*, 1908–1912; David Fairchild, "The Coming of the Winged Cycle," Bulletin No. 10, September 14, 1908, Bulletins of the Aerial Experiment Association, Aviation subject file, Aerial Experiment Association; both in Bell Papers, MDLC.

33. *New York Times*, 5 July 1908; *Hammondsport Herald*, 8 July 1908; Roseberry, *Glenn Curtiss*, p. 110; Bulletin No. 3, 27 July 1908, Bulletins of the Aerial Experiment Association, Aviation subject file, Aerial Experiment Association, Bell Papers, MDLC.

34. *New York Times*, 5 July 1908; *Hammondsport Herald*, 8 July 1908; Roseberry, *Glenn Curtiss*, pp. 110–11, 113; Curtiss and Post, *Curtiss Aviation Book*, p. 53.

35. *Hammondsport Herald*, 8 July 1908; Notes by Thomas E. Selfridge, September 24, 1907–July 24, 1908, Aviation subject file, *Aerial Experiment Association v. Myers*, 1908–1912; G. H. Curtiss, "Work of the Hammondsport Laboratory," Bulletin No. 5, August 10, 1908, Bulletins of the Aerial Experiment Association, Aviation subject file, Aerial Experiment Association; both in Bell Papers, MDLC; Roseberry, *Glenn Curtiss*, p. 114.

36. Roseberry, *Glenn Curtiss*, pp. 114–15.

37. Ibid., p. 115; Curtiss to Orville Wright, 24 July 1908, General Correspondence; Orville Wright to Wilbur Wright, 25 July 1908, Family Correspondence; both in Wilbur and Orville Wright Papers, Manuscript Division, Library of Congress (hereafter cited as Wright Papers, MDLC), http://memory.loc.gov/ammem/wrighthtml/wrighthome.html (accessed 9 November 2006–18 April 2007).

38. Roseberry, *Glenn Curtiss*, pp. 114, 117, 120–21; *Hammondsport Herald*, 15, 29 July, 5 August 1908.

39. *New York Times*, 20 November 1907; Crouch, *Bishop's Boys*, pp. 347–48; Roseberry, *Glenn Curtiss*, pp. 88–89; *Hammondsport Herald*, 26 February 1908; House, *Hell-Rider*, pp. 60–61, 85.

40. Roseberry, *Glenn Curtiss*, p. 122; *Hammondsport Herald*, 15 July 1908; *New York Times*, 26 July, 8, 9, 12 August 1908.

41. Roseberry, *Glenn Curtiss*, p. 123; *New York Times*, 15, 16 August 1908; *Hammondsport Herald*, 19 August, 2 September 1908.

42. Crouch, *Bishop's Boys*, pp. 372, 374; Roseberry, *Glenn Curtiss*, p. 124; Archibald D. Turnbull and Clifford L. Lord, *History of United States Naval Aviation* New Haven, CT: Yale University Press, 1949), p. 4.

43. Roseberry, *Glenn Curtiss*, pp. 124–25; Orville Wright to Wilbur Wright, 6 September 1908, Family Correspondence, Wright Papers, MDLC.

44. Crouch, *Bishop's Boys*, pp. 375–76.

45. Telegram, Fairchild to Bell, 17 September 1908, Bulletin No. 11, September 21, 1908, Bulletins of the Aerial Experiment Association, Aviation subject file, Aerial Experiment Association, Bell Papers, MDLC; *Hammondsport Herald*, 23 September 1908; Roseberry, *Glenn Curtiss*, p. 129.

46. Roseberry, *Glenn Curtiss*, p. 128; Curtiss to Aerial Experiment Association, 6 October 1908, Bulletin No. 16, October 26, 1908; G. H. Curtiss, "Lesson of the Wright Disaster," 10 November 1908, Bulletin No. 20, November 23, 1908; both in Bulletins of the Aerial Experiment Association, Aviation subject file, Aerial Experiment Association, Bell Papers, MDLC.

47. Crouch, *Bishop's Boys*, p. 378.

48. Roseberry, *Glenn Curtiss*, pp. 131–33.

49. Bell, "The Future of the A.E.A.," Bulletin No. 11, September 21, 1908, Bulletins of the Aerial Experiment Association, Aviation subject file, Aerial Experiment Association, Bell Papers, MDLC.

50. Roseberry, *Glenn Curtiss*, p. 142.

51. G. H. Curtiss, "Summary of the Work of the Hammondsport Laboratory from July 4 to September 1, 1908"; telegram, Curtiss to Bell, 9 September 1908; Curtiss to Bell, 11 September 1908; all in Bulletin No. 11, September 21, 1908, Bulletins of the Aerial Experiment Association, Aviation subject file, Aerial Experiment Association, Bell Papers, MDLC.

52. Casey, *Curtiss: The Hammondsport Era*, pp. 26–27; Curtiss to Bell, 2 December 1908, Bulletin No. 24, December 21, 1908, Bulletins of the Aerial Experiment Association, Aviation subject file, Aerial Experiment Association, Bell Papers, MDLC.

53. Roseberry, *Glenn Curtiss*, p. 138; House, *Hell-Rider*, p. 88.

54. Casey, *Curtiss: The Hammondsport Era*, pp. 29–32.

55. *Hammondsport Herald*, 23 September 1908; Curtiss to Aerial Experiment Association, 14 October 1908, Bulletin No. 16, October 26, 1908; AEA press release, 31 October 1908, Bulletin No. 18, November 9, 1908; Curtiss to Bell, 11 November 1908; Curtiss to Mabel Bell, 12 November 1908, Bulletin No. 20, November 23, 1908; all in Bulletins of the Aerial Experiment Association, Aviation subject file, Aerial Experiment Association, Bell Papers, MDLC; Roseberry, *Glenn Curtiss*, pp. 138, 144.

56. Curtiss to Bell, 8 December 1908, Bulletin No. 24, December 21, 1908; Bell, Visit to Hammondsport, 28 December 1908, Bulletin No. 26, January 4, 1909; Curtiss to Mabel Bell, 22 December 1908, Bulletin No. 26, January 4, 1909; all in Bulletins of the Aerial Experiment Association, Aviation subject file, Aerial Experiment Association, Bell Papers, MDLC; Roseberry, *Glenn Curtiss*, p. 146; Casey, *Curtiss: The Hammondsport Era*, p. 32; *New York Times*, 7, 18 December 1908.

57. Bell to AEA, 18 November 1908, Bulletin No. 24, November 23, 1908, Bulletins of the Aerial Experiment Association, Aviation subject file, Aerial Experiment Association, Bell Papers, MDLC; Roseberry, *Glenn Curtiss*, p. 143.

58. Casey, *Curtiss: The Hammondsport Era*, p. 32.

Chapter 3. The "Flying Bug"

1. *Hammondsport Herald*, 27 January 1909; Roseberry, *Glenn Curtiss*, pp. 148–49.

2. Roseberry, *Glenn Curtiss*, p. 147; Curtiss to Mabel Bell, 2 January 1909, Bulletin No. 28, January 18, 1909, Bulletins of the Aerial Experiment Association, Aviation subject file, Aerial Experiment Association, Bell Papers, MDLC.

3. Roseberry, *Glenn Curtiss*, p. 149.

4. Ibid., pp. 150–51.

5. Ibid., pp. 151–52.

6. Ibid., pp. 139–40; *Hammondsport Herald*, 28 October 1908.

7. Roseberry, *Glenn Curtiss*, pp. 149–50.

8. Casey, *Curtiss: The Hammondsport Era*, p. 32; Bell, Drome No. 5, 22 February 1909; Curtiss' Account, 23 February 1909; Curtiss' Account, 24 February 1909; Bell, Second Trial of *Cygnet II*, 24 February 1909; all in Bulletin No. 34, March 1, 1909, Bulletins of the Aerial Experiment Association, Aviation subject file, Aerial Experiment Association, Bell Papers, MDLC.

9. Bell, Departures from Beinn Bhreagh, 26 February 1909, Bulletin No. 34, March 1, 1909, Bulletins of the Aerial Experiment Association, Aviation subject file, Aerial Experiment Association, Bell Papers, MDLC; *Hammondsport Herald*, 3 March 1909.

10. Roseberry, *Glenn Curtiss*, p. 166; Casey, *Curtiss: The Hammondsport Era*, p. 41.

11. Roseberry, *Glenn Curtiss*, p. 153.

12. Ibid., p. 152; Crouch, *Dream of Wings*, pp. 219–20; Crouch, *Bishop's Boys*, pp. 380, 400; *New York Times*, 4 March 1909.

13. *Herring-Curtiss Company v. Glenn Curtiss, et al.*, State of New York Supreme Court (October 1921), vol. 9, pp. 5710–15, folder 2, box 5, Curtiss Coll., NASM (emphasis in document); Roseberry, *Glenn Curtiss*, p. 152.

14. *Herring-Curtiss Company v. Glenn Curtiss, et al.*, State of New York Supreme Court (October 1921), vol. 9, p. 5712, folder 2, box 5, Curtiss Coll., NASM; Roseberry, *Glenn Curtiss*, pp. 155–56, 158.

15. Telegram, Curtiss to Bell, 6 March 1909, Bulletin No. 37, March 22, 1909, Bulletins of the Aerial Experiment Association, Aviation subject file, Aerial Experiment Association, Bell Papers, MDLC; Roseberry, *Glenn Curtiss*, pp. 158–59.

16. *New York Times*, 5, 13 March 1909; *Hammondsport Herald*, 10 March 1909.

17. Roseberry, *Glenn Curtiss*, pp. 157–60; House, *Hell-Rider*, p. 92; *New York Times*, 21 March 1909.

18. Bell, *Scientific American* Trophy, 19 March 1909, Bulletin No. 37, March 22, 1909, Bulletins of the Aerial Experiment Association, Aviation subject file, Aerial Experiment Association; Deposition by J. A. D. McCurdy, 9 April 1920, Aviation subject file, Curtiss, Glenn H., 1920; both in Bell Papers, MDLC; Roseberry, *Glenn Curtiss*, pp. 161–62.

19. J. Lawrence Lee, e-mail message to author, 11 October 2007; AEA notes, folder 9, box 14, MS Group 77, Series 2, Alden Hatch Papers, Special Collections, George A. Smathers Libraries, University of Florida, Gainesville, FL (hereafter cited as Hatch Papers, UF); Curtiss to Washington I. Chambers, 30 October 1911, Corresp. 1910–1919, June 1911–October 1912 folder, Curtiss, Glenn H., box 13, General Correspondence, Papers of Washington Irving Chambers, Manuscript Division, Library of Congress (hereafter cited as Gen. Corresp., Chambers Papers, MDLC).

20. House, *Hell-Rider*, pp. 90, 116; Casey, *Curtiss: The Hammondsport Era*, p. 39.

21. Casey, *Curtiss: The Hammondsport Era*, pp. 39, 41, 44–45; Roseberry, *Glenn Curtiss*, pp. 468–69.

22. *Hammondsport Herald*, 26 May, 9 June 1909; *New York Times*, 11, 19, 25 June 1909; Roseberry, *Glenn Curtiss*, pp. 117, 171–72.

23. Roseberry, *Glenn Curtiss*, pp. 168–70, 172; Crouch, *Bishop's Boys*, p. 403.

24. Roseberry, *Glenn Curtiss*, pp. 172–73; *New York Times*, 27 June 1909; *Hammondsport Herald*, 7 July 1909.

25. Roseberry, *Glenn Curtiss*, p. 174; Crouch, *Bishop's Boys*, pp. 396–97.

26. Roseberry, *Glenn Curtiss*, pp. 174–75; *New York Times*, 15 July 1909.

27. Roseberry, *Glenn Curtiss*, pp. 176–77; *New York Times*, 18 July 1909; *Hammondsport Herald*, 21 July 1909.

28. *New York Times*, 18, 19 July 1909.

29. Roseberry, *Glenn Curtiss*, pp. 178–81.

30. *Hammondsport Herald*, 26 July 1909. Bleriot's flight covered about twenty-five miles.

31. Ibid., 4 August 1909; *New York Times*, 1, 4, 6, 8 August 1909.

32. *New York Times*, 3, 6 August 1909; *Hammondsport Herald*, 11 August 1909; Roseberry, *Glenn Curtiss*, p. 186.

33. Roseberry, *Glenn Curtiss*, p. 187; *Hammondsport Herald*, 18 August 1909.

34. Roseberry, *Glenn Curtiss*, pp. 185, 187–88, 192; *Hammondsport Herald*, 18 August 1909; *New York Times*, 19 August 1909.

35. *Hammondsport Herald*, 18 August 1909; Casey, *Curtiss: The Hammondsport Era*, pp. 47, 49–50.

36. *New York Times*, 17, 18 August 1909.

37. Ibid., 20, 22 August 1909; Roseberry, *Glenn Curtiss*, pp. 190–91.

38. Roseberry, *Glenn Curtiss*, p. 191; *New York Times*, 20, 21, 24 August 1909.

39. *New York Times*, 20, 21 August 1909; Roseberry, *Glenn Curtiss*, p. 192.

40. *New York Times*, 23, 24, 27, 28 August 1909; Roseberry, *Glenn Curtiss*, pp. 192–94.

41. *New York Times*, 29 August 1909; Roseberry, *Glenn Curtiss*, p. 197.

42. *New York Times*, 30 August 1909; *Hammondsport Herald*, 1, 8 September 1909; Roseberry, *Glenn Curtiss*, pp. 198–99.

43. Clifford L. Lord, "The History of Naval Aviation, 1898–1939," microfilm, Office of the Deputy Chief of Naval Operations (Air) (Washington, DC: Naval Aviation History Unit, 1946), p. 13.

44. *New York Times*, 3, 5, 8 September 1909.

45. Ibid., 12, 13, 14 September 1909.

46. Ibid., 19, 20, 21, 22, 23 September 1909.

47. *Hammondsport Herald*, 22, 29 September 1909.

48. Richard P. Hallion, *Taking Flight: Inventing the Aerial Age from Antiquity through the First World War* (Oxford and New York: Oxford University Press, 2003), p. 264; Robert Wohl, *A Passion for Wings: Aviation and the Western Imagination, 1908–1918* (New Haven, CT, and London: Yale University Press, 1994), pp. 2, 61–63, 122, 233–36, 250; *Hammondsport Herald*, 29 September 1909.

49. *Hammondsport Herald*, 15 September 1909; Roseberry, *Glenn Curtiss*, pp. 210–11; Casey, *Curtiss: The Hammondsport Era*, pp. 51–52.

50. *New York Times*, 27, 30 September, 1, 2 October 1909; Roseberry, *Glenn Curtiss*, pp. 216–18, 220–21; Crouch, *Bishop's Boys*, pp. 407–8.

51. James Joseph Horgan, "City of Flight: The History of Aviation in Saint Louis" (PhD diss., St. Louis University, 1965), pp. 178–83, 194, 199–200, 201–3; *Hammondsport Herald*, 6 October 1909; *New York Times*, 8 October 1909.

52. David M. Young, *Chicago Aviation: An Illustrated History* (DeKalb, IL: Northern Illinois University Press, 2003), p. 41; *Hammondsport Herald*, 20 October 1909.

53. *Hammondsport Herald*, 20 October 1909; Roseberry, *Glenn Curtiss*, pp. 225–27; *Herring-Curtiss Company v. Glenn Curtiss, et al.*, State of New York Supreme Court (August 1921), vol. 3, p. 2017, folder 10, box 3, Curtiss Coll., NASM.

54. *New York Times*, 13–15 November 1909; *Herring-Curtiss Company v. Glenn Curtiss, et al.*, State of New York Supreme Court (August 1921), vol. 3, p. 2022, folder 10, box 3, Curtiss Coll., NASM.

55. Roseberry, *Glenn Curtiss*, pp. 238–41; United States District Court, Western District of New York, *In the Matter of Herring-Curtiss Company Bankrupt* (20 July 1910), pp. 10–11, folder 5, box 3, Curtiss Coll., NASM.

56. Roseberry, *Glenn Curtiss*, pp. 243.

57. *New York Times*, 29 December 1909.

58. Roseberry, *Glenn Curtiss*, pp. 239, 471–72; *New York Times*, 17 October 1909.

59. Roseberry, *Glenn Curtiss*, pp. 222, 240; *Hammondsport Herald*, 20 October 1909.

60. *New York Times*, 15 December 1909; *Hammondsport Herald*, 15 December 1909; Crouch, *Bishop's Boys*, p. 413.

Chapter 4. The Exhibition Business

1. Crouch, *Bishop's Boys*, p. 403; *Fly* 3 (January 1911): p. 4, 1908–1912 Newspaper Clippings folder, Curtiss, Glenn H., box 16, Institute of the Aerospace Sciences, American Institute of Aeronautics and Astronautics, Aeronautical Archives, Manuscript Division, Library of Congress (hereafter cited as AIAA Archives, MDLC).

2. Roseberry, *Glenn Curtiss*, p. 224.

3. *New York Times*, 2 November 1909; *Hammondsport Herald*, 10 November 1909; Roseberry, *Glenn Curtiss*, pp. 227–28.

4. *New York Times*, 7 November 1909; *Hammondsport Herald*, 5 January 1910; *San Diego Union*, 6, 8 January 1910. The Curtisses' rail itinerary is conjectural, based on information supplied by J. Lawrence Lee.

5. Roseberry, *Glenn Curtiss*, pp. 334–35; *San Diego Union*, 6 January 1910; *New York Times*, 4 January 1910.

6. *San Diego Union*, 6 January 1910; Crouch, *Bishop's Boys*, pp. 412–13.

7. *San Diego Union*, 8, 11 January 1910; *New York Times*, 10, 11 January 1910; *Hammondsport Herald*, 12 January 1910.

8. *New York Times*, 12 January 1910.

9. Ibid., 13, 14, 15 January 1910.

10. Ibid., 16, 17, 18, 21 January 1910; *Hammondsport Herald*, 19 January 1910.

11. Roseberry, *Glenn Curtiss*, pp. 233–34; *Hammondsport Herald*, 4 May 1910.

12. *Hammondsport Herald*, 5 January, 2 February 1910.

13. Roseberry, *Glenn Curtiss*, pp. 179–80; *Hammondsport Herald*, 16 February, 9 March 1910; United States District Court, Western District of New York, *In the Matter of Herring-Curtiss Company Bankrupt* (20 July 1910), pp. 2–3, folder 5; *Herring-Curtiss Company v. Glenn Curtiss, et al.*, State of New York Supreme Court (August 1921), vol. 3, pp. 1815–16, folder 10; both legal folders are in box 3, Curtiss Coll., NASM.

14. Roseberry, *Glenn Curtiss*, pp. 253–54; United States District Court, Western District of New York, *In the Matter of Herring-Curtiss Company Bankrupt* (20 July 1910), pp. 7–9, folder 5, box 3, Curtiss Coll., NASM.

15. *Hammondsport Herald*, 6, 20 April, 10 August 1910; Curtiss testimony, 20 July, 3, 26 August 1910, United States District Court, Western District of New York, *In the Matter of Herring-Curtiss Company Bankrupt* (July, August 1910), pp. 5–11.,26–38, 57–65, folder 5, box 3, Curtiss Coll., NASM; Herring to Creditors of the Herring-Curtiss Co., undated, Legal Cases, Miscellaneous Documents, 1910–1911, Wright Papers, MDLC.

16. *Hammondsport Herald*, 16 February, 16 March 1910; James Lawrence Lee, "Into the Wind: A History of the American Wind Tunnel, 1896–1941" (PhD diss., Auburn University, 2002), pp. 40–45.

17. Roseberry, *Glenn Curtiss*, pp. 262–63.

18. Ibid., pp. 263–64; Casey, *Curtiss: The Hammondsport Era*, pp. 64–65.

19. *Hammondsport Herald*, 6, 13 April 1910; Roseberry, *Glenn Curtiss*, p. 264; *New York Times*, 28 March, 8, 11 April 1910.

20. *Hammondsport Herald*, 20 April, 4 May 1910; Roseberry, *Glenn Curtiss*, pp. 264–65; *New York Times*, 24 April 1910.

21. *Hammondsport Herald*, 25 May 1910; Roseberry, *Glenn Curtiss*, p. 265.

22. Roseberry, *Glenn Curtiss*, pp. 266–67.

23. *New York Times*, 28, 29 May 1910; Roseberry, *Glenn Curtiss*, pp. 268–72; Curtiss and Post, *Curtiss Aviation Book*, p. 97.

24. Roseberry, *Glenn Curtiss*, pp. 273–75. Times for takeoffs and landings are from the *New York Times*, 30 May 1910.

25. Roseberry, *Glenn Curtiss*, pp. 275–78; *New York Times*, 30 May 1910.

26. Roseberry, *Glenn Curtiss*, pp. 278–80; Curtiss and Post, *Curtiss Aviation Book*, p. 104; *New York Times*, 30 May 1910; *Birmingham News*, 30 May 1910; *Hammondsport Herald*, 1 June 1910; *New York World*, 1 June 1910.

27. *Hammondsport Herald*, 1 June 1910; Roseberry, *Glenn Curtiss*, p. 280; Casey, *Curtiss: The Hammondsport Era*, pp. 60–62.

28. Roseberry, *Glenn Curtiss*, p. 336; *New York Times*, 14, 15 June 1910.

29. *New York World*, 30 June, 1 July 1910.

30. Turnbull and Lord, *History of United States Naval Aviation*, pp. 6–7; *New York World*, 30 June, 1 July 1910.

31. *Hammondsport Herald*, 8, 29 June 1910; Crouch, *Bishop's Boys*, pp. 425–28; *New York Times*, 5, 10, 12, 13 July 1910.

32. Capt. Holden Richardson, "Reminiscences of Captain Holden Richardson," interview by Kenneth Leish, July 1960, Aviation Project, Oral History Research Office, Columbia University, pp. 1–6; William J. Armstrong, "Dick Richardson: His Life in Aeronautics," *Naval Aviation News* 59 (April 1977): p. 33.

33. *New York Times*, 24, 25 July 1910; William F. Trimble, *High Frontier: A History of Aeronautics in Pennsylvania* (Pittsburgh: University of Pittsburgh Press, 1982), pp. 61–62.

34. *New York Times*, 25 July, 12, 20, 21, 28 August 1910; Jane Morgan, "Wireless Begins to Talk—and Fly," Chap. 3 in *Electronics in the West: The First Fifty Years* (Palo Alto, CA: National Press Books, 1967), http://earlyradiohistory.us/1910enn2.htm (accessed 16 July 2008).

35. *New York Times*, 29 August, 2 September 1910.

36. Ibid., 4, 5, 8 September 1910; Casey, *Curtiss: The Hammondsport Era*, p. 71.

37. *New York Times*, 15, 16 September 1910.

38. Trimble, *High Frontier*, p. 62; *Allentown (Pa.) Morning Call*, 26 September 1910.

39. Roseberry, *Glenn Curtiss*, pp. 282–83; Emil M. Sholz to Curtiss, 28 May 1910, Corresp. 1910 folder, box 1, Curtiss Coll., NASM; *New York Times*, 12 July 1910; *Hammondsport Herald*, 3 August 1910.

40. Roseberry, *Glenn Curtiss*, p. 286; Certificate of Incorporation, 30 July 1910, brown envelope No. 21, box TY 1, Wright Collection, Museum of Flight, Seattle, WA (courtesy of Dan Hagedorn and Dennis Parks; hereafter cited as Wright Coll., Museum of Flight, Seattle); Crouch, *Bishop's Boys*, pp. 426–28.

41. Eileen F. Lebow, *Before Amelia: Women Pilots in the Early Days of Aviation* (Washington, DC: Brassey's, 2002), pp. 131–38; *Hammondsport Herald*, 28 September 1910; clipping, *New York World Telegram*, 28 January 1913, Blanche Stuart Scott, Miscellany folder, box 109, AIAA Archives, MDLC.

42. Unidentified, undated clipping, Beachey, Lincoln, Clippings folder; Beachey, Lincoln, Biographical Material folder; both in box 6, AIAA Archives, MDLC; Naval Aviators, Biographical Notebooks File, Associates and Contemporaries of Towers, pp. 1905–69, folder 7, box 11, Towers Papers, MDLC; Henry Serrano Villard, *Contact! The Story of the Early Birds* (New York: Thomas Y. Crowell Company, 1968), pp. 194–97.

43. *New York Times*, 1 June, 16 July, 10, 11 September 1910.

44. Ibid., 1, 2, 3, 5, 6, 9 October 1910; Roseberry, *Glenn Curtiss*, pp. 290–91.

45. *New York Times*, 10, 11, 12 October 1910.

46. Curtiss Schools of Aviation, Curtiss Aeroplane Co., Hammondsport, NY, no date [probably 1912], in Printed Matter folder, Curtiss Aero & Motor Company Incorporated, box 136, AIAA Archives, MDLC; *New York Times*, 11 September 1910; *Lexington (Ky.) Herald*, 30 April 1911; Roseberry, *Glenn Curtiss*, p. 302. For Rodgers' flight, see Eileen F. Lebow, *Cal Rodgers and the Vin Fizz* (Washington, DC: Smithsonian Institution Press, 1989), especially pp. 87–146.

47. Roseberry, *Glenn Curtiss*, pp. 291–93; Casey, *Curtiss: The Hammondsport Era*, p. 72.

Chapter 5. The Partnership

1. Lord, "History of Naval Aviation," p. 24; Casey, *Curtiss: The Hammondsport Era*, p. 72; *Hammondsport Herald*, 19 October 1910; *New York Times*, 21, 22 October 1910.

2. Stephen K. Stein, *From Torpedoes to Aviation: Washington Irving Chambers and Technological Innovation in the New Navy, 1876–1913* (Tuscaloosa: University of Alabama Press, 2007), especially pp. 1–2, 59–66, 117–25, 134–45, 155–59; Dewey endorsement, 7 October 1910, on H. I. Cone to SecNav, 7 October 1910, Corresp. 1910–1919, Aviation Progress folder, box 10, Gen. Corresp., Chambers Papers, MDLC.

3. *New York Times*, 26, 27, 29 October 1910; Washington Irving Chambers, "Aviation and Aeroplanes," United States Naval Institute *Proceedings* 37 (March 1911): pp. 163–69.

4. Lord, "History of Naval Aviation," pp. 24–25, 90; *New York Times*, 3, 4, 5, 9, 10 November 1910.

5. Turnbull and Lord, *History of United States Naval Aviation*, p. 10.

6. *New York Times*, 3, 4 November 1910.

7. Ibid., 5, 10 November 1910.

8. Ibid., 12, 13 November 1910.

9. Lord, "History of Naval Aviation," p. 28; Chambers, "Aviation and Aeroplanes," p. 174.

10. *New York Times*, 12, 14, 15 November 1910; Chambers, "Aviation and Aeroplanes," pp. 174–76.

11. *New York Times*, 15 November 1910; Chambers, "Aviation and Aeroplanes," p. 176.

12. Chambers, "Aviation and Aeroplanes," p. 176; *New York Times*, 15 November 1910; von L. Meyer to Ely, 17 November 1910, Corresp. 1910–1919, Ely, Eugene folder, box 15, Gen. Corresp., Chambers Papers, MDLC.

13. Chambers, "Aviation and Aeroplanes," pp. 176–77.

14. Lord, "History of Naval Aviation," p. 32.

15. Chambers, "Aviation and Aeroplanes," p. 184; Turnbull and Lord, *History of United States Naval Aviation*, p. 11; Roseberry, *Glenn Curtiss*, pp. 257–58, 337–38.

16. George van Deurs, *Anchors in the Sky: Spuds Ellyson, the First Naval Aviator* (San Rafael, CA: Presidio Press, 1978), pp. 13–14, 53–54.

17. Chambers to Ellyson, 11 January 1911, Corresp. 1910–1919, Ellyson, T. G., 3 January–27 February 1911 folder, box 14, Gen. Corresp., Chambers Papers, MDLC; van Deurs, *Anchors in the Sky*, pp. 54–56.

18. Van Deurs, *Anchors in the Sky*, p. 56; *Hammondsport Herald*, 30 November 1910; Roseberry, *Glenn Curtiss*, p. 310; Jerome S. Fanciulli to Chambers, 10 December 1910, Corresp. 1910–1919, Curtiss, Glenn H., November 1910–December 1911 folder, box 13; Ellyson to SecNav, 31 January 1911, Corresp. 1910–1919, Ellyson, T. G., 3 January–27 February 1911 folder, box 14; both in Gen. Corresp., Chambers Papers, MDLC.

19. *Hammondsport Herald*, 28 December 1910, 18 January 1911; *San Diego Union*, 1 January 1911; Sherwood Harris, *The First to Fly: Aviation's Pioneer Days* (New York: Simon and Schuster, 1970), pp. 216–19.

20. Curtiss and Post, *Curtiss Aviation Book*, pp. 124–25; Roseberry, *Glenn Curtiss*, p. 309.

21. *San Diego Union*, 5, 16, 19 January 1910; Bruce Linder, *San Diego's Navy: An Illustrated History* (Annapolis, MD: Naval Institute Press, 2001), pp. 23–24, 31–32, 37–38, 41; Elretta Sudsbury, *Jackrabbits to Jets: The History of North Island, San Diego, California* (San Diego: Neyenesch Printers, 1967), pp. 5–9.

22. "Colonel D. Charles Collier (1871–1934)," http://www.sandiegohistory.org/bio/collier/collier2.htm (accessed 20 September 2005); *San Diego Sun*, 21, 27 January 1931 (courtesy of George Cully); Ellyson to SecNav, 4 January 1911, Corresp. 1910–1919, Ellyson, T. G., 3 January–27 February 1911 folder, box 14, Gen. Corresp., Chambers Papers, MDLC; *San Diego Union*, 4 January 1911.

23. Roseberry, *Glenn Curtiss*, p. 311; *Hammondsport Herald*, 22 March 1911.

24. Linder, *San Diego's Navy*, p. 41; copy of agreement, 4 February 1911, enclosure in Curtiss to SecNav, 14 February 1911, Corresp. 1910–1919, Curtiss, Glenn H., November 1910–December 1911 folder, box 13; Ellyson to SecNav, 31 January 1911, Corresp. 1910–1919, Ellyson, T. G., 3 January–27 February 1911 folder, box 14; both papers in Gen. Corresp., Chambers Papers, MDLC; Gary F. Kurutz, "The Only Safe and Sane Method: The Curtiss School of Aviation," *Journal of San Diego History* 25 (Winter 1979): p. 4, http://www.sandiegohistory.org/journal/79winter/curtiss.htm (accessed 15 September 2005); *San Diego Union*, 12, 15 January 1911.

25. Ellyson to Chambers, 18 January 1911, Corresp. 1910–1919, Ellyson, T. G., 3 January–27 February 1911 folder, box 14, Gen. Corresp., Chambers Papers, MDLC; Curtiss and Post, *Curtiss Aviation Book*, p. 120.

26. Chambers, "Aviation and Aeroplanes," pp. 191–93; Ellyson to Chambers, 18 January 1911; Ellyson to Chambers, 1 February 1911; both in Corresp. 1910–1919, Ellyson, T. G., 3 January–27 February 1911 folder, box 14, Gen. Corresp., Chambers Papers, MDLC; *New York Times*, 19 January 1911.

27. *New York Times*, 19 January 1911; Chambers, "Aviation and Aeroplanes," pp. 193–95.

28. *New York Times*, 19 January 1911; *San Diego Union*, 19 January 1911; Curtiss to Ely, 9 February 1911, Corresp. 1910–1919, Ely, Eugene folder, box 15, Gen. Corresp., Chambers Papers, MDLC; Curtiss and Post, *Curtiss Aviation Book*, p. 122.

29. Lord, "History of Naval Aviation," p. 33; Washington I. Chambers, "Aviation in the Navy," United States Naval Institute *Proceedings* 38 (June 1912): p. 745.

30. Jerome S. Fanciulli to Chambers, 6 January 1911 and Chambers to Cdr. Yates Stirling, 20 January 1911; both in Corresp. 1910–1919, McCurdy, J. A. D. folder, box 18, Gen. Corresp., Chambers Papers, MDLC.

31. *New York Times*, 21, 23 January 1911; Chambers to Stirling, 14, 20 January 1911; E. E. Hayden, Commandant, U.S. Naval Station Key West, to Stirling, 23 January 1911; all in Corresp. 1910–1919, McCurdy, J. A. D. folder, box 18, Gen. Corresp., Chambers Papers, MDLC; Chambers, "Aviation and Aeroplanes," p. 185; Casey, *Curtiss: The Hammondsport Era*, pp. 70–71.

32. Chambers, "Aviation and Aeroplanes," pp. 186–87, 189; *New York Times*, 31 January 1911.

33. Chambers, "Aviation and Aeroplanes," pp. 187–89; *New York Times*, 31 January, 1 February 1911.

34. Ellyson to SecNav, 31 January 1911; Ellyson to Chambers, 18 January 1911; both in Corresp. 1910–1919, Ellyson, T. G., 3 January–27 February 1911 folder, box 14, Gen. Corresp., Chambers Papers, MDLC; Casey, *Curtiss: The Hammondsport Era*, pp. 85–88; George E. A. Hallett, "First Flight from Water," *AeroSpace Briefing* (a publication of the San Diego Aerospace Museum) 1 (October 1964): pp. 1–2 (courtesy of George Cully); *San Diego Union*, 19, 21 January 1911.

35. Casey, *Curtiss: The Hammondsport Era*, pp. 88–89; Curtiss and Post, *Curtiss Aviation Book*, p. 129.

36. *San Diego Union*, 25 January 1911; Casey, *Curtiss: The Hammondsport Era*, pp. 92–93.

37. Casey, *Curtiss: The Hammondsport Era*, pp. 89–92.

38. Ellyson to SecNav, 28 January, 2, 17 February 1911, Corresp. 1910–1919, Ellyson, T. G., 3 January–27 February 1911 folder, box 14, Gen. Corresp., Chambers Papers, MDLC; *New York Times*, 27 January 1911; *San Diego Union*, 28 January 1911; Curtiss and Post, *Curtiss Aviation Book*, pp. 130–31.

39. *San Diego Union*, 29 January 1911; Ellyson to Chambers, 1 February 1911, Corresp. 1910–1919, Ellyson, T. G., 3 January–27 February 1911 folder, box 14, Gen. Corresp., Chambers Papers, MDLC; Kurutz, "The Only Safe and Sane Method," pp. 5–6; van Deurs, *Anchors in the Sky*, pp. 63–64.

40. Van Deurs, *Anchors in the Sky*, pp. 64–66.

41. Ellyson to Chambers, 14 February 1911; Ellyson to SecNav, 17 Feb 1911; both in Corresp. 1910–1919, Ellyson, T. G., 3 January–27 February 1911 folder, box 14, Gen. Corresp., Chambers Papers, MDLC; Curtiss and Post, *Curtiss Aviation Book*, pp. 134–35; *San Diego Union*, 18 February 1911; Casey, *Curtiss: The Hammondsport Era*, pp. 94–95.

42. Curtiss and Post, *Curtiss Aviation Book*, pp. 136–37; Casey, *Curtiss: The Hammondsport Era*, pp. 96–98.

43. Ellyson to SecNav, 31 January 1911; Ellyson to Chambers, 1 February 1911; both in Corresp. 1910–1919, Ellyson, T. G., 3 January–27 February 1911 folder, box 14, Gen. Corresp., Chambers Papers, MDLC.

44. Ellyson to Chambers, 1, 14 February 1911, Corresp. 1910–1919, Ellyson, T. G., 3 January–27 February 1911 folder, box 14, Gen. Corresp., Chambers Papers, MDLC.

45. Ellyson to Chambers, 17 March 1911, Corresp. 1910–1919, Ellyson, T. G., 3 March–18 May 1911 folder; Chambers to Ellyson, undated, Corresp. 1910–1919 Ellyson, T. G., 26 November 1912–24 January 1914 folder; both in box 14, Gen. Corresp., Chambers Papers, MDLC; Chambers, "Aviation and Aeroplanes," p. 196.

46. Curtiss to SecNav, 14 February 1911, Corresp. 1910–1919, Curtiss, Glenn H., November 1910–December 1911 folder, box 13, Gen. Corresp., Chambers Papers, MDLC; van Deurs, *Anchors in the Sky*, pp. 75–80.

47. Van Deurs, *Anchors in the Sky*, pp. 80–82; Roseberry, *Glenn Curtiss*, p. 317.

48. Chambers to Ellyson, 24 January, 8 February 1911; Ellyson to Chambers, 14 February 1911; all in Corresp. 1910–1919, Ellyson, T. G., 3 January–27 February 1911 folder, box 14; Chambers to Ellyson, 11 March 1911, Corresp. 1910–1919, Ellyson, T. G., 3 March–18 May 1911 folder, box 14; Jerome Fanciulli to Chambers, 20 February 1911, Corresp. 1910–1919, Curtiss, Glenn H., November 1910–December 1911 folder, box 13; all in Gen. Corresp., Chambers Papers, MDLC.

49. Lord, "History of Naval Aviation," pp. 39, 45–46; van Deurs, *Anchors in the Sky*, p. 85.

50. *San Diego Union*, 24, 31 March, 3, 9 April 1911; *New York Times*, 9 April 1911; "Factsheets: Chapter Four: The April 1911 Aviation Carnival," http://www.hill.af.mil/library/factsheets/factsheet.asp?id=5964 (accessed 21 July 2008).

51. *Hammondsport Herald*, 12, 19 April 1911.

Chapter 6. High above Keuka's Waters

1. *Hammondsport Herald*, 19, 26 April 1911; Certificate of Incorporation, Curtiss Motor Co., 19 December 1911, brown envelope No. 21, box TY 1, Wright Coll., Museum of Flight, Seattle.

2. Ellyson to Chambers, 5 March 1911; Chambers to Ellyson, 11 March 1911; Ellyson to Chambers, 17 March 1911; all in Corresp. 1910–1919, Ellyson, T. G., 3 March–18 May 1911 folder, box 14, Gen. Corresp., Chambers Papers, MDLC.

3. Record of the Service of Lieutenant (Junior Grade) Theodore G. Ellyson, 10 October 1916, Ellyson, Theodore G., Case No. 25, vol. 495, box 344, Proceedings of Naval and Marine Examining Boards, 1890–1941, Records of the Office of the Judge Advocate General (Navy), Record Group 125, National Archives (hereafter cited as JAG Records, RG 125, NA); van Deurs, *Anchors in the Sky*, p. 85; Lord, "History of Naval Aviation," pp. 40–41; Chambers to SecNav, 3 April 1911, pp. 45A–46, Aviation No. 1, W. I. Chambers Letterbook, box 1, Letters Sent Concerning the Navy's Early Use of and Experimentation with Aircraft ("Aviation"), Records of the Bureau of Naval Personnel, Record Group 24, National Archives (hereafter cited as BuPers Records, RG 24, NA).

4. Ellyson to Chambers, 31 March 1911, Corresp. 1910–1919, Ellyson, T. G., 3 March–18 May 1911 folder, box 14, Gen. Corresp., Chambers Papers, MDLC; Chambers to SecNav, 3 April 1911, pp. 45A–46; Chambers to Jerome Fanciulli, 25 March 1911, p. 45; both in Aviation No. 1, W. I. Chambers Letterbook, box 1, Letters Sent Concerning the Navy's Early Use of and Experimentation with Aircraft ("Aviation"), BuPers Records, RG 24, NA; Specifications for one Curtiss eight cyl. biplane or "Triad" to be furnished on or about 1 July 1911 to Annapolis (no date), Corresp. 1910–1919, Triad 1911–1912 folder, Curtiss Aeroplane Co., box 13, Gen. Corresp., Chambers Papers, MDLC.

5. Roy A. Grossnick, ed., *United States Naval Aviation, 1910–1995* (Washington, DC: Naval Historical Center, 1997), pp. 4–5; Casey, *Curtiss: The Hammondsport Era*, p. 100; Peter M. Bowers, *Curtiss Aircraft, 1907–1947* (London: Putnam & Company, 1979), pp. 47–49, 52.

6. Chambers to Ellyson, 8 February 1911; Ellyson to Chambers, 14 February 1911; both in Corresp. 1910–1919, Ellyson, T. G., 3 January–27 February 1911 folder, box 14, Gen. Corresp., Chambers Papers, MDLC; Chambers to Chief BuNav (Bureau of Navigation), 1 May 1911, pp. 62–63, Aviation No. 1, W. I. Chambers Letterbook, box 1, Letters Sent Concerning the Navy's Early Use of and Experimentation with Aircraft ("Aviation"), BuPers Records, RG 24, NA; Lord, "History of Naval Aviation," p. 49.

7. Van Deurs, *Anchors in the Sky*, p. 90; Ellyson to Chambers, 3 May 1911, Corresp. 1910–1919, Ellyson, T. G.,3 March–18 May 1911 folder, and Ellyson to Chambers, 20 May 1911, Corresp. 1910–1919, Ellyson, T. G., 19 May–10 July 1911; both in box 14, Gen. Corresp., Chambers Papers, MDLC. For Mott's boardinghouse, see *Hammondsport Herald*, 4 March 1903.

8. Van Deurs, *Anchors in the Sky*, p. 87; Ellyson to Chambers, 17 May 1911, Corresp. 1910–1919, Ellyson, T. G., 3 March–18 May 1911 folder, box 14, Gen. Corresp., Chambers Papers, MDLC; *New York Times*, 12, 13, 14 May 1911.

9. Ellyson to Chambers, 17 May 1911; Ellyson to Chief BuNav, 18 May 1911; both in Corresp. 1910–1919, Ellyson, T. G., 3 March–18 May 1911 folder, box 14, Gen. Corresp., Chambers Papers, MDLC.

10. Ellyson to Chief BuNav, 18 May 1911, Corresp. 1910–1919, Ellyson, T. G., 3 March–18 May 1911 folder, box 14, Gen. Corresp., Chambers Papers, MDLC.

11. *Hammondsport Herald*, 31 May 1911; Curtiss to Chambers, 1 June 1911; Chambers to Curtiss; both in Corresp. 1910–1919, Curtiss, Glenn H., November 1910–December 1911 folder, box 13; Ellyson to Chief BuNav, 18 May 1911, Corresp. 1910–1919, Ellyson, T. G., 3 March–18 May 1911 folder, box 14; all in Gen. Corresp., Chambers Papers, MDLC.

12. Quoted in House, *Hell-Rider*, p. 192.

13. Ellyson to Chambers, 1, 6 June 1911; telegram, Ellyson to Chambers, 8 June 1911; all in Corresp. 1910–1919, Ellyson, T. G., 19 May–10 July 1911 folder, box 14, Gen. Corresp., Chambers Papers, MDLC.

14. Ellyson to Chambers, 12, 26 June 1911; Ellyson to Chief BuNav, 15 June 1911; all in Corresp. 1910–1919, Ellyson, T. G., 19 May–10 July 1911 folder, box 14, Gen. Corresp., Chambers Papers, MDLC; *Hammondsport Herald*, 5 July 1911.

15. Clark G. Reynolds, *Admiral John. H. Towers: The Struggle for Naval Air Supremacy* (Annapolis, MD: Naval Institute Press, 1991), pp. 29–33; Ellyson to Chambers, 17 May 1911, Corresp. 1910–1919, Ellyson, T. G., 3 March–18 May 1911 folder; Ellyson to Chambers, 22 May 1911, Corresp. 1910–1919, Ellyson, T. G., 19 May–10 July 1911 folder; both in box 14, Gen. Corresp., Chambers Papers, MDLC.

16. John H. Towers, "Twenty Years of Naval Aviation," Chap. 1 in undated and incomplete autobiography, Personal File, Speeches & Writings, folder 26, box 4, Towers Papers, MDLC; Reynolds, *Towers*, pp. 33–34.

17. Reynolds, *Towers*, pp. 35–36.

18. Curtiss to Chambers, 27 June 1911, Corresp. 1910–1919, Curtiss, Glenn H., June 1911–October 1912 folder, box 13; Ellyson to Chambers, 26 June 1911, Corresp. 1910–1919, Ellyson, T. G., 19 May–10 July 1911 folder, box 14; both in Gen. Corresp., Chambers Papers, MDLC.

19. Aviation Log, 27 June–2 July 1911, Curtiss Hydroaeroplane Navy No. A-1, 1 July 1911 to 16 October 1912, copy in GHCM; van Deurs, *Anchors in the Sky*, pp. 91–92; Reynolds, *Towers*, p. 42.

20. Van Deurs, *Anchors in the Sky*, pp. 92–94; Aviation Log, 2–3 July 1911, Curtiss Hydroaeroplane Navy No. A-1, 1 July 1911 to 16 October 1912, copy in GHCM; *Hammondsport Herald*, 5 July 1911; telegram, Curtiss to Chambers, 3 July 1911, Corresp. 1910–1919, Ellyson, T. G., 19 May–10 July 1911 folder, box 14, Gen. Corresp., Chambers Papers, MDLC.

21. Ellyson to Chambers, 1 June, 10 July 1911, Corresp. 1910–1919, Ellyson, T. G., 19 May–10 July 1911 folder, box 14, Gen. Corresp., Chambers Papers, MDLC; Aviation Log, 7–12 July, Curtiss Hydroaeroplane Navy No. A-1, 1 July 1911 to 16 October 1912, copy in GHCM; Logbook of Curtiss Hydro-Aeroplane No. A-2, 13 July 1911, Aviation Logs, Curtiss Single Pontoon A-1, July 1911–Nov 1915, box 37, Gen. Corresp., Chambers Papers, MDLC.

22. Ellyson to Chambers, 13 July, 23 August 1911, Corresp. 1910–1919, Ellyson, T. G., 11 July–16 December 1911 folder, box 14, Gen. Corresp., Chambers Papers, MDLC; Aviation Log, 30 August 1911, Curtiss Hydroaeroplane Navy No. A-1, 1 July 1911 to 16 October 1912, copy in GHCM; Reynolds, *Towers*, pp. 38–42.

23. Lord, "History of Naval Aviation," p. 47; Ellyson to Chambers, 1 June 1911, Corresp. 1910–1919, Ellyson, T. G., 19 May–10 July 1911 folder, box 14, Gen. Corresp., Chambers Papers, MDLC.

24. Telegram, Ellyson to Chambers, 17 August 1911; Ellyson to Chambers, 19, 30 August 1911; all in Corresp. 1910–1919, Ellyson, T. G., 11 July–16 December 1911 folder, box 14; Curtiss to Chambers, 27 June, 2 September 1911, Corresp. 1910–1919, Curtiss, Glenn H., June 1911–Oct 1912 folder, box 13; all in Gen. Corresp., Chambers Papers, MDLC.

25. Ellyson to Chambers, 7 September 1911; telegram, Ellyson to Chambers, 7 September 1911; both in Corresp. 1910–1919, Ellyson, T. G., 11 July–16 December 1911 folder, box 14, Gen. Corresp., Chambers Papers, MDLC; Chambers, "Aviation To-Day and Development in the United States Navy, Part II," *Flying and the Aero Club of America Bulletin* 1 (January 1913): p. 6; Aviation Log, 4 September, 30 September 1911, Curtiss Hydroaeroplane Navy No. A-1, 1 July 1911 to 16 October 1912, copy in GHCM. Some accounts state that the A-1 was used for the wire-cable launching tests, but the A-1 flight log shows no flights from 4 September until 30 September at Annapolis.

26. Ellyson to Chambers, 24 August, 7 September 1911; telegram, Ellyson to Chambers, 11 September 1911; all in Corresp. 1910–1919, Ellyson, T. G., 11 July–16 December 1911 folder, box 14, Gen. Corresp., Chambers Papers, MDLC; Reynolds, *Towers*, pp. 42–44.

27. Reynolds, *Towers*, p. 40.

28. Ibid., pp. 44–45; Ellyson to Chambers, 16 September 1911; telegram, Ellyson to Chambers, 18 September 1911; both in Corresp. 1910–1919, Ellyson, T. G., 11 July–16 December 1911 folder, box 14, Gen. Corresp., Chambers Papers, MDLC; Record of the Service of Lieutenant (Junior Grade) Theodore G. Ellyson, 10 October 1916, Ellyson, Theodore G., Case No. 25, vol. 495, box 344, Proceedings of Naval and Marine Examining Boards, 1890–1941, JAG Records, RG 125, NA; van Deurs, *Anchors in the Sky*, pp. 103–106; Lord, "History of Naval Aviation," p. 49.

29. Record of Service of Lieutenant John Rodgers, U.S. Navy, 3 October 1916; Report on the Fitness of Officers, John Rodgers, Lieut., Capt. T. W. Kinkaid, Head of Naval Engineering Experiment Station, 1 October 1911–11 January 1912; both in Rodgers, John, Aviation, Case No. 67, vol. 289, box 931, Proceedings of Naval and Marine Examining Boards, 1890–1941, JAG Records, RG 125, NA; Reynolds, *Towers*, pp. 8, 46; Grossnick, ed., *United States Naval Aviation*, p. 7.

30. Ellyson to Chambers, 7 September 1911, Corresp. 1910–1919, Ellyson, T. G., 11 July–16 December 1911 folder, box 14, Gen. Corresp., Chambers Papers, MDLC.

31. Aviation Log, 21–22 October 1911, Curtiss Hydroaeroplane Navy No. A-1, 1 July 1911 to 16 October 1912, copy in GHCM; Reynolds, *Towers*, p. 45.

32. Curtiss to Chambers, 19 October 1911, Corresp. 1910–1919, Curtiss, Glenn H., June 1911–October 1912 folder, box 13, Gen. Corresp., Chambers Papers, MDLC.

33. Reynolds, *Towers*, p. 45.

34. Ibid., pp. 45–46.

35. W. Irving Chambers, "Aviation To-Day, and the Necessity for a National Aerodynamic Laboratory," United States Naval Institute *Proceedings* 38 (December 1912): p. 1502.

36. Aviation Log, 15 November–17 December 1911, Curtiss Hydroaeroplane Navy No. A-1, 1 July 1911 to 16 October 1912, copy in GHCM; Reynolds, *Towers*, pp. 46–47.

37. Reynolds, *Towers*, p. 47; Ellyson to Chambers, 13 December 1911, Corresp. 1910–1919, Ellyson, T. G., 11 July–16 December 1911 folder, box 14, Gen. Corresp., Chambers Papers, MDLC.

38. Ellyson to Chambers, 29 November 1911, Corresp. 1910–1919, Ellyson, T. G., 11 July–16 December 1911 folder, box 14; telegram, Chambers to Curtiss, 23 December 1911; Curtiss to Chambers, 23 December 1911; both in Corresp. 1910–1919, Curtiss, Glenn H., November 1910–December 1911 folder, box 13; all in Gen. Corresp., Chambers Papers, MDLC; *Hammondsport Herald*, 20 September, 29 November 1911; Roseberry, *Glenn Curtiss*, p. 318.

39. G. H. Curtiss, Hydroaeroplane, Patent No.1,420,609, applied for 22 August 1911, patented 20 June 1922, http://www.uspto.gov (accessed 30 January 2007); Robie, *For the Greatest Achievement*, pp. 82–84; *New York Times*, 19 November 1911.

40. Chambers, "Report on Aviation, 1912," in Alex Roland, *Model Research: The National Advisory Committee for Aeronautics, 1915–1958* (Washington, DC: National Aeronautics and Space Administration, 1985), 2: pp. 573–77.

Chapter 7. The Navy's Wings

1. *San Diego Union*, 5 March 1913; Ellyson to Chambers, 14 December 1911, Corresp. 1910–1919, Ellyson, T. G., 11 July–16 December 1911 folder; Ellyson, "Address before the New York Electrical Society: Safe Flying and the Flying Boat," no date, Corresp. 1910–1919, Ellyson, T.G., undated folder; both in box 14, Gen. Corresp., Chambers Papers, MDLC; Chambers, "Aviation To-Day—Part II," p. 5. For a general history of the flying boat, see Richard C. Knott, *The American Flying Boat: An Illustrated History* (Annapolis, MD: Naval Institute Press, 1979).

2. Chambers to Curtiss, 18 November 1911; Curtiss to Chambers, 20 November 1911; both in Corresp. 1910–1919, Curtiss, Glenn H., June 1911–Oct 1912 folder, box 13, Gen. Corresp., Chambers Papers, MDLC.

3. Casey, *Curtiss: The Hammondsport Era*, pp. 108–11.

4. Ellyson, "Address before the New York Electrical Society: Safe Flying and the Flying Boat," no date, Corresp. 1910–1919, Ellyson, T.G., undated folder, box 14, Gen. Corresp., Chambers Papers, MDLC.

5. Record of the Service of Lieutenant (Junior Grade) Theodore G. Ellyson, 10 October 1916, Ellyson, Theodore G., Case No. 25, vol. 495, box 344; Record of Service of Lieutenant John Rodgers, U.S. Navy, 3 October 1916, Rodgers,

John, Aviation, Case No. 67, vol. 289, box 931; both in Proceedings of Naval and Marine Examining Boards, 1890–1941, JAG Records, RG 125, NA; Ellyson to Chambers, 3 February 1912, Corresp. 1910–1919, Ellyson, T. G., 3 January–6 August 1912 folder, box 14, Gen. Corresp., Chambers Papers, MDLC; Reynolds, *Towers*, p. 48.

6. Chambers to F. H. Russell (Burgess Co.), 27 November 1911, pp. 213–14, Aviation No. 1, W. I. Chambers Letterbook, box 1, Letters Sent Concerning the Navy's Early Use of and Experimentation with Aircraft ("Aviation"), BuPers Records, RG 24, NA; Reynolds, *Towers*, p. 48; Curtiss to Chambers, 4 April 1912, Corresp. 1910–1919, Curtiss Aeroplane Co., July 1912 folder, box 13, Gen. Corresp., Chambers Papers, MDLC.

7. Aviation Log, 30 January–14 February 1912, Curtiss Hydroaeroplane Navy No. A-1, 1 July 1911 to 16 October 1912, copy in GHCM; Reynolds, *Towers*, p. 49; Sudsbury, *Jackrabbits to Jets*, p. 24.

8. Armstrong, "Dick Richardson," pp. 33–34; James R. Hansen, *First Man: The Life of Neil A. Armstrong* (New York: Simon & Schuster, 2005), pp. 115, 119–20.

9. Towers, "Twenty Years of Naval Aviation," Chap. 1 in undated and incomplete autobiography, Personal File, Speeches & Writings, folder 26, box 4, Towers Papers, MDLC; Richardson to Chambers, 29 February, 9 March 1912, Corresp. 1910–1919, Richardson, H. C. folder, box 21; Curtiss to Chambers, March 6, 1912, Corresp. 1910–1919, Curtiss Aeroplane Co., July 1912 folder, box 13; all in Gen. Corresp., Chambers Papers, MDLC.

10. Richardson to Chambers, 16 March 1912, Corresp. 1910–1919, Richardson, H.C. folder, box 21; Towers to Chambers, 15 March 1912, Corresp. 1910–1919, Towers, J. H. folder, box 22; both in Gen. Corresp., Chambers Papers, MDLC; Report of Medical Officer to Bureau of Medicine and Surgery, March 28, 1912, in W. C. Braisted to Chief, BuNav, 16 October 1916, Medical Record for promotion of Lieut. Theodore G. Ellyson, U.S. Navy, since 15 November 1910, Ellyson, Theodore G., Case No. 25, vol. 495, box 344, Proceedings of Naval and Marine Examining Boards, 1890–1941, JAG Records, RG 125, NA; Reynolds, *Towers*, pp. 49–50.

11. Richardson to Chambers, 16 March, 13, 26 April 1912, Corresp. 1910–1919, Richardson, H. C. folder, box 21, Gen. Corresp., Chambers Papers, MDLC; Reynolds, *Towers*, p. 50.

12. Richardson to Chambers, 13, 26 April 1912, Corresp. 1910–1919, Richardson, H.C. folder, box 21, Gen. Corresp., Chambers Papers, MDLC; Reynolds, *Towers*, p. 50; Richardson to Chambers, 22 June 1920, file 57-1, box 57, Richard K. Smith Papers, Special Collections and Archives, Auburn University, Auburn, AL (hereafter cited as Smith Papers, AU).

13. Richardson to Chambers, 13, 17, 26 April 1912, Corresp. 1910–1919, Richardson, H.C. folder, box 21, Gen. Corresp., Chambers Papers, MDLC; Aviation Log, 25 March–23 April 1912, Curtiss Hydroaeroplane Navy No. A-1, 1 July 1911 to 16 October 1912, copy in GHCM.

14. Kurutz, "The Only Safe and Sane Method," pp. 10–13; Reynolds, *Towers*, p. 48.

15. Roseberry, *Glenn Curtiss*, pp. 299–300; telegram, Callan to Genung, 6 December 1911, Correspondence 1911 folder, box 2, John Lansing Callan Papers, Manuscript Division, Library of Congress (hereafter cited as Callan Papers, MDLC); *Aero* 3 (9 March 1912): p. 461.

16. *Hammondsport Herald*, 24 April 1912; Record of the Service of Lieutenant (Junior Grade) Theodore G. Ellyson, 10 October 1916, Ellyson, Theodore G., Case No. 25, vol. 495, box 344, Proceedings of Naval and Marine Examining Boards, 1890–1941, JAG Records, RG 125, NA; van Deurs, *Anchors in the Sky*, pp. 125–26; Chambers, "Aviation To-day—Part II," pp. 3–4; Reynolds, *Towers*, p. 53.

17. Roseberry, *Glenn Curtiss*, pp. 324–25.

18. Casey, *Curtiss: The Hammondsport Era*, pp. 118–20; Reynolds, *Towers*, p. 49.

19. House, *Hell-Rider*, pp. 132, 161–62; Roseberry, *Glenn Curtiss*, p. 324; Laurence K. Loftin Jr., *Quest for Performance: The Evolution of Modern Aircraft* (Washington, DC: National Aeronautics and Space Administration, 1985), pp. 168–70. For the "Eureka moment," see James R. Hansen, *Engineer in Charge: A History of the Langley Aeronautical Laboratory, 1917–1958* (Washington, DC: National Aeronautics and Space Administration, 1987), pp. 334–35. Roseberry and House, relying on Henry Kleckler's reminiscences, state that Richardson assisted in the flying boat experiments in the spring of 1912, but no records verify that he was in Hammondsport at that time.

20. Telegram, Ellyson to Chambers, 5 July 1912, Corresp. 1910–1919, Ellyson, T. G., 3 January–6 August 1912 folder, box 14; Curtiss to Chambers, 9 July 1912, Corresp. 1910–1919, Curtiss Aeroplane Co., July 1912 folder, box 13; Curtiss to Chambers, 17 July 1912, Corresp. 1910–1919, Curtiss, Glenn H., June 1911–October 1912 folder, box 13; all in Gen. Corresp., Chambers Papers, MDLC.

21. *New York Times*, 14 July 1912; *Hammondsport Herald*, 24 July 1912; Robie, *For the Greatest Achievement*, p. 84; G. H. Curtiss, Flying Boat, Patent No. 1,142,754, applied for 4 June 1913, patented 8 June 1915, http://www.uspto.gov (accessed 30 January 2007).

22. Curtiss to Chambers, 27 July, 9 August 1912, Corresp. 1910–1919, Curtiss, Glenn H. June 1911–October 1912 folder, box 13; Richardson to Chambers, 9, 14 August 1912, Corresp. 1910–1919, Richardson, H. C. folder, box 21; all in Gen. Corresp., Chambers Papers, MDLC; *Rochester Democrat and Chronicle*, 22 August 1912.

23. *Hammondsport Herald*, 28 August, 4 September, 9 October 1912.

24. Reynolds, *Towers*, p. 54; Lord, "History of Naval Aviation," pp. 66b–67, 79; Ellyson to Chambers, 3 October 1912, Corresp. 1910–1919, Ellyson, T.G., 16 August–24 November 1916 folder, box 14, Gen. Corresp., Chambers Papers, MDLC.

25. Chambers to Curtiss, 26 December 1911, confidential, handwritten draft, Corresp. 1910–1919, Curtiss, Glenn H. November 10–December 1911 folder; Curtiss to Chambers, 3 January 1912, Corresp. 1910–1919, Curtiss Aeroplane Co., July 1912 folder; both in box 13; Richardson to Chambers, 13, 26 April 1912, Corresp. 1910–1919, Richardson, H. C. folder, box 21; all in Gen. Corresp., Chambers Papers, MDLC.

26. Armstrong, "Richardson," pp. 35–36; Ellyson to Chambers, 26 May 1912, Corresp. 1910–1919, Ellyson, T. G., 3 January–6 August 1912 folder, box 14, Gen. Corresp., Chambers Papers, MDLC.

27. Armstrong, "Richardson," pp. 35–36; van Deurs, *Anchors in the Sky*, p. 140; Chambers, "Aviation To-Day—Part II," p. 1509; Chambers to Lt. Cdr. G. L. Smith, 12 July 1917, Official Correspondence January–August 1917 folder, box 4, Gen. Corresp., Chambers Papers, MDLC.

28. Roland, *Model Research*, 2: p. 572.

29. Ibid., pp. 573–84; Turnbull and Lord, *History of United States Naval Aviation*, p. 21.

30. Ellyson, "Address before the New York Electrical Society: Safe Flying and the Flying Boat," no date, Corresp. 1910–1919, Ellyson, T. G., undated folder, box 14, Gen. Corresp., Chambers Papers, MDLC.

31. Ibid.; Casey, *Curtiss: The Hammondsport Era*, p. 225; *Rochester Democrat and Chronicle*, 11, 13, 14 October 1912.

32. *Hammondsport Herald*, 9 October, 29 November, 1 December 1912; Chief BuNav to Chambers, 5 October 1912, Corresp. 1910–1919, Official Correspondence 1912 folder, box 4; Ellyson to Chambers, 26, 29 November, 1 December 1912, Corresp. 1910–1919, Ellyson, T. G., 26 November 1912–24 January 1914 folder, box 14; all in Gen. Corresp., Chambers Papers, MDLC; van Deurs, *Anchors in the Sky*, p. 143.

33. William F. Trimble, *Jerome C. Hunsaker and the Rise of American Aeronautics* (Washington, DC: Smithsonian Institution Press, 2002), pp. 4–26, 73.

34. Van Deurs, *Anchors in the Sky*, p. 140; Reynolds, *Towers*, pp. 56–59.

35. Sudsbury, *Jackrabbits to Jets*, p. 27.

36. *San Diego Union*, 1, 3, 20 January, 4, 5 March 1913.

37. Roseberry, *Glenn Curtiss*, pp. 337–38; Crouch, *Bishop's Boys*, pp. 448–51, 456–57.

38. Casey, *Curtiss: The Hammondsport Era*, pp. 146–51; *San Diego Union*, 5, 12, 19, 24 February, 15 March 1913.

39. Genung to Chambers, 2 January 1913, Corresp. 1910–1919, Curtiss Aeroplane Co. August 1912 folder, box 13; Richardson to Chambers, 5 October 1913, Corresp. 1910–1919, Sperry Gyroscope Co. folder, box 22; both in Gen. Corresp., Chambers Papers, MDLC; Richardson to Chambers, 5 October 1913, Chambers files 252, 253, "Chronology of U.S. Naval Aviation," 1913–14, no date, Biographical Notebooks File, Chronological 1919, folder 12, box 10, Towers Papers, MDLC; *Hammondsport Herald*, 17 December 1913; Casey, *Curtiss: The Hammondsport Era*, pp. 104–105.

40. *Hammondsport Herald*, 17 December, 4 February 1914; Casey, *Curtiss: The Hammondsport Era*, pp. 105–6; Stein, *From Torpedoes to Aviation*, pp. 173–74,

41. Crouch, *Bishop's Boys*, p. 443; Thomas Parke Hughes, *Elmer Sperry: Inventor and Engineer* (Baltimore: The Johns Hopkins University Press, 1971), pp. 174–75, 178; *Hammondsport Herald*, 14 October 1908; Roland, *Model Research*, 2: p. 577; Ellyson to Chambers, 22 March 1911, Corresp. 1910–1919, Ellyson, T. G., 3 March–18 May 1911 folder, box 14, Gen. Corresp., Chambers Papers, MDLC; Chambers to SecNav, 3 April 1911, pp. 45A–46, Aviation No. 1, W. I. Chambers Letterbook,

box 1, Letters Sent Concerning the Navy's Early Use of and Experimentation with Aircraft ("Aviation"), BuPers Records, RG 24, NA.

42. Hughes, *Elmer Sperry*, pp. 179–81; Curtiss to Chambers, 27 July 1912, Corresp. 1910–1919, Curtiss, Glenn H., June 1911–October 1912 folder, box 13; Chambers to Lt.(jg) R. E. Gillmor, 29 June 1912; Curtiss to Elmer Sperry, 11 July 1912, Corresp. 1910–1919, Sperry Gyroscope Co. folder, box 22; all in Gen. Corresp., Chambers Papers, MDLC.

43. Hughes, *Elmer Sperry*, pp. 181, 184–85; *Hammondsport Herald*, 9 October 1912; Ellyson to Chambers, 24 November 1912, Corresp. 1910–1919, Ellyson, T. G., 16 August–24 November 1912 folder, box 14; Ellyson to Chambers, 4 December 1912, Corresp. 1910–1919, Ellyson, T. G., 26 November 1912–24 January 1914 folder, box 14; telegram, Elmer Sperry to Chambers, 30 December 1912, Corresp. 1910–1919, Sperry Gyroscope Co. folder, box 22; all in Gen. Corresp., Chambers Papers, MDLC.

44. Elmer Sperry to Chambers, 31 December 1912, Corresp. 1910–1919, Sperry Gyroscope Co. folder, box 22, Gen. Corresp., Chambers Papers, MDLC; *San Diego Union*, 29 January, 2, 19 February, 3, 23, 28 March, 4, 9 April 1913; Hughes, *Elmer Sperry*, pp. 185–86.

45. Elmer Sperry to Chambers, 19 April, 14 May 1913; Chambers to Chief BuNav, 28 April 1913, Corresp. 1910–1919, Sperry Gyroscope Co. folder; both in box 22; Victor Blue (Acting Chief of BuNav) to Chambers, 5 July 1913, Official Correspondence July 1913 folder, box 4; all in Gen. Corresp., Chambers Papers, MDLC; Reynolds, *Towers*, p. 56; *Hammondsport Herald*, 2, 16 July 1913.

46. Elmer Sperry to Chambers, 11 September 1913; Bellinger to Chambers, 14 September 1913; both in Corresp. 1910–1919, Sperry Gyroscope Co. folder, box 22, Gen. Corresp., Chambers Papers, MDLC; *Hammondsport Herald*, 17 December 1913; Hughes, *Elmer Sperry*, pp. 187–90; Lord, "History of Naval Aviation," pp. 91–92.

47. Hughes, *Elmer Sperry*, pp. 190–99.

48. *Hammondsport Herald*, 6, 27 August, 15 October 1913; *New York Times*, 30 August, 30 September 1913; unidentified clipping, 27 October 1913, 1912–1940 Newspaper Clippings folder, Curtiss, Glenn H., box 16, AIAA Archives, MDLC; Roseberry, *Glenn Curtiss*, p. 349; Casey, *Curtiss: The Hammondsport Era*, p. 134; Larry Rinek, "Curtiss Aviation Engines: An American Success Story," *Torque Meter: Journal of the Aircraft Engine Historical Society* 6 (Spring 2007): pp. 12–17.

49. *Hammondsport Herald*, 10 December 1913, 18, 25 February 1914; *New York Times*, 4 January, 10 February 1914; unidentified clipping, 4 December 1913, 1912–1940 Newspaper Clippings folder, Curtiss, Glenn H., box 16, AIAA Archives, MDLC; Roseberry, *Glenn Curtiss*, pp. 349–51.

Chapter 8. Headwinds

1. *New York Times*, 10, 11 February 1914.

2. Crouch, *Bishop's Boys*, pp. 460–62; Roseberry, *Glenn Curtiss*, pp. 342–47, 357. An undated photograph (Roseberry, *Glenn Curtiss*, no. 78) shows Curtiss and Ford standing next to one of Curtiss' flying boats at Hammondsport.

3. Roseberry, *Glenn Curtiss*, pp. 357–59; *Hammondsport Herald*, 9 December 1914.

4. Smith, *First Across!*, pp. 5–6.

5. Chambers to J. E. Beatty, 26 May 1913, Corresp. 1910–1919, Transatlantic folder, box 22, Gen. Corresp., Chambers Papers, MDLC; Roseberry, *Glenn Curtiss*, pp. 363–64; Casey, *Curtiss: The Hammondsport Era*, p. 180.

6. *New York Times*, 1 April 1913, 5 February 1914; Roseberry, *Glenn Curtiss*, pp. 364–65.

7. Roseberry, *Glenn Curtiss*, pp. 365–66.

8. Casey, *Curtiss: The Hammondsport Era*, pp. 180–81; Roseberry, *Glenn Curtiss*, p. 366; *Hammondsport Herald*, 10 December 1913; *New York Times*, 4 January, 11 February 1914.

9. Roseberry, *Glenn Curtiss*, pp. 366–67.

10. *New York Times*, 5 February 1914; Bristol to Chief BuNav, 17 February 1914, Biographical Notebooks File, Naval Aviators, Photocopies of Correspondence, January–May 1914, folder 1, box 12, Towers Papers, MDLC; Reynolds, *Towers*, pp. 74–75.

11. *New York Times*, 25, 27 February 1914; Reynolds, *Towers*, p. 75; Towers report, 10 March 1914, Towers biog. ms., undated (from tape), Biographical Notebooks File, Chronological 1914, folder 1, box 7, Towers Papers, MDLC.

12. Roseberry, *Glenn Curtiss*, p. 367; *New York Times*, 27, 28 February 1914.

13. Casey, *Curtiss: The Hammondsport Era*, pp. 181–83; Jas. H. Smellie press release, 3 March 1914, "America" misc. info. folder, Flying Boats file, GHCM; Towers report, 10 March 1914, Biographical Notebooks File, Chronological 1914, folder 2, box 7, Towers Papers, MDLC.

14. *New York Times*, 12, 25 February 1914; Casey, *Curtiss: The Hammondsport Era*, pp. 180–84; Bowers, *Curtiss Aircraft*, pp. 58–60.

15. Jas. H. Smellie press release, 3 March 1914, "America" misc. info. folder, Flying Boats file, GHCM; *Hammondsport Herald*, 15, 29 April 1914.

16. Turnbull and Lord, *History of United States Naval Aviation*, pp. 41–42.

17. Curtiss to Towers, 5 May 1914, Biographical Notebooks File, Chronological 1914, folder 2, box 7, Towers Papers, MDLC; Reynolds, *Towers*, pp. 77–80.

18. *New York Times*, 18, 19 June 1914; Roseberry, *Glenn Curtiss*, pp. 369–70, 372; Smith, *First Across!*, p. 49.

19. Callan to Curtiss, 29 March 1913, Correspondence January–May 1913 folder; Chevalier to Callan, 11 December 1913, Correspondence September–December 1913 folder; box 2, Callan Papers, MDLC; *Hammondsport Herald*, 11 June 1913, 18 February 1914; Reynolds, *Towers*, pp. 61, 71–72; Grossnick, ed., *United States Naval Aviation*, p. 12.

20. *New York Times*, 20 June 1914; Roseberry, *Glenn Curtiss*, pp. 371–72, 377; Callan, Azores, Pathfinder and Relief Pilot for Transatlantic Flight, no date, Proposed "America" Flight folder, box 7, Callan Papers, MDLC.

21. *New York Times*, 25 February 1914; Smith, *First Across!*, p. 20. For a perspective on weight and load capacities of airplanes, see Smith, "Weight Envelope," pp. 30–44, especially pp. 31–32, and Smith's "The Superiority of the American Transoceanic

Airliner, 1932–1939: Sikorsky S-42 vs. Short S. 23," *American Aviation Historical Society Journal* 29 (Summer 1984): pp. 82–94.

22. Reynolds, *Towers*, p. 81; Roseberry, *Glenn Curtiss*, pp. 372–74; *New York Times*, 21, 23 June 1914; *Hammondsport Herald*, 24 May 1899, 24 June 1914.

23. *New York Times*, 24 June 1914.

24. Ibid., 28 June, 1 July 1914; *Hammondsport Herald*, 1 July 1914.

25. *New York Times*, 2, 3, 6, 9, 11, 12 July 1914.

26. Ibid., 19 July 1914; *Hammondsport Herald*, 15 July 1914.

27. Richardson to Bristol, 19 July 1914, op 5 946-14, folders 901-14 to 950-14, box 3, General Correspondence of Office of Naval Aeronautics, 1914–17, Records of the Bureau of Aeronautics, Record Group 72, National Archives (hereafter cited as BuAer Records, RG 72, NA) ; H. C. Richardson, "Big Flying Boats," (no date), Special Article, Book File, box 5, Holden Chester Richardson Papers, Manuscript Division, Library of Congress; Reynolds, *Towers*, p. 83; *New York Times*, 19 July 1914.

28. *New York Times*, 24, 25, 26 July 1914; *Hammondsport Herald*, 22 July 1914; Towers to Bristol, 28 July 1914, folder 142851, box 1, General Correspondence, Bureau of Steam Engineering, Records of Predecessor Offices, BuAer Records, RG 72, NA.

29. *New York Times*, 26 July 1914; *Hammondsport Herald*, 12 August 1914; Roseberry, *Glenn Curtiss*, p. 379.

30. Roseberry, *Glenn Curtiss*, pp. 381–82; Crouch, *Bishop's Boys*, p. 486.

31. *New York Times*, 26 January 1914; Roseberry, *Glenn Curtiss*, pp. 382–84.

32. Roseberry, *Glenn Curtiss*, pp. 384–85.

33. Ibid., p. 386.

34. *Hammondsport Herald*, 20 May 1914; Roseberry, *Glenn Curtiss*, pp. 386–88; C. G. Abbot, "The 1914 Tests of the Langley 'Aerodrome,'" *Smithsonian Miscellaneous Collections* 103 (24 October 1942): pp. 3–6, available online at http://cr.nps.gov/history/online_books/daav/appendix-c.htm (accessed 5 December 2006).

35. Roseberry, *Glenn Curtiss*, p. 389; *New York Times*, 29 May 1914.

36. Crouch, *Bishop's Boys*, pp. 488–89; *New York Times*, 22 June 1914.

37. *New York Times*, 22, 23 June 1914.

38. *Hammondsport Herald*, 2, 23 September 1914, 7 April 1915; Roseberry, *Glenn Curtiss*, pp. 391–92; House, *Hell-Rider*, pp. 145–46.

39. Roseberry, *Glenn Curtiss*, pp. 392–93; Crouch, *Bishop's Boys*, pp. 465–66, 489.

40. Crouch, *Bishop's Boys*, pp. 465–66, 487, 489–501, 520, 527–29.

41. Ibid., pp. 489–90; Bowers, *Curtiss Aircraft*, pp. 87–88; Hallion, *Taking Flight*, pp. 126–27, 290, 292; House, *Hell-Rider*, pp. 176–77. Curtiss' biographer C. R. Roseberry does not mention the Goupil Duck.

42. Richard K. Smith, "Not a Success—But a Triumph: 80 Years since Kitty Hawk," *Naval War College Review* 36 (November–December 1983): p. 17; Shulman, *Unlocking the Sky*, pp. 65, 220–21; Crouch, *Bishop's Boys*, p. 490.

43. *New York Times*, 5 August 1914.

44. Bristol to SecNav, 26 September 1914, folder 1251-14 to 1300-14, box 4, General Correspondence of Office of Naval Aeronautics, 1914–17, BuAer Records,

RG 72, NA; Richardson to Chambers, 19 October 1913, Corresp. 1910–1919, Richardson, H. C. folder, box 21; and H. C. Genung to Chambers, 22 October 1913, Corresp. 1910–1919, Curtiss, Glenn H., 1913 folder, box 13; both in Gen. Corresp., Chambers Papers, MDLC.

45. Casey, *Curtiss: The Hammondsport Era*, pp. 134–35, 168–73, 191–92; *Hammondsport Herald*, 9, 30 September 1914; Bowers, *Curtiss Aircraft*, p. 90.

46. Genung to Bristol, 6 June 1914, folder 651–14 to 700–14, box 2; Bristol to Curtiss Aeroplane Co., 6 July 1914, folder 851–14 to 900–14, box 3; both in General Correspondence of Office of Naval Aeronautics, 1914–1917, BuAer Records, RG 72, NA.

47. *Hammondsport Herald*, 4 November 1914; Mark Goldman, *High Hopes: The Rise and Decline of Buffalo, New York* (Albany: State University of New York Press, 1983).

48. *Hammondsport Herald*, 2 September, 9 December 1914; Roseberry, *Glenn Curtiss*, pp. 394–95; Surrogate's Court, Steuben County, New York, in the Matter of the Probate of the Last Will and Testament of Glenn H. Curtiss, no date (probably 1931), file CC-840000-05, Curtiss file, Archives and Library, NASM; Plan and Contract, Curtiss Aeroplane . . . and Erie Finance Corp., 17 August 1916, brown envelope No. 34, box TY 1, Wright Coll., Museum of Flight, Seattle.

49. Richard J. Beiter, "Curtiss Plants–Buffalo, NY," in Curtiss Co., Buffalo Street Plans folder, GHCM; memo, C. S. Ashdown to BuC&R (Bureau of Construction and Repair), Report on Plant—Curtiss Aeroplane and Motor Corporation, Buffalo, New York, 30 November 1917, pp. 115–19, vol. 1, file QM (28) Curtiss Engineering Corp., box 4363, Records of Divisions and Offices, Office Services Division, Administrative Services, General Correspondence, 1925–1942, BuAer Records, RG 72, NA; Roseberry, *Glenn Curtiss*, pp. 397–98; *Aerial Age Weekly* 1 (24 May 1915): p. 225.

50. Trimble, *Hunsaker*, pp. 27–32.

51. Casey, *Curtiss: The Hammondsport Era*, pp. 176–77, 188–89; *Hammondsport Herald*, 20 May 1914; Bristol to Herbster, 11 November 1914, Op. 5 1371-14 Ans, folder 1351-14 to 1375-14, box 5, General Correspondence of Office of Naval Aeronautics, 1914–17, BuAer Records, RG 72, NA; Bowers, *Curtiss Aircraft*, pp. 63–66, 143–60.

52. William O. Shanahan, "Procurement of Naval Aircraft, 1907–1939," vol. 17, Deputy Chief of Naval Operations (Air) (Washington, DC: Naval Aviation History Unit, 1946), pp. 92, 97; Trimble, *Hunsaker*, pp. 40–41.

53. Mustin to Chief of Operations (Air), 26 October 1915, July–December 1915 folder, box 30, General Correspondence, Papers of Mark L. Bristol, Manuscript Division, Library of Congress; Turnbull and Lord, *History of United States Naval Aviation*, pp. 47, 55–56; Roseberry, *Glenn Curtiss*, pp. 396–98; *Hammondsport Herald*, 15 September 1915; *New York Times*, 14 January 1916.

54. Roseberry, *Glenn Curtiss*, p. 401; *Hammondsport Herald*, 19 January 1916; *Aerial Age Weekly* 3 (4 September 1916): p. 745, 4 (2 July 1917): pp. 522–23.

55. Timothy Wilson, "Broken Wings: The Curtiss Aeroplane Company, K-Boats, and the Russian Navy, 1914–1916," *Journal of Military History* 66 (October 2002): pp. 1061–83; Bowers, *Curtiss Aircraft*, pp. 82–83, 106–7; Statement of Mr. Glenn H. Curtiss, undated, *U.S. v. Curtiss Aeroplane Company*—Statements of Witnesses folder, box TY 3, Wright Coll., Museum of Flight, Seattle.

56. Trimble, *Hunsaker*, pp. 41–42.

57. Westervelt to Hunsaker, 15, 17 May 1917, file W, box 6, Jerome C. Hunsaker Papers, Archives and Library, National Air and Space Museum, Washington, DC (hereafter cited as Hunsaker Papers, NASM).

58. *New York Times*, 29 June, 14 July 1917; Roseberry, *Glenn Curtiss*, pp. 402–3, 406; Jerome C. Hunsaker, "The Reminiscences of Jerome C. Hunsaker," interview by Donald Shaughnessy, April 1960, Aviation Project, Oral History Research Office, Columbia University, p. 92 (hereafter cited as Hunsaker interview, April 1960, OHRO, Columbia University).

59. Chambers to Ellyson, 16 February 1911, Corresp. 1910–1919, Ellyson, T. G., 3 January–27 February 1911 folder, box 14, Gen. Corresp., Chambers Papers, MDLC; Roseberry, *Glenn Curtiss*, pp. 322, 407, 424; Helen Muir, *Miami, U.S.A.* (Gainesville: University Press of Florida, 2000), pp. 87–91.

60. Muir, *Miami, U.S.A.*, pp. 99, 102, 114; Surrogate's Court, Steuben County, New York, in the Matter of the Probate of the Last Will and Testament of Glenn H. Curtiss, no date (probably 1931), file CC-840000-05, Curtiss file, Archives and Library, NASM; *Hammondsport Herald*, 12 January 1916; *Miami Herald*, 29 October, 24 November, 9 December 1916, 11 January 1917; *Aviation and Aeronautical Engineering* 1 (15 November 1916): p. 260; Callan to Harold Kantner, 24 November 1916, November 1916 folder, box 3, General Correspondence, Callan Papers, MDLC.

61. *New York Times*, 29 June, 14 July 1917; Roseberry, *Glenn Curtiss*, pp. 402–3, 406; Richard J. Beiter, "Curtiss Plants–Buffalo, NY," in Curtiss Co., Buffalo Street Plans folder, GHCM; Certificate of Incorporation, Curtiss Engineering Corporation, 13 August 1917, brown envelope No. 21, box TY 1, Wright Coll., Museum of Flight, Seattle; Hunsaker interview, April 1960, OHRO, Columbia University; Director of Naval Intelligence to Taylor, 2 February 1918, vol. 1, file QM(28) Curtiss Eng. Corp., box 4363, Records of Divisions and Offices, Office Services Division, Administrative Services, General Correspondence, BuAer Records, RG 72, NA; memo, Hunsaker to Taylor, 12 November 1917, file C, box 1, Hunsaker Papers, NASM.

62. Roseberry, *Glenn Curtiss*, pp. 328, 361, 474–75; *Hammondsport Herald*, 8 September 1915; *Aerial Age Weekly* 2 (27 September 1915): p. 32; Crouch, *Wings*, p. 148.

63. Roland, *Model Research*, 1: pp. 37–41.

64. Crouch, *Bishop's Boys*, pp. 463, 466; Hallion, *Taking Flight*, pp. 288–90.

65. Director of Naval Intelligence to Taylor, 2 February 1918; memo, Lt. (jg) L. M. Ream to Hunsaker, 13 April 1918, 401-Z-6; Westervelt to Bureau of Construction and Repair, 27 July 1918, no. 1400; R. S. Griffin to SecNav, 27 July 1918; all in

vol. 1, file QM(28), Curtiss Engineering Corp., box 4363, Records of Divisions and Offices, Office Services Division, Administrative Services, General Correspondence, BuAer Records, RG 72, NA; *New York Times*, 22 June 1918.

66. Jacob A. Vander Meulen, *The Politics of Aircraft; Building an American Military Industry* (Lawrence: University Press of Kansas, 1991), pp. 31–40.

67. Bowers, *Curtiss Aircraft*, pp. 73–74; *Hammondsport Herald*, 20 November 1918. A seventh plant in Buffalo, on Bradley Street, may have produced parts only.

Chapter 9. Challenges Old and New

1. Curtiss to J. C. Porte, 26 March 1915; Agreement between the Curtiss Aeroplane Company . . . and Rodman Wanamaker, 2 September 1915; Agreement between the Curtiss Aeroplane Company . . . and the America Trans Oceanic Company, Inc., 31 March 1916; all in small brown envelope, box TY 4, Wright Coll., Museum of Flight, Seattle; Roseberry, *Glenn Curtiss*, p. 406; *New York Times*, 2 April 1916.

2. Bowers, *Curtiss Aircraft*, pp. 136–37; Henry Woodhouse, "The Fifteen-Ton Curtiss Air Cruiser," *Flying* 5 (March 1916): pp. 63, 73–74; "A New Curtiss Air Cruiser," *Aeronautics* 18 (12 July 1916), p. 23; Rinek, "Curtiss Aviation Engines," p. 17; clippings in file AC-903400-01, Curtiss T. Wanamaker Triplane, Model 3, Archives and Library, NASM.

3. Smith, *First Across!*, pp. 16–18; G. C. Westervelt, H. C. Richardson, and A. C. Read, *The Triumph of the NCs* (Garden City, NY: Doubleday, Page & Co., 1920), pp. 4, 16.

4. Smith, *First Across!*, p. 20; Roseberry, *Glenn Curtiss*, pp. 412–13.

5. Louis S. Casey, "Curtiss Flying Lifeboat," *American Aviation Historical Society Journal* 10 (Summer 1965): pp. 102–4 (courtesy of George Cully).

6. Smith, *First Across!*, pp. 20–21; J. C. Hunsaker, "Progress in Naval Aircraft," *Journal of the Society of Automotive Engineers* 5 (July 1919): p. 32.

7. Hunsaker, "Progress in Naval Aircraft," p. 32; Taylor to Cuthell, White, Bayles, and Appel, 23 March 1920, vol. 3, file QM(28), Curtiss Eng. Corp., box 4364, Records of Divisions and Offices, Office Services Division, Administrative Services, General Correspondence, 1925–1942, BuAer Records, RG 72, NA.

8. Smith, *First Across!*, pp. 21–22, 29; Bowers, *Curtiss Aircraft*, p. 120; Hunsaker, "Progress in Naval Aircraft," p. 33; C. J. McCarthy to R. K. Smith, 30 September 1968, file 57-2, box 57, Smith Papers, AU; Smith, "Superiority of the American Transoceanic Airliner," p. 85.

9. Smith, *First Across!*, p. 22; Transcript of Dinner Comments, Toastmaster Irvin S. Cobb, 10 July 1919, folder 28, box 14, MS Group 77, Series 2, Hatch Papers, UF.

10. Roseberry, *Glenn Curtiss*, pp. 406–7; Curtiss Aeroplane and Motor Company, Inc., information booklet, file CC-840000-02, Curtiss file, Archives and Library, NASM; unidentified clipping, 9 December 1917, 1912–1940 Newspaper Clippings folder, Curtiss, Glenn H., box 16, AIAA Archives, MDLC; *Aerial Age Weekly* 6 (11 February 1918); *Hammondsport Herald*, 6 February 1918.

11. Smith, *First Across!*, pp. 22–23; Hunsaker, "Progress in Naval Aircraft," p. 38.

12. Westervelt to Hunsaker, 5 April 1918, file W, box 6, Hunsaker Papers, NASM; Smith, *First Across!*, pp. 26–28.

13. Smith, *First Across!*, p. 27; Westervelt to Hunsaker, 24 July 1918, file W, box 6, Hunsaker Papers, NASM.

14. Smith, *First Across!*, pp. 28–29; Roseberry, *Glenn Curtiss*, p. 415.

15. Roseberry, *Glenn Curtiss*, p. 415; Smith, *First Across!*, pp. 30–31.

16. Smith, *First Across!*, pp. 31–34.

17. Ibid., pp. 37–47, 49, 100, 177.

18. Ibid., pp. 56–57.

19. Ibid., pp. 58–59.

20. Ibid., p. 213; Hunsaker, "Progress in Naval Aircraft," p. 42.

21. Smith, *First Across!*, pp. 63–64.

22. Hunsaker interview, April 1960, OHRO, Columbia University, pp. 59, 63; Smith, *First Across!*, pp. 68–92, 97.

23. *New York Times*, 11 May 1919.

24. Smith, *First Across!*, pp. 104–16, 120–22, 133–37.

25. Ibid., pp. 122–26, 137–43.

26. Ibid., pp. 112–15, 119, 126–30, 150–53, 163–71.

27. Ibid., pp. 179–89, 192–94.

28. *New York Times*, 11 July 1919; Roseberry, *Glenn Curtiss*, pp. 422–23; Reynolds, *Towers*, p. 164; Transcript of Dinner Comments, Toastmaster Irvin S. Cobb, 10 July 1919, folder 28, box 14, MS Group 77, Series 2, Hatch Papers, UF.

29. *Aerial Age Weekly* 3 (4 September 1916): p. 743, 6 (21 January 1918): p. 833; *New York Times*, 31 October 1915, 26 August 1916; SecNav to Alan R. Hawley, Aero Club of America, 29 March 1915, Op.5 259-15, folder 243-15 to 302-15, box 8, General Correspondence of Office of Naval Aeronautics, 1914–17, BuAer Records, RG 72, NA; Bowers, *Curtiss Aircraft*, p. 165.

30. Curtiss to Hunsaker, 30 April 1920, folder 3, file C, box 1, Hunsaker Papers, NASM.

31. Thomas G. Foxworth, *The Speed Seekers* (New York: Doubleday & Company, 1976), pp. 173, 177–84, 428.

32. Roseberry, *Glenn Curtiss*, pp. 426–27, 453; Bowers, *Curtiss Aircraft*, pp. 138–43; Grossnick, ed., *United States Naval Aviation*, p. 36; Foxworth, *Speed Seekers*, p. 190.

33. Curtiss to Hunsaker, 26 November 1920; Hunsaker to Curtiss, 29 November 1920; both in folder 3, file C, box 1, Hunsaker Papers, NASM; Foxworth, *Speed Seekers*, pp. 29–31, 173–74, 190, 446–50; Trimble, *Hunsaker*, pp. 85–86.

34. Louis R. Eltscher and Edward M. Young, *Curtiss-Wright: Greatness and Decline* (New York: Twayne Publishers, 1998), pp. 26–27; U.S. Congress, House, *Hearing before a Subcommittee of the Committee on Military Affairs, United Air Service*, 66th Cong., 2d sess. (Washington, DC: Government Printing Office, 1919), pp. 244–45; *Hammondsport Herald*, 20 November, 25 December 1918, 22 January, 5 February 1919; House, *Hell-Rider*, p. 200.

35. *Hammondsport Herald*, 6 August, 31 December 1919; Roseberry, *Glenn Curtiss*, pp. 429–30.

36. Eltscher and Young, *Curtiss-Wright*, pp. 28–29, 32; C. M. Keys, "The Curtiss Aeroplane and Motor Corporation after the War," *Aerial Age Weekly* 13 (6 June 1921): pp. 295–96.

37. Foxworth, *Speed Seekers*, pp. 33–34, 193–98.

38. Ibid., pp. 191–92; Ladislas d'Orcy, "The Curtiss Marine Flying Trophy Race," *Aviation* 13 (16 October 1922): pp. 490–92.

39. Foxworth, *Speed Seekers*, pp. 34–35, 199–201, 209–10, 244–47, 494–95, 519; Roseberry, *Glenn Curtiss*, pp. 427–28; *New York Times*, 1 October 1922.

40. Foxworth, *Speed Seekers*, pp. 36–37, 52–53, 201–4, 217–21, 248–55, 472–73; *New York Times*, 4 October 1923.

41. Roseberry, *Glenn Curtiss*, p. 428; Bowers, *Curtiss Aircraft*, p. 186.

42. J. C. Hunsaker, memo for file, 27 September 1922, vol. 3, file QM(28), Curtiss Eng. Corp., box 4364, Records of Divisions and Offices, Office Services Division, Administrative Services, General Correspondence, 1925–1942, BuAer Records, RG 72, NA.

Epilogue

1. *Miami Herald*, 15 July 1918; Roseberry, *Glenn Curtiss*, pp. 424–25; Grossnick, ed., *United States Naval Aviation*, p. 34.

2. Roseberry, *Glenn Curtiss*, pp. 425, 430; Surrogate's Court, Steuben County, New York, in the Matter of the Probate of the Last Will and Testament of Glenn H. Curtiss, no date (probably 1931), file CC-840000-05, Curtiss file, Archives and Library, NASM.

3. Roseberry, *Glenn Curtiss*, pp. 426, 431; *New York Times*, 16 January 1925.

4. Roseberry, *Glenn Curtiss*, pp. 431–32; "Glenn H. Curtiss—Miami Springs Historical Hike," http://www.acgweb.com/Spring/index.html (accessed 17 July 2008); Surrogate's Court, Steuben County, New York, in the Matter of the Probate of the Last Will and Testament of Glenn H. Curtiss, no date (probably 1931), file CC-840000-05, Curtiss file, Archives and Library, NASM.

5. C. L. Waters to Nancy Hutches, no date, file #574, Rutha Curtiss folder, GHCM; Hunsaker to Curtiss, 11 January 1928, Personal Correspondence, 1928, folder 25, box 7; and Westervelt to Hunsaker, 31 January 1928, Personal Correspondence, 1928, folder 12, box 8; both in Hunsaker Papers, NASM.

6. Roseberry, *Glenn Curtiss*, pp. 432–33; Muir, *Miami, U.S.A.*, pp. 134–35; T. D. Allman, *Miami: City of the Future* (New York: Atlantic Monthly Press, 1987), pp. 196–97.

7. Roseberry, *Glenn Curtiss*, pp. 439–40. For an overview of the boom and bust, see William Frazer and John J. Guthrie Jr., *The Florida Land Boom: Speculation, Money, and the Banks* (Westport, CT: Quorum Books, 1995).

8. *Aviation* 21 (27 December 1926): p. 1091; *Aviation* 21 (29 August 1927): pp. 490–91; *Aviation* 26 (6 July 1929): p. 55; *Aviation* 27 (20 July 1929): p. 178; *New York Times*, 2 July 1928, 8, 9, 10 January 1929. The Pan American Field became Miami International Airport; the Opa-locka facility is now Opa-locka Executive Airport.

9. *Hammondsport Herald*, 15 September 1915; undated, unidentified newspaper clipping, Hammondsport, file #595, GHCM; *New York Times*, 5 July 1928; Roseberry, *Glenn Curtiss*, pp. 446–47.

10. Kirk W. House, "Modern Transportation: Curtiss Aerocar," *Invention and Technology* 23 (Fall 2008): pp. 40–47; *New York Times*, 14 September 1928.

11. Roseberry, *Glenn Curtiss*, pp. 433–34; *New York Times*, 13 October 1918.

12. Roseberry, *Glenn Curtiss*, pp. 434–35; *New York Times*, 19 July 1926.

13. Eltscher and Young, *Curtiss-Wright*, pp. 29–52.

14. Bowers, *Curtiss Aircraft*, pp. 215–17.

15. Roseberry, *Glenn Curtiss*, pp. 451–53.

16. Ibid., pp. 445, 453–55; Curtiss to Towers, 5 July 1930, folder 5, Biographical Notebooks File, Chronological 1928–30, box 8, Towers Papers, MDLC; telegram, Towers to Curtiss, 12 July 1930, file 600, GHCM; *New York Times*, 24 July 1930.

17. Roseberry, *Glenn Curtiss*, p. 456; Reynolds, *Towers*, p. 230.

18. Chambers to Lena Curtiss, 25 July 1913 [1930; misdated 1913], 1913 folder, Corresp., 1910–1919, box 13, Curtiss Aeroplane Co., Gen. Corresp., Chambers Papers, MDLC.

19. USS *Curtiss, Dictionary of American Naval Fighting Ships*, http://www.history.navy.mil/danfs/c16/curtiss.htm (accessed 29 December 2008); USS *Hammondsport, Dictionary of American Naval Fighting Ships*, http://www.history.navy.mil/danfs/h2/hammondsport.htm (accessed 29 December 2008).

Bibliography

Manuscript and Archival Material

Auburn University, Special Collections and Archives, Auburn, AL.
    Smith, Richard K. Papers.
Glenn Hammond Curtiss Museum, Hammondsport, NY.
Library of Congress, Manuscript Division, Washington, DC.
    American Institute of Aeronautics and Astronautics. Aeronautical Archives.
    Bell Family, Alexander Graham. Papers.
        http://memory.loc.gov/ammem/bellhtml/bellhome.html (accessed
        11 December 2002–21 March 2007)
    Bristol, Mark L. Papers.
    Callan, John Lansing. Papers.
    Chambers, Washington Irving. Papers.
    Richardson, Holden Chester. Papers.
    Towers, John H. Papers.
    Wright, Wilbur and Orville. Papers.
        http://memory.loc.gov/ammem/wrighthtml/wrighthome.html http://
        memory.loc.gov/ammem/bellhtml/bellhome.html (accessed
        9 November 2006–18 April 2007)
Museum of Flight, Seattle, WA.
    Wright Collection.
National Air and Space Museum, Archives and Library, Washington, DC.
    Curtiss, Glenn H. Biographical file.
    Curtiss, Glenn H. Collection.
    Hunsaker, Jerome C. Papers.
National Archives and Records Administration, Washington, DC.
    Records of the Bureau of Aeronautics, Record Group 72.
        General Correspondence of Office of Naval Aeronautics, 1914–17.
        Records of Divisions and Offices, Office Services Division,
            Administrative Services, General Correspondence, 1925–1942.
    Records of the Bureau of Naval Personnel, Record Group 24.
        Letters Sent Concerning the Navy's Early Use of and Experimentation
        with Aircraft ("Aviation").
    Records of the Office of the Judge Advocate General (Navy), Record Group
        125.

Proceedings of Naval and Marine Examining Boards, Proceedings, 1890–1941.
    Washington I. Chambers.
    Theodore G. Ellyson.
    John Rodgers.
University of Florida, Special Collections, George A. Smathers Libraries,
    Gainesville, FL.
    Hatch, Alden. Papers.

Public Document

U.S. Congress. House. *Hearing before a Subcommittee of the Committee on
    Military Affairs, United Air Service.* 66th Cong., 2d sess. Washington, DC:
    Government Printing Office, 1919.

Books and Articles

Abbot, C. G. "The 1914 Tests of the Langley 'Aerodrome.'" *Smithsonian
    Miscellaneous Collections* 103 (24 October 1942). Available online at
    http://cr.nps.gov/history/online_books/daav/appendix-c.htm (accessed
    5 December 2006).
Allman, T. D. *Miami: City of the Future.* New York: Atlantic Monthly Press, 1987.
Armstrong, William J. "Dick Richardson: His Life in Aeronautics." *Naval
    Aviation News* 59 (April 1977): pp. 32–39.
Bowers, Peter M. *Curtiss Aircraft, 1907–1947.* London: Putnam & Company, 1979.
Brayer, Elizabeth. *George Eastman: A Biography.* Baltimore and London: The
    Johns Hopkins University Press, 1996.
Bruce, Robert V. *Bell: Alexander Graham Bell and the Conquest of Solitude.*
    Boston: Little, Brown and Company, 1973.
Carpenter, Jack. *Pendulum: The Story of America's Three Aviation Pioneers.* San
    Juan Capistrano, CA: Arsdalen, Bosch & Co., 2003.
Casey, Louis S. "Curtiss Flying Lifeboat." *American Aviation Historical Society
    Journal* 10 (Summer 1965): pp. 102–4.
———. *Curtiss: The Hammondsport Era, 1907–1915.* New York: Crown Publishers,
    1981.
Chambers, Washington Irving. "Aviation and Aeroplanes." United States Naval
    Institute *Proceedings* 37 (March 1911): pp. 163–207.
———. "Aviation in the Navy." United States Naval Institute *Proceedings* 38
    (June 1912): pp. 744–46.
———. "Aviation To-Day and Development in the United States Navy, Part II."
    Flying and the Aero Club of America Bulletin 1 (January 1913): pp. 3–7.
———. "Aviation To-Day, and the Necessity for a National Aerodynamic
    Laboratory." United States Naval Institute *Proceedings* 38 (December 1912):
    pp. 1491–1528.

Champlin, Charles. *Back There Where the Past Was: A Small-Town Boyhood.* Syracuse, NY: Syracuse University Press, 1988.

Crouch, Tom D. *The Bishop's Boys: A Life of Wilbur and Orville Wright.* New York: W.W. Norton & Company, 1989.

———. *A Dream of Wings: Americans and the Airplane, 1875–1905.* New York and London: W. W. Norton & Company, 1981.

———. *The Eagle Aloft: Two Centuries of the Balloon in America.* Washington, DC: Smithsonian Institution Press, 1983.

———. "How the Bicycle Took Wing." *American Heritage of Invention and Technology* 2 (Summer 1986): pp. 10–16.

———. *Wings: A History of Aviation from Kites to the Space Age.* New York: W. W. Norton & Company, 2003.

Curtiss, G. H. "An Airship Chauffeur." *The American Aeronaut* 1 (January 1908): pp. 27–28.

Curtiss, Glenn H., and Augustus Post. *The Curtiss Aviation Book.* New York: Frederick A. Stokes Company, 1912.

D'Orcy, Ladislas. "The Curtiss Marine Flying Trophy Race." *Aviation* 13 (16 October 1922): pp. 490–92.

Eltscher, Louis R., and Edward M. Young. *Curtiss-Wright: Greatness and Decline.* New York: Twayne Publishers, 1998.

Foxworth, Thomas G. *The Speed Seekers.* New York: Doubleday & Company, 1976.

Frazer, William, and John J. Guthrie Jr. *The Florida Land Boom: Speculation, Money, and the Banks.* Westport, CT: Quorum Books, 1995.

Goldman, Mark. *High Hopes: The Rise and Decline of Buffalo, New York.* Albany: State University of New York Press, 1983.

Grossnick, Roy A., ed. *United States Naval Aviation, 1910–1995.* Washington, DC: Naval Historical Center, 1997.

Hallett, George E. A. "First Flight from Water." *AeroSpace Briefing* (a publication of the San Diego Aerospace Museum) 1 (October 1964): pp. 1–2.

Hallion, Richard P. *Taking Flight: Inventing the Aerial Age from Antiquity through the First World War.* Oxford and New York: Oxford University Press, 2003.

Hansen, James R. *Engineer in Charge: A History of the Langley Aeronautical Laboratory, 1917–1958.* Washington, DC: National Aeronautics and Space Administration, 1987.

———. *First Man: The Life of Neil A. Armstrong.* New York: Simon & Schuster, 2005.

Harris, Sherwood. *The First to Fly: Aviation's Pioneer Days.* New York: Simon & Schuster, 1970.

Hatch, Alden. *Glenn Curtiss: Pioneer of Naval Aviation.* New York: J. Messner, 1942.

Hough, Richard, and L. J. K. Setright. *A History of the World's Motorcycles.* New York: Harper & Row Publishers, 1966.

House, Kirk W. *Hell-Rider to King of the Air: Glenn Curtiss's Life of Innovation.* Warrendale, PA: SAE International, 2003.

———. "Modern Transportation: Curtiss Aerocar." *Invention and Technology* 23 (Fall 2008): pp. 40–47.

Hughes, Thomas Parke. *Elmer Sperry: Inventor and Engineer.* Baltimore: The Johns Hopkins University Press, 1971.

Hunsaker, J. C. "Progress in Naval Aircraft." *Journal of the Society of Automotive Engineers* 5 (July 1919): pp. 31–44.

Jakab, Peter L. *Visions of a Flying Machine: The Wright Brothers and the Process of Invention.* Washington, DC: Smithsonian Institution Press, 1990.

Jakab, Peter L., and Rick Young. *The Published Writings of Wilbur and Orville Wright.* Washington, DC and London: Smithsonian Institution Press, 2000.

Keys, C. M. "The Curtiss Aeroplane and Motor Corporation after the War." *Aerial Age Weekly* 13 (6 June 1921): pp. 295–96.

Knott, Richard C. *The American Flying Boat: An Illustrated History.* Annapolis, MD: Naval Institute Press, 1979.

Kurutz, Gary F. "The Only Safe and Sane Method: The Curtiss School of Aviation." *Journal of San Diego History* 25 (Winter 1979): 4. Available online at http://www.sandiegohistory.org/journal/79winter/curtiss.htm (accessed 15 September 2005).

Lebow, Eileen F. *Before Amelia: Women Pilots in the Early Days of Aviation.* Washington, DC: Brassey's, 2002.

———. *Cal Rodgers and the Vin Fizz.* Washington, DC: Smithsonian Institution Press, 1989.

Linder, Bruce. *San Diego's Navy: An Illustrated History.* Annapolis, MD: Naval Institute Press, 2001.

Loening, Grover. *Our Wings Grow Faster.* Garden City, NY: Doubleday, Doran & Co., 1935.

Loftin, Laurence K. Jr. *Quest for Performance: The Evolution of Modern Aircraft.* Washington, DC: National Aeronautics and Space Administration, 1985.

Markides, Constantinos C., and Paul A. Geroski. *Fast Second: How Smart Companies Bypass Radical Innovation to Enter and Dominate New Markets.* San Francisco: Jossey-Bass, 2005.

McKelvey, Blake. *Rochester on the Genesee: The Growth of a City.* 2nd ed. Syracuse, NY: Syracuse University Press, 1993.

Muir, Helen. *Miami, U.S.A.* Gainesville: University Press of Florida, 2000.

Reynolds, Clark G. *Admiral John H. Towers: The Struggle for Naval Air Supremacy.* Annapolis, MD: Naval Institute Press, 1991.

Rinek, Larry M. "Curtiss Aviation Engines: An American Success Story." *Torque Meter: Journal of the Aircraft Engine Historical Society* 6 (Spring 2007): pp. 6–23.

Robie, Bill. *For the Greatest Achievement: A History of the Aero Club of America and the National Aeronautic Association.* Washington, DC and London: Smithsonian Institution Press, 1993.

Roland, Alex. *Model Research: The National Advisory Committee for Aeronautics, 1915–1958.* 2 vols. Washington, DC: National Aeronautics and Space Administration, 1985.

Roseberry, C. R. *Glenn Curtiss: Pioneer of Flight.* 1972. Reprint, Syracuse, NY: Syracuse University Press, 1991.

Seely, Lyman J. *Flying Pioneers at Hammondsport, N.Y., 1904–1914.* Auburn, NY: Fenton Press, 1929.

Shulman, Seth. *Unlocking the Sky: Glenn Hammond Curtiss and the Race to Invent the Airplane.* New York: HarperCollins Publishers, 2002.

Smith, Richard K. *First Across! The U.S. Navy's Transatlantic Flight of 1919.* Annapolis, MD: Naval Institute Press, 1973.

———. "Not a Success--But a Triumph: 80 Years since Kitty Hawk." *Naval War College Review* 36 (November–December 1983): pp. 4–20.

———. "The Superiority of the American Transoceanic Airliner, 1932–1939: Sikorsky S-42 vs. Short S. 23." *American Aviation Historical Society Journal* 29 (Summer 1984): pp. 82–94.

———. "The Weight Envelope: An Airplane's Fourth Dimension." *Aerospace Historian* 33 (Spring/March 1986): pp. 30–44.

Smith, Robert A. *A Social History of the Bicycle: Its Early Life and Times in America.* New York: American Heritage Press, 1972.

Spector, Ronald H. *At War at Sea: Sailors and Naval Combat in the Twentieth Century.* New York: Viking Press, 2001.

Stein, Stephen K. *From Torpedoes to Aviation: Washington Irving Chambers and Technological Innovation in the New Navy, 1876–1913.* Tuscaloosa: University of Alabama Press, 2007.

Studer, Clara. *Sky Storming Yankee: The Life of Glenn Curtiss.* New York: Stackpole Sons, 1937.

Sudsbury, Elretta. *Jackrabbits to Jets: The History of North Island, San Diego, California.* San Diego: Neyenesch Printers, 1967.

Trimble, William F. *High Frontier: A History of Aeronautics in Pennsylvania.* Pittsburgh: University of Pittsburgh Press, 1982.

———. *Jerome C. Hunsaker and the Rise of American Aeronautics.* Washington, DC: Smithsonian Institution Press, 2002.

———. "The Narrow and Pitching Deck: The Navy's Special Requirements for Aircraft." In *1998 National Aerospace Conference Proceedings*, pp. 215–19. Dayton, OH: Wright State University, 1999.

Turnbull, Archibald D., and Clifford L. Lord. *History of United States Naval Aviation*. New Haven, CT: Yale University Press, 1949.

"USS *Curtiss*." In *Dictionary of American Naval Fighting Ships*, 2: pp. 220–21. Washington, DC: Naval History Division, 1963. Also available online at http://www.history.navy.mil/danfs/c16/curtiss.htm.

"USS *Hammondsport*." In *Dictionary of American Naval Fighting Ships*, 3: p. 227. Washington, DC: Naval History Division, 1968. Also available online at http://www.history.navy.mil/danfs/h2/hammondsport.htm.

Vander Meulen, Jacob A. *The Politics of Aircraft; Building an American Military Industry*. Lawrence: University Press of Kansas, 1991.

Van Deurs, George. *Anchors in the Sky: Spuds Ellyson, the First Naval Aviator*. San Rafael, CA: Presidio Press, 1978.

Villard, Henry Serrano. *Contact! The Story of the Early Birds*. New York: Thomas Y. Crowell Company, 1968.

Westervelt, G. C., H. C. Richardson, and A. C. Read. *The Triumph of the NCs*. Garden City, NY: Doubleday, Page & Co., 1920.

Wilson, Timothy. "Broken Wings: The Curtiss Aeroplane Company, K-Boats, and the Russian Navy, 1914–1916." *Journal of Military History* 66 (October 2002): pp. 1061–83.

Wohl, Robert. *A Passion for Wings: Aviation and the Western Imagination, 1908–1918*. New Haven, CT and London: Yale University Press, 1994.

Young, David M. *Chicago Aviation: An Illustrated History*. DeKalb,: Northern Illinois University Press, 2003.

Interviews and Oral Histories

Hunsaker, Jerome C. "The Reminiscences of Jerome C. Hunsaker." Interview by Donald Shaughnessy. April 1960. Aviation Project, Oral History Research Office, Columbia University, New York, NY.

Richardson, Holden C. "Reminiscences of Captain Holden Richardson." Interview by Kenneth Leish. July 1960. Aviation Project, Oral History Research Office, Columbia University, New York, NY.

Dissertations, Papers, Web Sites, and Other Materials

"Colonel D. Charles Collier (1871–1934)." http://www.sandiegohistory.org/bio/collier/collier2.htm (accessed 20 September 2005).

Crouch, Tom D. "Some Notes on the History of the Aileron." Undated.

"Curtiss Characteristics." San Diego Aerospace Museum (courtesy of George Cully).

"Factsheets: Chapter Four: The April 1911 Aviation Carnival." http://www.hill.af.mil/library/factsheets/factsheet.asp?id=5964 (accessed 21 July 2008).

"Glenn H. Curtiss--Miami Springs Historical Hike." http://www.acgweb.com/Spring/index.html (accessed 17 July 2008).

Horgan, James Joseph. "City of Flight: The History of Aviation in Saint Louis." PhD diss., St. Louis University, 1965.

Lee, James Lawrence. "Into the Wind: A History of the American Wind Tunnel, 1896–1941." PhD diss., Auburn University, 2002.

Lord, Clifford L. "The History of Naval Aviation, 1898–1939." Microfilm. Office of the Deputy Chief of Naval Operations (Air). Washington, DC: Naval Aviation History Unit, 1946.

Morgan, Jane. "Wireless Begins to Talk--and Fly." Chap. 3 in *Electronics in the West: The First Fifty Years*. http://earlyradiohistory.us/1910enn2.htm (accessed 16 July 2008). Book also available in print, Palo Alto, CA: National Press Books, 1967.

Shanahan, William O. "Procurement of Naval Aircraft, 1907–1939." Vol. 17. Deputy Chief of Naval Operations (Air). Washington, DC: Department of the Navy, Naval Aviation History Unit, 1946.

Stein, Stephen K. "Washington Irving Chambers: Innovation, Professionalization, and the New Navy." PhD diss., The Ohio State University, 1999.

Sullivan, James, ed. "The History of New York State Biographies, Part 3." http://www.usgennet.org/usa/ny/state/his/bio/pt3.html (accessed 30 April 2007).

U.S. Patent and Trademarks Office. U.S. Department of Commerce. http://www.uspto.gov.

Newspapers and Periodicals

Aerial Age Weekly

Aero

Aeronautics

Aeronautics (London)

AeroSpace Briefing

Aerospace Historian

Allentown (Pa.) Morning Call

The American Aeronaut

American Aviation Historical Society Journal

American Heritage of Invention and Technology

Aviation

Aviation and Aeronautical Engineering

Birmingham News

Fly

Flying

Flying and the Aero Club of America Bulletin

Hammondsport Herald

Invention and Technology: Journal of the Society of Automotive Engineers

Journal of Military History
Journal of San Diego History
Lexington (Ky.) Herald
Miami Herald
Naval Aviation News
Naval War College Review
New York Herald
New York Times
New York World
Rochester Democrat and Chronicle
San Diego Sun
San Diego Union
Scientific American
Torque Meter: Journal of the Aircraft Engine Historical Society
United States Naval Institute *Proceedings*

Index

Acosta, Bert, 202
Adams, G. Carl, 4, 103–4, 106, 113, 117, 134, 205, 209
Adams, J. Charles, 4
advanced base concept, Marine, 151
Aerial Experiment Association, 22–23, 45–46; and Aero Club of America, 28, 33; airplanes, 26–29, 55; and airplane control systems, 29, 31, 33, 42; and airplane exhibitions, 48, 51; and Alexander Graham Bell, 41–42; American Aerodrome Company, 48–49; and *Cygnet*, 24; and *Cygnet II*, 36, 49–50; and death of Selfridge, 40, 41; dissolution of, 54; future of, 48; glider, 24–26; and Herring-Curtiss Manufacturing Company, 52–53; and *June Bug*, 31–35, 38, 42–43, 44, 45; organization of, 23; and patents, 26, 32, 36, 41–42, 45, 47–48, 73, 170; and *Red Wing*, 26–29; relocation to Hammondsport, 24; and *Scientific American* trophy, 35, 54; and *Silver Dart*, 36, 43–45, 47, 50, 54; six-month extension of, 41; and Thomas Selfridge, 39–41; and *White Wing*, 29–31; and Wright brothers, 26, 29
Aero Club of America, xi, 14, 28, 32, 33, 34, 35, 45, 49, 57, 58, 65–67, 73, 76, 82, 84, 87, 96, 126, 129, 134–35, 144, 159, 160, 161, 167, 175, 198, 199, 200; San Diego chapter, 105, 106, 113; and *Scientific American* trophy, 49, 54
Aero Club of California, 76
Aero Club de France, 66
Aero Club of New York, 58
Aero Club of Pittsburgh, 89
Aerocar Corporation, 209
Aeronautic Society of New York, 45, 49, 50, 53, 56–57, 61, 63; and *Scientific American* trophy, 56; and Wright patent, 55
Aeronautical Annual, 45
Aeronautics, 45
aileron, 29–30, 42, 45
aircraft: Aeronautic Society of New York airplane, 55–62; airships, 11–12, 158; Antoinette, 62, 64, 98, 115; Bleriot, 60, 62, 64, 77, 78, 91, 97, 98, 115, 159; Farman, 70, 77, 78; NW racers, 202–3; *Red Devil*, 83; Verville VCP racer, 200; Voisin, 62, 66–67; Vought VE-7, 200; Wright F2W-1 racer, 203. *See also* Aerial Experiment Association; Baldwin, Thomas S.; Bell, Alexander Graham; Curtiss airplanes; Wright brothers
aircraft engines, 11–12, 15–16, 18, 159, 176, 181, 183, 187–89, 192, 199, 200, 202, 203; Kirkham K-12, 200. *See also* Curtiss aircraft engines; Liberty engine
aircraft industry, 200–1; and World War I, 183–84, 186
airplane: accidents, 39–41, 83, 104, 116, 122–24, 125–26, 127–28, 133, 139–40, 141, 146, 153, 154; automatic stability of, 53, 152–55; bombing experiments, 87–88; catapult, 145–46, 149; as component of fleet, 133, 136;

control systems, xiii, 29, 31, 33, 36,
87, 117, 138, 174; and the imagination, 68; inherent stability of, 19;
launching devices, 145–46; and naval
warfare, 87, 88, 89,147; over-water
flights, 131; patents, 35, 36; at sea,
xi–xii, 99–102, 109, 114; on ships,
128–29; weight, 27, 30, 31, 44, 56,
96, 164–65, 187, 189, 192–93, 194–95;
wire-launching system, 128–29. *See
also* Aerial Experiment Association;
aircraft; Curtiss, Glenn H.
Airships, Inc., 201
Albany-New York flight, xi–xii, 82–86,
211
America Trans Oceanic Company, 187
Andrews, William S., 212
Annapolis, 130, 146; flight training facility at, 121
Army, 73; airplane competition, 51; airship contract, 103; flight instruction, 116; and Curtiss, 149–50, 179;
and North Island, 153–54, 179;
Signal Corps, and airplane, 37;
Signal Corps airship contract, 37
aspect ratio, wing, 26, 27, 44, 55, 62
aviation exhibitions and meets, 57,
61–66, 69–70, 95, 104; Akron,
124; Allentown, 91–92; Atlantic
City, 88–89; Belmont Park, 96–98;
Boston-Harvard, 90–91; Brescia,
66–67; Bridgeport, 122; Charlotte,
92; Chicago, 70, 94–95; Cincinnati,
71; Cleveland, 90; Coronado,
113; Fall River, 124; Fort Wayne,
93; Halethorpe, 98–99, 100;
Havana, 109; Hempstead Plains,
58–59; Hudson-Fulton, 68–69;
Indianapolis, 93; Los Angeles
(Dominguez field, 1910), 76–79,
104, 105 (Dominguez Field, 1911),
103–4; Memphis, 83; Minneapolis,
90; Morris Park, 56–57; Niagara
Falls, 93–94; Omaha, 89, 90;

Pittsburgh, 89; Rheims, 57, 58,
60–66; Sacramento, 94; St. Louis,
69–70; Salt Lake City, 117–18, 120;
San Antonio, 83; San Francisco,
94, 104, 107; Sheepshead Bay
(Brooklyn), 90, 103; Washington,
DC, 93; Winona Lake, 95
Azores, 163, 164, 165, 189,193, 195, 196,
197

Baddeck, 22–23
Baker, Robert H., 112
Baldwin, Frederick W. ("Casey"), 21, 23,
25, 27, 28–30, 36, 42, 48, 54
Baldwin, Thomas S., 11–13, 15, 17, 18,
23–24, 33, 34, 44, 51, 61, 69, 70, 83;
and A. Roy Knabenshue, 12–13;
and Army airship contract, 37–39,
103; and *California Arrow*, 12–13,
14; and Curtiss, 20–21, 23–24; and
Hammondsport, 15; and Hudson-
Fulton celebration, 82; and Lincoln
Beachey, 24; and *Red Devil*, 83, 89;
and *Signal Corps I* airship, 37–39
Barrin, Louis T., 195
Beach, Stanley Y., 34, 152
Beachey, Lincoln, 24, 70, 71, 93, 148;
and Bridgeport exhibition, 122; and
Curtiss, 169–70; and Curtiss exhibition team, 93–94; and Langley
aerodrome, 169–70
Beck, Paul W., 79, 116
Bedwin, William, 49
Bell, Alexander Graham, 18, 26, 33–34;
and Aerial Experiment Association,
22–25, 41–42, 46, 48, 51, 54; and
aileron, 29–30; and airplane control systems, 42; airplane stability,
19, 29; and American Aerodrome
Company, 48–49, 52, 53; and
Baddeck, 47; and Baddeck aero lab,
19, 20, 21, 23; and *Cygnet*, 24, 26;
and *Cygnet II*, 36, 42, 47, 49, 50;
and death of Selfridge, 40, 41; and

About the Author

A professor of history and former department chair at Auburn University in Alabama, William F. Trimble received his Ph.D. from the University of Colorado, Boulder. He is the author, coauthor, or editor of seven books, including *Attack from the Sea: A History of the U.S. Navy's Seaplane Striking Force,* published by the Naval Institute Press in 2005. His book *Admiral William A. Moffett: Architect of Naval Aviation* was reprinted in 2007 as one of the Naval Institute Press' Bluejacket Books.

The Naval Institute Press is the book-publishing arm of the U.S. Naval Institute, a private, nonprofit, membership society for sea service professionals and others who share an interest in naval and maritime affairs. Established in 1873 at the U.S. Naval Academy in Annapolis, Maryland, where its offices remain today, the Naval Institute has members worldwide.

Members of the Naval Institute support the education programs of the society and receive the influential monthly magazine *Proceedings* or the colorful bimonthly magazine *Naval History* and discounts on fine nautical prints and on ship and aircraft photos. They also have access to the transcripts of the Institute's Oral History Program and get discounted admission to any of the Institute-sponsored seminars offered around the country.

The Naval Institute's book-publishing program, begun in 1898 with basic guides to naval practices, has broadened its scope to include books of more general interest. Now the Naval Institute Press publishes about seventy titles each year, ranging from how-to books on boating and navigation to battle histories, biographies, ship and aircraft guides, and novels. Institute members receive significant discounts on the Press's more than eight hundred books in print.

Full-time students are eligible for special half-price membership rates. Life memberships are also available.

For a free catalog describing Naval Institute Press books currently available, and for further information about joining the U.S. Naval Institute, please write to:

Member Services
U.S. Naval Institute
291 Wood Road
Annapolis, MD 21402-5034
Telephone: (800) 233-8764
Fax: (410) 571-1703
Web address: www.usni.org